Titles in This Series

DIMACS
Series in Discrete Mathematics
and Theoretical Computer Science

Volume 14

Coding and Quantization

DIMACS/IEEE Workshop
October 19–21, 1992

Robert Calderbank
G. David Forney, Jr.
Nader Moayeri
Editors

NSF Science and Technology Center
in Discrete Mathematics and Theoretical Computer Science
A consortium of Rutgers University, Princeton University,
AT&T Bell Labs, Bellcore

American Mathematical Society

This Dimacs volume on coding and quantization contains papers from a workshop held at DIMACS from October 19 to October 21, 1992, as well as two papers that record results obtained in discussion outside the formal sessions.

1991 *Mathematics Subject Classification.* Primary 94A05, 94A29, 94B05, 94B10, 94B12.

Library of Congress Cataloging-in-Publication Data

Workshop on Coding and Quantization (1992: Princeton University)
Coding and quantization: DIMACS/IEEE Workshop, October 19–21, 1992/Robert Calderbank, G. David Forney, Jr., Nader Moayeri, editors.
p. cm. — (DIMACS series in discrete mathematics and theoretical computer science; no. 14)
On t.p.: "NSF Science and Technology Center in Discrete Mathematics and Theoretical Computer Science, a consortium of Rutgers University, Princeton University, AT&T Bell Labs, Bellcore."
Workshop co-sponsored by the Center for Discrete Mathematics and Theoretical Computer Science (DIMACS) and the Information Theory Society of the Institute of Electrical and Electronics Engineers (IEEE).
Includes bibliographical references.
ISBN 0-8218-6603-6 (alk. paper)
1. Telecommunication systems—Congresses. 2. Coding theory—Congresses. I. Calderbank, Robert, 1954– . II. Forney, G. David. III. Moayeri, Nader, 1956– . IV. NSF Science and Technology Center in Discrete Mathematics and Theoretical Computer Science. V. DIMACS (Group) VI. IEEE Information Theory Society. VII. Title. VIII. Series.
TK5102.5.W69 1992 93-29283
621.382—dc20 CIP

Printed in the United States of America.

♾ The paper used in this book is acid-free and falls within the guidelines
established to ensure permanence and durability.
♻ Printed on recycled paper.

This volume was prepared by the authors using AMS-TEX and AMS-LATEX,
the American Mathematical Society's TEX macro systems.

10 9 8 7 6 5 4 3 2 1 98 97 96 95 94 93

Contents

Foreword

This DIMACS volume on coding and quantization contains papers from a workshop held October 19–21, 1992, as well as two papers that record results obtained in discussion outside the formal sessions. The workshop was cosponsored by DIMACS and IEEE (Information Theory Society of the Institute of Electrical and Electronics Engineers).

We especially thank the workshop organizers, Robert Calderbank, G. David Forney, Jr., and Nader Moayeri, for organizing this workshop, which brought together so many outstanding participants in this field.

Fred Roberts, Acting Director
Robert Tarjan, Co-Director
Diane Souvaine, Associate Director

Preface

This volume is devoted to the Proceedings of the Workshop on Coding and Quantization. This workshop was cosponsored by the Center for Discrete Mathematics and Theoretical Computer Science (DIMACS) and the Information Theory Society of the Institute of Electrical and Electronics Engineers (IEEE). Approximately one hundred and twenty researchers attended one or more days of the workshop which took place October 19–21, 1992. About eighty percent of the attendees were from university engineering departments, with the remainder from local industry and government organizations. We begin these Proceedings with a short perspective on the themes of the workshop.

In 1948 Shannon developed fundamental limits on the efficiency of communication over noisy channels. It is coding that makes reliable communication possible, and discrete mathematics is central to coding theory. Multidimensional Euclidean geometry (especially lattice theory) and finite state machines are of particular importance within coding theory.

Discrete mathematics has had a significant impact on coded transmission over bandlimited channels; this is already an important subject, and will become more so in the coming years, with the advent of better cellular networks, personal communications devices and the wireless office.

A bandlimited channel such as a telephone channel supports transmission only of continuous functions that contain no frequencies higher than W Hz. The sampling theorem allows us to replace a continuous bandlimited function by a discrete sequence of its samples without any loss of information. Now signals become simply vectors in $\mathbb{R}^N$ consisting of N consecutive samples. Typically these signals are drawn from a finite dimensional lattice; the signal constellation consists of all lattice points that lie within some region $\mathcal{R}$ whose centroid is the origin. Now the goal is to design a low complexity signaling scheme that maximizes the minimum squared distance d^2 between distinct signal sequences. The power required to transmit a lattice point x is $||x||^2$, and the figure of merit for the signaling scheme is d^2/P, where P is the average transmitted signal power. Typically encoding is accomplished through a finite state machine, and decoding is accomplished by dynamic programming. It is these techniques from discrete mathematics that have made possible (in the last 5 years) practical systems that approach the Shannon limit on Gaussian noise channels.

It is natural to ask the question why these developments took over 40 years to emerge. Part of the answer is that only recently has it become possible to do signal processing in silicon at high speeds. Now that we have that capability there will be more opportunities for coding theory.

It is important to notice that the fields of communication and quantization are very closely related. A signal constellation bounded by a region $\mathcal{R}$ can be used to quantize source samples that fall within $\mathcal{R}$. Here the goal is to distribute quantization points so as to minimize mean squared error. The focus of much recent work is to combine transform techniques with quantization schemes in order to compress speech and images.

It is clear from even this brief introduction that the theory of communication and that of quantization overlap significantly, and that many fundamental questions are of central interest to researchers in both fields. However, it was the sense of the organizers that there had been little crosspollination between the two communities. The main goal of the workshop was to promote more interaction. There were thirty-five presentations at the workshop spanning a wide range of topics, from the difficulty of compressing songs by Suzanne Vega for digital audio broadcasting, to the Minkowski-Hlawka theorem in geometric number theory. The papers that appear in these Proceedings are, for the most part, accounts of these presentations. However, two of the papers (one by G. D. Forney, Jr., N. J. A. Sloane and M. D. Trott, the other by Y. Levy, D. J. Costello, Jr., and A. R. Calderbank) record results that were obtained in discussion outside the formal sessions. All papers are in final form.

AT&T Bell Laboratories contributed to the publication of these Proceedings by providing technical support. The contributions were typeset in DIMACS format by Susan Pope, without whom we would not have attempted this project. Thanks are also due to Joan Stortz for her cheerful administrative assistance, and to Pat Toci of DIMACS for her organizational support during the workshop. Finally, and most important, we would like to thank the authors of the outstanding articles assembled here, and we hope that you the reader will enjoy these Proceedings.

Organizing Committee

Robert Calderbank
G. David Forney, Jr.
Nader Moayeri

Joint DIMACS/IEEE Workshop on Coding and Quantization

Rutgers University, Piscataway, NJ, USA October 19–21, 1992

Technical Program

Session I: LATTICES, DUALITY, AND SHANNON THEORY
Monday Morning, 9:00–12:00
Chair: N.J.A. Sloane

9:00–9:30	New Lattices and Designs — *N.J.A. Sloane*
9:30–9:50	Existence proofs for good Euclidean-space codes — *A. Loeliger*
9:50–10:10	Asymptotically optimal noisy channel quantization via random coding — *K. Zeger and V. Manzella*
10:10–10:30	BREAK
10:30–10:50	Duality between packing and covering problems for lattices — *G.D. Forney, Jr.*
10:50–11:10	Generalized theta functions for lattice vector quantization — *P. Solé*
11:10–11:30	A coding theorem for low-rate transform codes — *D.F. Lyons and D.L. Neuhoff*
11:30–12:00	Tree-structured signal space codes — *C.F. Barnes*

Session II: QUANTIZATION
Monday Afternoon, 2:00–5:00
Chair: D.L. Neuhoff

Part A:	HIGH-RATE THEORY
2:00–2:20	The other asymptotic theory of lossy source coding — *D.L. Neuhoff*
2:30–2:50	Block-constrained quantizers: introduction and asymptotic analysis — *A.S. Balamesh and D.L. Neuhoff*
2:50–3:10	Syndrome-based VQ codebooks — *P.F. Swaszek*

3:10–3:30 BREAK

Part B: FUNDAMENTALS AND COMBINED SOURCE-CHANNEL CODING

3:30–4:00 The quantization problem for coded systems — *E. Zehavi*

4:00–4:20 The optimality of the natural binary code — *S.W. McLaughlin, D.L. Neuhoff, and J. Ashley*

4:20–4:40 Multiple-description scalar quantizer design: good index assignments — *V. Vaishnampayan*

4:40–5:00 Structured vector quantizers as generalized product codes — *W.-Y. Chan and A. Gersho*

Session III: TRELLIS-CODED QUANTIZATION
Tuesday Morning, 9:00–12:00
Chair: T.R. Fischer

9:00–9:30 Pyramid cubic lattice and trellis codes — *T.R. Fischer and J. Pan*

9:30–9:50 A new construction of trellis-coded quantizers — *R.J. van der Vleuten and J.H. Weber*

9:50–10:10 Wavelet coding of images using trellis-coded quantization — *P. Sriram and M.W. Marcellin*

10:10–10:30 BREAK

10:30–11:00 Trellis-based scalar-vector quantizer for memoryless sources — *R. Laroia and N. Farvardin*

11:00–11:20 Vector quantization using lattice and trellis-bounded codebooks — *M.V. Eyuboglu and A. Balamesh*

11:20–11:40 Bounds on the sizes of constant-weight covering codes — *T. Etzion, V.K. Wei and Z. Zhang*

Session IV: FINITE-STATE MACHINES
Tuesday Afternoon, 2:00–3:30
Chair: A.R. Calderbank

2:00–2:30 Sliding block codes for finite-state machines with forbidden submachines — *R. Karabed and P.H. Siegel*

2:30–2:50 Covering properties of convolutional codes and associated lattices — *A.R. Calderbank, P.C. Fishburn, and A. Rabinovich*

2:50–3:10 Trellis codes, symbolic dynamics, and isometries — *C. Heegard and E. Rossin*

3:10–3:30 The design of finite-state machines for quantization using simulated annealing — *E. Ayanoglu and E.E. Kuroglu*

3:30–3:50 BREAK

3:50–5:00 DISCUSSIONS

Session V: CODING APPLICATIONS
Wednesday Morning, 9:00–12:00
Chair: D.J. Costello, Jr.

9:00–9:30	The M-algorithm, the failure of reduced-state sequence detection with good convolutional codes, and some implications for trellis coding — *J.B. Anderson and E. Offer*
9:30–9:50	An algebraic approach to constructing convolutional codes from quasi-cyclic codes — *Y. Levy and D.J. Costello, Jr.*
9:50–10:10	Table-driven decoding of convolutional codes with soft decisions — *H. Koorapaty, D.L. Bitzer, A. Dholokia, and M.A. Vouk*
10:10–10:30	BREAK
10:30–10:50	Rotationally invariant multilevel codes — *J.N. Livingston*
10:50–11:10	Constellations for diversity — *K. Kerpez*
11:10–11:30	Bounded-expansion codes for error control — *A.S. Khayrallah*
11:30–11:50	A bound on zero-error list coding capacity — *E. Arikan*

Session VI: QUANTIZATION APPLICATIONS
Wednesday Afternoon, 2:00–4:00
Chair: J. Johnston

2:00–2:30	Geometric vector quantization for subband-based video coding — *C. Podilchuk and A. Jacquin*
2:30–2:50	Quantization analysis in multirate filter banks by spectral theory — *C.W. Kok and S.H. Leung*
2:50–3:10	Recursively indexed differential pulse code modulation — *K. Sayood and S. Na*
3:10–3:30	BREAK
3:30–4:00	Quantization with perceptual criteria — *J. Johnston*

Workshop Participants

Behnaam Aazhang, Rice Univ., Houston, TX
aaz@rice.edu

Jean-Pierre Adoul, Univ. of Sherbrooke, Sherbrooke, CANADA
adoul@gel.usherb.ca

John B. Anderson, Rensselaer Poly. Inst., Troy, NY
anderson@ecse.rpi.edu

Erdal Arikan, Bilkent Univ., Ankara, TURKEY
arikan@trbilun.bitnet

Ender Ayanoglu, AT&T Bell Labs, Holmdel, NJ
ender@boole.att.com

Ahmed S. Balamesh, King Abdul-Aziz University, Jeddah, SAUDI ARABIA
CCP3017@SAKKAU03.BITNET

Christopher F. Barnes, Georgia Inst. of Tech., Atlanta, GA
cbarnes@mal-s2.gatech.edu

Sankar Basu, Stevens Inst. of Tech., Hoboken, NJ
SBASU@vaxc.stevens-tech.edu

Gal Ben-David, Technion, Haifa, ISRAEL
GAL@neptun.technion.ac.il

Donald L. Bitzer, North Carolina State Univ., Raleigh, NC
bitzer@bvcd.csc.ncsu.edu

Richard E. Blahut, IBM, Owego, NY
blahut@owgvm3.vnet.ibm.com

A. R. Calderbank, AT&T Bell Labs, Murray Hill, NJ
rc@research.att.com

C. V. Chakravarthy, Stevens Inst. of Tech., Hoboken, NJ
SGN_CCHAKRAV@vaxc.stevens-tech.edu

Wai-Yip Chan, McGill Univ., Montreal, CANADA
chan@aldebaran.insl.mcgill.ca

Gerard J. Chang, Rutgers Univ., Piscataway, NJ
gjchang@dimacs.rutgers.edu

Bing Chen, AT&T Bell Labs, Murray Hill, NJ
bing@ulysses.att.com

King-Wai Chow, Princeton University, Princeton, NJ
kingchow@ee.princeton.edu

Sean Coffey, The Univ. of Michigan, Ann Arbor, MI
scoffey@eecs.umich.edu

Daniel J. Costello, Jr., Univ. of Notre Dame, Notre Dame, IN
costello@saturn.ece.nd.edu

Thomas M. Cover, Stanford Univ., Stanford, CA
cover@isl.stanford.edu

Rene Cruz, Univ. of California, San Diego, CA
cruz@ece.ucsd.edu

David G. Daut, Rutgers Univ., Piscataway, NJ
daut@caip.rutgers.edu

Ajay Dholakia, North Carolina State Univ., Raleigh, NC
ajay@bvcd.csc.ncsu.edu

Anthony D. DiBiase, EkTRON Applied Imaging, Bedford, MA
tdb@ektron.kodak.com / nobody@kodak.com

Wei Ding, Princeton University, Princeton, NJ
weiding@ee.princeton.edu

Steven C. Dzik, AT&T Image Solutions, Middletown, NJ

Anthony Ephremides, Univ. of Maryland, College Park, MD
tony@eng.umd.edu

M. Vedat Eyuboglu, Motorola Codex, Mansfield, MA
vedat_eyuboglu@mcimail.com

Thomas R. Fischer, Washington State Univ., Pullman, WA
fischer@eecs.wsu.edu

G. David Forney, Jr., Motorola Codex, Mansfield, MA
david_forney@mcimail.com

Richard L. Frost, Brigham Young Univ. Provo, UT
rickf@ee.byu.edu

Tom Fuja, Univ. of Maryland, College Park, MD
fuja@ra.src.umd.edu

Ehud Gelblum, Columbia Univ., New York, NY
gelblum@ctr.columbia.edu

Jerry D. Gibson, Texas A&M Univ., College Station, TX
gibson@ee.tamu.edu

Bruce Hajek, Univ. of Illinois, Urbana, IL
hajek@uicsl.csl.uiuc.edu

Chris Heegard, Cornell Univ., Ithaca, NY
heegard@ee.cornell.edu

Shay-Jan Huang, Univ. of Maryland, College Park, MD
shayjan@eng.umd.edu

Arnaud Jacquin, AT&T Bell Labs, Murray Hill, NJ
jacquin@chitra.att.com

Branko Jelicic, Univ. of Pennsylvania, Philadelphia, PA

Frederick Jelinek, IBM T.J. Watson Res. Center, Yorktown Heights, NY
jelinek@watson.ibm.com

Jim Johnston, AT&T Bell Labs, Murray Hill, NJ
jj@research.att.com

Mark Kahrs, Rutgers Univ., Piscataway, NJ
kahrs@winlab.rutgers.edu

Rama Kalluri, Rutgers Univ., Piscataway, NJ

Razmik Karabed, IBM Almaden Res. Center, San Jose, CA
karabed@almaden.ibm.com

Kenneth J. Kerpez, Bellcore, Morristown, NJ
kerpez@aries.bellcore.com

Ali S. Khayrallah, Univ. of Delaware, Newark, DE
ali@udel.edu

Ken Kishi, Princeton, NJ

C. W. Kok, City Polytechnic of Hong Kong, HONG KONG
90910434@CPHKVX.BITNET

Havish Koorapaty, North Carolina State Univ., Raleigh, NC
havish@bvcd.csc.ncsu.edu

Frank R. Kschischang, Univ. of Toronto, Toronto, CANADA
frank@comm.toronto.edu

P. Sarath Kumar, Univ. of Pennsylvania, Philadelphia, PA

Rajiv Laroia, AT&T Bell Labs, Murray Hill, NJ
laroia@research.att.com

Cheng Chieh Lee, Univ. of Maryland, College Park, MD
cclee@src.umd.edu

Don H. Lee, IBM T.J. Watson Res. Center, Yorktown Heights, NY
dhl@watson.ibm.com

Jungwoo Lee, Princeton Univ., Princeton, NJ
junglee@ee.princeton.edu

Yannick Levy, Univ. of Notre Dame, Notre Dame, IN
ylevy@dvorak.helios.nd.edu

Pascal Ligdas, Univ. of Maryland, College Park, MD
pascal@src.umd.edu

Shu Lin, Univ. of Hawaii, Honolulu, HI
slin@wiliki.eng.hawaii.edu

Jay N. Livingston, Texas A&M Univ., College Station, TX
jnl@jeeves.tamu.edu

Hans-Andrea Loeliger, Linkoping Univ., Linkoping, SWEDEN
andi@isy.liu.se

Minsky Lou, AT&T Bell Labs, Murray Hill, NJ
ml@ulysses.att.com

Daniel F. Lyons, Mitre Corp., McLean, VA
dflyons@mitre.org

Michael W. Marcellin, Univ. of Arizona, Tucson, AZ
marcellin@ece.arizona.edu

James Mazo, AT&T Bell Labs, Murray Hill, NJ

Steven W. McLaughlin, Rochester Inst. of Tech., Rochester, NY
swmeee@ritvax.isc.rit.edu

Nader Mehravari, IBM, Owego, NY
nader@owgvm0.vnet.ibm.com

Laurence B. Milstein, Univ. of California, San Diego, CA
milstein@celece.ucsd.edu

Nader Moayeri, Rutgers University, Piscataway, NJ
moayeri@winlab.rutgers.edu

Nader Mohsenian, Princeton Univ., Princeton, NJ
naderm@ee.princeton.edu

David L. Neuhoff, The Univ. of Michigan, Ann Arbor, MI
neuhoff@eecs.umich.edu

Antonio Ortega, Columbia Univ., New York, NY
antonio@ctr.columbia.edu

Nam Phamdo, Univ. of Maryland, College Park, MD
nam@src.umd.edu

Christine Podilchuk, AT&T Bell Labs, Murray Hill, NJ
chrisp@research.att.com

H. Vincent Poor, Princeton Univ., Princeton, NJ
poor@ivy.princeton.edu

Mohendra Pratap, AT&T Image Solutions, Middletown, NJ

Asya Rabinovich, Stanford University, Stanford, CA
asya@playfair.stanford.edu

M. V. Raganath, AT&T Image Solutions, Middletown, NJ

Kannan Ramchandran, Columbia Univ., New York, NY
kannan@ctr.columbia.edu

Ramesh Rao, Univ. of California, San Diego, CA
rrao@ucsd.edu

Eric Rossin, Cornell Univ., Ithaca, NY
ejr@ee.cornell.edu

Summit Roy, Univ. of Pennsylvania, Philadelphia, PA
roy@pender.ee.upenn.edu

Noel Rozario, GE Astro Space, Princeton, NJ

Burt Saltzberg, AT&T Bell Labs, Middletown, NJ

Khalid Sayood, Univ. of Nebraska, Lincoln, NE
ksayood@eecomm.unl.edu / EERDKS@engvms.unl.edu

Stuart C. Schwartz, Princeton University, Princeton, NJ
stuart@ivy.princeton.edu

Mutsumu Serizawa, Rutgers Univ., Piscataway, NJ
serizawa@winlab.rutgers.edu

Homayoun Shahri, AT&T Bell Labs, Murray Hill, NJ
hsa@ulysses.att.com

Talal Shamoon, Cornell Univ., Ithaca, NY
talal@ee.cornell.edu

Vincent Shaw, LSI International, Marlboro, NJ

Nagabhushana Sindhushayana, Cornell Univ., Ithaca, NY
bhushan@ee.cornell.edu

Paul H. Siegel, IBM Almaden Res. Center, San Jose, CA
siegelph@almaden.ibm.com

Neil J. A. Sloane, AT&T Bell Labs, Murray Hill, NJ
njas@research.att.com

Jakov Snyders, New Jersey Inst. of Tech., Newark, NJ
snyders@hertz.njit.edu

Patrick Solé, CNRS, Valbonne, FRANCE
sole@mimosa.unice.fr

Peter F. Swaszek, Univ. of Rhode Island, Kingston, RI
swaszek@ele.uri.edu

I. Emre Telatar, AT&T Bell Labs, Murray Hill, NJ
telatar@research.att.com

Steven A. Tretter, Univ. of Maryland, College Park, MD
tretter@eng.umd.edu

Mitchell D. Trott, Mass. Inst. of Technology, Cambridge, MA
trott@lids.mit.edu

David N. Tse, Mass. Inst. of Technology, Cambridge, MA
dntse@lids.mit.edu

Vinay Vaishampayan, Texas A&M Univ., College Station, TX
vinay@varun.tamu.edu

Rene J. van der Vleuten, Delft Univ. of Tech., Delft, The NETHERLANDS
rene@duteinm.et.tudelft.nl

Sridhar Vembu, Princeton University, Princeton, NJ
vembu@ee.princeton.edu

Sergio Verdu, Princeton Univ., Princeton, NJ
verdu@princeton.edu

Victor K. Wei, Bellcore, Morristown, NJ
wekowe@bellcore.com

Aaron D. Wyner, AT&T Bell Labs, Murray Hill, NJ
adw@research.att.com

Jian Yang, Univ. of Pennsylvania, Philadelphia, PA

Xiancheng Yuan, PictureTel Corp., Danvers, MA
yuan@pictel.com

Rami Zamir, Tel-Aviv Univ., Tel-Aviv, ISRAEL
zamir@genius.eng.tau.ac.il

Kenneth A. Zeger, Univ. of Illinois, Urbana, IL
zeger@ai.mit.edu

Ephraim Zehavi, Technion, Haifa, Israel
ezehavi@ee.technion.ac.il

DIMACS Series in Discrete Mathematics
and Theoretical Computer Science
Volume **14**, 1993

On the Duality of Coding and Quantizing

G. DAVID FORNEY, JR.

December 7, 1992

ABSTRACT. The coding gain $\gamma_c(\Lambda)$ (Hermite's parameter) and the shaping gain $\gamma_s(\Lambda)$ (or equivalently the normalized second moment $G(\Lambda)$) are geometrical invariants of a lattice Λ that are figures of merit for coding and quantizing, respectively.

These quantities appear in low-order terms of the series expansions of the normalized (relevant) theta series of Λ and the normalized moment-generating function of Λ, respectively. The asymptotic behavior of the normalized error function of Λ, which is equivalent to the normalized moment-generating function of Λ, is governed by $\gamma_c(\Lambda)$ at high SNRs and by $\gamma_s(\Lambda)$ at low SNRs. The performance of a high-rate Voronoi codebook $C(\Lambda/\Lambda')$ for transmission is a function of $\gamma_c(\Lambda)$ and $\gamma_s(\Lambda')$, whereas for quantization it is a function of $\gamma_c(\Lambda')$ and $\gamma_s(\Lambda)$. The duals of the best known lattices in terms of $\gamma_c(\Lambda)$ are the best known lattices in terms of $\gamma_s(\Lambda)$ in 1-8, 12, 16 and 24 dimensions. Other empirical evidence suggests that the duals of lattices that are good for coding are good for quantizing, although this rule has exceptions, and the converse often does not hold.

Consequently it appears that the coding and shaping gains are approximate duals. It is conjectured that this may be a first-order approximation to a more precise duality relationship, perhaps between the normalized (relevant?) theta series of Λ and the normalized moment-generating (error) function of the dual of Λ.

1. Introduction

It is commonly understood that the packing and covering problems, or alternatively the coding and quantizing problems, are in some sense duals. The objective of this paper is to make more precise statements in this vein.

Our working hypotheses are:

- The dual of the packing radius is not the covering radius, but rather the normalized second moment, at least to a first-order approximation.

1991 *Mathematics Subject Classification.* Primary 94A05, 94A29.

- The dual of a Euclidean-space code that is good for coding is good for quantizing (and *vice versa*?)

We give empirical evidence that tends to support these hypotheses. However, the evidence indicates that at best they can be only approximately true. We conjecture that they are first-order approximations to a more precise duality relationship.

Our basic text is the comprehensive treatise of Conway and Sloane [**CS88**].

2. Geometrical Parameters of Lattices

This section discusses the basic geometrical parameters of a lattice Λ, such as its packing radius $\rho(\Lambda)$, kissing number $K(\Lambda)$, theta series $\Theta_\Lambda(q)$, covering radius $\tau(\Lambda)$, and second moment per dimension $P(\Lambda)$. We show how to normalize these parameters so that they become geometrical invariants of Λ. Finally, after [**CS88**], we review the various optimization problems that they suggest.

2.1. Geometrical parameters of Λ. An n-dimensional *lattice* Λ is a discrete additive subgroup of real Euclidean n-space $\mathbf{R}^n$. We assume that Λ spans $\mathbf{R}^n$.

(More generally, the parameters discussed in this section are well defined for: an n-dimensional lattice translate, which is a discrete subset of $\mathbf{R}^n$ that is generated by a group of translations; an n-dimensional regular array, which is a discrete subset of $\mathbf{R}^n$ that is generated by a group Γ of isometries of $\mathbf{R}^n$; or a geometrically uniform code, which is a discrete subset of $(\mathbf{R}^n)^I$ that is generated by a subgroup of Γ^I, where $I \subseteq \mathbf{Z}$ is an index set and Γ is a group of isometries of $\mathbf{R}^n$ [**Fo91**]. These geometrical sets all have congruent Voronoi regions. However, for simplicity we discuss only lattices.)

Except for the theta series $\Theta_\Lambda(q)$, the geometrical parameters that we discuss are all defined by the *Voronoi region* $R(\Lambda)$ of the lattice Λ, which is the set of points in $\mathbf{R}^n$ that are at least as close to the origin $\mathbf{0}$ as to any other point in Λ:

$$R(\Lambda) \triangleq \{\mathbf{x} \in \mathbf{R}^n : \|\mathbf{x}\|^2 = \min_{\mathbf{c}\in\Lambda} \|\mathbf{x} - \mathbf{c}\|^2\} .$$

The set of points in $\mathbf{R}^n$ that are at least as close to a lattice point $\mathbf{c} \in \Lambda$ as to any other point in Λ is then the translate $R(\Lambda) + \mathbf{c}$. The set of translates $\{R(\Lambda) + \mathbf{c},\ \mathbf{c} \in \Lambda\}$ is the set of decision regions of a minimum-distance decision rule; this set covers n-space $\mathbf{R}^n$, with overlaps only on the region boundaries, which have zero volume.

There is a well-defined *volume* $V(\Lambda)$ per lattice point, namely the volume of the Voronoi region $R(\Lambda)$:

$$V(\Lambda) \triangleq \int_{R(\Lambda)} d\mathbf{x} .$$

By the group property of Λ, the *minimum squared distance* between lattice points is the minimum nonzero norm of any lattice point $\mathbf{c} \in \Lambda$:

$$d^2_{\min}(\Lambda) \triangleq \min_{\substack{\mathbf{c}\in\Lambda \\ \mathbf{c}\neq 0}} \|\mathbf{c}\|^2 \ .$$

The *packing radius* of Λ is then

$$\rho(\Lambda) \triangleq d_{\min}(\Lambda)/2 \ ,$$

the radius of the greatest sphere that can be inscribed within $R(\Lambda)$.

The *kissing number* of Λ is the number of nearest neighbors to any lattice point, which by the group property is the number of lattice points of norm $d^2_{\min}(\Lambda)$:

$$K(\Lambda) \triangleq | \{\mathbf{c} \in \Lambda : \ \|\mathbf{c}\|^2 = d^2_{\min}(\Lambda)\} | \ .$$

$K(\Lambda)$ is the number of faces of $R(\Lambda)$ at distance $\rho(\Lambda)$ from $\mathbf{0}$.

The *theta series* $\Theta_\Lambda(q)$ of Λ is the generating function of the norms $N(\mathbf{c}) \triangleq \|\mathbf{c}\|^2$:

$$\Theta_\Lambda(q) \triangleq \sum_{\mathbf{c}\in\Lambda} q^{N(\mathbf{c})} = 1 + K(\Lambda) q^{d^2_{\min}(\Lambda)} + \dots ,$$

where the last expression exhibits the first two terms in a series expansion of $\Theta_\Lambda(q)$.

Each face of the Voronoi region $R(\Lambda)$ is defined by a *relevant* (face-defining) lattice point $\mathbf{c} \in \Lambda$, and consists of a portion of the hyperplane bisecting the line between $\mathbf{0}$ and $\mathbf{c}$. The set of relevant lattice points will be denoted by $S(\Lambda)$. All minimum-norm lattice points are relevant. The *relevant theta series* $\Theta'_\Lambda(q)$ of Λ is the generating function of the norms of the relevant lattice points:

$$\Theta'_\Lambda(q) \triangleq \sum_{\mathbf{c}\in S(\Lambda)} q^{N(\mathbf{c})} = K(\Lambda) q^{d^2_{\min}(\Lambda)} + \dots .$$

Unlike the global function $\Theta_\Lambda(q)$, the relevant theta series $\Theta'_\Lambda(q)$ is a local function determined by $R(\Lambda)$. As we shall see, it yields a slightly tighter bound on error probability than $\Theta_\Lambda(q)$.

The *covering radius* of Λ is the radius of the least sphere that contains $R(\Lambda)$:

$$\tau(\Lambda) \triangleq \max_{\mathbf{x}\in R(\Lambda)} \|\mathbf{x}\| \ .$$

The *second moment per dimension* of Λ is the average value of $\|\mathbf{x}\|^2/n$ under a uniform probability density over $R(\Lambda)$, namely $p(\mathbf{x}) = 1/V(\Lambda)$, $\mathbf{x} \in R(\Lambda)$:

$$P(\Lambda) \triangleq [1/V(\Lambda)] \int_{R(\Lambda)} (\|\mathbf{x}\|^2/n) \, d\mathbf{x} \ .$$

2.2. Geometrical invariants of Λ. We now normalize these parameters to be the same for any version of Λ. A *version of* Λ is obtained by any combination of:

Scaling:	$\Lambda \to \alpha\Lambda,$	$\alpha \in \mathbf{R} > 0;$
Translation:	$\Lambda \to \alpha\Lambda + \mathbf{x},$	$\mathbf{x} \in \mathbf{R}^n;$
Orthogonal transformation:	$\Lambda \to T\Lambda,$	$TT^T = I;$
Cartesian product:	$\Lambda \to \Lambda^m,$	$m \in \mathbf{Z} > 0.$

A parameter that is invariant under these operations is a *geometrical invariant* of Λ.

The first three operations are conventional similarity transformations. Since scaling by α increases $V(\Lambda)$ by a factor of α^n, we normalize parameters for scale by using the one-dimensional scale factor $V(\Lambda)^{1/n}$. We normalize for translation by measuring all parameters with respect to a lattice point, which may be taken as $\mathbf{0}$. All parameters defined in terms of norms (Euclidean squared distances) are automatically invariant to orthogonal transformations.

The Cartesian product operation is included in order to ensure proper normalization for dimension. An n-dimensional lattice Λ and an m-dimensional lattice Λ' may be compared by comparing Λ^m to $(\Lambda')^n$ in nm-space $\mathbf{R}^{nm}$.

Any function of a geometrical invariant is another geometrical invariant. We shall say that two geometrical invariants are *equivalent* if one is a one-to-one function of the other.

The normalized minimum squared distance is obtained by dividing $d^2_{\min}(\Lambda)$ by the scale factor $V(\Lambda)^{2/n}$ to obtain *Hermite's parameter*

$$\gamma_c(\Lambda) \triangleq d^2_{\min}(\Lambda)/V(\Lambda)^{2/n} ,$$

which in the coding literature is called the nominal (fundamental, asymptotic) *coding gain* of Λ. Since $d^2_{\min}(\Lambda^m) = d^2_{\min}(\Lambda)$, the coding gain $\gamma_c(\Lambda)$ is a geometrical invariant of Λ (unlike the center density $\delta(\Lambda) \triangleq [\rho(\Lambda)]^n/V(\Lambda)$). The coding gain of any version of the integer lattice $\mathbf{Z}$ (including $\mathbf{Z}^m$, for any m) is $\gamma_c(\mathbf{Z}) = 1$, which may be taken as a baseline coding gain. We shall sometimes measure coding gain in dB:

$$\gamma_c(\Lambda) \text{ (in dB) } = 10 \log_{10} \gamma_c(\Lambda) .$$

Since $K(\Lambda^m) = mK(\Lambda)$, the normalized kissing number is

$$\kappa(\Lambda) \triangleq K(\Lambda)/n .$$

Since $\Theta_\Lambda m(q) = [\Theta_\Lambda(q)]^m$, and norms are normalized by dividing by $V(\Lambda)^{2/n}$, the correct normalization of the theta series of Λ is given by

$$\begin{aligned} T_\Lambda(q) &\triangleq [\Theta_\Lambda(q^{V(\Lambda)^{-2/n}})]^{1/n} \\ &= [1 + K(\Lambda) q^{d^2_{\min}(\Lambda)/V(\Lambda)^{2/n}} + \ldots]^{1/n} \\ &= 1 + \kappa(\Lambda) q^{\gamma_c(\Lambda)} + \ldots . \end{aligned}$$

We call $T_\Lambda(q)$ the *normalized theta series* of Λ; it is a geometrical invariant of Λ. The fact that the second term of the series expansion of $T_\Lambda(q)$ is $\kappa(\Lambda)q^{\gamma_c(\Lambda)}$ shows that both $\kappa(\Lambda)$ and $\gamma_c(\Lambda)$ are geometrical invariants of Λ. Similarly, the coefficients and exponents of all higher-order terms of the series expansion of the normalized theta series of Λ are geometrical invariants of Λ.

The Voronoi region $R(\Lambda^m)$ is the Cartesian product $[R(\Lambda)]^m$. It has $|S(\Lambda)|^m$ faces, defined by the set $S(\Lambda^m)$ of m-tuples in Λ^m with $m-1$ zero components and a single component from $S(\Lambda)$. The relevant theta series of Λ^m is therefore simply given by $\Theta'_{\Lambda^m}(q) = m\Theta'_\Lambda(q)$. The *normalized relevant theta series* of Λ is then

$$\begin{aligned} T'_\Lambda(q) &\triangleq \Theta_\Lambda(q^{V(\Lambda)^{-2/n}})/n \\ &= [K(\Lambda) q^{d^2_{\min}(\Lambda)/V(\Lambda)^{2/n}} + \ldots]/n \\ &= \kappa(\Lambda) q^{\gamma_c(\Lambda)} + \ldots . \end{aligned}$$

Since $T'_\Lambda(q)$ is another geometrical invariant of Λ, the fact that the first term of its series expansion is $\kappa(\Lambda)q^{\gamma_c(\Lambda)}$ again shows that both $\kappa(\Lambda)$ and $\gamma_c(\Lambda)$ are geometrical invariants of Λ.

Since $\tau^2(\Lambda^m) = m\tau^2(\Lambda)$, the normalized squared covering radius is

$$[\tau^2(\Lambda)/n]/V(\Lambda)^{2/n} .$$

In other words, unlike the squared packing radius, the squared covering radius must be normalized per dimension to become a geometrical invariant. This hints at a lack of duality between $\rho(\Lambda)$ and $\tau(\Lambda)$.

Since $P(\Lambda^m) = P(\Lambda)$ and $P(\alpha\Lambda) = \alpha^2 P(\Lambda)$, the *normalized second moment* of Λ is

$$G(\Lambda) \triangleq P(\Lambda)/V(\Lambda)^{2/n} = 1/[nV(\Lambda)^{1+2/n}] \int_{R(\Lambda)} \|\mathbf{x}\|^2 \, d\mathbf{x} .$$

The normalized second moment $G(\Lambda)$ is a geometrical invariant of Λ that is generally taken as the figure of merit of Λ as a quantizer.

The normalized second moment of any version of the integer lattice $\mathbf{Z}$ (including $\mathbf{Z}^n$, for any n) is $G(\mathbf{Z}) = 1/12$, which may be taken as a baseline normalized second moment. The *shaping gain* of Λ is then defined as

$$\gamma_s(\Lambda) \triangleq G(\mathbf{Z})/G(\Lambda) = (1/12)/G(\Lambda) ,$$

which will also sometimes be measured in dB. It is known that the maximum possible shaping gain is $\pi e/6$ (1.53 dB), which is derived from the limit $(1/2\pi e)$ of the normalized second moment of the n-sphere as $n \to \infty$.

More generally, consider the moment-generating function $E_\Lambda(e^{-\lambda\|\mathbf{x}\|^2})$, defined as the expectation of $e^{-\lambda\|\mathbf{x}\|^2}$ under a uniform distribution $p_u(\mathbf{x}) = 1/V(\Lambda)$ over $R(\Lambda)$:

$$E_\Lambda(e^{-\lambda\|\mathbf{x}\|^2}) \triangleq [1/V(\Lambda)] \int_{R(\Lambda)} \exp -\lambda\|\mathbf{x}\|^2 \, d\mathbf{x} \; .$$

Since $E_{\Lambda^m}(e^{-\lambda\|\mathbf{x}\|^2}) = [E_\Lambda(e^{-\lambda\|\mathbf{x}\|^2})]^m$, and norms are normalized by dividing by $V(\Lambda)^{2/n}$, the *normalized moment-generating function*

$$U_\Lambda(\lambda) \triangleq \{[1/V(\Lambda)] \int_{R(\Lambda)} \exp -\lambda\|\mathbf{x}\|^2/V(\Lambda)^{2/n} \, d\mathbf{x}\}^{1/n}$$

is another geometrical invariant of Λ. From the series expansion $e^x = \sum_{n\geq 0} (n!)^{-1}x^n$,

$$U_\Lambda(\lambda) = \{1 - n\lambda G(\Lambda) + \ldots\}^{1/n} \; .$$

As $\lambda \to 0$, we have the first-order approximation

$$U_\Lambda(\lambda) \cong 1 - \lambda G(\Lambda) + \ldots \; .$$

2.3. Figures of merit for packing, covering and quantizing. The use of Hermite's parameter $\gamma_c(\Lambda)$ as a figure of merit for packing is well accepted. Indeed, Conway and Sloane [**CS88**] refer to maximization of $\gamma_c(\Lambda)$ (or equivalently $\delta(\Lambda)$) in a given dimension as 'the (lattice) packing problem.' [The (lattice) 'kissing number problem' is to maximize $K(\Lambda)$ in a given dimension; this can be viewed as a packing problem on the surface of an n-sphere.]

In coding, the nominal coding gain $\gamma_c(\Lambda)$ is widely accepted as a good single-parameter figure of merit of the coding efficiency of Λ in the presence of white Gaussian noise; however, it is recognized that the kissing number ('error coefficient') must also be taken into account for a more accurate estimate of 'effective coding gain.' A better measure is the probability of error in white Gaussian noise, which is determined by the normalized error function of Λ that will be introduced in the next section.

The 'covering problem' is to minimize the normalized squared covering radius $[\tau^2(\Lambda)/n]/V(\Lambda)^{2/n}$ in a given dimension. Conway and Sloane state [**CS88**, p. 31] that 'the problem of finding the best covering of space by overlapping spheres [is] a kind of dual to the packing problem.' This paper offers little support for this view.

The 'quantizing problem' is to minimize the normalized second moment $G(\Lambda)$, or equivalently to maximize the shaping gain $\gamma_s(\Lambda)$. We shall argue that this problem is more nearly dual to the packing problem than is the covering problem.

3. The Normalized Error Function of Λ

In this section we introduce a figure of merit for a lattice Λ for the channel coding problem, which is seen to be equivalent to the normalized moment-generating function. Interestingly, at high signal-to-noise ratios this geometrical invariant becomes equivalent to the normalized theta series (or to the normalized relevant theta series), and its behavior is governed by the coding gain $\gamma_c(\Lambda)$, whereas at low signal-to-noise ratios its behavior is governed by the shaping gain $\gamma_s(\Lambda)$.

3.1. Definitions. If a lattice point in Λ is transmitted in white Gaussian noise of variance σ^2 per dimension, then the probability of error using Voronoi decision regions is

$$\Pr_\Lambda(E \mid \sigma^2) = 1 - \int_{R(\Lambda)} p_{\sigma^2}(\mathbf{x})\, d\mathbf{x} ,$$

where $p_{\sigma^2}(\mathbf{x})$ is the n-dimensional Gaussian density

$$p_{\sigma^2}(\mathbf{x}) = (2\pi\sigma^2)^{-n/2} \exp -\|\mathbf{x}\|^2/2\sigma^2 .$$

This can be expressed in terms of a *generalized error function*, defined as the probability of no error when $\sigma^2 = 1/8y^2$:

$$\mathrm{erf}_\Lambda(y^2) \triangleq \int_{R(\Lambda)} p_{1/8y^2}(\mathbf{x}) d\mathbf{x} = 1 - \Pr_\Lambda(E \mid 1/8y^2) .$$

The parameter y^2 may be regarded as a kind of signal-to-noise ratio. It is left squared to avoid tedious square roots. Clearly $\mathrm{erf}_\Lambda(y^2)$ is a monotonic function of y^2, and

$$\begin{aligned} \mathrm{erf}_\Lambda(y^2) &\to 0 \quad \text{as} \quad y^2 \to 0; \\ \mathrm{erf}_\Lambda(y^2) &\to 1 \quad \text{as} \quad y^2 \to \infty . \end{aligned}$$

The complement of the generalized error function is

$$\mathrm{erfc}_\Lambda(y^2) \triangleq 1 - \mathrm{erf}_\Lambda(y^2) = \Pr_\Lambda(E \mid 1/8y^2) .$$

For the integer lattice $\mathbf{Z}$, since $R(\mathbf{Z})$ is the interval $[-1/2,\ 1/2]$, we have

$$\begin{aligned} \mathrm{erf}_{\mathbf{Z}}(y^2) &= \int_{[-1/2,\ 1/2]} (2\pi/8y^2)^{-1/2} \exp -4x^2y^2\, dx \\ &= \int_{[-y,y]} (\pi)^{-1/2} \exp -z^2\, dz \\ &= \mathrm{erf}(y), \end{aligned}$$

where $\mathrm{erf}(y)$ is the conventional one-dimensional Gaussian error function.

Since $\mathrm{erf}_{\Lambda^m}(y^2) = [\mathrm{erf}_\Lambda(y^2)]^m$ and $\mathrm{erf}_{\alpha\Lambda}(y^2) = \mathrm{erf}_\Lambda(\alpha^2 y^2)$, the proper normalization of $\mathrm{erf}_\Lambda(y^2)$ is

$$E_\Lambda(y^2) \triangleq \{ \mathrm{erf}_\Lambda[y^2/V(\Lambda)^{2/n}\}^{1/n} = \left[\int_{R(\Lambda)} p_{V(\Lambda)^{2/n}/8y^2}(\mathbf{x})\, d\mathbf{x} \right]^{1/n} ,$$

which we define as the *normalized error function* $E_\Lambda(y^2)$. This function is another geometrical invariant of Λ. Like $\mathrm{erf}_\Lambda(y^2)$, $E_\Lambda(y^2)$ is a monotonic function of y^2 that ranges from 0 to 1. Its complement is the *normalized error probability*

$$P_\Lambda(y^2) \triangleq 1 - E_\Lambda(y^2) \ .$$

The 'channel coding problem' is then to maximize the function $E_\Lambda(y^2)$, or to minimize its complement $P_\Lambda(y^2)$. (If the answer is not independent of y^2, then we choose a target normalized error probability $P_\Lambda(y^2)$ and seek the Λ for which the target is achieved with the minimum y^2.)

Note that

$$\begin{aligned} E_\Lambda(y^2) &= \left\{ \left[8y^2/2\pi V(\Lambda)^{2/n}\right]^{n/2} \int_{R(\Lambda)} \exp -4y^2\|\mathbf{x}\|^2/V(\Lambda)^{2/n} d\mathbf{x} \right\}^{1/n} \\ &= [8y^2/2\pi]^{1/2} U_\Lambda(4y^2) \ . \end{aligned}$$

Therefore the geometrical invariants $E_\Lambda(y^2)$ and $U_\Lambda(\lambda)$ are equivalent. As $y^2 \to 0$,

$$E_\Lambda(y^2) \cong [8y^2/2\pi]^{1/2}[1 - 4y^2 G(\Lambda)] \ .$$

3.2. Relation to normalized theta series. There is an interesting relation between the normalized error function of Λ and the normalized theta series of Λ (see [**CS88**, p. 73]). Let K_{w^2} denote the number of lattice points of norm w^2; then

$$\Theta_\Lambda(q) = \sum_{w^2} K_{w^2} q^{w^2} \ .$$

By the *union bound*, the probability of error is bounded by

$$\Pr_\Lambda(E \mid \sigma^2) \le \sum_{w^2>0} K_{w^2} \Pr_{w\mathbf{Z}}(E \mid \sigma^2)/2 \ .$$

But

$$\Pr_{w\mathbf{Z}}(E \mid \sigma^2) = \Pr_{\mathbf{Z}}(E \mid \sigma^2/w^2) = \ \mathrm{erfc}_{\mathbf{Z}}(w^2/8\sigma^2) \ .$$

By the Chernoff bound, which is exponentially tight,

$$\mathrm{erfc}_{\mathbf{Z}}(w^2/8\sigma^2) \le \exp -w^2/8\sigma^2 \ .$$

Therefore

$$\begin{aligned} \Pr_\Lambda(E \mid \sigma^2) &\le (1/2) \sum_{w^2>0} K_{w^2} \exp -w^2/8\sigma^2 \\ &= (1/2)[\Theta_\Lambda(\exp -1/8\sigma^2) - 1] \ . \end{aligned}$$

It follows that

$$\begin{aligned} E_\Lambda(y^2) &= \{\mathrm{erf}_\Lambda[y^2/V(\Lambda)^{2/n}]\}^{1/n} \\ &= \{1 - \Pr_\Lambda(E \mid V(\Lambda)^{2/n}/8y^2)\}^{1/n} \\ &\geq \{1/2[1 - \Theta_\Lambda(\exp -y^2/V(\Lambda)^{2/n})]\}^{1/n} \\ &= 2^{-1/n}[1 - [T_\Lambda(e^{-y^2})]^n]^{1/n} \ . \end{aligned}$$

This expression shows that a high signal-to-noise ratios the normalized error function $E_\Lambda(y^2)$ (or equivalently $U_\Lambda(\lambda)$) tends to become equivalent to the normalized theta series $T_\Lambda(q)$.

A tighter union bound is derived from the relevant theta series:

$$\Pr_\Lambda(E \mid \sigma^2) \leq (1/2)\Theta'_\Lambda(\exp -1/8\sigma^2) \ .$$

This yields

$$\begin{aligned} E_\Lambda(y^2) &\geq \{[1 - (1/2)\Theta'_\Lambda(\exp -y^2/V(\Lambda)^{2/n})]\}^{1/n} \\ &= \{1 - (n/2)[T'_\Lambda(e^{-y^2})]\}^{1/n} \\ &\geq 1 - (1/2)T'_\Lambda(e^{-y^2}) \ , \end{aligned}$$

so

$$P_\Lambda(y^2) \leq (1/2)T'_\Lambda(e^{-y^2}) = (1/2)\kappa(\Lambda)e^{-y^2\gamma_c(\Lambda)} + \dots \ .$$

As $y^2 \to \infty$, this upper bound becomes exponentially tight; thus there is an even closer connection between $E_\Lambda(y)$ and the normalized relevant theta series $T'_\Lambda(q)$.

Note that the coding gain enters as a multiplicative factor in the exponent, where it raises the 'signal-to-noise ratio' from y^2 to $y^2\gamma_c(\Lambda)$.

3.3. Asymptotic behavior at the two extremes. We now examine the asymptotic behavior of $E_\Lambda(y)$ at the two extremes, $y^2 \to \infty$ and $y^2 \to 0$. We find that its behavior is governed by $\gamma_c(\Lambda)$ in the former case, and by $G(\Lambda)$ or $\gamma_s(\Lambda)$ in the latter. (The gist of this argument is in [**CS88**, p. 70].)

As $y^2 \to \infty$, or $\sigma^2 \to 0$, the error probability $\Pr_\Lambda(E \mid \sigma^2)$ is well approximated by the first term of the union bound:

$$\Pr_\Lambda(E \mid \sigma^2) \cong (1/2)K(\Lambda)\ \mathrm{erfc}[(d^2_{\min}(\Lambda)/8\sigma^2)^{1/2}] \ .$$

Then the normalized error function is well approximated by

$$\begin{aligned} E_\Lambda(y^2) &= \{1 - \Pr_\Lambda[E \mid V(\Lambda)^{2/n}/8y^2]\}^{1/n} \\ &\cong 1 - (1/n)\Pr_\Lambda[E \mid V(\Lambda)^{2/n}/8y^2] \\ &\cong 1 - [K(\Lambda)/2n]\ \mathrm{erfc}_{\mathbf{Z}}[y^2 d^2_{\min}(\Lambda)/V(\Lambda)^{2/n}] \\ &= 1 - [\kappa(\Lambda)/2]\ \mathrm{erfc}_{\mathbf{Z}}[y^2\gamma_c(\Lambda)] \ . \end{aligned}$$

Thus in the limit as $y^2 \to \infty$ the behavior of $E_\Lambda(y^2)$ is governed by the coding gain $\gamma_c(\Lambda)$ and the normalized kissing number $\kappa(\Lambda)$ (normalized by $\kappa(\mathbf{Z}) = 2$).

Ultimately the former dominates, so the best lattice for channel coding at high signal-to-noise ratios is the lattice with the best coding gain $\gamma_c(\Lambda)$.

As $y^2 \to 0$, or $\sigma^2 \to \infty$, we have seen that the normalized error function becomes

$$E_\Lambda(y^2) \cong (8y^2/2\pi)^{1/2}[1 - 4y^2 G(\Lambda)] \ .$$

Thus in the limit as $y^2 \to 0$ the behavior of $E_\Lambda(y^2)$ is governed by the normalized second moment $G(\Lambda)$. In this sense the best lattice for channel coding at low signal-to-noise ratios is the lattice with the best shaping gain $\gamma_s(\Lambda)$.

This result is a first strong suggestion of duality between $\gamma_c(\Lambda)$ and $\gamma_s(\Lambda)$.

4. Voronoi Codebooks

Let Λ' be a sublattice of Λ. A *Voronoi codebook* $C(\Lambda/\Lambda')$ is the set of points of Λ (or of a translate $\Lambda + \mathbf{a}$) that lie in $R(\Lambda')$ [**CS83**],[**Fo89**].

A Voronoi codebook $C(\Lambda/\Lambda')$ contains one point (the minimum-norm point) from each of the $|\Lambda/\Lambda'|$ cosets of Λ' whose union is $\Lambda + \mathbf{a}$, assuming resolution of ties on the boundary of $R(\Lambda')$. The size of $C(\Lambda/\Lambda')$ is therefore $|\Lambda/\Lambda'|$, which is equal to

$$|\Lambda/\Lambda'| = V(\Lambda')/V(\Lambda) \ ,$$

and its *rate* is

$$R = (2/n)\log_2 V(\Lambda')/V(\Lambda) \quad \text{bits per two dimensions.}$$

For transmission, as shown in [**Fo89**] using the high-rate approximations

$$\Pr_\Lambda(E \mid \sigma^2) \cong [K(\Lambda)/2]\ \mathrm{erfc}_{\mathbf{Z}}[d^2_{\min}(\Lambda)/8\sigma^2];$$

$$E_C[\|\mathbf{x}\|^2/n] \cong P(\Lambda')$$

$$2^R - 1 \cong 2^R = V(\Lambda')^{2/n}/V(\Lambda)^{2/n},$$

where $E_C[\|\mathbf{x}\|^2/n]$ is the average norm per dimension of a uniform discrete probability distribution over $C(\Lambda/\Lambda')$, the error probability is well approximated by

$$\Pr_\Lambda(E \mid \sigma^2) \cong [K(\Lambda)/2]\ \mathrm{erfc}_{\mathbf{Z}}[3\gamma_c(\Lambda)\gamma_s(\Lambda')\mathrm{SNR}_{\mathrm{norm}}/2],$$

where the *normalized signal-to-noise ratio* is defined by

$$\mathrm{SNR}_{\mathrm{norm}} \triangleq \{E_C[\|\mathbf{x}\|^2/n]/\sigma^2\}(2^R - 1) \ .$$

Thus, to the accuracy of these approximations, the probability of error of a Voronoi transmission codebook is a function only of

(a) the coding gain $\gamma_c(\Lambda)$ of the granular lattice Λ, and its kissing number $K(\Lambda)$,

(b) the shaping gain of the sublattice Λ', and

(c) the normalized signal-to-noise ratio $\mathrm{SNR}_{\mathrm{norm}}$.

On the other hand, for quantization of a white Gaussian source of variance σ^2 per dimension, it is shown in [**EF93**] using the high-rate approximations

$$\Pr(\text{overload}) = \Pr'_{\Lambda}(E \mid \sigma^2) \cong [K(\Lambda')/2] \operatorname{erfc}_{\mathbf{Z}}[d^2_{\min}(\Lambda')/8\sigma^2];$$

$$\text{MSE} \cong P(\Lambda);$$

where Pr (overload) is the probability that the source vector falls outside the support region $R(\Lambda')$ and MSE is the average quantization error per dimension within the support region, that the overload probability is well approximated by

$$\Pr(\text{overload}) \cong [K(\Lambda')/2] \operatorname{erfc}_{\mathbf{Z}}[3\gamma_c(\Lambda')\gamma_s(\Lambda)/(2\,\text{SQNR}_{\text{norm}})],$$

where the *normalized signal-to-quantization-noise-ratio* is defined by

$$\text{SQNR}_{\text{norm}} \triangleq (\sigma^2/\text{MSE})/2^R .$$

Thus, to the accuracy of these approximations, the probability of overload of a Voronoi quantization codebook is a function only of

(a) the shaping gain $\gamma_s(\Lambda)$ of the granular lattice Λ;
(b) the coding gain of the sublattice Λ' and its kissing number $K(\Lambda')$, and
(c) the normalized signal-to-quantization-noise ratio $\text{SQNR}_{\text{norm}}$.

The objective in transmission is typically to minimize average signal power $E_C[\|\mathbf{x}\|^2/n]$ or maximize the rate R for a given average noise variance σ^2 and probability of error. If the objective in quantization is dual, namely to minimize MSE and/or rate for a given source variance σ^2 and probability of overload, then we see that the roles of the granular lattice Λ and the boundary lattice Λ' are interchanged. Equally, in the dual problem, the roles of coding gain and shaping gain are interchanged, suggesting again that these two figures of merit are duals.

5. Dual Lattices: Empirical Evidence

In this section we give empirical evidence showing that the duals of lattices with good coding gains have good shaping gains. We see that if one n-dimensional lattice is superior to another in terms of coding gain, then it is generally superior in terms of shaping gain, although there are exceptions to this rule. We note also that there is little evidence that the dual of a lattice with a good shaping gain will necessarily be good for coding.

The *dual lattice* Λ^* to an n-dimensional lattice Λ is defined as

$$\Lambda^* = \{\mathbf{b} \in \mathbf{R}^n : \ (\mathbf{b}, \mathbf{c}) \in \mathbf{Z} \text{ for all } \mathbf{c} \in \Lambda\},$$

where $(\mathbf{b}, \mathbf{c})$ is the usual inner product. If $G \in \mathbf{R}^{n \times n}$ is a *basis* for Λ, so that

$$\Lambda = \{\mathbf{x}G : \ \mathbf{x} \in \mathbf{Z}^n\} ,$$

then a basis for Λ^* is $[G^{-1}]^T$. The volume of Λ^* is $V(\Lambda^*) = 1/V(\Lambda)$.

A lattice is *self-dual* (or 'iso-dual') if its dual is a version of itself.

5.1. Best known packings, coverings and quantizers. Conway and Sloane [**CS88**] give a comprehensive survey of the best known packings, coverings and quantizers. The packing problem is an ancient one in mathematics, and has been extremely well studied. The covering problem is of comparable age, but fewer results are known because it is more difficult to compute covering radii. The quantizer problem has been studied only recently, and the results in this area are quite sparse.

Table 1.1 of [**CS88**] shows the best known (a) packings, (b) coverings and (c) quantizers in 1-8, 12, 16 and 24 dimensions:

	1	2	3	4	5	6	7	8	12	16	24
(a)	$\mathbf{Z}$	A_2	A_3	D_4	D_5	E_6	E_7	E_8	K_{12}	BW_{16}	L_{24}
(b)	$\mathbf{Z}^*$	A_2^*	A_3^*	A_4^*	A_5^*	A_6^*	A_7^*	A_8^*	A_{12}^*	A_{16}^*	L_{24}^*
(c)	$\mathbf{Z}^*$	A_2^*	A_3^*	D_4^*	D_5^*	E_6^*	E_7^*	E_8^*	K_{12}^*	BW_{16}^*	L_{24}^*

Here $\mathbf{Z}$ is the integer lattice; A_n, D_n and E_n are n-dimensional root lattices; K_{12} is the 12-dimensional Coxeter-Todd lattice; BW_{16} is the 16-dimensional Barnes-Wall lattice; and L_{24} is the famous 24-dimensional Leech lattice. Of these lattices, $\mathbf{Z}$, A_2 (the hexagonal lattice), D_4, E_8, K_{12}, BW_{16} and L_{24} are self-dual.

The sparsest coverings known in dimensions 2 to 21 are the duals A_n^* of the root lattices A_n. Apart from this covering property, in dimensions 4 and above, these lattices are inferior in other respects.

In particular, the coding gains of the root lattices A_n are given by

$$\gamma_c(A_n) = 2(n+1)^{-1/n} ,$$

which increase slowly from the optimal 1.337 (1.00 dB) at $n = 3$ to an asymptote of 2 (3.01 dB) as $n \to \infty$. The coding gains of the lattices A_n^* are equal to

$$\gamma_c(A_n^*) = n(n+1)^{-1+1/n} ,$$

which are worse for $n > 3$; they reach a maximum of 1.196 (0.78 dB) at $n = 4$, and then decrease to 1 as $n \to \infty$.

The shaping gains of A_n and A_n^* are computed in [**CS88**, Ch. 21] and plotted in [**CS88**, Fig. 2.9]. The shaping gains of the root lattices A_n are distinctly suboptimal for $n \geq 3$; they reach a maximum value of 1.0768 (0.32 dB) at $n = 8$, and then decrease to 1 as $n \to \infty$. The shaping gains of the dual lattices A_n^* are better, but distinctly suboptimal for $n \geq 4$; they reach a value of 1.1039 (0.43 dB) at $n = 16$.

A striking feature of the table above is that the best known lattices in terms of shaping gain are the duals of the best known lattices in terms of coding gain. Conway and Sloane comment [**CS88**, p. 62]:

> It is worth remarking that the best n-dimensional quantizers presently known are always the duals of the best packings known.

However, we do not expect that this will always be the case. It would be nice to have more data.

5.2. More empirical data. More data are available from [**Fo89**], in which the shaping gains of a number of 'mod-2' (Construction A) lattices were computed.

Given a linear binary block code $C_{(n,k)}$ of length n and dimension k, the corresponding *mod-2 lattice* is the lattice $\Lambda_{(n,k)}$ consisting of all integer n-tuples that are congruent mod 2 to a codeword in C:

$$\Lambda_{(n,k)} \triangleq \{\mathbf{x} \in \mathbf{Z}^n : \mathbf{x} \equiv \mathbf{c} \pmod 2 \text{ for some } \mathbf{c} \in C_{(n,k)}\} .$$

The dual of a mod-2 lattice $\Lambda_{(n,k)}$ is the mod-2 lattice $\Lambda^*_{(n,k)} = \Lambda_{(n,n-k)}$ corresponding to the linear binary block code $C^*_{(n,k)} = C_{(n,n-k)}$ that is dual to $C_{(n,k)}$.

The following table gives the shaping gains of certain mod-2 lattices in 16, 24 and 32 dimensions, as well as of the optimal lattices BW_{16} and L_{24}, and the coding gains of their duals.

Λ	$\gamma_s(\Lambda)$	dB	Λ^*	$\gamma_c(\Lambda^*)$	dB
BW_{16}	1.220	0.86	BW_{16}	2.828	4.52
$\Lambda_{(16,5)}$	1.206	0.81	$\Lambda_{(16,11)}$	2.594	4.14
$\Lambda_{(16,4)}$	1.167	0.67	$\Lambda_{(16,12)}$	1.414	1.51
L_{24}	1.267	1.03	L_{24}	4.000	6.02
$\Lambda_{(24,6)}$	1.215	0.84	$\Lambda_{(24,18)}$	2.828	4.52
$\Lambda_{(24,5)}$	1.192	0.76	$\Lambda_{(24,19)}$	1.498	1.76
$\Lambda_{(24,9)}$	1.183	0.73	$\Lambda_{(24,15)}$	2.378	3.76
$\Lambda_{(32,7)}$	1.217	0.85	$\Lambda_{(32,25)}$	2.954	4.70
$\Lambda_{(32,6)}$	1.200	0.79	$\Lambda_{(32,26)}$	3.084	4.89
$\Lambda_{(32,13)}$	1.176	0.70	$\Lambda_{(32,19)}$	2.278	3.57

It can be seen from the above table that the duals of lattices that are good for coding are good for shaping, and that in general the better a lattice is for coding, the better its dual is for shaping.

However, this rule fails to hold for lattices that are not good for coding; e.g., $\Lambda_{(24,19)}$ has a poor minimum distance (2) and thus a poor coding gain, but its dual $\Lambda_{(24,5)}$ is better than $\Lambda_{(24,9)}$ for shaping, even though $\Lambda_{(24,15)}$ is substantially better than $\Lambda_{(24,19)}$ for coding. Thus we cannot expect in general that the duals of lattices that are good for shaping will be good for coding. Coding gain can be destroyed by a small number of near neighbors, whereas the normalized second moment is not very sensitive to the movement of a few Voronoi faces.

In 32 dimensions, there is a clear counterexample involving two lattices that are quite similar and that are both reasonably good for coding (relative to the best known 32-dimensional lattice coding gain of slightly more than 6 dB): $\Lambda_{(32,26)}$ is slightly better than $\Lambda_{(32,25)}$ for coding, but its dual $\Lambda_{(32,6)}$ is slightly worse than $\Lambda_{(32,7)}$ for shaping. Thus the hypothesis that if Λ and Λ' are good for coding, with Λ being better, then Λ^* will be better than $(\Lambda')^*$ for shaping, is at best only approximately true.

6. Discussion

The results of Sections 3, 4 and 5.1 lead us to conjecture that coding gain and shaping gain are dual quantities, and that there is a strong relationship between the coding gain of an optimal lattice and the shaping gain of the dual lattice.

The evidence of Section 5.2 forces us to modify the latter conjecture, since there can at best be only an approximate relationship between the coding gain of a lattice and the shaping gain of the dual lattice.

The geometrical invariants introduced in Section 2 show that coding gain and shaping gain are only first-order approximations to more global expressions. The asymptotic relationships of Section 3.3 are also suggestive.

A conjecture such as the following is suggested by these relationships:

Conjecture. The normalized (relevant?) theta series $T'_\Lambda(q)$ of a lattice Λ and the normalized moment-generating function $U_{\Lambda^*}(\lambda)$ of the dual lattice Λ^* are equivalent.

Acknowledgment

I am grateful to N.J.A. Sloane for assistance with the lattice literature.

References

[CS83] J. H. Conway and N.J.A. Sloane, "A fast encoding method for lattice codes and quantizers," *IEEE Trans. Inform. Theory*, vol. IT-29, pp. 820–824, 1983.

[CS88] J. H. Conway and N.J.A. Sloane, *Sphere Packings, Lattices and Groups.* New York: Springer-Verlag, 1988.

[EF93] M. V. Eyuboglu and G. D. Forney, Jr., "Lattice and trellis quantization with lattice- and trellis-bounded codebooks — High-rate theory for memoryless sources," *IEEE Trans. Inform. Theory*, vol. 39, pp. 46–59, Jan. 1993.

[Fo89] G. D. Forney, Jr., "Multidimensional constellations — Part II: Voronoi constellations," *IEEE J. Select Areas Commun.*, vol. 7, pp. 941–958, Sept. 1989.

[Fo91] G. D. Forney, Jr., "Geometrically uniform codes," *IEEE Trans. Inform. Theory*, vol. 37, pp. 1241–1260, Sept. 1991.

Motorola Codex, Mansfield, MA 02048, USA
E-mail address: david_forney@mcimail.com

DIMACS Series in Discrete Mathematics
and Theoretical Computer Science
Volume **14**, 1993

On Existence Proofs for Asymptotically Good Euclidean-Space Group Codes

HANS-ANDREA LOELIGER

January 11, 1993

ABSTRACT. It is pointed out that a standard proof of the Minkowski-Hlawka theorem is naturally interpreted as an averaging argument using linear codes over finite fields. In particular, it is shown that the existence of lattices with asymptotic density D satisfying $\lim_{n\to\infty} 1/n \log D = -\log 2$ (the best existence result known) is easily proved with a Gilbert-Varshamov-type argument for such codes.

1. Introduction

All previously known existence proofs for asymptotically good group codes rely on linear codes over finite fields — except, seemingly, the asymptotic results for lattices, which are based on the Minkowski-Hlawka theorem from geometric number theory [**1**] [**2**] [**3**]. This anomaly will be removed in this paper: it will be shown that the proof of the Minkowski-Hlawka theorem can be interpreted as an averaging argument for linear codes over finite fields.

It will be instructive to consider the *mod-M Gaussian channel*, which is created by an M-level amplitude-modulation (AM) signal set, additive white Gaussian noise, and a 'demodulator' that wraps the reals axis around a circle of circumference M (Fig. 1). More mathematically, the channel output is $(x+n)$ mod M, where (for odd M) $x \in \{-(M-1)/2, -(M-1)/2+1, \ldots, 0, \ldots, (M-1)/2\}$ is the channel input and n is a Gaussian random variable.

The natural codes for the mod-M channel are linear codes over Z_M, the integers modulo M. With any such code of length n is associated the corresponding mod-M lattice, which consists of all points in Z^n that are congruent mod M^n to a codeword.

1991 *Mathematics Subject Classification.* Primary 94A05; Secondary 94B75.

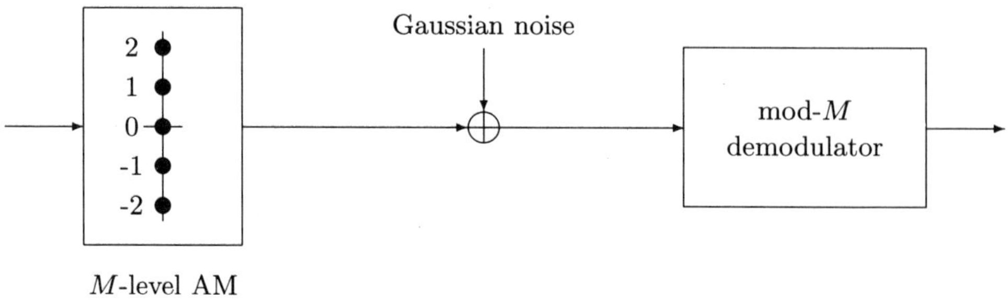

FIGURE 1. Mod-M Gaussian channel (for $M = 5$).

The lattices whose existence is proved by the Minkowski-Hlawka theorem are of this type, with M prime. Moreover, the proof of that theorem contains a limit $M \to \infty$; this implies (as will be shown in detail) that, for all practical purposes, only the corresponding linear codes are actually used. In other words, those lattice codes that are known to be asymptotically good are precisely the linear codes over Z_M, M prime, for the mod-M channel! We will also demonstrate that the existence of n-dimensional lattices with density D satisfying $\lim_{n\to\infty} 1/n \log D = -\log 2$ — the best result known and previously always derived from the Minkowski-Hlawka theorem — follows directly from the Gilbert-Varshamov bound for mod-M linear codes.

The paper is structured as follows. The necessary averaging arguments for linear codes are stated in Section 2; Section 3 reviews the proof of the Minkowski-Hlawka theorem and relates it to linear codes; and Section 4 contains the derivation of the asymptotic density result by means of the Gilbert-Varshamov bound.

2. Averaging Arguments

Following [**2**], we will adopt the notation $f(C) \triangleq \sum_{x\in C\setminus\{0\}} f(x)$ for the sum of a function $f : C \to R$ over all nonzero elements of a linear code C.

All averaging arguments for linear codes (and lattices) are based on the fact that, for fixed blocklength n, dimension k, and alphabet F_q, every nonzero element of F_q^n is contained in the same number of q-ary linear (n, k) codes. This implies the following well-known fact.

LEMMA 2.1 (BASIC AVERAGING LEMMA). Let $f(\cdot)$ be any real valued function defined on F_q^n. Then the average, over all q-ary linear (n, k) codes C, of $f(C)$ is

$$\overline{f(C)} = \frac{q^k - 1}{q^n - 1} f(F_q^n).$$

We will see in Section 3 that Lemma 2.1 is the basic argument in the proof of the Minkowski-Hlawka theorem. An immediate consequence is the following lemma, which we will use in Section 4.

LEMMA 2.2 (AVERAGE INTERSECTION CARDINALITY). Let E be an arbitrary nonempty subset of F_q^n that does not contain zero. Then the average, over all q-ary linear (n, k) codes C, of $|C \cap E|$ is

$$\overline{|C \cap E|} = \frac{q^k - 1}{q^n - 1} \cdot |E|.$$

PROOF. Let $f : F_q^n \to \{0, 1\}$ be the indicator function for E and apply Lemma 2.1. $\square$

3. The Minkowski-Hlawka Theorem and Linear Codes

We present a proof of the Minkowski-Hlawka theorem that is based on the mod-M channel used with linear codes. In fact, our proof is actually a reinterpretation of a standard one, as the reader may verify by comparing this section with the appendix of [**2**]. We will consider linear (n, k) codes over F_q, q prime. For any such code C, let $\Lambda_C \subset \rho Z^n$, for some scale parameter ρ, be the corresponding Euclidean-space image as induced by the mod-q channel mapping (Fig. 1); let $\Theta \subset \rho Z^n$ be the corresponding hypercubic image of all of F_q^n, i.e., $\Theta = \{(x_1, \dots, x_n) \in \rho Z^n : |x_i| \le \rho q/2,\ 0 \le i \le n\}$. Let $f(\cdot)$ be some given function $R^n \to R$. For any subset W of R^n, let $f(W)$ denote the sum $f(W) \triangleq \sum_{x \in W \setminus \{0\}} f(x)$. Application of Lemma 2.1 yields

$$\overline{f(\Lambda_C)} = \lambda q^{k-n} f(\Theta),$$

where $\lambda \triangleq q^{n-k}(q^k - 1)/(q^n - 1) \approx 1$. There thus exists a q-ary linear code C such that

$$f(\Lambda_C) \cdot V(\Lambda_C) \le \lambda f(\Theta) \cdot V(\Theta) \tag{3.1}$$

where $V(\Theta) = \rho^n$ and $V(\Lambda_C) = q^{n-k}\rho^n$ are the fundamental volumes of the lattices corresponding to Θ and Λ_C, respectively. We now pass to the limit $\rho \to 0$ and $q \to \infty$ such that $V(\Lambda_C)$ approaches some fixed value. Since $q = (1/\rho)^{n/(n-k)} \cdot V(\Lambda_C)^{1/(n-k)}$, the product $q\rho$ will, in this limit, grow over all bounds; i.e., Θ will densely cover any finite region of R^n. The right side of (3.1) will thus converge to the integral $\int f(x)\, dV(x)$. Passing from Λ_C to the associated lattice yields:

MINKOWSKI-HLAWKA THEOREM. *For any Riemann integrable function $f : R^n \to R$, any real $V(\Lambda_C) > 0$ and any $\epsilon > 0$, there exists a lattice Λ with fundamental volume $V(\Lambda)$ such that*

$$V(\Lambda) \cdot f(\Lambda) < \int f(x)\, dV(x) + \epsilon.$$

We have thus demonstrated that, in a certain sense, the Minkowski-Hlawka theorem deals with linear codes for the mod-M channel rather than with lattices!

4. Asymptotic Density

One of the applications of the Minkowski-Hlawka theorem is the derivation of an existence proof for n-dimensional lattices with a density D larger than 2^{-n}, cf. [**1**, p. 14]. We show that this result follows easily from a Gilbert-Varshamov-type argument.

Let $S_{n,r} = \{x \in R^N : \|x\| \leq r\}$ be the n-dimensional sphere (or rather ball) of radius r centered at the origin; let $\tilde{S}_{n,r} = \{x \in Z^n : 0 < \|x\| \leq r\}$ be the corresponding discrete sphere without its center; and let $|S_{n,r}|$ and $|\tilde{S}_{n,r}|$ denote the volume (discrete case: the cardinality) of these spheres.

THEOREM 4.1. (Gilbert-Varshamov Bound for Lattices) For any prime q and integers n and k such that $0 < k < n$, there exists a mod-q sublattice of Z^n whose minimum Euclidean distance d satisfies either $d \geq q/2$ or $|\tilde{S}_{n,d}| > q^{n-k}$.

PROOF. Assume, contrary to the claim, that the largest minimum distance d among such lattices satisfies both $d < q/2$ and $|\tilde{S}_{n,d}| \leq q^{n-k}$. Since $d < q/2$, $\tilde{S}_{n,d}$ lies entirely in F_q^n, where we regard F_q^n as embedded in Z^n by the mod-q channel mapping, cf. Fig. 1. Thus $|\Lambda \cap \tilde{S}_{n,d}| = |C \cap \tilde{S}_{n,d}|$ for any mod q lattice Λ and its associated linear code C. Applying Lemma 2.2 to $E = \tilde{S}_{n,d}$ yields $|C \cap \tilde{S}_{n,d}| = (q^k - 1)/(q^n - 1) \cdot |\tilde{S}_{n,d}| \leq (q^k - 1)/(q^n - 1) \cdot q^{n-k} < 1$. There thus exists at least one lattice Λ such that $|\Lambda \cap \tilde{S}_{n,d}| = 0$, i.e., whose minimum distance is larger than d, a contradiction. □

For $d < q/2$, the density D of these lattices is

$$\begin{aligned} D &= |S_{n,d/2}| \,/\, q^{n-k} \\ &> |S_{n,d/2}| \,/\, |\tilde{S}_{n,d}| \\ &\approx |S_{n,d/2}| \,/\, |S_{n,d}| \qquad (4.1) \\ &= 2^{-n}, \end{aligned}$$

and the approximation (4.1) becomes exact in the limit for $d \to \infty$.

References

1. J. H. Conway and N. J. A. Sloane, *Sphere Packings, Lattices and Groups*, New York: Springer Verlag, 1988.
2. R. de Buda, 'The upper error bound of a new near-optimal code', *IEEE Trans. Inform. Theory*, vol. 21, pp. 441–445, July 1975.
3. R. de Buda, 'Some optimal codes have structure', *IEEE J. Select. Areas Comm.*, vol. 7, pp. 893–899, Aug. 1989.

ISY, Linköping University, S-58183 Linköping, Sweden
E-mail address: andi@isy.liu.se

DIMACS Series in Discrete Mathematics
and Theoretical Computer Science
Volume **14**, 1993

The Nordstrom-Robinson Code is the Binary Image of the Octacode

G. D. FORNEY, JR., N. J. A. SLOANE AND M. D. TROTT

December 1, 1992

ABSTRACT. The Nordstrom-Robinson code, a nonlinear binary code of length 16 and minimal Hamming distance 6, is the binary image of the octacode, a linear self-dual code over $\mathbb{Z}_4$ of length 8 and minimal Lee distance 6. Since the octacode is the $\mathbb{Z}_4$-analogue of a Hamming code, this provides an extremely simple definition of the Nordstrom-Robinson code.

1. Introduction

This note records an interesting result of the DIMACS/IEEE Workshop that was obtained outside of the formal sessions.

Briefly, as the Workshop began, one of us (Trott), acting on a suggestion by Forney, had just succeeded in proving that the Nordstrom-Robinson (or NR) code was the binary image of a linear code over $\mathbb{Z}_4$, the integers mod 4. Trott asked Sloane if this result was known previously. Sloane thought not,[1] but immediately recognized that the NR code must be the binary image of the octacode, a self-dual code over $\mathbb{Z}_4$ which is used as a glue code in a construction of the Leech lattice from the face-centered cubic lattice [**CS92**, Chaps. 16, 24], [**CS93**].

The purpose of this note is to establish this result, to show that there is no analogous self-dual code of length 12 whose binary image is the Golay code, and to give a simple construction for the E_8 lattice from the octacode.

1991 *Mathematics Subject Classification.* Primary 94B05.

M. D. Trott wishes to thank his student Rajeev Surati for his assistance.

[1]He was wrong! R. Hammons and P. V. Kumar had noticed this in June, although they had not identified the $\mathbb{Z}_4$-code as the octacode. For further details see [**CHKSS**], [**HKCSS**].

2. Preliminaries

The symmetry group of binary Hamming n-space $\mathbb{Z}_2^n$ is a semidirect product of the group of translations by elements of $\mathbb{Z}_2^n$ (isomorphic to $\mathbb{Z}_2^n$) by the group of coordinate permutations (the symmetric group S_n). In particular, the symmetry group of $\mathbb{Z}_2^2$ is a semidirect product of $\mathbb{Z}_2^2$ by $\mathbb{Z}_2$, which is isomorphic to the dihedral group of order 8. This group has a subgroup isomorphic to $\mathbb{Z}_4$, namely the group $R = \langle\rho\rangle$ generated by the isometry $\rho = \{$swap coordinates and add 01$\}$. ρ induces the permutation

$$00 \to 01 \to 11 \to 10 \to 00$$

on $\mathbb{Z}_2^2$. Thus R is a sharply transitive generating group of $\mathbb{Z}_2^2$.

This leads to an 'isometric labeling' [**Fo91**] of $\mathbb{Z}_2^2$ by $\mathbb{Z}_4$, namely

$$00 \leftrightarrow 0,\ 01 \leftrightarrow 1,\ 11 \leftrightarrow 2,\ 10 \leftrightarrow 3\ . \tag{2.1}$$

We use (2.1) to define a mapping from $\mathbb{Z}_4^n$ to $\mathbb{Z}_2^{2n}$ as follows. Let $\alpha, \beta : \mathbb{Z}_4 \to \mathbb{Z}_2$ be given by

i	$\alpha(i)$	$\beta(i)$
0	0	0
1	0	1
2	1	1
3	1	0

Then the *binary image* $C = \phi(D)$ of a code D in $\mathbb{Z}_4^n$ is defined to be the image of D under the map $\phi : \mathbb{Z}_4^n \to \mathbb{Z}_2^{2n}$ given by

$$\phi(a_1, a_2, \ldots, a_n) = (\alpha(a_1), \beta(a_1), \alpha(a_2), \ldots, \beta(a_n))\ . \tag{2.2}$$

A linear code D of length n over $\mathbb{Z}_4$ is an additive subgroup of $\mathbb{Z}_4^n$. We define an inner product on $\mathbb{Z}_4^n$ by $a \cdot b = a_1b_1 + \cdots + a_nb_n \pmod 4$, and then the notions of dual code (D^*) and self-dual code ($D = D^*$) are defined in the usual way (cf. [**Kl87**], [**MS77**]).

The symmetrized weight enumerator (s.w.e.) of a linear code D over $\mathbb{Z}_4$ is

$$swe_D(x, y, z) = \sum_{a \in D} x^{N_0(a)} y^{N_1(a)} z^{N_2(a)}\ ,$$

where $N_i(a)$ is the number of components of a congruent to $\pm i \pmod 4$. The Lee weight enumerator of D is given by

$$Lee_D(x) = swe_D(1, x, x^2)\ . \tag{2.3}$$

(The Lee weights of $0, 1, 2, 3$ are respectively $0, 1, 2, 1$.)

The binary image $C = \phi(D)$ is in general nonlinear. (Necessary and sufficient conditions for $\phi(D)$ to be linear are given in [**HKCSS**].) We say that a binary code is $\mathbb{Z}_4$-*linear* if after a suitable permutation of coordinates it has the form $\phi(D)$ for some linear code D.

Although a binary $\mathbb{Z}_4$-linear code C need not be linear, it follows from the fact that D is linear that $C = \phi(D)$ is 'a geometrically uniform code' in Hamming space [**Fo91**]. In particular, C is distance invariant: the set of Hamming distances from any word in C to all other words is the set of Lee weights in D. The weight enumerator $W_C(x)$ of C is therefore well-defined, and is given by

$$W_C(x) = Lee_D(x) = swe_D(1, x, x^2) \ . \tag{2.4}$$

If we replace $\{0,1\}$ by $\{+1,-1\}$, the binary image $\phi(x)$ of a vector $x \in \mathbb{Z}_4^n$ is a vertex of the $2n$-cube. The transformation ρ now becomes a 90° rotation in 2-space, Lee distance becomes Euclidean distance, and the image of a linear code over $\mathbb{Z}_4$ becomes a geometrically uniform subset of the hypercube in Euclidean $2n$-space (a 'group code for the Gaussian channel', in the sense of Slepian [**Sl68**]). The codewords of D become a group of vectors of rotations of 2-space, and then $C = \phi(D)$ is the image of a vertex of the $2n$-cube under this group. Each codeword in D is a symmetry of C.

EXAMPLE 2.1. The binary image of the $\mathbb{Z}_4$ code with generator matrix

$$\begin{bmatrix} 0 & 0 & 0 & 0 & 2 & 2 & 2 & 2 \\ 0 & 0 & 2 & 2 & 0 & 0 & 2 & 2 \\ 0 & 2 & 0 & 2 & 0 & 2 & 0 & 2 \\ 1 & 1 & 1 & 1 & 1 & 1 & 1 & 1 \end{bmatrix} \tag{2.5}$$

is the first-order Reed-Muller code $\mathcal{R}$ of length 16. (In [**HKCSS**] it is shown that any binary Reed-Muller code of length 2^m and order $0, 1, 2, m-1$ or m is $\mathbb{Z}_4$-linear.)

3. The Nordstrom-Robinson code

The NR code has an interesting history, recounted in [**Be74**]. In the course of a public lecture in 1967, Robinson pointed out that the smallest parameters allowed by known distance bounds for which a linear code was not yet known to exist were $[15, 8, 5]$. Nordstrom, then a high-school student, succeeded in constructing a nonlinear code with these parameters [**NR67**]. The NR code of this paper is obtained by extending Nordstrom's code with an overall parity check. It is now known that no linear code exists with these parameters, and in fact that the NR code is the unique code of length 16, minimal distance 6 and containing 256 words (Snover [**Sn73**]).

The usual definition of the NR code is the following [**MS77**, Chaps. 2, 15]. Let $\mathcal{G}$ denote the $[24, 12, 8]$ Golay code with coordinates arranged so that $1^8 0^{16} \in \mathcal{G}$. The $[16, 5, 8]$ first-order Reed-Muller code $\mathcal{R}$ consists of all vectors $v \in \mathbb{Z}_2^{16}$ such that $0^8 v \in \mathcal{G}$. The NR code consists of all vectors $v \in \mathbb{Z}_2^{16}$ such that $uv \in \mathcal{G}$, where u is one of the eight vectors

$$00000000, \ 11000000, \ 10100000, \ldots, 10000001 \ .$$

$\mathcal{N}$ is the union of eight translates of $\mathcal{R}$, and is a nonlinear code of length 16 containing 256 words with minimal Hamming distance 6. $\mathcal{N}$ has weight enumerator

$$1 + 112x^6 + 30x^8 + 112x^{10} + x^{16} \ . \tag{3.1}$$

This definition makes it easy to study the properties of the NR code, via the properties of the Golay code and its symmetry group $Aut(\mathcal{G})$, since that group is well understood [**CS92**, Chaps. 10, 11]. For example, [**CS90**] classifies all vectors of $\mathbb{Z}_2^{16}$ into orbits under the symmetry group $Aut(\mathcal{N})$ of the NR code.

One property that is not stated in [**CS90**] but which is very easy to establish is that NR is geometrically uniform. As in [**CS90**], [**CS92**] we describe words in the Golay code by coordinates arranged in 4×6 arrays consisting of three 4×2 arrays called 'bricks' (these are the Miracle Octad Generator or MOG coordinates for $\mathcal{G}$). $\mathcal{N}$ is formed by taking all words of $\mathcal{G}$ whose left brick is one of

$$\begin{array}{|cc|}\hline \ & \ \\ \ & \ \\ \ & \ \\ \ & \ \\ \hline\end{array}\ , \begin{array}{|cc|}\hline 1 & \ \\ 1 & \ \\ \ & \ \\ \ & \ \\ \hline\end{array}\ , \begin{array}{|cc|}\hline 1 & \ \\ \ & \ \\ 1 & \ \\ \ & \ \\ \hline\end{array}\ , \begin{array}{|cc|}\hline 1 & \ \\ \ & \ \\ \ & \ \\ 1 & \ \\ \hline\end{array}\ , \begin{array}{|cc|}\hline 1 & 1 \\ \ & \ \\ \ & \ \\ \ & \ \\ \hline\end{array}\ , \begin{array}{|cc|}\hline 1 & \ \\ \ & 1 \\ \ & \ \\ \ & \ \\ \hline\end{array}\ , \begin{array}{|cc|}\hline 1 & \ \\ \ & \ \\ \ & 1 \\ \ & \ \\ \hline\end{array}\ , \begin{array}{|cc|}\hline 1 & \ \\ \ & \ \\ \ & \ \\ \ & 1 \\ \hline\end{array}\ , \tag{3.2}$$

and projecting onto the other two bricks. The words corresponding to the first figure in (3.2) comprise the Reed-Muller code $\mathcal{R}$.

If we translate $\mathcal{N}$ by adding to it a vector from one of the nonzero cosets of $\mathcal{R}$ in $\mathcal{N}$, say that corresponding to the second figure in (3.2), we obtain a code $\mathcal{N}'$ which is formed from the Golay words whose left brick is one of

$$\begin{array}{|cc|}\hline 1 & \ \\ 1 & \ \\ \ & \ \\ \ & \ \\ \hline\end{array}\ , \begin{array}{|cc|}\hline \ & \ \\ \ & \ \\ \ & \ \\ \ & \ \\ \hline\end{array}\ , \begin{array}{|cc|}\hline \ & \ \\ 1 & \ \\ 1 & \ \\ \ & \ \\ \hline\end{array}\ , \begin{array}{|cc|}\hline \ & \ \\ 1 & \ \\ \ & \ \\ 1 & \ \\ \hline\end{array}\ , \begin{array}{|cc|}\hline \ & 1 \\ 1 & \ \\ \ & \ \\ \ & \ \\ \hline\end{array}\ , \begin{array}{|cc|}\hline \ & \ \\ 1 & 1 \\ \ & \ \\ \ & \ \\ \hline\end{array}\ , \begin{array}{|cc|}\hline \ & \ \\ 1 & \ \\ \ & 1 \\ \ & \ \\ \hline\end{array}\ , \begin{array}{|cc|}\hline \ & \ \\ 1 & \ \\ \ & \ \\ \ & 1 \\ \hline\end{array}\ . \tag{3.3}$$

But $Aut(\mathcal{G})$ contains permutations that fix the left brick as a whole and apply any even permutation inside it, thus sending (3.2) to (3.3) (see [**CS92**, Chap. 11, §10]). So $\mathcal{N}$ and $\mathcal{N}'$ are geometrically congruent.

This result is also a consequence of Theorem 4.1 below. However, arguments such as this demonstrate that the old definition of the NR code is not totally superseded by the new one from the octacode. For one thing, the symmetry group of the NR code has order $2^4 \cdot 7! = 80640$, while the group of the octacode (the group of all permutations and sign-changes of coordinates that preserve the set of codewords, which in this case is isomorphic to $GL(4, 2)$), has order only 1344.

4. The octacode

The octacode $\mathcal{O}_8$ may be defined in several equivalent ways. The first definition guarantees that the definitions are equivalent.

(i) $\mathcal{O}_8$ is the unique self-dual code of length 8 over $\mathbb{Z}_4$ with minimal Lee distance 6 [**CS93**, Theorem 2]. It has symmetrized weight enumerator

$$x^8 + 16y^8 + 14x^4z^4 + z^8 + 112xy^4z(x^2+z^2)\ . \tag{4.1}$$

(ii) Form the cyclic code of length 7 over $\mathbb{Z}_4$ with generator polynomial $g(X) = X^3 + 3X^2 + 2X + 3$, and add an overall parity check to make the coordinates sum to zero. The result is $\mathcal{O}_8$. $g(X)$ is a divisor of $X^7 - 1 \pmod 4$ and reduces to $X^3 + X^2 + 1 \pmod 2$, so $\mathcal{O}_8$ may be regarded as a $\mathbb{Z}_4$-analogue of a Hamming code. Then $\mathcal{O}_8$ is the code of length 8 over $\mathbb{Z}_4$ with generator matrix

$$\begin{array}{cccccccc} \infty & 0 & 1 & 2 & 3 & 4 & 5 & 6 \\ \hline 3 & 3 & 2 & 3 & 1 & 0 & 0 & 0 \\ 3 & 0 & 3 & 2 & 3 & 1 & 0 & 0 \\ 3 & 0 & 0 & 3 & 2 & 3 & 1 & 0 \\ 3 & 0 & 0 & 0 & 3 & 2 & 3 & 1 \end{array}\ , \tag{4.2}$$

or equivalently

$$\begin{array}{|cccccccc|} \hline 2 & 0 & 0 & 0 & 1 & 3 & 1 & 1 \\ 2 & 0 & 1 & 1 & 2 & 2 & 3 & 1 \\ 0 & 1 & 0 & 1 & 2 & 3 & 0 & 1 \\ 1 & 1 & 1 & 1 & 1 & 1 & 1 & 1 \\ \hline \end{array}\ . \tag{4.3}$$

The order-2 words in (4.2) and (4.3) are generated by

$$\begin{array}{|cccccccc|} \hline 2 & 2 & 2 & 0 & 2 & 0 & 0 & 0 \\ 2 & 0 & 2 & 2 & 0 & 2 & 0 & 0 \\ 2 & 0 & 0 & 2 & 2 & 0 & 2 & 0 \\ 2 & 0 & 0 & 0 & 2 & 2 & 0 & 2 \\ \hline \end{array} \text{ and } \begin{array}{|cccccccc|} \hline 0 & 0 & 0 & 0 & 2 & 2 & 2 & 2 \\ 0 & 0 & 2 & 2 & 0 & 0 & 2 & 2 \\ 0 & 2 & 0 & 2 & 0 & 2 & 0 & 2 \\ 2 & 2 & 2 & 2 & 2 & 2 & 2 & 2 \\ \hline \end{array}\ ,$$

respectively. These are familiar generator matrices for the $[8, 4, 4]$ binary Hamming code, multiplied by 2.

(iii) $\mathcal{O}_8$ is the 'glue code' used in the 'holy construction' of the Leech lattice from eight copies of the face-centered cubic lattice A_3 [**CS92**, Chaps. 16, 24]. The connection between these lattices and codes over $\mathbb{Z}_4$ arises from the fact that the quotient A_3^*/A_3 of the dual lattice A_3^* by A_3 is isomorphic to $\mathbb{Z}_4$.

The main result of this note is the following.

THEOREM 4.1. *The image $\phi(\mathcal{O}_8)$ is the Nordstrom-Robinson code.*

PROOF. It follows from (2.4) and (4.1) that the binary image of $\mathcal{O}_8$ has minimal distance 6. From Snover's uniqueness theorem [**Sn73**], this code is equivalent to the NR code. □

Here is an explicit isomorphism. We use (4.2) to define $\mathcal{O}_8$, labeling the coordinates as shown in that matrix, and map the words of $\mathcal{O}_8$ to binary vectors of length 16 by sending $a_\infty\ a_0\ a_1 \ldots a_6$ to the MOG vector

$\alpha(a_\infty)$	$\alpha(a_0)$	$\beta(a_\infty)$	$\beta(a_0)$
$\alpha(a_3)$	$\alpha(a_2)$	$\beta(a_3)$	$\beta(a_2)$
$\alpha(a_5)$	$\alpha(a_1)$	$\beta(a_5)$	$\beta(a_1)$
$\alpha(a_6)$	$\alpha(a_4)$	$\beta(a_6)$	$\beta(a_4)$

(cf. [**CS92**, Figure 11.28]). It is now a routine calculation to verify that this map sends the words of $\mathcal{O}_8$ to words of the NR code as defined by (3.2).

In [**HKCSS**] it is shown that Kerdock and (slightly modified) Preparata codes are also binary images of linear codes over $\mathbb{Z}_4$, as are the Goethals and Delsarte-Goethals nonlinear codes. In fact the Kerdock and Preparata codes are the binary images of a dual pair of extended cyclic codes over $\mathbb{Z}_4$.

5. The Golay code

Because of the relationship between the NR code and the Golay code, it is natural to ask if the Golay code itself is the image of a self-dual code over $\mathbb{Z}_4$. It is not.

THEOREM 5.1. There is no self-dual code of length 12 over $\mathbb{Z}_4$ whose binary image is the $[24, 12, 8]$ Golay code.

PROOF. It follows from Theorem 6 of [**CS93**] that the symmetrized weight enumerator of any self-dual code over $\mathbb{Z}_4$ is a polynomial function of the three generators

$$\begin{aligned} f_1 &= x + z\ , \\ f_4 &= 2y^4 - xz(x^2 + z^2)\ , \\ f_8 &= y^4(x - z)^4\ . \end{aligned}$$

A self-dual code of length 12 therefore has s.w.e. of the form

$$a_1 f_8 f_1^4 + a_2 f_8 f_4 + a_3 f_4^3 + a_4 f_4^2 f_1^4 + a_5 f_4 f_1^8 + a_6 f_1^{12}\ , \tag{5.1}$$

where the a_i are integers. The condition that this should collapse to the weight enumerator of the Golay code when x, y, z are replaced respectively by $1, x, x^2$ implies $a_1 = 6 - a_4$, $a_2 = 64 - a_3$, $a_5 = 12$, $a_6 = 1$. When these values are substituted in (5.1), the coefficient of x^3y^8z becomes -512, which is impossible. □

By using further properties of the Golay code, one can show that there is no linear code over $\mathbb{Z}_4$ whose binary image is the Golay code — see [**HKCSS**]. Of course there *is* a nonlinear code with this property: just map the Golay code into a $\mathbb{Z}_4$-code using (2.1).

6. The E_8 lattice

One of the standard constructions for the 8-dimensional lattice E_8 is that it consists of all vectors $u \in \mathbb{Z}^8$ such that $u(\text{mod } 2)$ is in the $[8,4,4]$ Hamming code ([**CS92**, Chaps. 5,7]). There is a similar construction from $\mathcal{O}_8$.

THEOREM 6.1. The set of vectors $u \in \mathbb{Z}^8$ such that $u \pmod 4$ is in the octacode is isomorphic to the E_8 lattice.

PROOF. It is easy to see that this set of vectors forms a lattice Λ. By an argument similar to that used to prove Theorem 6.1 of [**CS92**, Chap. 7], the theta series of Λ is obtained from the s.w.e. of the octacode by replacing x, y, z by

$$1 + 2q^{16} + 2q^{64} + \cdots ,$$

$$q + q^9 + q^{25} + \cdots ,$$

$$2q^4 + 2q^{36} + 2q^{100} + \cdots$$

respectively. From Eq. (4.1) we find that the theta series of Λ begins $1 + 240q^8 + \cdots$. But Bannai and Sloane (see Chapter 14 of [**CS92**]) have shown that E_8 is the unique 8-dimensional lattice with kissing number 240. □

It can be seen in retrospect that this version of the E_8 lattice was used in a construction of the Leech lattice in [**Fo88**].

REFERENCES

[Be74] E. R. Berlekamp, editor, *Key papers in the development of coding theory*, IEEE Press, NY, 1974, p. 101.

[CHKSS] A. R. Calderbank, R. Hammons, P. V. Kumar, N. J. A. Sloane and P. Solé, *A linear construction for certain Kerdock and Preparata codes*, Bull. Amer. Math. Soc., submitted, 1992.

[CS90] J. H. Conway and N. J. A. Sloane, *Orbit and coset analysis of the Golay and related codes*, IEEE Trans. Inform. Theory, **36** (1990), 1038–1050.

[CS92] J. H. Conway and N. J. A. Sloane, *Sphere-packings, lattices and groups*, 2nd ed., Springer-Verlag, NY 1992.

[CS93] J. H. Conway and N. J. A. Sloane, *Self-dual codes over the integers modulo 4*, J. Comb. Theory, Ser. A, **62** (1993), 30–45.

[Fo88] G. D. Forney, Jr., *Coset codes — part II: binary lattices and related codes*, IEEE Trans. Inform. Theory, **34** (1988), 1152–1187.

[Fo91] G. D. Forney, Jr., *Geometrically uniform codes*, IEEE Trans. Inform. Theory, **37** (1991), 1241–1260.

[HKCSS] R. Hammons, P. V. Kumar, A. R. Calderbank, N. J. A. Sloane and P. Solé, *The $\mathbb{Z}_4$-linearity of Kerdock, Preparata, Goethals and related codes*, IEEE Trans. Inform. Theory, submitted, 1992.

[Kl87] M. Klemm, *Über die Identität von MacWilliams für die Gewichtsfunktion von Codes*, Arch. Math., **49** (1987), 400–406.

[MS77] F. J. MacWilliams and N. J. A. Sloane, *The theory of error-correcting codes*, North-Holland, Amsterdam, 1977.

[NR67] A. W. Nordstrom and J. P. Robinson, *An optimum nonlinear code*, Inform. Control, **11** (1967), 613–616. Reprinted in [**Be74**].

[Sl68] D. Slepian, *Group codes for the Gaussian channel*, Bell Syst. Tech. J., **47** (1968), 575–602.

[Sn73] S. L. Snover, *The uniqueness of the Nordstrom-Robinson and the Golay binary codes*, Ph.D. Dissertation, Math. Dept., Michigan State Univ., 1973.

Motorola Codex, Mansfield, MA 02048
E-mail address: david_forney@mcimail.com

Mathematical Sciences Research Center, AT&T Bell Laboratories, Murray Hill, New Jersey 07974
E-mail address: njas@research.att.com

Department of Electrical Engineering and Computer Science, M. I. T., Cambridge, MA 02139
E-mail address: trott@lids.mit.edu

DIMACS Series in Discrete Mathematics
and Theoretical Computer Science
Volume **14**, 1993

Generalized Theta Functions for Lattice Vector Quantization

PATRICK SOLÉ

March 25, 1993

ABSTRACT. Estimates of the size of VQ codebooks consisting of lattice points within a sphere for the L^p distance are given. Geometric upper and lower bounds based on volume ratios are derived. Generalized theta functions are introduced and computed when a coding theoretic construction of type A,B, or D of the lattice exists and weight enumerators of the codes are known. A new class of unimodular lattices with known theta function is introduced. An elementary expression is given for the theta function of the Leech lattice.

1. Problem and Motivation

When quantizing a multidimensional source with given probability density function (pdf), the asymptotic equipartition principle of information theory tells us that the samples of the source will concentrate on or about the equiprobable surface. In the case of a Gaussian law, these surfaces are Euclidean spheres. If a lattice Λ is used for quantizing the source with a sphere-shaped codebook then counting the number of points inside the sphere is essential for determining the transmission rate.

We shall enumerate such codebooks when the equiprobable surfaces are spheres for the L^p metric of the type

$$S_p(n,m) = \{x \in \mathbf{R}^n |\ ||x||_p \leq m\},$$

where $||x||_p^p = \sum_{i=1}^n |x_i|^p$. When the source is Laplacian, $p = 1$, and $S_1(n,m)$ is a so-called pyramid (or cross-polytope, or hyperoctahedron). This case has practical applications in image processing [**4**].

1991 *Mathematics Subject Classification.* Primary 94B75.
We thank M. Barlaud, D. Gardy, G. Lachaud, A. M. Odlyzko, N. J. A. Sloane and K. Yang for helpful discussions.

The paper is organized as follows. Section 2 recalls a classical asymptotic approximation which is refined in Section 3, where upper and lower bounds are derived. Section 4 is devoted to an exact enumeration approach by means of generating functions which coincides with the classical theta function of a lattice for $p = 2$.

2. Volume Approximation

Gauss' counting principle says that the number of points with integer coordinates in a convex body is well approximated by its volume. This was proved to fail for $S_2(n, \sqrt{n})$ and large n in [**2**]. If, however, n and p are fixed and m is large this is a simple application of Riemann sums. If points are drawn from a lattice Λ with fundamental volume $vol(\Lambda)$ then

$$|S_p(n,m) \cap \Lambda| \sim \frac{vol(S_p(n,m))}{vol(\Lambda)}. \tag{2.1}$$

A more explicit formula for the numerator of (2.1) can be given as

$$vol(S_p(n,m)) = \frac{\Gamma(1+\frac{1}{p})^n}{\Gamma(1+\frac{n}{p})},$$

as can be found e.g. in [**2**]. The denominator is equal to the square root of the determinant of the Gram matrix of the lattice [**1**]. In the next section, we will derive upper and lower bounds which are asymptotically equivalent to this approximation.

3. Voronoi Packing and Covering Bounds

In the special case $p = 2$, let R denote the covering radius of the lattice. Then the Voronoi cells centered on lattice points within $S_2(n, m)$ are packed into $S_2(n, m + p)$ (up to negligible sets of points). This yields the upper bound

$$|\Lambda \cap S_2(n,m)| \leq \frac{vol(S_2(n, m+R))}{vol(\Lambda)}.$$

This approach does not generalize easily for $p \neq 2$, since the Voronoi cells can then overlap significantly. If we keep the Voronoi domains for L^2 to pack L^p spheres we have to replace R by the largest L^p norm of a point of the boundary of the Voronoi cell; call this quantity R_p^2. Note that for $0 < p \leq 2$, one has $R_p^2 \leq R_2^2 = R$. Then, we get

$$|\Lambda \cap S_p(n,m)| \leq \frac{vol(S_p(n, m+R_p^2))}{vol(\Lambda)}.$$

If instead of packing spheres of radius $m+R_p^2$ we cover spheres of radius $m-R_p^2$ we obtain as a lower bound the RHS of equation (2.1), that is

$$|S_p(n,m)\cap\Lambda| \geq \frac{vol(S_p(n,m-R_p^2))}{vol(\Lambda)}. \tag{3.1}$$

These two bounds are, for fixed n and large m, asymptotically equivalent to equation (2.1).

4. Generalized Theta Function

Let

$$\theta_{p,\Lambda}(q) = \sum_{x\in\Lambda} q^{||x||_p^p}. \tag{4.1}$$

When $p=2$, Equation (4.1) is just the definition of the classical theta function [**1**], and when $p=1$ it is the Nu function of [**4, 5**]. In general for $p\neq 2$ the isometry group of L^p is much smaller than the orthogonal group $O(n,\mathbf{R})$ [1], so that the preceding definition is not invariant under rotations. Two versions of E_8 with different Nu functions can be found in [**5**]. When Λ is obtained from a binary code C by construction A, we have

$$\theta_{p,\Lambda}(q) = W_C(\theta_{p,2Z}(q), \theta_{p,2Z+1}(q)), \tag{4.2}$$

where W_C is the weight enumerator of C. Equation (4.2) is a generalization of Equation (6) of [**1**, p.183]. It is a corollary of Theorem 1 below. More generally, given a *flag* F of codes,

$$C_1 \subseteq C_2 \subseteq \cdots \subseteq C_m,$$

a lattice can be constructed by the following *code formula* [**6**]

$$\Lambda = C_1 + 2C_2 + \cdots + 2^{m-1}C_m + 2^m\mathbf{Z}^n.$$

Up to a scaling factor this is construction D of [**1**, p.232]. Code nesting ensures that we obtain a lattice and not only a sphere packing. In particular, for $m=2$, and for C_2 a parity-check code, we recover the classical construction B [**1**, p.191] up to normalization. Our approach to computing the theta series of this lattice is to consider the flag as a code over the alphabet $\mathbf{Z}_{2^m}$. Let L_F denote the *Lee shape enumerator* of that code, a polynomial in $2^{m-1}-1$ variables. Recall that the *Lee shape* of a vector x of length n over $\mathbf{Z}_{2^m}$ is the vector of length $2^{m-1}-1$ and i^{th} coordinate $n_i(x)$ equal to the number of coordinates of x equal to $\pm i$. The Lee shape enumerator is then the counting function for this vector of integers. In symbols:

$$L_F(t_0,t_1,\ldots,t_m) = \sum_{x\in C}\prod_{i=0}^{2^{m-1}} t_i^{n_i(x)}.$$

By means of a variation on a theme of Maher [**9**] we obtain

[1] it is indeed the *hyperoctahedral* group, a finite group of size $2^n n!$

THEOREM 4.1. Let θ_i be a shorthand for $\theta^p_{2^m\mathbf{Z}+i}(q)$. A binary lattice Λ constructed from the flag of binary codes F has theta function given by

$$\theta_{p,\Lambda}(q) = L_F(\theta_0, \theta_1, \dots, \theta_{2^{m-1}}).$$

PROOF. For $x \in F$ let $\Lambda_x = \{y \in \mathbf{Z}^n | y \equiv x \ mod \ 2^m\}$ Clearly these sets partition Λ and each of them is a Cartesian product of one dimensional lattice cosets as follow.

$$\Lambda_x = (2^m\mathbf{Z} + 2^{m-1})^{n_{2^{m-1}}(x)} \prod_{i=0}^{2^{m-1}-1} (2^m\mathbf{Z} \pm i)^{n_i(x)}.$$

Note[2] that θ_i is the generalized theta function for both $2^m\mathbf{Z}+i$ and $2^m\mathbf{Z}-i$ Hence

$$\theta^p_{\Lambda_x}(q) = \theta_{2^{m-1}} \prod_{i=0}^{2^{m-1}-1} \theta_i^{n_i(x)},$$

and we conclude by observing that

$$\theta^p_{\Lambda}(q) = \sum_{x\in F} \theta^p_{\Lambda_x}(q).$$

□

An immediate corollary is Equation (4.2) obtained for $m = 1$ and $C_1 = C$.

A more recent application of this theorem is in [8] where the lattice E_8 is constructed from the octacode by Construction A modulo 4. A version of this theorem for $p = 2$ is invoked to show that the kissing number of the lattice is indeed 240.

To obtain the generalized theta function for Construction B, we consider codes over $Z_4 = \{0, \pm 1, 2\}$. First, we express the Lee shape enumerator of $C_1 + 2C_2$ as a function of the joint weight enumerator of C_1 and C_2, usually denoted by J_{C_1,C_2}, and given by

$$J_{C_1,C_2}(a,b,c,d) = \sum_{x\in C_1, y\in C_2} a^{i(x,y)} b^{j(x,y)} c^{k(x,y)} d^{l(x,y)},$$

with the integers i, j, k, l counting patterns 00,01,10,11 in the ordered pair x, y.

LEMMA 4.1.

$$L_{C_1+2C_2}(x_0, x_1, x_2) = J_{C_1,C_2}(x_0, x_2, x_1, x_1).$$

PROOF. Counting in base 2, mod 4, with the more significant bit on the right, we see that $00 = 0$, $01 = 2$, $10 = 1$, $11 = 1$. □

Second, we can use known facts on joint weight enumerators to derive a general formula for construction B lattices (Theorem 2 below), and a new family of unimodular lattices with known theta series.

[2]Otherwise we should have used the complete w.e.

THEOREM 4.2. Let C denote a binary even code and $B(C)$ the lattice $C + 2P_n + 4\mathbf{Z}^n$.

$$\theta^p_{B(C)}(q) = \frac{1}{2}W_C(\theta_0, \theta_1) + \frac{1}{2}(\theta_0(q^{2^p}) - \theta_1(q^{2^p}))^n$$

PROOF. A known fact [**10**] about joint weight enumerators is

$$J_{C,P_n}(a,b,c,d) = \frac{1}{2}W_C(a+b, c+d) + \frac{1}{2}W_C(a-b, c-d).$$

Hence we obtain

$$J_{C,P_n}(a,b,c,c) = \frac{1}{2}W_C(a+b, 2c) + \frac{1}{2}(a-b)^n.$$

The result follows by substituting for $a, b, 2c$ using the theta series for $4\mathbf{Z}, 4\mathbf{Z}+2, 4\mathbf{Z}\pm 1$, respectively. □

For any integer $m \geq 3$ let L_m be the lattice in dimension $n = 2^m$ defined by the code formula

$$L_m = \frac{1}{2}[RM(1,m) + 2RM(m-2,m) + 4Z^n].$$

Since the joint weight enumerator for $RM(1,m)$ with itself is known [**10**], the joint weight enumerator for $RM(1,m)$ with its dual can be computed by the (generalized) MacWilliams transform. The first few theta functions (for $p = 2$) are

$$\begin{aligned} \theta^2_{L_4}(q) &= 1 + 480q^8 + 61920q^{16}... \\ \theta^2_{L_5}(q) &= 1 + 146880q^{16} + .. \\ \theta^2_{L_6}(q) &= 1 + 166784q^{16} + ... \end{aligned}$$

The kissing number of L_5 is the same as that of the Barnes-Wall lattice of dimension 32 [**1**, Section 8.2(g)]. It is shown by Forney [**7**, p. 1069] that $L_5 = \Lambda_{32}$. Since the dual code of $RM(1,m)$ is $RM(m-2,m)$, it is easy to check that $L_m \subseteq L_m^*$. A determinant calculation shows then that $L_m = L_m^*$. Another application of Theorem 1 is to compute in an elementary way the theta function of the Leech lattice which may be defined via the code formula [**1**, Chapter 4, Section 11]

$$\frac{1}{2\sqrt{2}}(C_8 + 8Z^{24}) \cup (\mathbf{51} + C_8 + 8Z^{24}),$$

where C_8 denotes the code over the integers mod 8 defined via the [24,12,8] Golay code G_{24} as

$$C_8 = 2G_{24} + 4P_{24},$$

where P_{24} is the vector with first coordinate 5 and remaining coordinates equal to 1. So the first half of the Leech lattice code formula can be thought of as Construction A applied to C_8 and is usually called "the even centers set", and the second half as Construction A applied to a coset of C_8 and usually called "the odd centers set." The even centers part can be reduced to Construction B (mod 2) applied to G_{24}, while the Lee enumerator needed for the odd centers is easily seen to be

$$L(a, b, c, d, e) = J_{G_{24}, \overline{P_{24}}}(b, d, d, b),$$

which reduces to

$$2^{11}((b + d)^{24} - (b - d)^{24}).$$

Now b and d have to be replaced by the theta functions for $8\mathbf{Z}$ and $8\mathbf{Z} + 1$ respectively. Some Maple procedures for computing the first few terms of the theta function of the Leech lattice are available from the author.

References

1. J.H. Conway and N.J.A. Sloane "Sphere Packings, Lattices and Groups" Springer Verlag, Second Edition (1990).
2. J. E. Mazo and A. M. Odlyzko, "Lattice Points in High-Dimensional Spheres", Monatshefte Math. 110, 47-61 (1990).
3. N.D. Elkies, A.M. Odlyzko, and J.A. Rush," On the Packing Densities of Superballs and Other Bodies." Inventiones Math. 105 (1991) 613-640.
4. M. Barlaud, P. Solé, M. Antonini, P. Mathieu, and T. Gaidon, "Pyramidal Lattice Vector Quantization for multiscale image coding", submitted to IEEE Trans. on Image Processing.
5. P. Solé, "Counting Lattice Points in Pyramids", submitted to the proceedings of Formal Power Series and Algebraic Combinatorics, Montréal, Canada, June 1992.
6. G.D. Forney, Jr., "Coset Codes-Part I: Introduction and Geometrical Classification", IEEE Trans. Inform. Theory, IT-34, 5 (1988) 1123-1151.
7. G.D. Forney, Jr., "Coset Codes-Part II: Binary Lattices and Related Codes", IEEE Trans. Inform. Theory, IT-34 (1988), 1123-1151.
8. G.D. Forney, Jr., N.J.A Sloane, and M.D. Trott,"The Nordstrom-Robinson Code is the Binary Image of the Octacode", these Proceedings.
9. D. Maher,"Lee Enumerators of Codes and Theta Series of Lattices", Canadian J. of Math 30 (1978), 738-747.
10. F.J. MacWilliams, C.L. Mallows, and N.J.A. Sloane, "Generalization of Gleason's Theorem on Weight Enumerators of Self-Dual Codes" IEEE Trans. Inform. Theory, IT-18, 6 (1972), 794-805.

CNRS, I3S, 250, rue A. Einstein, 06 560 Valbonne, France
E-mail address: sole@mimosa.unice.fr

DIMACS Series in Discrete Mathematics
and Theoretical Computer Science
Volume **14**, 1993

Tree Structured Signal Space Codes

CHRISTOPHER F. BARNES

January 20, 1993

ABSTRACT. Abstract groups are used in coded modulation for two important reasons. First, a normal subgroup induces a partition of the group into a factor group. Second, there exist groups in metric spaces with subgroup chains that have progressively expanded intra–subgroup distances. Lattices in Euclidean space have proved particularly useful. In this paper, a multidimensional tree structure that corresponds to a direct sum signal set is reviewed which has the desirable partition and distance properties useful in coded modulation, and, in general, may be used in most signal space code constructions. Unlike lattices, direct sum signal sets do not necessarily form a group under ordinary vector addition and hence are unencumbered by a unnecessary linearity constraint, viz., closure under vector addition. It is demonstrated that the class of direct sum signal sets includes lattices and certain lattice subsets as a constrained special case. The tree structures associated with direct sum signal sets permit labelings such that the distance properties of the labels assumes a geometric significance in the signal space. A method of designing direct sum signal constellations is reviewed which is based on an iterative algorithm that uses training data drawn from multidimensional probability distribution functions. Several two and four dimensional direct sum signal constellations designed with this algorithm are presented.

1. Direct Sum Coset Codes

Coded modulation constructions rely very little on the linearity properties of the groups on which they are based, viz., that the sum of any two members of the group yields another group member [**1**]. The two essential properties of group based constructions are that normal subgroups induce partitions via coset decompositions and that there exist subgroup chains with expanded intra–subgroup minimum distances. A direct sum discrete subset of $\Re^N$ which corresponds to a geometric structure which we call a σ–tree does not necessarily form an algebraic

---

1991 *Mathematics Subject Classification.* Primary 94B12.

group under vector addition; but interestingly, σ–trees and their associated direct sum signal sets retain the two properties of abstract groups that are useful in the application of coded modulation [**2, 3**]. In particular, there exist subtrees $\mathcal{T}'$ of a σ–tree $\mathcal{T}$ that induce partitions (via geometric properties) of $\mathcal{T}$ into partition chains with expanded intra–subtree minimum distances. In this introductory section we give a review of lattice coset codes and direct sum coset code constructions. We show that σ–tree coset codes may be considered a natural generalization of lattice–type coset codes.

A *lattice coset code* $\mathcal{C}(\Lambda/\Lambda'; C)$ consists of a binary encoder C, a lattice Λ in $\Re^N$ (or translate of Λ) and a sublattice Λ' of Λ. Since Λ is a group under vector addition, the sublattice Λ' induces a partition of Λ into the factor group Λ/Λ'. During each signaling interval the coset code accepts n input bits and operates on k bits to provide $k+r$ *coded bits.* The coded bits select one of the cosets of Λ' in the partition Λ/Λ' and the remaining $n-k$ information bits select a signal point from the selected coset [**1, 5**]. The assignment of coded bits to unique cosets of Λ' in the partition Λ/Λ' is called a *labeling.* If $|\Lambda/\Lambda'| = 2^{k+r}$, the labeling may be defined by a function $\boldsymbol{\lambda}(\boldsymbol{j})$, where $\boldsymbol{j}$ is any binary $(k+r)$–tuple, called a *label,* and $\boldsymbol{\lambda}(\boldsymbol{j})$ is a N–tuple coset representative of the coset of Λ' specified by $\boldsymbol{j}$. A complete collection of coset representatives $\{\boldsymbol{\lambda}(\boldsymbol{j})\}$ gives a coset decomposition $\Lambda = \{\boldsymbol{\lambda}(\boldsymbol{j})\} + \Lambda'$. If Λ is a mod–2 lattice, then a special class of labels are the *Ungerboeck labels* which can be written

$$\boldsymbol{\lambda}(\boldsymbol{j}) = \sum_{p=1}^{k+r} j^p \boldsymbol{g}^p, \tag{1.1}$$

where j^p is the pth element of the label $\boldsymbol{j}$, and $\boldsymbol{g}^p$ is a row vector of a $(k+r) \times N$ generator matrix G of some binary block code. Moreover, Ungerboeck labelings result in decompositions given by $\Lambda = \{\sum j^p \boldsymbol{g}^p\} + \Lambda'$ where the labeling is linear in the sense that the set $\{\sum j^p \boldsymbol{g}^p\}$ is closed under vector addition modulo 2 [1]. More generally, $\{\boldsymbol{\lambda}(\boldsymbol{j})\}$ is an *Ungerboeck labeling* if it is linear modulo Λ'.

A *direct sum signal constellation* is a discrete set of points in N–space that is formed from the direct sum of a collection of *constituent* (discrete) subsets of N–space (that is, one vector (point) is selected from each constituent set and all selected vectors are summed to form an element of the direct sum set). A σ*–tree* is a tree structure that may be associated with each unique ordering (permutation) of the constituent subsets of the direct sum signal constellation. That is, if the origin is the root node, then the first constituent set defines the set of nodes at the first level of the tree, the direct sum of the first and second constituent sets define the nodes at the second level, and so forth. Within the class of general tree structures, σ–trees are distinguished in that a σ–tree has subtrees that are mutually congruent at each level of the tree (for examples, see Figures 1 and 2). To illustrate the potential utility of σ–trees in coded modulation schemes, we next show that lattice coset codes can be generalized to yield direct sum coset codes.

A *direct sum coset code* $\mathcal{C}(\mathcal{T}/\mathcal{T}'; C)$ is based on a σ–tree $\mathcal{T}$ and σ–subtree $\mathcal{T}'$ in $\Re^N$ with *nonlinear labelings* of the form

$$t(j) = \sum_{p=1}^{k+r} g^p(j^p). \tag{1.2}$$

Note that lattice coset codes described by (1.1) may be considered a "linearized" version of (1.2). Hence, lattice coset codes may be interpreted as a special case of the more general class of direct sum coset codes.

Each set of N–tuples $G^p = \{g^p(j^p) : j^p \in Z_M\}$ used in (1.2) is called a *translate constituent set* and the set of all possible sums $G = G^1 + \cdots + G^{k+r}$ forms a set of *translates* $G = \{\sum g^p(j^p)\}$. A σ–subtree $\mathcal{T}'$ is likewise generated by an ordered $(n-k)$–member collection of M–ary *subtree constituent sets* $\mathcal{T}^q = \{g^q(j^q) : j^q \in Z_M\}$, that is, $\mathcal{T}' = \mathcal{T}^1 + \cdots + \mathcal{T}^{n-k}$. A $(n+r)$–level σ–tree $\mathcal{T}$ is formed by all translations G of the subtree $\mathcal{T}'$, that is

$$\mathcal{T} = G + \mathcal{T}', \tag{1.3}$$

$$= \sum_{p=1}^{k+r} G^p + \sum_{q=1}^{n-k} \mathcal{T}^q, \tag{1.4}$$

The M^{n+r}–member direct sum set of N–tuples is completely specified by the $M \times (n+r)$ constituents comprising the $\mathcal{T}^q$ and the G^p. (As we show in Section 2, this fact has significant implications on the simplicity of implementing the mapping of coded and uncoded information bits to multidimensional direct sum signal space points.) When used in a direct sum coset code with $M = 2$, the coded binary $(k+r)$–tuple j is a label that selects a translate $g(j) \in G$ to form a "coset" $g(j) + \mathcal{T}'$ of the subtree $\mathcal{T}'$ in a "natural" partition of $\mathcal{T}$ denoted $\mathcal{T}/\mathcal{T}'$. The remaining $n-k$ uncoded bits select a single point from the selected subtree coset.

2. Direct Sum Trellis Codes

Ungerboeck introduced a concept which he called "mapping by set partitioning" that assigned convolutionally coded bits to a sequence of subsets of the signal constellation [**4**]. The key idea in Ungerboeck's method was that the minimum intra–subset distance progressively increased in a subset chain associated with the coded bits. Other researchers have since shown [**5**] that this partitioning process can be interpreted as a mapping of coded bits into a partition chain of factor groups. For example, given Z as the group and the subgroup partition chain $Z/2Z/4Z/8Z\cdots$, the first coded bit selects an element of $Z/2Z$, the second coded bit selects an element of $2Z/4Z$, and so on. In this section we show how this process can be reinterpreted as a mapping of coded and uncoded bits into a fully "entangled" σ–tree structure. The advantage of this approach is that it is not necessary to rely on the algebraic properties of group theory to induce the partition chain, rather, the geometric properties of the σ–tree provide the required partitioning and distance properties.

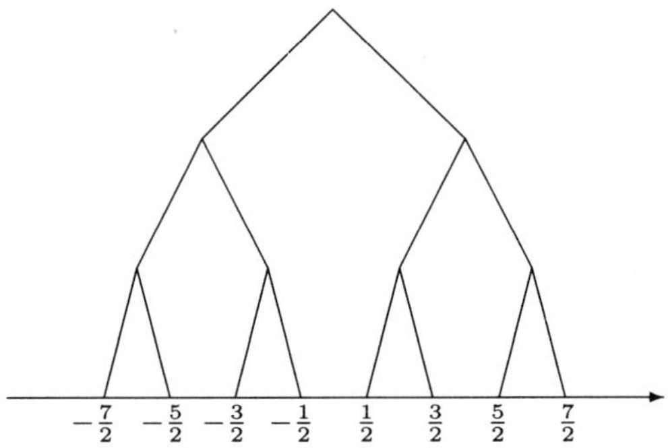

FIGURE 1. The σ–tree structure $\mathcal{T} = G^1 + G^2 + G^3$ corresponding to a direct sum PAM signal set.

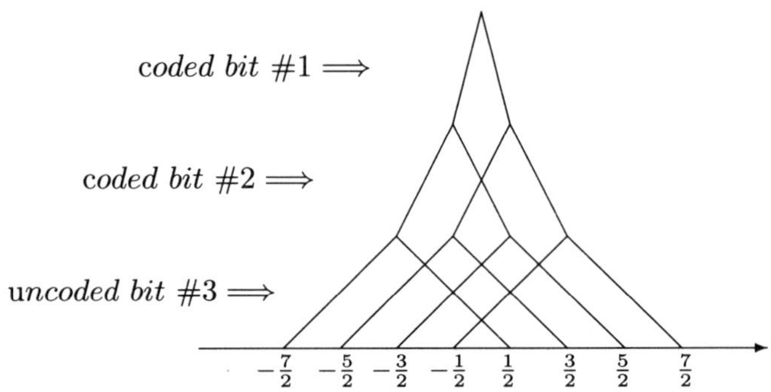

FIGURE 2. Direct sum PAM signal set partitioning via the σ–tree structure $\mathcal{T} = G^3 + G^2 + G^1$.

Consider the one–dimensional two–sided binary constituent sets $G^1 = \{-2, 2\}$, $G^2 = \{-1, 1\}$, and $G^3 = \{-\frac{1}{2}, \frac{1}{2}\}$. The associated direct sum signal constellation is the 8–member pulse amplitude modulation (PAM) set $\{-\frac{7}{2}, -\frac{5}{2}, -\frac{3}{2}, -\frac{1}{2}, \frac{1}{2}, \frac{3}{2}, \frac{5}{2}, \frac{7}{2}\}$. A corresponding σ–tree $\mathcal{T} = G^1 + G^2 + G^3$ is shown in Figure 1. This σ–tree has the undesirable property that any subtree has the same minimum intra–subtree distance (where minimum intra–subtree distance is defined as the minimum distance that separates the terminating leaf nodes of any subtree originating at a node in an interior level of the σ–tree). However, consider what happens when the constituents G^1, G^2, and G^3 are used in inverse order (permuted) to form the σ–tree $\mathcal{T} = G^3 + G^2 + G^1$ shown in Figure 2. This "entangled" σ–tree clearly has expanded intra–subtree distance properties which would be useful in coded modulation and suggests a reinterpretation of Ungerboeck's method of "mapping by set partitioning". Specifically, Figure 2 shows an example of how a mapping of the output of a rate 1/2 convolutional code combined with one additional uncoded bit in a trellis code would be implemented. The first coded bit selects one of the branches at the first level of the σ–tree to choose a subtree with minimum intra–subtree distance of two. The second coded bit selects a branch of the selected subtree to choose a smaller subtree with minimum intra–subtree distance of four. The remaining uncoded bit selects one of the branches of this last subtree.

This entangled tree–structured formulation of coded modulation has a significant implication on the complexity of mapping a large block of data often associated with high–dimensional signaling into a corresponding large signal set. In particular, to send $L \times n$ bits per $L \times 2$ dimensional composite symbol, some sort of mapping must be made from the input bit block onto a 2^{Ln}–member signal constellation in $L \times 2$ space. Usually this is done with a read–only–memory (ROM) with 2^{Ln} members. In practice, the implementation complexity of such a scheme has generally outweighed the performance gain for large values of Ln. However, the approach illustrated in Figure 2 would replace the single ROM with 2^{Ln} entries with a bank of Ln ROMs with only two (Ln–dimensional vector) entries each, followed by a Ln–input vector addition operation.

3. The Design of Direct Sum Constellations

Various σ–tree structures were first investigated in the source coding problem where the source coding dual of a σ–tree structure is a vector quantizer with a direct sum codebook [**6**]. The direct sum vector quantizer design problem is the covering design problem, and since the sphere packing problem is in some sense the dual of the covering problem [**7**], there should exist σ–tree structures that provide good packings. The hypothesis tested in this paper is that direct sum vector quantizers designed for uniformly distributed hypercubes and hyperspheres in N–space should have sufficient regularity and structure to allow consideration of the resulting quantization constellations as constellations for the channel signaling problem. For example, the familiar hexagonal A_2 lattice solves both the packing and covering problems in 2–space [**7**], and as we show in Sections 4 and 5, there exist direct sum vector quantizers and hence σ–trees corresponding to finite subsets of the A_2 lattice. In this section we give a review of optimality conditions and design methods for direct sum vector quantizers. More extensive details are available in [**6, 8, 9**].

Consider using a one–dimensional direct sum set $\mathcal{T}$ as a quantizer constellation for a one dimensional source with probability density function $f(x)$. The output representation generated by such a quantizer is the direct sum of points selected from P sets $G^p = \{g^p(j^p) : j^p \in Z_M\}$. This structure is readily recognized as the output of a *multistage residual quantizer* where G^p is the pth stage codebook. Conditions necessary for the *joint* local optimality of the codebooks G^p, or more specifically, the constituents $g^p \in G^p$ (i.e., *quanta*) are as follows. If $S(j)$ is the subset of $\Re$ that is mapped to $t(\boldsymbol{j}) \in \mathcal{T}$, where, in general, $\boldsymbol{j}$ is a M–ary P–tuple, the mean squared error of this quantizer is given by

$$D_{MSE} = \sum_{\text{all } \boldsymbol{j}} \int_{S(\boldsymbol{j})} [x - t(\boldsymbol{j})]^2 f(x)dx, \tag{3.1}$$

$$= \sum_{\text{all } \boldsymbol{j}} \int_{S(\boldsymbol{j})} \left[x - \sum_{p=1}^{P} g^p(j^p)\right]^2 f(x)dx, \tag{3.2}$$

where j^p is the pth element of $\boldsymbol{j}$. A direct minimization of D_{MSE} with respect to a particular $g^\rho(k^\rho)$ with $\rho \in \{1, 2, \ldots, P\}$ and $k^\rho \in Z_M$, assuming that all other quantizer parameters are held fixed yields the following necessary condition for optimality,

$$g^\rho(k^\rho) = \frac{\sum_{\boldsymbol{j} \in H_{k^\rho}} \int_{S(\boldsymbol{j})} \left[x - \sum_{\substack{p=1 \\ p \neq \rho}}^{P} g^p(j^p)\right] f(x)dx}{\sum_{\boldsymbol{j} \in H_{k^\rho}} \int_{S(\boldsymbol{j})} f(x)dx}, \tag{3.3}$$

where H_{k^ρ} is the set of all $\boldsymbol{j}$ with ρth element equal to k^ρ. Equation (3.3) may be generalized to the vector case and shown to be a centroid of a certain residual random variable [**10**]. Conversely, if $\mathcal{T}$ is held fixed and the partition cells $S(\boldsymbol{j})$ are chosen to minimize D_{MSE}, then the best $S(\boldsymbol{j})$ are *nearest–neighbor* or *Voronoi* cells with respect to the $t(\boldsymbol{j}) \in \mathcal{T}$. These two conditions are necessary for the local optimality of $\mathcal{T}$. An iterative algorithm has been developed [**6, 9**] for finding constituents $\boldsymbol{g}^p(j^p)$ of arbitrary dimensionality that simultaneously satisfy (3.3) for all j^p and $1 \leq p \leq P$. All examples of σ–trees given in this paper were generated by this algorithm.

4. Direct Sum Signal Constellations

Since the covering problem is in some sense the dual of the sphere packing problem, there should be σ–trees that give good performances as signal constellations. To investigate this possibility, several binary (two constituents per constituent set) two and four dimensional σ–trees were designed with an iterative computer algorithm more fully described in [**6, 9**].

4.1. Two Dimensional Constellations. The direct sum constellations shown in Figure 3 were designed with one million training data vectors uniformly distributed inside the square shown by dotted lines. All initial constituents used at the start of the iterative algorithm were chosen by a "splitting" process [**6**]. The design process was allowed to continue until the relative change in the covering (quantization) distortion fell below a predetermined threshold. It is important to note that the results shown in Figure 3 were obtained without any attempt to encourage lattice– and array–like structures. These direct sum signal sets are the natural products of the iterative design algorithm. Constellations (a) through (f) have numbers of binary constituent sets varying from 3 through

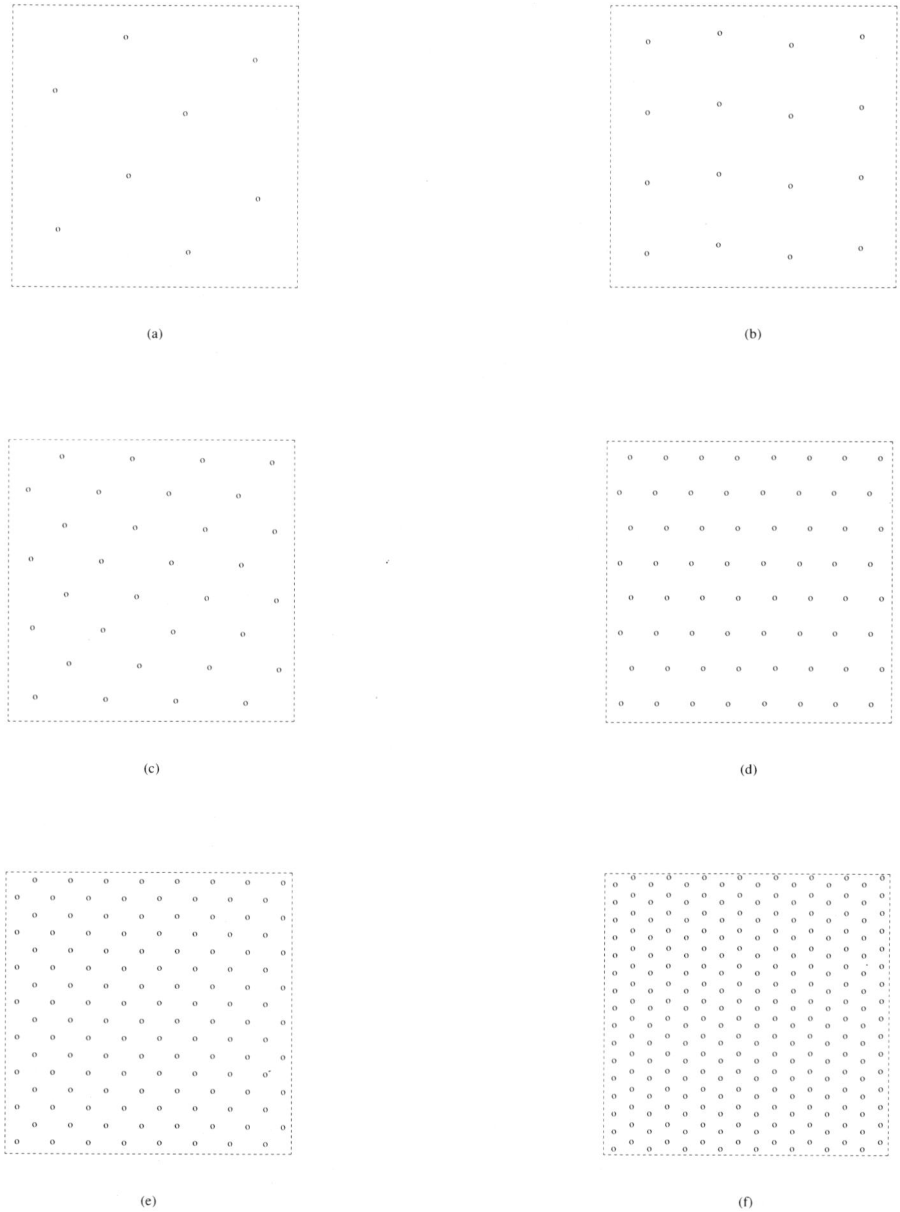

FIGURE 3. Cubical two dimensional σ–tree signal constellations.

8, respectively. Constellations (a), (c) and (e) seem to be subsets of the rotated two dimensional integer lattice RZ^2. However, careful examination of these direct sum constellations shows that (a) and (c) are not true lattice subsets: the points are slightly perturbed away from the RZ^2 points in order to satisfy the conditions described in Section 3. These signal sets are therefore not subsets of lattice groups closed under vector addition. Sets (a) and (c) together with constellations (b) and (d) are recognized as subsets of regular arrays [**11**]. The 256–point direct sum constellation of Figure 3(f) seems to be a subset of the hexagonal A_2 lattice: the best packing and covering in two dimensions. Considering the duality of the sphere packing problem and the covering problem, it is not surprising that a 256–point σ–tree was generated that corresponds to the optimal hexagonal A_2 lattice, but it is surprising that this subset of A_2 was generated by the direct sum of only eight binary constituent sets consisting of a total of only 16 two dimensional points.

We also generated σ–tree constellations with data uniformly distributed inside the circular enclosing boundaries shown in Figure 4. Constellations (a) through (f) have numbers of binary constituent sets varying from 1 through 6, respectively. It seems apparent that designing constellations with spherical boundaries allow more flexibility in obtaining shape gain than designing direct sum constellations with square boundaries. In addition, observe that the constellation of Figure 4(f) has points which are nearly hexagonal in spite of the training set boundary being circular. It is also interesting to note that some of the $\boldsymbol{t} \in \mathcal{T}$ in the constellations of Figure 4 have escaped the spherical boundary of the training data. This phenomenon represents a compromise between the need to minimize distortion and the structural constraint imposed by the σ–tree structure.

As a concluding two dimensional example, shown in Figure 5 are two dimensional direct sum 2–way and 4–way partitions induced by the σ–tree in a manner completely analogous to the one–dimensional example of Figure 2.

4.2. Four Dimensional Constellations. Shown in Figure 6 are the two dimensional projections of four dimensional σ–trees. That is, if $\boldsymbol{t} = (t_1, t_2, t_3, t_4)$ is a leaf node of a four dimensional tree, then the figures contain plots of both (t_1, t_2) and (t_3, t_4). These σ–trees were designed using training data drawn from four dimensional uniformly distributed hyper–cubes. Figures 6(a)–(c) correspond to a non–uniform, five–level σ–tree that had the direct sum structure $2 \times 2 \times 2 \times 2 \times 16$. That is, the constituent sets at levels one through four had binary constituent sets, and the last level constituent set contained 16 generators. Hence, this σ–tree has 256 leaf nodes in 4–space. Figure 6(a) shows the two dimensional projections of the entire σ–tree. Figure 6(b) shows the two dimensional projections of the σ–tree after the top two constituent sets have been removed, leaving only a three level subtree with 64 leaf nodes. Figure 6(c) shows the two dimensional projections of the σ–tree after the top four constituent sets have been removed, leaving only a single level subtree with 16 leaf nodes (a total

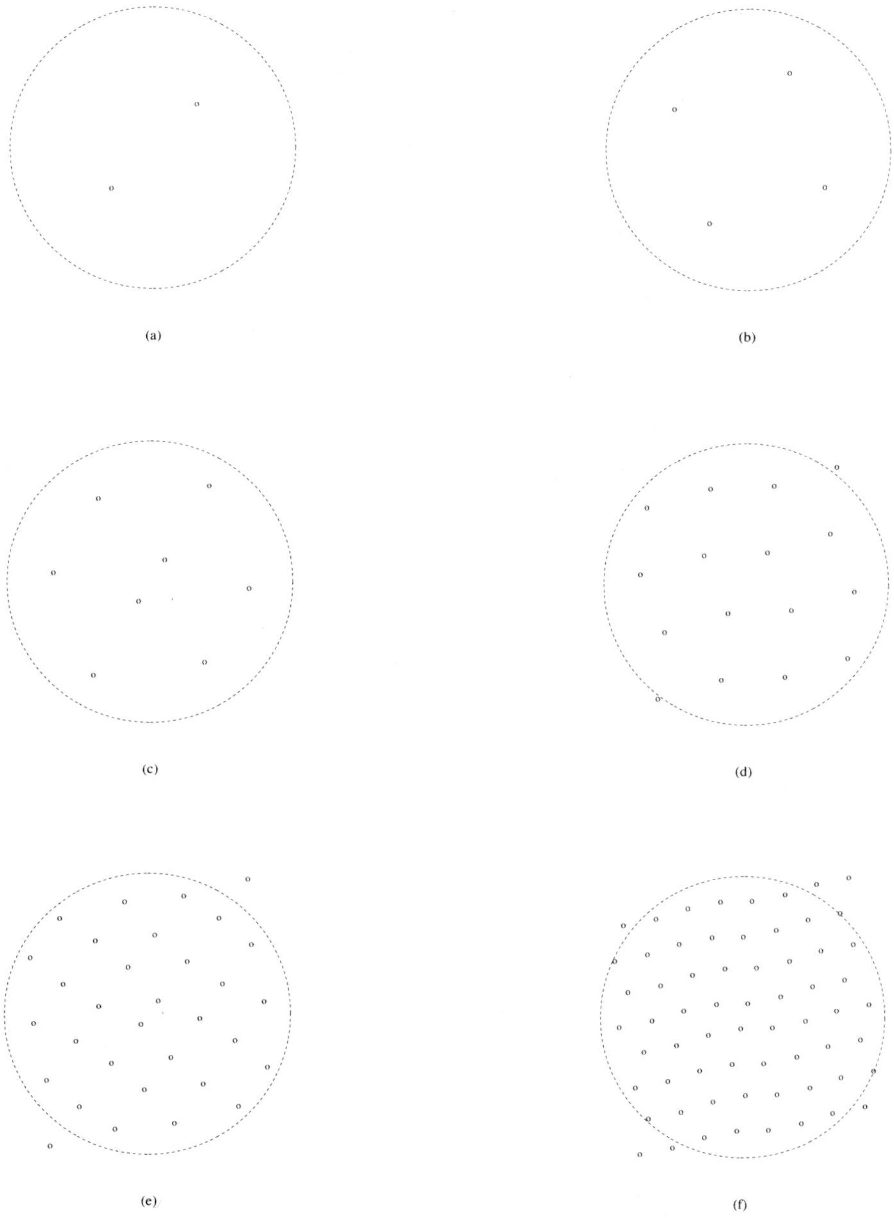

FIGURE 4. Circular two dimensional σ–tree signal constellations.

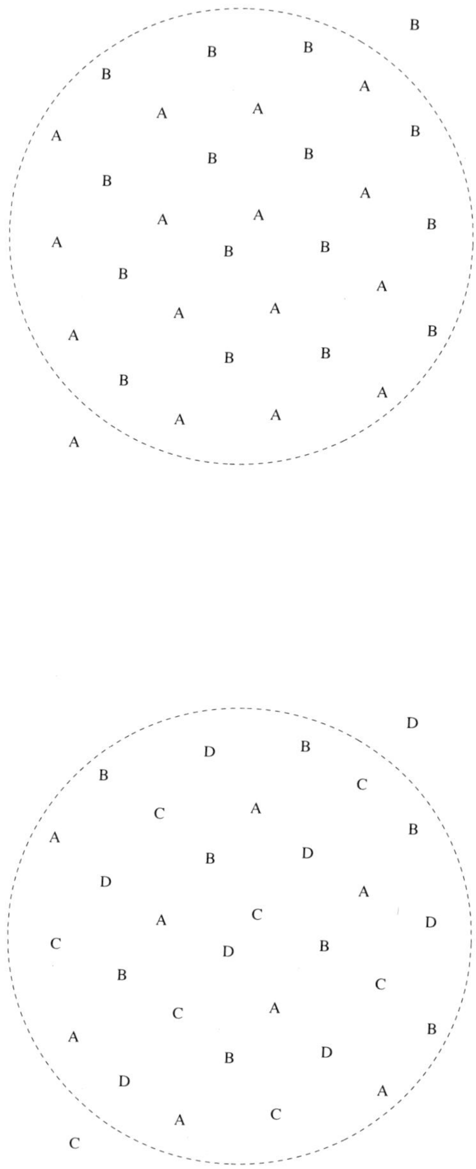

FIGURE 5. Two–way and four–way partitions of the 32–point circular direct sum constellation as induced by the first and second levels of the σ–tree, respectively.

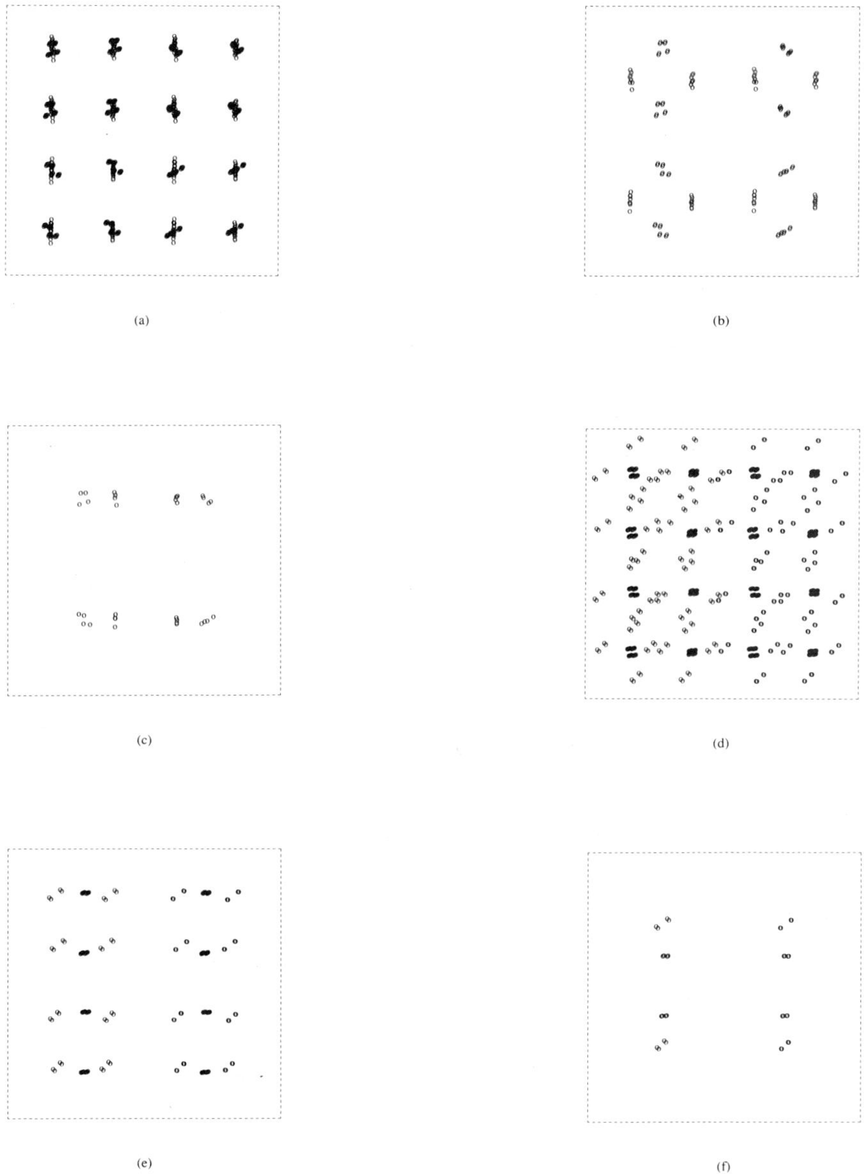

FIGURE 6. Two dimensional projections of four dimensional hyper–cube σ–tree signal constellations.

of 32 two dimensional projections are shown in Figure 6(c)). Examination of these figures seems to indicate that the intra–subtree distances in this sequence of subtrees expand as levels are removed from the σ–tree. In fact, examination of the corresponding intra–subtree distance profiles (not given here) confirms that this is true. Another four dimensional σ–tree is shown in Figures 6(d)–(f). This direct sum structure is $4 \times 4 \times 4 \times 4$, where only one level is removed each time to form a subtree.

5. Direct Sum Decompositions of Lattices

In this section we show that there exist direct sum decompositions of lattices and of certain finite subsets of lattices.

For every N–dimensional lattice it is possible to find a set of N *basis vectors* $\boldsymbol{g}_1, \boldsymbol{g}_2, \ldots, \boldsymbol{g}_N$ such that the $\boldsymbol{\lambda} \in \Lambda$ can be described as $\boldsymbol{\lambda} = \sum \xi_i \boldsymbol{g}_i$ where the ξ_i are integers. The $N \times M$ matrix G with $N \leq M$ and the rows equal to the $\boldsymbol{g}_i$ (it is sometimes convenient to use $M > N$ coordinates to describe an N–dimensional lattice [**7**]) is called a *generator matrix* for the lattice. Using G and the integer N–tuples $\boldsymbol{\xi} = (\xi_1, \xi_2, \ldots, \xi_N)$ the corresponding lattice can be written as

$$\Lambda = \{\boldsymbol{\xi} G : \boldsymbol{\xi} \in Z^N\}. \tag{5.1}$$

In source and channel coding applications which use lattices as the bases for quantization or signaling constellations, it is often useful to consider only a finite subset $\mathcal{T}$ of Λ. One way to describe such a subset is to allow $\boldsymbol{\xi}$ to assume values only in a finite subset of Z^N. One such subset is

$$Z_k^N = \underbrace{Z_k \times Z_k \times \cdots \times Z_k}_{N\ terms}, \tag{5.2}$$

where $Z_k = \{0, 1, \ldots, k-1\}$ and where for convenience it is assumed that k is a power of 2. The corresponding finite subset of Λ is then given by

$$\mathcal{T} = \{\boldsymbol{\xi} G : \boldsymbol{\xi} \in Z_k^N\} \tag{5.3}$$

and has $|Z_k^N|$ members.

Much insight into the structure of the subset $\mathcal{T}$ can be obtained if the integer N–tuples $\boldsymbol{\xi} \in Z_k^N$ are written as $\boldsymbol{\xi} = \boldsymbol{\beta} J$ where $\boldsymbol{\beta} = (1, 2, 4, 8, \ldots, 2^{\log_2(k)-1})$ and where

$$J = \begin{bmatrix} j_1^1 & j_2^1 & \cdots & j_N^1 \\ j_1^2 & j_2^2 & \cdots & j_N^2 \\ \cdots & & & \\ j_1^P & j_2^P & \ddots & j_N^P \end{bmatrix} \tag{5.4}$$

with $j_i^p \in Z_2$ and $P = \log_2(k)$. The ith column vector $\boldsymbol{\nu}_i$ of J contains the standard binary representation of ξ_i. This representation of the integer N–tuple

$\boldsymbol{\xi}$ permits each point $\boldsymbol{t} \in \mathcal{T}$ to be written $\boldsymbol{t} = \boldsymbol{\beta} JG$ for some J matrix with binary (0 or 1) elements and the lattice subset $\mathcal{T}$ to be written

$$\mathcal{T} = \{\boldsymbol{\beta} JG : J \in \boldsymbol{Z}_2^{P \times N}\}, \tag{5.5}$$

where $\boldsymbol{Z}_2^{P\times N}$ is the set of all possible $P \times N$ matrices with zero–one elements.

Next, consider the row vectors $\boldsymbol{j}^p = (j_1^p, j_2^p, \ldots, j_N^p)$ of J and let $\boldsymbol{\beta}$ be more generally expressed by $\boldsymbol{\beta} = (\beta^1, \beta^2, \ldots, \beta^l)$ and observe that for each $\boldsymbol{t} \in \mathcal{T}$,

$$\boldsymbol{t} = [\beta^1 \beta^2 \cdots \beta^P] \begin{bmatrix} \boldsymbol{j}^1 G \\ \boldsymbol{j}^2 G \\ \vdots \\ \boldsymbol{j}^P G \end{bmatrix}, \tag{5.6}$$

for some set of $\boldsymbol{j}^p \in Z_2^N, 1 \leq p \leq P$. Hence, we have

$$\boldsymbol{t}(\boldsymbol{j}) = \sum_{p=1}^{P} \beta^p \boldsymbol{j}^p G \tag{5.7}$$

where $\boldsymbol{j} = (\boldsymbol{j}^1, \ldots, \boldsymbol{j}^P)$, and if we consider all $\boldsymbol{j}$,

$$\mathcal{T} = \{\beta^1 \boldsymbol{j}^1 G\} + \{\beta^2 \boldsymbol{j}^2 G\} + \cdots + \{\beta^P \boldsymbol{j}^P G\}, \tag{5.8}$$

where $+$ denotes the direct or Cartesian sum of set elements. The insight gained from (5.8) is that each $\boldsymbol{t} \in \mathcal{T}$ is a vector sum of scaled versions of different linear combinations of the rows of G and hence is a direct sum set and has an associated σ–tree. Next, note from (5.8) that the sets $\Gamma^p = \{\boldsymbol{j}^p G : \boldsymbol{j}^p \in Z_2^N\}$ are identical for all p, hence we may let $\Gamma = \Gamma^p$ and write (5.8) as

$$\mathcal{T} = \beta^1 \Gamma + \beta^2 \Gamma + \cdots + \beta^P \Gamma, \tag{5.9}$$

where $\beta^p \Gamma$ denotes that all elements of Γ are scaled by β^p. Equation (5.9) introduces a representation of a certain class of finite subsets of lattices (described by (5.3)) which allows the σ–tree based partitioning concepts of Section 2 to be applied to lattice subsets (or their translates). As we show next, generalizations of (5.9) remove the linearity constraint associated with group alphabets.

Since every $\gamma \in \Gamma$ is the image of some $\boldsymbol{j}^p \in Z_2^N$, the set Γ may be considered the range of a function with domain Z_2^N and we may write $\gamma(\boldsymbol{j}^p) = \boldsymbol{j}^p G$ and (5.7) becomes

$$\boldsymbol{t}(\boldsymbol{j}) = \sum_{p=1}^{P} \beta^p \gamma(\boldsymbol{j}^p). \tag{5.10}$$

Even more generally, if we let $\boldsymbol{g}^p(\boldsymbol{j}^p) = \beta^p \gamma(\boldsymbol{j}^p)$, then we have

$$\boldsymbol{t}(\boldsymbol{j}) = \sum_{p=1}^{P} \boldsymbol{g}^p(\boldsymbol{j}^p), \tag{5.11}$$

where each $\boldsymbol{j}^p$ selects one of the elements of the constituent set $\beta^p\Gamma = G^p$. In its most general form, (5.9) can be written

$$\mathcal{T} = G^1 + G^2 + \cdots + G^P, \tag{5.12}$$

which reveals the σ–tree associated with (5.3) (where in general, the G^p are arbitrary subsets of $\Re^N$). If the $\boldsymbol{g}^p \in G^p$ of (5.11) have the form $\boldsymbol{g}^p = \beta^p \boldsymbol{j}^p G$ for some generator matrix G, then $\mathcal{T}$ is a subset of the lattice corresponding to G. In addition, if the sum of (5.11) ranges from $-\infty$ to $+\infty$ where $\boldsymbol{\beta} = (\cdots - 4, -2, -1, 1, 2, 4 \cdots)$, then

$$\Lambda = \sum_{\substack{i \in Z \\ i \neq 0}} G^i. \tag{5.13}$$

However, there is no requirement that the $\boldsymbol{g}^p \in G^p$ must obey such a relationship, and, in general, the constituents $\boldsymbol{g}^p$ may be completely arbitrary.

6. Signal Space Codes

In this section we formalize much of the material of the previous sections by giving definitions and lemmas related to σ–tree structures. We also show that generalized tree–structured alphabets permit labelings of direct sum signal sets such that the distance properties of the labels assumes a geometric significance in the signal space.

6.1. σ–Tree Structures. Let $\mathcal{P}$ denote the ordered set $(1, 2, \ldots, P)$ and let $\sigma : \mathcal{P} \mapsto \mathcal{P}$ be a permutation of $\mathcal{P}$. Let $\sigma(p)$ denote the pth element of $\sigma(\mathcal{P})$. Also, let the notation $\sigma(Q : P)$ denote the last $P - Q + 1$ elements of $\sigma(\mathcal{P})$ where $Q \leq P$, that is, $\sigma(Q : P) = (\sigma(Q), \sigma(Q+1), \ldots, \sigma(P))$. In particular, we note that $\sigma(\mathcal{P}) = \sigma(1 : P)$.

DEFINITION 6.1. The *leaf nodes* of a P–level, M–ary, uniform *σ–tree* $\mathcal{T}_{\sigma(1:P)}$ is the set of M^P possible sums of vectors in real Euclidean N–space with one vector selected from each of an ordered P–member collection of M–ary sets $(G^{\sigma(1)}, G^{\sigma(2)}, \cdots, G^{\sigma(P)})$. That is, $\mathcal{T}_{\sigma(1:P)}$ is the direct sum set $G^{\sigma(1)} + G^{\sigma(2)} + \cdots + G^{\sigma(P)}$. The sets $G^{\sigma(p)}$ are called *constituent sets* and the N–tuples, $\boldsymbol{g}_j^{\sigma(p)} \in G^{\sigma(p)}, j \in \{0, 1, \ldots, M-1\}$ are called *generators.*

The number of elements in each constituent set $G^{\sigma(\cdot)}$ is written $|G^{\sigma(\cdot)}|$. If the number of elements in each $G^{\sigma(p)}$ varies with p, the σ–tree is said to be *non–uniform.* For ease of notation, only uniform σ–trees with $|G^{\sigma(\cdot)}| = M$ are considered here.

Although Definition 6.1 pertains mainly to the leaf nodes of the tree structure, the internal nodes of the structure are implicitly represented by the notation $\mathcal{T}_{\sigma(1:P)}$, that is, if the origin of N–space is the root node of the σ–tree, then $\mathcal{T}_{\sigma(1:1)}$ represents the M nodes at the first level of the tree structure, $\mathcal{T}_{\sigma(1:2)}$

represents the M^2 nodes at the second level, and so forth. In this way, if $\sigma_1(\cdot)$ and $\sigma_2(\cdot)$ are two different permutations of $\mathcal{P}$ (and the associated constituents $G^{\sigma(\cdot)}$), then $\mathcal{T}_{\sigma_1(1:P)}$ and $\mathcal{T}_{\sigma_2(1:P)}$ also represent two different tree structures, although, the set of leaf nodes (and hence the corresponding direct sum set) of the two tree structures are identical.

DEFINITION 6.2. A $(P-Q+1)$–level, *subtree* $\mathcal{T}_{\sigma(Q:P)}$ of $\mathcal{T}_{\sigma(1:P)}$ is a σ–tree that is formed from the last $P-Q+1$ elements of the ordered set $(G^{\sigma(1)}, G^{\sigma(2)}, \ldots, G^{\sigma(P)})$; that is, $\mathcal{T}_{\sigma(Q:P)} = G^{\sigma(Q)} + G^{\sigma(Q+1)} + \cdots + G^{\sigma(P)}$.

6.2. σ–Tree Partitions. A *partition* of a σ–tree $\mathcal{T}$ is a collection of disjoint subsets $S(j)$ whose union is $\mathcal{T}$, where j is a *label* for the subsets. The partition is denoted by $\mathcal{T}/S$ and the *order* (denoted by $|\mathcal{T}/S|$) of the partition is the number of disjoint subsets in the collection. A *partition subset labeling* is any one–to–one map between partition subsets and a set of $|\mathcal{T}/S|$ labels.

A *coset* $\boldsymbol{c}+\mathcal{T}$ of a σ–tree $\mathcal{T}$ is the set of all N–tuples of the form $\boldsymbol{c}+\boldsymbol{t}$ where $\boldsymbol{t}$ is any point in $\mathcal{T}$, and $\boldsymbol{c}$, called a *translate*, is some constant N–tuple that specifies the coset.

LEMMA 6.1. A $(P-Q+1)$–level subtree $\mathcal{T}_{\sigma(Q:P)}$ of a M–ary σ–tree $\mathcal{T}_{\sigma(1:P)}$ induces a *partition* $\mathcal{T}_{\sigma(1:P)}/\mathcal{T}_{\sigma(Q:P)}$ consisting of a collection of $|\mathcal{T}_{\sigma(1:P)}/\mathcal{T}_{\sigma(Q:P)}| = M^{(Q-1)}$ cosets of $\mathcal{T}_{\sigma(Q:P)}$. The cosets of $\mathcal{T}_{\sigma(Q:P)}$ have translates $\boldsymbol{c}$ determined by the $Q-1$ constituent sets used in the construction of $\mathcal{T}_{\sigma(1:P)}$ but omitted from the construction of $\mathcal{T}_{\sigma(Q:P)}$, that is, $\boldsymbol{c} \in \mathcal{T}_{\sigma(1:Q-1)}$.

PROOF. Let $\mathcal{T}_{\sigma(1:P)}$ be a σ–tree with P constituent M–ary sets $G^{\sigma(p)}, 1 \leq p \leq P$. Let $\mathcal{T}_{\sigma(Q:P)}$ be a $(P-Q+1)$–level subtree of $\mathcal{T}_{\sigma(1:P)}$. Then $\mathcal{T}_{\sigma(1:P)}$ may be written as

$$\mathcal{T}_{\sigma(1:P)} = G^{\sigma(1)} + G^{\sigma(2)} + \cdots + G^{\sigma(Q-1)} + \mathcal{T}_{\sigma(Q:P)}. \tag{6.1}$$

Each $\boldsymbol{c} \in \{G^{\sigma(1)} + G^{\sigma(2)} + \cdots + G^{\sigma(Q-1)}\}$ is a translate for a coset $\boldsymbol{c}+\mathcal{T}_{\sigma(Q:P)}$ of the subtree $\mathcal{T}_{\sigma(Q:P)}$, and since the union of $\boldsymbol{c}+\mathcal{T}_{\sigma(Q:P)}$ over all $\boldsymbol{c} \in \{G^{\sigma(1)} + G^{\sigma(2)} + \cdots + G^{\sigma(Q-1)}\}$ gives $\mathcal{T}_{\sigma(1:P)}$, we have a partition of $\mathcal{T}_{\sigma(1:P)}$ into subsets $\boldsymbol{c}+\mathcal{T}_{\sigma(Q:P)}$. Since $|G^{\sigma(1)} + G^{\sigma(2)} + \cdots + G^{\sigma(Q-1)}| = M^{(Q-1)}$, hence $|\mathcal{T}_{\sigma(1:P)}/\mathcal{T}_{\sigma(Q:P)}| = M^{(Q-1)}$. □

Lemma 6.1 shows that the ordered collection of constituents $(G^{\sigma(1)}, G^{\sigma(2)}, \ldots, G^{\sigma(Q-1)})$ omitted in forming a particular subtree $\mathcal{T}_{\sigma(Q:P)}$ yields a set of translates for the cosets of $\mathcal{T}_{\sigma(Q:P)}$ in the partition $\mathcal{T}_{\sigma(1:P)}/\mathcal{T}_{\sigma(Q:P)}$. This set of translates is written as $[\mathcal{T}_{\sigma(1:P)}/\mathcal{T}_{\sigma(Q:P)}]$. Every element of $\mathcal{T}_{\sigma(1:P)}$ can be written uniquely as a sum $\boldsymbol{t} = \boldsymbol{c} + \boldsymbol{t}'$, where $\boldsymbol{c} \in [\mathcal{T}_{\sigma(1:P)}/\mathcal{T}_{\sigma(Q:P)}]$ is the translate of the coset of $\mathcal{T}_{\sigma(Q:P)}$ in which $\boldsymbol{t}$ lies, and $\boldsymbol{t}' = \boldsymbol{t} - \boldsymbol{c}$ is an element of the subtree $\mathcal{T}_{\sigma(Q:P)}$. The σ–tree $\mathcal{T}_{\sigma(1:P)}$ may be expressed by a *subtree decomposition*,

$$\mathcal{T}_{\sigma(1:P)} = [\mathcal{T}_{\sigma(1:P)}/\mathcal{T}_{\sigma(Q:P)}] + \mathcal{T}_{\sigma(Q:P)}. \tag{6.2}$$

A short hand notation for (6.2) is $\mathcal{T}_1 = [\mathcal{T}_1/\mathcal{T}_Q] + \mathcal{T}_Q$.

Since $|\mathcal{T}_1/\mathcal{T}_Q| = M^{(Q-1)}$, a set of M–ary $(Q-1)$–tuples $\boldsymbol{j}$ may be used as a partition subset labeling $\mathcal{T}_Q(\boldsymbol{j})$. Since a unique translate is associated with every coset $\mathcal{T}_Q(\boldsymbol{j})$, we may label cosets by labeling the respective translate $\mathcal{T}_Q(\boldsymbol{j}) = \boldsymbol{c}(\boldsymbol{j}) + \mathcal{T}_Q$.

As an example of a subtree decomposition, consider constituent sets that are binary ($M = 2$), and in particular, the constituent sets,

$$G^1 = \{0,1\}, \tag{6.3}$$
$$G^2 = \{0,2\}, \tag{6.4}$$
$$\vdots \tag{6.5}$$
$$G^P = \{0,2^{P-1}\}. \tag{6.6}$$

Also assume for this example that $\sigma(\cdot)$ is the identity permutation, $\sigma(\mathcal{P}) = \mathcal{P}$, and hence, $\sigma(p) = p$. The leaf nodes of the σ–tree $\mathcal{T}_{\sigma(1:P)}$ are $\{0,1,2,\dots,2^P-1\}$, which is the set of integers Z_{2^P}. In general, if $P = \infty$, then the corresponding σ–tree is the set of all non–negative integers $\mathcal{T}_{\sigma(1:\infty)} = Z^+$, where $|\mathcal{T}_{\sigma(1:\infty)}| = \infty$. The partition $\mathcal{T}_{\sigma(1:\infty)}/\mathcal{T}_{\sigma(2:\infty)}$ gives the subtree decomposition

$$\mathcal{T}_{\sigma(1:\infty)} = [\mathcal{T}_{\sigma(1:\infty)}/\mathcal{T}_{\sigma(2:\infty)}] + \mathcal{T}_{\sigma(2:\infty)}, \tag{6.7}$$
$$= G^1 + \mathcal{T}_{\sigma(2:\infty)}, \tag{6.8}$$
$$= \{0,1\} + \{0,2,4,\dots\}. \tag{6.9}$$

The cosets of $\mathcal{T}_{\sigma(2:\infty)}$ may be labeled such that $\mathcal{T}_{\sigma(2:\infty)}(0) = 0 + \{0,2,4,\dots\}$ and $\mathcal{T}_{\sigma(2:\infty)}(1) = 1 + \{0,2,4,\dots\}$, and hence $\cup_{j\in\{0,1\}}\mathcal{T}_{\sigma(2:\infty)}(j) = Z^+$. We note that the set $\mathcal{T}_{\sigma(2:\infty)} = \{0,2,4\dots,\}$ is equivalent to the semi–infinite sublattice $2Z^+$ of Z^+ and from (6.9) we have $\mathcal{T}_{\sigma(1:\infty)} = \{0,1\} + 2Z^+$. Which is essentially $Z^+ = [Z^+/2Z^+] + 2Z^+$ where $[Z^+/2Z^+] = \{0,1\}$ is a set of coset representatives of the semi–infinite sublattice $2Z^+$.

As another example, consider the same constituent sets and the permutation of the positive non–zero integers, $\sigma(1,2,3,4,5,\cdots) = (2,1,3,4,5,\cdots)$, where 1 and 2 are permuted, i.e., $\sigma(1) = 2$, $\sigma(2) = 1$ and $\sigma(p) = p$, otherwise. Then $\mathcal{T}_{\sigma(2:P)}$ is the set of every other pair of non–negative integers starting with $Z_2 = \{0,1\}$ and the subtree decomposition is

$$\mathcal{T}_{\sigma(1:\infty)} = \{0,2\} + \{0,1,4,5,8,9,12,13,\dots\}. \tag{6.10}$$

The coset $\mathcal{T}_{\sigma(2:\infty)}(0) = 0 + \{0,1,4,5,\dots\}$ gives replicated translates of $Z_2 = \{0,1\}$ and $\mathcal{T}_{\sigma(2:\infty)}(1) = 2 + \{0,1,4,5,\dots\}$ gives replicated translates of $2 + Z_2 = \{2,3\}$ such that $\cup_{j\in\{0,1\}}\mathcal{T}_{\sigma(2:\infty)}(j) = Z^+$.

6.3. σ–Tree Partition Chains. A *Q–level partition chain* $\mathcal{T}_1/\mathcal{S}_2/\cdots/\mathcal{S}_Q$ is obtained by repeated partitioning of subsets; i.e., the σ–tree $\mathcal{T}_1$ is first partitioned into $|\mathcal{T}_1/\mathcal{S}_2|$ subsets $\mathcal{S}_2(j^1)$, then each subset $\mathcal{S}_2(j^1)$ of $\mathcal{T}_2$ is partitioned, and so forth. It is convenient to label a Q–level partition chain by a $(Q-1)$–*tuple label*

$\boldsymbol{j} = (j^1, j^2, \ldots, j^{Q-1})$, where j^p is one of a set of M indexes used at the pth level. The subsets at the pth level are then labeled by the first $p-1$ parts of the label; e.g., $S_2(j^1), S_3(j^1, j^2)$, and so forth. Since all partitions at any given level have the same order M, the order of $|\mathcal{T}_1/S_Q|$ is the product of $|\mathcal{T}_1/S_2|$ and the common orders $|S_{p-1}(j^{p-2})/S_p(j^{p-1})|$ for $2 < p \leq Q$.

The next lemma shows first, that any partition $\mathcal{T}_1/\mathcal{T}_Q$ of a M–ary σ–tree can be broken up into a Q–level partition chain of M–way partitions $\mathcal{T}_{p-1}/\mathcal{T}_p; 1 < p \leq Q$; second, that there is a labeling

$$\mathbf{c}(\boldsymbol{j}) = \sum_{p=1}^{Q-1} \boldsymbol{g}_{j^p}^{\sigma(p)} \tag{6.11}$$

where $\boldsymbol{g}_{j^p}^{\sigma(p)}$ is an element of the pth constituent set $G^{\sigma(p)}$, and j^p is the pth member of the M–ary $(Q-1)$–tuple $\boldsymbol{j}$. This implies that the M vectors in $G^{\sigma(p-1)}$ are a system of translates for the cosets of $\mathcal{T}_p$ in the partition $\mathcal{T}_{p-1}/\mathcal{T}_p$, and that the $M^{(Q-1)}$ linear combinations $\{\sum \boldsymbol{g}_{j^p}^{\sigma(p)}\}$ of the *generators* $\boldsymbol{g}_{j^p}^{\sigma(p)} \in G^{\sigma(p)}$ are a system of translates $[\mathcal{T}_1/\mathcal{T}_Q]$ for the cosets of $\mathcal{T}_Q$ in the partition $\mathcal{T}_1/\mathcal{T}_Q$, and hence,

$$\mathcal{T}_1 = [\mathcal{T}_1/\mathcal{T}_Q] + \mathcal{T}_Q, \tag{6.12}$$

$$= \{\mathbf{c}(\boldsymbol{j})\} + \mathcal{T}_Q, \tag{6.13}$$

$$= \left\{\sum_{p=1}^{Q-1} \boldsymbol{g}_{j^p}^{\sigma(p)}\right\} + \mathcal{T}_Q. \tag{6.14}$$

LEMMA 6.2. Given a subtree $\mathcal{T}_{\sigma(Q:P)}$ of $\mathcal{T}_{\sigma(1:P)}$, let $\mathcal{T}_{\sigma(1:P)}/\mathcal{T}_{\sigma(Q:P)}$ be a partition of $\mathcal{T}_{\sigma(1:P)}$ of order $M^{(Q-1)}$. Then there is a partition chain $\mathcal{T}_{\sigma(1:P)}/\mathcal{T}_{\sigma(2:P)}/\cdots/\mathcal{T}_{\sigma(Q:P)}$ where each partition $\mathcal{T}_{p-1}/\mathcal{T}_p$ has order M for $1 < p \leq Q$ and such that

$$\mathcal{T}_{\sigma(1:P)} = [\mathcal{T}_{\sigma(1:P)}/\mathcal{T}_{\sigma(Q:P)}] + \mathcal{T}_{\sigma(Q:P)}, \tag{6.15}$$

$$= [\mathcal{T}_{\sigma(1:P)}/\mathcal{T}_{\sigma(2:P)}] + \cdots + [\mathcal{T}_{\sigma(Q-1:P)}/\mathcal{T}_{\sigma(Q:P)}] + \mathcal{T}_{\sigma(Q:P)}, \tag{6.16}$$

$$= G^{\sigma(1)} + \cdots + G^{\sigma(Q-1)} + \mathcal{T}_{\sigma(Q:P)}, \tag{6.17}$$

$$= \left\{\sum_{p=1}^{Q-1} \boldsymbol{g}_{j^p}^{\sigma(p)}\right\} + \mathcal{T}_{\sigma(Q:P)}. \tag{6.18}$$

That is, each $[\mathcal{T}_{p-1}/\mathcal{T}_p] = G^{\sigma(p-1)}$ is a system of translates of $\mathcal{T}_p$ in the partition $\mathcal{T}_{p-1}/\mathcal{T}_p$ for $1 < p \leq Q$, and $G^{\sigma(p)} + \cdots + G^{\sigma(Q-1)} = \{\sum \boldsymbol{g}_{j^p}^{\sigma(p)}\}$ is a system of translates for $\mathcal{T}_{\sigma(Q:P)}$ in the partition $\mathcal{T}_{\sigma(1:P)}/\mathcal{T}_{\sigma(Q:P)}$.

PROOF. Each partition $\mathcal{T}_{p-1}/\mathcal{T}_p$ has order M since

$$\begin{aligned} \mathcal{T}_{p-1} &= [\mathcal{T}_{p-1}/\mathcal{T}_p] + \mathcal{T}_p, && (6.19)\\ &= G^{\sigma(p-1)} + \mathcal{T}_p, && (6.20)\end{aligned}$$

where $G^{\sigma(p-1)}$ is a constituent used to form $\mathcal{T}_{p-1}$ and omitted in forming $\mathcal{T}_p$, and where $|G^{\sigma(p-1)}| = M$. Hence, in a M–way partition $\mathcal{T}_{p-1}/\mathcal{T}_p$, each $\boldsymbol{g}^{\sigma(p-1)}_{j^{p-1}} \in G^{\sigma(p-1)}$ is a translate for a coset of the subtree $\mathcal{T}_p$. Next consider that $\mathcal{T}_{\sigma(1:P)} = G^{\sigma(1)} + \cdots + G^{\sigma(Q-1)} + T_{\sigma(Q:P)}$. Hence, $\mathcal{T}_{\sigma(1:P)} = [\mathcal{T}_{\sigma(1:P)}/\mathcal{T}_{\sigma(2:P)}] + \cdots + [\mathcal{T}_{Q-1}/\mathcal{T}_{\sigma(Q:P)}] + \mathcal{T}_{\sigma(Q:P)}$ and the $\boldsymbol{c}(\boldsymbol{j}) \in \left\{\sum \boldsymbol{g}^{\sigma(p)}_{j^p}\right\}$ are a system of translates of $\mathcal{T}_{\sigma(Q:P)}$ in the partition $\mathcal{T}_{\sigma(1:P)}/\mathcal{T}_{\sigma(Q:P)}$. □

Once again, using the example of the 1–dimensional 1–sided binary canonical constituents with the identity permutation, and where $P = 5$ and $Q = 5$, the partition $\mathcal{T}_1/\mathcal{T}_5$ has a partition chain decomposition given by

$$\begin{aligned} \mathcal{T}_1 &= [\mathcal{T}_1/\mathcal{T}_2] + [\mathcal{T}_2/\mathcal{T}_3] + [\mathcal{T}_3/\mathcal{T}_4] + [\mathcal{T}_4/\mathcal{T}_5] + \mathcal{T}_5, && (6.21)\\ &= G^1 + G^2 + G^3 + G^4 + G^5, && (6.22)\\ &= \{0,1\} + \{0,2\} + \{0,4\} + \{0,8\} + \{0,16\}, && (6.23)\\ &= \{j^1\cdot 1 + j^2\cdot 2 + j^3\cdot 4 + j^4\cdot 8 + j_5\cdot 16\}. && (6.24)\end{aligned}$$

In this case, the 5–tuple $\boldsymbol{j} = (j^1, \ldots, j^5)$ with $j^p \in \{0,1\}$ gives the standard binary representation of any integer $0 \le z < 2^P$. Also, note that the generators are decomposed as in (1.1) where $\boldsymbol{g}^{\sigma(p)}_{j^p} = j^p \boldsymbol{g}^{\sigma(p)}$ and $\boldsymbol{g}^{\sigma(p)} = 2^{\sigma(p)-1}$.

6.4. σ–Tree Permutations. Since there are $P!$ different permutations of the integers $(1, 2, \ldots, P)$, we have the following lemma

LEMMA 6.3. *There exists $P!$ different partition chain decompositions $\mathcal{T}_1/\mathcal{T}_2/\ldots/\mathcal{T}_P$ of $\mathcal{T}_1/\mathcal{T}_P$ determined by the $P!$ different permutations of $\mathcal{P}$.*

The proof of this lemma follows directly from the definitions of a σ–tree partition chain. Each permutation of the constituent sets represents a different σ–tree structure. For example, given the 1–dimensional 2–sided binary constituent sets $G^1 = \{-\frac{1}{2}, \frac{1}{2}\}$, $G^2 = \{-\frac{3}{2}, \frac{3}{2}\}$, and $G^3 = \{-\frac{5}{2}, \frac{5}{2}\}$, the *identity* permutation $\sigma(1,2,3,) = (1,2,3)$ gives the σ tree structure shown in Figure 1. The *inverting* permutation $\sigma(1,2,3) = (3,2,1)$ gives the σ–tree structure shown in Figure 2.

In the next section we examine the distance properties of permuted σ–tree partition chains. It is the constituent set permutations that determine the label and signal set distance properties which are most useful in trellis codes.

6.5. σ–Tree Distance Properties. We assume a distance metric $d(\boldsymbol{t}, \boldsymbol{t}')$ is defined between pairs $(\boldsymbol{t}, \boldsymbol{t}')$ of elements of $\mathcal{T}$ and that $d(\boldsymbol{t}, \boldsymbol{t}')$ is zero if $\boldsymbol{t} = \boldsymbol{t}'$ and greater than zero if $\boldsymbol{t} \neq \boldsymbol{t}'$ (which is an implicit constraint on the M–ary constituent sets G^p such that all leaf nodes are distinct). We define the *minimum distance* $d(\mathcal{T})$ of $\mathcal{T}$ as the minimum non–zero $d(\boldsymbol{t}, \boldsymbol{t}')$ for $\boldsymbol{t}$ and $\boldsymbol{t}'$ in $\mathcal{T}$.

If $d(\cdot,\cdot)$ is translation invariant, then all cosets of $\mathcal{T}_Q$ have the same minimum distance $d(\mathcal{T}_Q)$. We assume that $d(\cdot,\cdot)$ is translation invariant. We are generally interested in partitions for which $d(\mathcal{T}_Q) > d(\mathcal{T})$ and assume we are dealing with σ–tree structures that have this property.

If $\mathcal{T}_Q(\boldsymbol{j})$ and and $\mathcal{T}_Q(\boldsymbol{j}')$ are cosets of $\mathcal{T}_Q$, the *coset distance* $d(\boldsymbol{j},\boldsymbol{j}')$ is defined as the minimum distance between the elements of the union $\mathcal{T}_Q(\boldsymbol{j}) \cup \mathcal{T}_Q(\boldsymbol{j}')$. If $\boldsymbol{j} = \boldsymbol{j}'$, then $d(\boldsymbol{j},\boldsymbol{j}) = d(\mathcal{T}_Q)$. In a single–level partition $\mathcal{T}_1/\mathcal{T}_Q$, $d(\boldsymbol{j},\boldsymbol{j}')$ is lower–bounded by $d(\mathcal{T}_1)$ in general, but if $\boldsymbol{j} = \boldsymbol{j}'$, then $d(\boldsymbol{j},\boldsymbol{j}') = d(\mathcal{T}_Q)$. If $j^1 = (j^1)'$, then $d(\boldsymbol{j},\boldsymbol{j}') \geq d(\mathcal{T}_2)$, because $\mathcal{T}_2(\boldsymbol{j})$ and $\mathcal{T}_2(\boldsymbol{j}')$ are both subtrees of the first–level subtree $\mathcal{T}_2(j^1)$;

The general version of these observations is the essential distance property used in coset code constructions based on set partitions, that is, if $\mathcal{T}_1/\mathcal{T}_2/\cdots/\mathcal{T}_Q$ is a M–ary partition chain with distances such that $d(\mathcal{T}_1) < d(\mathcal{T}_2) < \cdots < d(\mathcal{T}_Q)$ and $d(\mathcal{T}_Q(\boldsymbol{j}))$ and $d(\mathcal{T}_Q(\boldsymbol{j}'))$ are subtrees with multipart labels, then the coset distance $d(\boldsymbol{j},\boldsymbol{j}')$ is lower–bounded by $d(\mathcal{T}_p)$, where if $\boldsymbol{j} \neq \boldsymbol{j}'$, p is the smallest index such that $j^{p-1} \neq (j^{p-1})'$, while if $\boldsymbol{j} = \boldsymbol{j}'$, p is equal to $Q-1$.

This lower bound thus depends only on whether the first $Q-1$ parts of the label are the same or different; i.e., on the Hamming distances between parts of the label, where the *Hamming distance* between two quantities is defined as zero if they are the same and one if they are different.

6.6. Label Isomorphisms. The group $(Z_M)^P$ is a natural label group for the elements of the direct sum set $\mathcal{T}$ comprised of P constituent sets with M constituents each. A one–to–one label map $m : (Z_M)^P \mapsto \mathcal{T}$ induces a group structure on $\mathcal{T}$ under the following binary operation: the sum $\boldsymbol{t}(\boldsymbol{j}) + \boldsymbol{t}(\boldsymbol{k})$ is defined as $\boldsymbol{t}(\boldsymbol{j} \oplus \boldsymbol{k})$ where $\boldsymbol{j}$ and $\boldsymbol{k}$ are in $(Z_M)^P$ and $\oplus$ denotes mod–M vector addition. Hence, we have the *label isomorphism* $< (Z_M)^P, \oplus > \simeq < \mathcal{T}, + >$.

6.7. Multi–Resolution Signal Sets. Examination of (5.9) reveals a notion of self–similarity in a certain class of σ–trees; that is, it is possible to generate a self–similar image or discrete fractal if the $\boldsymbol{\beta}$ sequence is made *contractive* instead of *expansive*, e.g., $\boldsymbol{\beta} = (1, 1/2, 1/4, 1/8\cdots)$ and if certain of the $\boldsymbol{g} \in \Gamma$ are connected by line segments to form a fundamental image element (if the line segments are not used, a discrete fractal is obtained as the number of stages approaches infinity). As an example, Shown in Figure 7 is a self–similar image (shown only for two scale levels $\boldsymbol{\beta} = (\beta_1, \beta_2)$) that is based on a σ–tree corresponding to a 7–ary direct sum signal set $\mathcal{T}$ related to the hexagonal A_2 lattice. The vertices of the hexagons in Figure 7 represent the $\boldsymbol{t} \in \mathcal{T}$. Such constellations may prove useful in so called multiresolution broadcast schemes [**12**].

7. Summary

A direct sum generalization of coset codes was introduced and a new interpretation of Ungerboeck's method of mapping by set partitioning was presented. The new partitioning method is based on certain permutations of the constituent

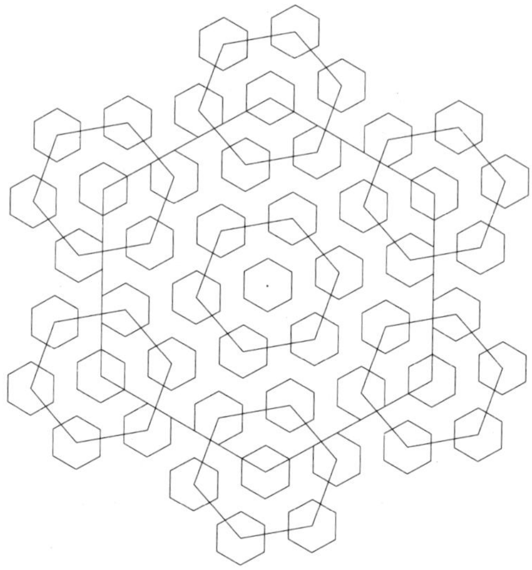

FIGURE 7. The hexagonal self–similar image generated by a contractive σ–tree.

sets of direct sum signal sets and the associated σ–tree structures. Design methods for σ–trees and local optimality conditions for the direct sum constituents for the covering problem were reviewed. Several two and four dimensional direct sum signal sets were designed with an iterative algorithm and the results support the hypothesis that direct sum quantization constellations have sufficient regularity and structure for consideration as signal sets. It was demonstrated that this approach has the flexibility of searching for signal sets that are more spherical in shape in spaces of arbitrary dimensionality. Also shown was that lattices and certain lattice subsets have direct sum decompositions. The direct sum formulation presented in this paper is related to work on multilevel code constructions. For example, Forney [**13**] used multipart labels to select points in a multilevel direct sum construction of lattice coset representatives. Kschischang, *et al.,* [**14**] proposed a multilevel direct sum structure using block codes and block subcode alphabets. More generally, multilevel σ–trees can be related to the hierarchical and multilevel code constructions of [**15, 16, 17**]. As a concluding observation, we note that it may be advantageous to use different permutations of the constituent sets of a given direct sum set at the transmitter and receivers. A permutation that entangles the tree for desirable partition chain distance properties would be useful at the modulator, a permutation that unentangles the tree and hence yields a tree structure with efficient sequential search properties would be useful in reducing the search complexity of a soft–decision demodulator.

References

1. G. D. Forney. Coset codes—Part I: Introduction and geometric classification. *IEEE Transactions on Information Theory*, IT-34(5):1123–1151, Sept. 1988.
2. C. F. Barnes. Two-dimensional signal constellations for non-linear coset codes based on multistage codes. In *Proc. 1991 Conference on Information Sciences and Systems*, page 405, The Johns Hopkins University, March 10–22 1991.
3. C. F. Barnes. Direct sum signal constellations for coded modulation. In *Proc. 1992 Conference on Information Sciences and Systems*, volume I, pages 300–306, Princeton University, 1992.
4. G. Ungerboeck. Channel coding with multilevel/phase signals. *IEEE Transactions on Information Theory*, IT-28(1):55–67, Jan. 1982.
5. A. R. Calderbank and N. J. A. Sloane. New trellis codes based on lattices and cosets. *IEEE Transactions on Information Theory*, IT–33(2):177–195, Mar. 1987.
6. C. F. Barnes and R. L. Frost. Vector quantizers with direct sum code books. *To appear in IEEE Transactions on Information Theory.*
7. J. H. Conway and N. J. A. Sloane. *Sphere Packings, Lattices and Groups.* Springer-Verlag, New York, 1988.
8. C. F. Barnes. *Rsidual Quantizers.* PhD thesis, Brigham Young University, Provo, UT, Dec. 1989.
9. C. F. Barnes and R. L. Frost. Residual vector quantizers with jointly optimized code books. In *Advances in Electronics and Electron Phytsics; Image Mathematics and Image Processing*, volume 84, pages 1–59. Academic Press, 1992.
10. C. F. Barnes and R. L. Frost. Necessary conditions for the optimality of residual vector quantizers. In *Abstracts of the IEEE International Symposium on Information Theory*, San Diego, CA, Jan. 14–19, 1990.
11. G. D. Forney. Geometrically uniform codes. *IEEE Transactions on Information Theory*, IT-37(5):1241–1260, Sept. 1991.
12. K. Ramchandran, A. Ortega, K. M. Uz, and M. Vetterli. Embedded multiresolution digital HDTV broadcast using joint source-channel coding. In *Proc. 1992 Conference on Information Sciences and Systems*, volume I, page 145, Princeton University, 1992.
13. G. D. Forney. Multidimensional constellations—Part II: Voronoi constellations. *IEEE Journal on Selected Areas in Communications*, SAC-7(6):941–958, Aug. 1989.
14. F. R. Kschischang, P. G. de Buda, and S. Pasupathy. Block coset codes for M-ary phase shift keying. *IEEE journal on Selected Areas in Communications*, 7(6):900–913, Aug. 1989.
15. H. Imai and S. Hirakawa. A new multilevel coding method using error-correcting codes. *IEEE Transactions on Information Theory*, IT–23(3):371–377, May 1977.
16. V. V. Ginzburg. Multidimensional signals for a continuous channel (English translation). *Probl. Inf. Transmission*, 23(4):20–34, Jan.–Mar. 1984.
17. G. J. Pottie and D. P. Taylor. Multilevel codes based on partitioning. *IEEE Transactions on Information Theory*, IT–35(1):87–98, Jan. 1989.

Georgia Tech Research Institute, Georgia Institute of Technology, Atlanta, Georgia 30332

E-mail address: cbarnes@mal-s1.gatech.edu

DIMACS Series in Discrete Mathematics
and Theoretical Computer Science
Volume **14**, 1993

The Other Asymptotic Theory of Lossy Source Coding

DAVID L. NEUHOFF

February 4, 1993

ABSTRACT. Rate-distortion theory, as initiated by Shannon in his celebrated 1948 paper, is a well known theory of lossy source coding. It is an asymptotic theory in the sense that the performance it prescribes is approachable only in the limit as code dimension increases. Less well known is the "other" asymptotic theory of lossy source coding, which goes by the names of high-rate, high-resolution or asymptotic quantization theory. This theory prescribes the performance of codes with a given dimension and asymptotically large rate. The purpose of the present paper is to compare and contrast the two theories, and to highlight some recent results in high-rate quantization theory. It is the thesis of this paper that high-rate quantization theory has surpassed rate-distortion theory in its relevance to practical code design, because of its ability to identify key characteristics of good codes and to analyze the performance of codes with complexity-reducing structure.

1. Introduction

Source coding is the process of encoding to produce a binary representation of the data from some source and decoding to create a reproduction of the data from the binary representation. In this paper, we are concerned with the data from discrete-time, real-valued, stationary sources – the most illuminating case. As these cannot be encoded and decoded without introducing errors, the codes that are used are often called *lossy*.

The efficiency or compression of a lossy source code is measured by its *rate*, which is the average number of bits produced by the encoder per source symbol. The accuracy or fidelity of such a code is characterized by its *distortion*, which is a measure of the average loss associated with substituting the reproductions for

---

1991 *Mathematics Subject Classification.* Primary 94A29, 94A34.
This work was supported by NSF grant NCR-9105647.

the original data. Another important aspect of a source code is the complexity of implementing its encoder and decoder, as for example measured by the amount of storage required and the number of arithmetic operations required per sample.

The principal goals of a source coding theory include finding the following (for a given source):

(1) the least distortion of codes with rate R;
(2) the least distortion of codes with dimension k and rate R;
(3) the least distortion of codes with complexity c (with respect to some appropriate measure of complexity) and rate R;
(4) the least distortion of codes in a given class C with rate R;
(5) the key characteristics of codes that are optimal (or nearly so) in the above senses; and
(6) methods to design optimal (or nearly optimal) codes.

In this paper, we compare and contrast how two competing theories of lossy source coding attempt to serve these goals. The most well known is Shannon's rate-distortion theory. The "other", lesser-known theory has been called high-rate, high-resolution or asymptotic quantization theory.

2. Background

We focus on *vector quantizers* (VQ's). These are characterized by a *dimension* k, a *size* N, a *quantizing partition* $S = \{S_1, \ldots, S_N\}$ of $\Re^k$ into N *cells*, a *codebook* of *quantization points* $C = \{v_1, \ldots, v_N\} \subset \Re^k$ and a set of *binary codewords* $B = \{b_1, \ldots, b_N\}$, each having $\lceil \log_2 N \rceil$ bits. (The restriction to fixed-length binary codewords is for simplicity of discussion and implementation.) When a source sequence $x = (x_1 \ldots x_k)$ lies in cell S_i of the quantizing partition, the encoder produces b_i as the binary representation of x, and the decoder produces $y = v_i$ as the reproduction of x. Overall, the VQ is characterized by the *quantization rule* $Q(x) = v_i$ when $x \in S_i$.

The rate of a vector quantizer is $R = k^{-1} \log_2 N$. (We choose this instead of $\lceil \log_2 N \rceil / N$ to simplify discussion.) As a measure of distortion, we choose mean squared error $D = k^{-1} E\|X - Q(X)\|^2$, where $\|x - y\|$ denotes k-dimensional Euclidean distance and where the expectation is with respect to the k-dimensional source distribution, which we presume to be characterized by a density $p_k(x)$. (Later, we mention generalizations to other distortion measures.)

Given a codebook, the conceptually simplest method of encoding with the best quantizing partition is to compute the squared distance between the given source vector x and each quantization point. The encoder outputs the binary codeword corresponding to the closest quantization point. The decoder uses the binary codeword to address a table containing the quantization points. This *full search* method of quantization requires storage and arithmetic complexity proportional to $N = 2^{kR}$, which grows exponentially with kR, the dimension-rate product. Thus complexity is a serious issue in vector quantization. Indeed, finding low-complexity codes is a principal goal of modern source coding.

As indicated by the first of the aforementioned goals, given a source, we would like to find the least distortion of any VQ with rate R. Viewed as a function of R, this least distortion is called the VQ Operational Distortion-Rate Function (ODRF)[1] and denoted $\delta(R)$. Therefore, the first goal is equivalent to finding $\delta(R)$. Similarly, each of the second through fourth goals is equivalent to finding a corresponding ODRF. For example, $\delta_k(R)$ denotes the least distortion of k-dimensional VQ's with rate R. In summary, a principal goal of source coding theory is to find the ODRF's of various classes of codes.

Of special interest is finding how the ODRF's of various classes of codes relate to their complexity. For instance, one would like to know how close $\delta_k(R)$ is to $\delta(R)$ for small to moderate values of k, because the complexity of coding increases rapidly with k.[2] As another example, the ODRF for a class of structured vector quantizers will indicate how its complexity-reducing structure affects its performance.

3. Rate-Distortion Theory

Shannon's rate-distortion theorem, the third theorem of his celebrated 1948 paper [**1**] (expanded upon in his 1959 paper [**2**] and generalized by others [**3, 4**]) achieves the first goal by showing that for stationary, ergodic sources (satisfying a moment finiteness condition)

$$\delta(R) = \mathcal{D}(R) \ ,$$

where $\mathcal{D}(R)$ is the information-theoretic *distortion-rate function* (DRF)[3], defined as follows (c.f. [**3, 5, 6**]):

$$\mathcal{D}(R) \triangleq \lim_{k\to\infty} \mathcal{D}_k(R) \ .$$

where

$$\mathcal{D}_k(R) \triangleq \inf_{q \in Q_k(R)} \frac{1}{k} E\|X - Y\|^2 \ ,$$

where $Y = (Y_1 \ldots Y_k)$ is the output of the *test channel* q with X as the input, where $Q_k(R) \triangleq \{q(y|x) : k^{-1} I_q(X;Y) \le R\}$, is a collection of k-dimensional test channels, and where $I_q(X;Y) \triangleq \int p_k(x) q(y|x) \log_2 (p_k(x) q(y|x)/p(y))\, dx$ is the *information* between input and output of the test channel q. In other words, rate-distortion theory relates the operational quantity $\delta(R)$ that we wish to know to the information-theoretic quantity $\mathcal{D}(R)$. The latter can be evaluated analytically (cf. [**5, 6**]) or numerically [**7**].

[1] An ODRF, sometimes called an OPTA function, need only be "attainable" in the sense that there are codes whose performance comes arbitrarily close to it.

[2] It is straightforward to show that $\delta_k(R)$ approaches $\delta(R)$ from above as k tends to infinity (by showing subadditivity).

[3] Actually, Shannon showed the equivalent result that the least rate achievable by codes with distortion D is given by the rate-distortion function $\mathcal{R}(D)$, which is the inverse of $\mathcal{D}(R)$.

It is well known that, except for degenerate cases,

$$\delta_k(R) > \mathcal{D}_k(R) \ .$$

For small k, this bound is usually rather weak, and the kth-order distortion-rate function cannot be viewed as having much operational significance.

There are several well-known bounds to $\mathcal{D}(R)$ and $\mathcal{D}_k(R)$ (cf. [**5, 6**]). An upper bound derives from known parametric formulas for $\mathcal{D}_k(R)$ and $\mathcal{D}(R)$ for Gaussian sources and from the fact that among sources with a given covariance function, the Gaussian distortion-rate function is largest. The simplest and most widely used lower bounds are the Shannon lower bounds:

$$\begin{aligned} \mathcal{D}(R) &\geq \frac{1}{2\pi e} 2^{2(h-R)} \triangleq \mathcal{D}_{slb}(R) \\ \mathcal{D}_k(R) &\geq \frac{1}{2\pi e} 2^{2(h_k-R)} \triangleq \mathcal{D}_{k,slb}(R) \end{aligned}$$

where h is the source *differential entropy* and h_k is the *kth-order differential entropy*, given, respectively, by $h \triangleq \lim_{k\to\infty} h_k$ and $h_k \triangleq k^{-1} \int p_k(x) \log_2 p_k(x) dx$. Both of these bounds are asymptotically tight in the sense that the ratio of the DRF to the lower bound goes to one as R tends to infinity.

4. High-Rate Quantization Theory

The central result of high-rate quantization theory is Zador's theorem [**8, 9**], which shows that

$$\lim_{R\to\infty} \frac{\delta_k(R)}{Z_k(R)} = 1 \tag{4.1}$$

where $Z_k(R)$ is the Zador-Gersho function, defined as

$$Z_k(R) \triangleq c_k \alpha_k 2^{-2R} \tag{4.2}$$

where $\alpha_k \triangleq \left(\int p_k(x)^{k/(k+2)} dx\right)^{(k+2)/k}$ depends on the source distribution and c_k, called the *tiling moment* of k-dimensional space, is the least *normalized moment of inertia* (n.m.i.) among k-dimensional polyhedra that tesselate. The n.m.i. of a cell P about a point y is $k^{-1} \int_P \|x - y\|^2 dx \ \mathrm{vol}(P)^{-(k+2)/k}$. It follows from (4.1) that

$$\lim_{R\to\infty} \frac{\delta(R)}{Z(R)} = 1$$

where

$$Z(R) \triangleq \lim_{k\to\infty} Z_k(R) \ .$$

Another important result of high-rate quantization theory is Bennett's integral for scalar quantizers [**10**] and its recent extension to VQ's [**11**]. The latter shows that for a VQ with many, mostly small cells, and neighboring cells having similar sizes and shapes

$$D \cong \frac{1}{N^{2/k}} \int \frac{m(x)}{\lambda(x)^{2/k}} \, p_k(x) dx \ , \tag{4.3}$$

where $\lambda(x)$ is the point density and $m(x)$ is the *inertial profile* of the VQ. As suggested by its name, $\lambda(x)$ is the density of quantization points in the vicinity of x, normalized to integrate to one. ($\lambda(x) \cong (N\text{vol}(S_i))^{-1}$ when $x \in S_i$.) The inertial profile $m(x)$ is a function that equals, approximately, the normalized moment of inertia of the cells in the vicinity of x.[4]

Bennett's integral shows that the inertial profile (cell shapes) and the point density (cell sizes) are key characteristics of a VQ with many points. It is natural, then, to seek the best inertial profile and point density. Although never formally proved, there is a widely believed conjecture due to Gersho **[9]** that, for large N, most cells of the best k-dimensional quantizers are congruent, approximately, to the tesselating polytope with minimum normalized moment of inertia. Assuming this to be the case, the best inertial profile is the constant function $m(x) = c_k$. Assuming a constant inertial profile such as this, either calculus of variations or Hölder's inequality can be used to show that Bennett's integral is minimized by the point density

$$\lambda_k^*(x) = \frac{p_k(x)^{k/k+2}}{\int p_k(x)^{k/k+2} dx} \ . \tag{4.4}$$

Substituting $\lambda_k^*(x)$ and c_k in Bennett's integral gives the Zador-Gersho formula[5].

5. Comparisons

We now compare and contrast rate-distortion theory with high-rate quantization theory.

(1) The two theories are complementary: Rate-distortion theory prescribes the best possible performance of codes with a given rate and asymptotically large dimension. High-rate quantization theory prescribes the best possible performance of codes with a given dimension and asymptotically large rate. That is,

$$\delta_k(R) \cong \begin{cases} \mathcal{D}(R) \text{ for large } k \text{ and any } R \\ Z_k(R) \text{ for large } R \text{ and any } k. \end{cases}$$

(2) History: Both theories originated in 1948. Rate-distortion theory had a spectacular beginning and rapidly became well known. It was mostly developed by Shannon **[1, 2]** and is now fairly mature. See **[5]** (pp. 291-293) for a survey

[4] Eq. (4.3) is made precise **[11]** by showing that $N^{2/k} D_N$ converges to the integral in (4.3), where $\{D_N\}$ are the distortions of a sequence of quantizers whose point densities and inertial profiles converge to λ and m, respectively, as the size N increases to infinity.

[5] Zador **[8]** found the form of (4.2); Gersho **[9]** recognized that the multiplicative constant is c_k.

of other early contributors, and [**12**] for a survey of more recent work. High-rate quantization theory had humble beginnings in Bennett's paper on scalar quantizers [**10**], developed slowly through the years through the efforts of many [**13-21, 9, 22-29**], and is not so well known. Recent results have significantly expanded its usefulness [11, 30-32], and it is still developing.

(3) Underlying principles: Rate-distortion theory is a deep and elegant theory based on the law of large numbers. High-rate quantization theory is a simpler, less elegant theory based on geometric characterizations and integral approximations over small cells.

(4) Siblings: Rate-distortion theory has siblings, also based on the law of large numbers, in almost lossless block source coding, channel coding and multiuser information theory. Siblings of high-rate quantization theory are the error probability analyses in channel coding based on minimum distances and average power analyses for the additive Gaussian channel based on the continuous approximation.

(5) Distortion measures: Rate-distortion theory requires a per-letter fidelity criteria, whereas high-rate quantization theory requires a difference distortion measure. Both, however, provide the most results for the squared-error distortion measure. Each requires the source to satisfy a finite moment condition, related to the specific distortion measure.

(6) Sources: Rate-distortion theory is intended primarily for stationary, ergodic sources, although there are generalizations to asymptotically stationary and nonergodic sources (cf. [**12**]). High-rate quantization theory is, fundamentally, a theory devoted to finite-dimensional random vectors, as opposed to random processes. However, for stationary sources, one may let dimension increase and obtain nice limiting formulas. Both theories give nice analytical formulas for Gaussian sources.

(7) Code structures: Rate-distortion theory applies primarily to vector quantizers, or *block codes* as they were originally called. However, there are converse theorems that show that no codes of any kind with rate R or less achieve distortion less than $\mathcal{D}(R)$. And other code structures, such as variable-length, sliding-block, tree and trellis have been shown to contain codes achieving $\mathcal{D}(R)$.

High-rate quantization theory was also developed primarily for vector quantizers. However, its ability to focus on vector quantizers with a specific dimension is a major strength. Another is that it can be tailored to specific classes of VQ's. For example, it has long been used to find the ODRF's of various scalar quantizer based codes such as PCM, transform coding and even DPCM, which is not a VQ. It has also been used to analyze lattice codes. And the recent extension of Bennett's integral to vector quantizers has led to finding the ODRF's for tree-structured VQ [**31**] and two-stage VQ [**32**].

(8) Performance vs. complexity: Rate-distortion theory specifies the fundamental limits to the performance of lossy source coding without regard to cost or complexity. On the other hand, high-rate quantization theory, which analyzes

the performance of codes with a given dimension and, sometimes, with a given structure, may be viewed as taking complexity into account, or at least quantitatively showing the effects of complexity-reducing structure. For example, in lattice quantization, the point density is a constant (far from optimal), in TSVQ the point density is good but the cell shapes are no better than cubes [**31**], and in two-stage VQ, the point density is affected but the cell shapes are optimal [**32**].

(9) Relationships: The following relations hold between distortion-rate functions and Zador-Gersho functions (cf. [**6**]). The inequalities marked with "•" become tight as dimension k increases. Those marked with "+" become tight as R increases.

$$
\begin{array}{ccccc}
\mathcal{D}(R) & \overset{+}{\geq} & \mathcal{D}_{slb}(R) & = & Z(R) \\
\rotatebox{90}{$\geq$}\,\bullet & & \rotatebox{90}{$\geq$}\,\bullet & & \rotatebox{90}{$\geq$}\,\bullet \\
\mathcal{D}_k(R) & \overset{+}{\geq} & \mathcal{D}_{k,slb}(R) & \overset{\bullet}{<} & Z_k(R)
\end{array}
$$

Thus, the Shannon lower bound and Zador's function are closely related.

(10) How large is "sufficiently large"? Both theories predict the performance of optimal codes as a certain parameter (k or R) becomes large. We now examine how large these parameters must be for the predictions to be reasonably accurate. Consider the case of an IID Gaussian source. By designing VQ's with the LBG algorithm [**33**] at low rates and by using high-rate theory at high rates, we find that a dimension of 8 to 14 is needed to give distortion within 1 dB of $\mathcal{D}(R)$. Thus, one may say that rate-distortion theory is applicable for VQ's with dimensions of the order of 10 or greater. For sources with memory, the dimension needs to be larger, roughly by the "length" of the memory.

On the other hand, designing VQ's with the LBG algorithm shows that, as a general rule, the Zador-Gersho formula is very accurate (to within tenths of a dB) for rates 3 or greater. It has also been found that Bennett's integral and other asymptotic analyses are accurate for roughly the same range of rates (cf. [**31**]). Thus, one may say that high-rate quantization theory is accurate for rates 3 and up. Moreover, it is generally accurate enough at rate 2 to give indicative results.

(11) Code design: Each theory leads to its own design philosophy. On the one hand, rate-distortion theory shows that good high-dimensional codes have quantization points that are typical of the output distribution of the test channel that achieves the distortion-rate function. Indeed, one can obtain a good code by randomly generating such quantization points. In the special case of IID Gaussian sources, the quantization points can be uniformly distributed either in a sphere or on the surface of a sphere. More generally, the points can be uniformly distributed in the region of *typical sequences*, where the source density is approximately uniform (from the *asymptotic equipartition property* (AEP) [**5**]).

On the other hand, high-rate quantization theory indicates that one obtains a good code with dimension k by making the quantization cells as spherical as possible, i.e. they should be shaped like the polyhedron with n.m.i. equal to c_k, and by causing the quantization points to be distributed according to the optimal point density, λ_k^*. For example, one can design essentially optimal scalar quantizers by choosing $y_i = F^{-1}((2i-1)/2N)$ [**10, 13, 27**], where $F(x) = \int_{-\infty}^{x} \lambda_k^*(u)du$ is the distribution function corresponding to the optimal point density.

These two design philosophies are not inconsistent. When both k and R are large, high-rate theory shows that the points of an optimal k-dimensional VQ are distributed as $\lambda_k^*(x)$, which in this case is approximately equal to $p_k(x)$. It follows, then, from the AEP, that the points of an optimal k-dimensional VQ are spread uniformly throughout the typical sequences, just as rate-distortion theory indicates.

Which design philosophy is more useful? At low rates (say 1 bit per sample or less), one has no choice but to look to rate-distortion theory. But at moderate to high rates, we argue that the high-rate philosophy is the better choice. The reason is that codes designed by the rate-distortion theory approach require very large dimensions. To see this consider an IID Gaussian source, a desired rate R and a VQ of dimension k with 2^{kR} points distributed uniformly throughout a spherical support region. This is the ideal code suggested by rate-distortion theory. One may lower bound its distortion by assuming that source vectors outside the spherical support region are quantized to the closest point on the surface of the sphere, and by assuming that the cells within the support region are perfect k-dimensional spheres. In this case, at moderate to large rates (say rate 10), after choosing the diameter of the support region to minimize this lower bound to distortion, it has been found [**34**] that the dimension k must be larger than 250 in order that the mean squared error is within 1 dB of the distortion-rate function.

We conclude that the fact that VQ's with dimension about 10 can have distortion within 1 dB of the distortion-rate function is not due to the rate-distortion theory design philosophy, the AEP, nor the use of ideal spherical codes. Rather it is due to the fact that good codes with small to moderate dimensions have appropriately tapered point densities, as suggested by high-rate theory.[6]

12. <u>The nature of the error process:</u> From rate-distortion theory, we know that good VQ's with large dimension have codewords typical of the output of the test channel that achieves the distortion-rate function. One can use this fact to learn something about the error process resulting from an optimal high-dimensional VQ. For example, for a Gaussian source with memory, one discovers how the spectrum of the noise relates to that of the source (cf. [**5**]).

Recently, in high-rate theory there has been developed an asymptotic formula for the density of the error that results from a VQ with many mostly small cells, with neighboring cells having similar sizes and shapes [**30**]. Taking the second

[6]It is likely that the originally perceived need for high dimensions (based on the AEP) delayed the serious consideration of vector quantizers. The breakthrough was the paper by Linde, Buzo and Gray [**33**], which showed that VQ's with moderate dimension were both good and feasible.

moment of this density yields, of course, Bennett's integral. The form of the density depends intimately on the point density and the cell shapes. The original motivation for finding the asymptotic error density was a high-rate analysis of two-stage VQ [**32**], where a second stage VQ is fed the error resulting from a first-stage VQ. With knowledge of the first-stage error density, Bennett's integral may be used to determine the overall distortion. It turned out that the formula is very sensitive to the shapes of the quantization cells. Thus, it has also proved useful in understanding the cell shapes of other VQ's, for example TSVQ [**31**].

13. Successive approximation: Many vector quantizers operate in a *successive approximation* or *progressive* fashion, whereby a low-rate coarse quantization is followed by a sequence of finer and finer quantizations, which add to the rate. Tree-structured, multi-stage and hierarchical VQ's are examples of such. Successive approximation is useful in situations where the decoder needs to produce rough approximations of the data from the first bits it receives and, subsequently, to refine the approximation as more bits are received. Moreover, successive-approximation VQ's are often structured in a way that makes them simpler than unstructured VQ's. Indeed, the three examples just cited are known more for their good performance with low complexity than for their progressive nature. An important question is whether the distortion of a successive-refinement code will be larger than a one-shot code. On the one hand, a recent rate-distortion theory analysis [**35**] has shown there are situations where successive approximation can be done without loss of optimality. On the other hand, recent high-rate analyses of TSVQ [**31**] and two-stage VQ [**32**] have quantified the loss of these particular codes. Thus, both theories have something to say about successive refinement.

6. Conclusions

As indicated in the abstract, the thesis of this paper is that high-rate quantization theory has surpassed rate-distortion theory in its relevance to practical code design and analysis, because of its ability to identify key characteristics of good codes and to be specialized to particular codes with complexity-reducing structure.

High-rate quantization theory also provides results concerning the performance of scalar and vector quantizers with variable-length binary codes [**8, 18, 5(p. 173), 20, 9, 22**], which space has precluded discussing.

References

1. C.E. Shannon, "A mathematical theory of communication," *Bell Syst. Tech. J.*, vol. 27, pp. 397-423, 623-656, 1948.
2. C.E. Shannon, "Coding theorems for a discrete source with a fidelity criterion," *IRE Nat'l. Conv. Rec. part 4*, pp. 142-163, 1959.
3. R.G. Gallager, *Information Theory and Reliable Communication*, New York: Wiley, 1968.
4. T. Berger, "Rate distortion theory for sources with abstract alphabets and memory," *Information and Control*, vol. 13, pp. 254-273, 1968.

5. T. Berger, *Rate Distortion Theory,* Englewood Cliffs, NJ: Prentice-Hall, 1971.
6. R.M.Gray, *Source Coding Theory,* Boston: Kluwer, 1990.
7. R.E. Blahut, "Computation of channel capacity and rate-distortion functions," *IEEE Trans. Inform. Theory,* vol. IT-18, pp. 460-473, July 1972.
8. P. Zador, "Development and Evaluation of Procedures for Quantizing Multivariate Distributions," Ph.D. dissertation, Stanford Univ., Stanford, CA, 1964.
9. A. Gersho, "Asymptotically optimal block quantization," *IEEE Trans. Inform. Theory,* vol. IT-23, pp. 373-380, July 1979.
10. W.R. Bennett, "Spectra of quantized signals," *B.S.T.J.,* vol. 27, pp. 446-472, July 1948.
11. S. Na and D.L. Neuhoff, "Bennett's integral for vector quantizers, and applications," *1990 IEEE Int'l Symp. on Inform. Theory*, Jan. 1990.
12. J.C. Kieffer, "A survey of the theory of source coding," to appear in *IEEE Trans. Inform. Theory.*
13. P.F. Panter and W. Dite, "Quantization distortion in pulse count modulation with nonuniform spacing of levels," *Proc. IRE,* vol. 39, pp. 44-48, Jan. 1951.
14. S.P. Lloyd, "Least squares quantization in PCM," Bell Laboratories Memorandum 1957, also published in *IEEE Trans. Inform. Theory,* vol. IT-28, pp. 129-137, March 1982.
15. M.P. Schutzenberger, "On the quantization of finite-dimensional messages," *Inform. and Control,* vol. 1, pp. 153-158, 1958.
16. J.J.Y. Huang and P.M. Schultheiss, "Block quantization of correlated Gaussian variables," *IEEE Trans. Commun.,* vol. COM-11, pp. 289-296, Sept. 1963.
17. V.R. Algazi, "Useful approximations to optimum quantization, "*IEEE Trans. Commun.,* vol. COM-14, pp. 297-301, June 1966.
18. H. Gish and J.R. Pierce, "Asymptotically efficient quantizing," *IEEE Trans. Inform. Theory,* vol. IT-14, pp. 676-683, Sept. 1968.
19. P. Elias, "Bounds on performance of optimum quantizers," *IEEE Trans. Inform. Theory,* vol. IT-16, pp. 172-184, March 1970.
20. I. Csiszar, "Generalized entropy and quantization problems," 6th Prague Conference, 1973.
21. R.M. Gray and A.H. Gray, "Asymptotically optimal quantizers," *IEEE Trans. Inform. Theory,* pp. 143-144, Jan. 1977.
22. J.A. Bucklew and N.C. Gallagher, "Some properties of uniform step size quantizers," *IEEE Trans. Inform. Theory,* vol. IT-26, pp. 610-613, Sept. 1980.
23. Y. Yamada, S. Tazaki and R.M. Gray, "Asymptotic performance of block quantizers with difference distortion measures," *IEEE Trans. Inform. Theory,* vol. IT-26, pp. 6-14, Jan. 1980.
24. J. A. Bucklew, "Companding and random quantization in several dimensions," *IEEE Trans. Inform. Theory,* vol. IT-27, pp. 207-211, March 1981.
25. J.A. Bucklew and G.W. Wise, "Multidimensional asymptotic quantization theory with r th power distortion measures," *IEEE Trans. Inform. Theory,* Vol. IT-28, pp. 239-247, Mar. 1982.
26. N.C. Gallagher, J.A. Bucklew, "Properties of minimum mean squared error block quantizers," *IEEE Trans. Inform. Thy.,* vol. IT-28, pp. 105-107, Jan. 1983.
27. S. Cambanis and N. Gerr, "A simple class of asymptotically optimal quantizers," *IEEE Trans. Inform. Theory,* vol. IT-29, pp. 664-676, Sept. 1983.
28. J.A. Bucklew, "A note on optimal multidimensional companders," *IEEE Trans. Inform. Theory,* vol. IT-29, pp. 279, March 1983.
29. J.A. Bucklew, "Two results on the asymptotic performance of quantizers," *IEEE Trans. Inform. Theory,* vol. IT-30, pp. 341-348, Mar. 1984.
30. D.H. Lee and D.L. Neuhoff, "The asymptotic distribution of the error in scalar and vector quantizers," *1990 IEEE Int'l Symp. Inform. Theory,* San Diego, Jan. 1990.
31. D.L. Neuhoff and D.H. Lee, "On the Performance of Tree-Structured Vector Quantization," *ICAASP91*, vol. 4, pp. 2277-2280, Toronto, May 1991.
32. D.H. Lee and D.L. Neuhoff, "An Asymptotic Analysis of Two-Stage Vector Quantization," *1991 IEEE Int'l Symp. on Inform. Theory,* p. 316, Budapest, June 1991.
33. Y. Linde, A. Buzo and R.M. Gray, "An algorithm for vector quantizer design," *IEEE*

Trans. Commun., vol. COM-28, pp. 84-95, Jan. 1980.
34. A. Balamesh and D. L. Neuhoff, unpublished notes, 1992.
35. W.H.R. Equitz and T.M. Cover, "Successive refinement of information," *IEEE Trans. Inform. Theory*, vol. IT-37, pp. 268-275, Mar. 1991.

Department of Electrical Engineering and Computer Science, University of Michigan, Ann Arbor, MI 48109

E-mail address: neuhoff@eecs.umich.edu

DIMACS Series in Discrete Mathematics
and Theoretical Computer Science
Volume **14**, 1993

Block-Constrained Quantization: Asymptotic Analysis

AHMED S. BALAMESH AND DAVID L. NEUHOFF

January 11, 1993

ABSTRACT. Block-constrained quantization (BCQ) is an efficient fixed-rate quantization method that has been recently introduced. In this paper, we summarize our results on the asymptotic analysis of BCQ. We give explicit forms for the asymptotic rate and distortion of BCQ. Also, we give the OPTA's for several classes of BCQ.

1. Introduction

Entropy-coded scalar quantization is one of the most efficient methods of source coding. Its main disadvantage is variable rate which necessitates buffering if transmission over a fixed-rate channel is intended. With a finite buffer, there is often a non-zero probability of overflow and underflow. In the literature, buffer-instrumented methods have been proposed to prevent overflow and underflow by monitoring the buffer and adjusting the quantizer in order to control the number of bits fed to the buffer. Block-constrained methods [**1, 2, 3, 4**] are a fixed-rate alternative, with a performance-complexity tradeoff that makes them more practical than vector quantization (even tree-structured) at moderate-to-high rates (3 bits per dimension or higher).

We illustrate the basic idea of block-constrained quantization (BCQ) by a simple example. Consider an m-level scalar quantizer (SQ) with levels $\underline{q} = \{q_1, \ldots, q_m\}$ and thresholds $\underline{t} = \{t_1, \ldots, t_{m-1}\}$, and a prefix code with codeword lengths $l_1, \ldots, l_m$ where the codeword c_j of length l_j corresponds to level q_j and quantization cell $[t_{j-1}, t_j)$ and $t_0 = -\infty, t_m = \infty$. We define $l_{\min} \triangleq \min_j l_j$ and $l_{\max} \triangleq \max_j l_j$.

1991 *Mathematics Subject Classification.* Primary 94A29, 94A34.

This work was supported in part by a scholarship from King Abdul-Aziz University, Jeddah, Saudi Arabia and by NSF grant NCR-9105647.

Given a block size n and a desired rate r bits/sample, consider quantizing a vector $\underline{x} = (x_1, \ldots, x_n)$ of n source samples. The usual *prefix-encoded* scalar quantizer (pe-SQ), quantizes each source sample x_i to a level $y_i = Q_{\underline{q},\underline{t}}(x_i)$ given by the *quantization rule* $Q_{\underline{q},\underline{t}}(x) = q_j$ if $x \in [t_{j-1}, t_j]$ and then transmits the codeword $f_e(y_i)$ corresponding to the level y_i. The total number of bits produced is $\ell(\underline{y}) = \sum_{i=1}^{n} l(y_i)$, where $l(q_j) \triangleq l_j$. For a desired rate r, we need to produce no more than nr bits per n source samples. Thus, if $\ell(\underline{y}) \leq nr$, then we can make nr bits by adding dummy bits and the decoder will still be able to decode correctly. On the other hand, if $\ell(\underline{y}) > nr$, then we need to reduce the number of bits to nr. A naive way to do this is to drop the extra bits and accept some decoding errors by the decoder, where the prefix code decoder will reproduce the mean of the source whenever it runs out of bits. A better approach is for the encoder to search for the best sequence of n levels whose binary encoding has no more than nr bits. This is equivalent to a vector quantizer having the codebook

$$\mathcal{C}_{\mathrm{bcq}}(\underline{q}, \underline{l}, n, L) = \{\underline{y} \in (\underline{q})^n : \ell(\underline{y}) \leq L\}, \tag{1.1}$$

where, in this case, $L = nr$. We call such a quantizer *prefix-encoded, block-constrained quantizer* (pe-BCQ). We call the elements of $\mathcal{C}_{\mathrm{bcq}}$ codevectors and L the *length threshold.*

More generally, a block-constrained quantizer (BCQ) has a codebook given by (1.1), where $\underline{l}$ can consist of arbitrary real numbers (not necessarily the lengths of prefix codewords) and L is chosen so that the desired rate is obtained. In this case, the binary encoding may not necessarily be done using a prefix code. The smallest rate is obtained by fixed-length, block encoding of the codebook $\mathcal{C}_{\mathrm{bcq}}$, which results in rate

$$R_{\mathrm{bcq}}^{\mathrm{be}}(\underline{l}, n, L) \triangleq \frac{1}{n} \left\lceil \log \left| \mathcal{C}_{\mathrm{bcq}}(\underline{q}, \underline{l}, n, L) \right| \right\rceil .$$

Other binary encoding schemes are also possible, e.g. arithmetic coding. The choice of $\underline{l}$ and L depends on the particular binary encoding scheme in use. See [**5**] for more details.

We consider block-constrained quantization to minimize the mean-squared-error (MSE) distortion, i.e. given a source n-vector, a vector $\hat{\underline{y}}$ that minimizes $\|\underline{x} - \underline{y}\|^2$ over all $\underline{y} \in \mathcal{C}_{\mathrm{bcq}}(\underline{q}, \underline{l}, n, L)$ is found; ties are resolved arbitrarily. We denote the quantization rule by $Q_{\mathrm{bcq}}^{(\underline{q}, \underline{l}, n, L)}$, i.e. for the above example, $Q_{\mathrm{bcq}}^{(\underline{q}, \underline{l}, n, L)}(\underline{x}) = \hat{\underline{y}}$. The distortion of the BCQ is then defined by $\bar{d}_{\mathrm{bcq}}(\underline{q}, \underline{l}, n, L) \triangleq E d_{\mathrm{bcq}}(\underline{q}, \underline{l}, n, L; \underline{X})$, where $d_{\mathrm{bcq}}(\underline{q}, \underline{l}, n, L; \underline{x}) \triangleq \|\underline{x} - Q_{\mathrm{bcq}}^{(\underline{q}, \underline{l}, n, L)}(\underline{x})\|^2/n$.

For a more detailed introduction to BCQ, see [**4**].

There are several issues of interest here. The question "How well does a particular class of BCQ's perform?" is at the top of our list. In other words, we would like to find the optimum performance theoretically achievable (OPTA) for different classes of BCQ. In this paper, we present such OPTA's for certain classes and some asymptotically (in n) achievable bounds for others.

The asymptotic rate of BCQ is of interest in its own right, particularly for those classes of BCQ that use suboptimal binary encoding (i.e. binary encoding other than block encoding). We find the asymptotic loss of such schemes.

An issue that is directly related to the complexity of the BCQ search is the asymptotic behavior of the length threshold L, particularly for block-encoded BCQ (be-BCQ). We show that, when properly chosen, L is asymptotically linear in n.

The results presented here summarize (without proof) those shown in [**5**, Chapter VI].

2. Asymptotic Distortion of BCQ

In this section, we study the asymptotic behavior of the distortion of a BCQ with given $m, \underline{q}$ and $\underline{l}$ and with a length threshold L_n that is adjusted with the dimension n to satisfy a certain criterion (e.g. rate r).

The major result of this section (and probably, the most important in the paper) is the following theorem, which relates the asymptotic distortion of BCQ based on $(\underline{q}, \underline{l})$ to the minimum distortion

$$\bar{d}_{\mathrm{sq}}(\underline{q}, \underline{t}) \triangleq \sum_{j=1}^{m} \int_{t_{j-1}}^{t_j} (x - q_j)^2 \, dF(x),$$

of the scalar quantizer $(\underline{q}, \underline{t})$ over all choices of $\underline{t}$ satisfying a constraint on the average length

$$\bar{l}_{\mathrm{sq}}(\underline{t}, \underline{l}) \triangleq \sum_{j=1}^{m} l_j \int_{t_{j-1}}^{t_j} dF(x),$$

where $F(\cdot)$ is the probability distribution function of the source.

THEOREM 2.1. Given $m, \underline{q}, \underline{l}$ and L_n such that $L_n/n \to R$ as $n \to \infty$, then, for an ergodic source,

$$(a) \qquad \delta_{\mathrm{sq}}(\underline{q}, \underline{l}, R+) \leq \liminf_{n \to \infty} d_{\mathrm{bcq}}(\underline{q}, \underline{l}, n, L_n; \underline{X}) \leq \limsup_{n \to \infty} d_{\mathrm{bcq}}(\underline{q}, \underline{l}, n, L_n; \underline{X}) \leq \delta_{\mathrm{sq}}(\underline{q}, \underline{l}, R-),$$

with probability one and

$$(b) \qquad \delta_{\mathrm{sq}}(\underline{q}, \underline{l}, R+) \leq \liminf_{n \to \infty} \bar{d}_{\mathrm{bcq}}(\underline{q}, \underline{l}, n, L_n) \leq \limsup_{n \to \infty} \bar{d}_{\mathrm{bcq}}(\underline{q}, \underline{l}, n, L_n) \leq \delta_{\mathrm{sq}}(\underline{q}, \underline{l}, R-),$$

where $\delta_{\mathrm{sq}}(\underline{q}, \underline{l}, R)$ is defined as

$$\delta_{\mathrm{sq}}(\underline{q}, \underline{l}, R) \triangleq \inf_{\underline{t}: \bar{l}_{\mathrm{sq}}(\underline{t}, \underline{l}) \leq R} \bar{d}_{\mathrm{sq}}(\underline{q}, \underline{t}),$$

$f(x+) = \lim_{\Delta\downarrow 0} f(x+\Delta)$ and $f(x-) = \lim_{\Delta\downarrow 0} f(x-\Delta)$.

REMARK. Theorem 2.1 holds for any stationary, ergodic source and for a wide range of distortion measures, including the absolute measure. See [**5**] for more details.

Theorem 2.1 is very useful since it relates the asymptotic distortion of a BCQ to that of a scalar quantizer. Hence, it enables us to study the asymptotic OPTA's of several classes of BCQ's, as we will see in Section 6. We remark that δ_{sq} is perhaps the most important function we introduce in this paper.

If $\delta_{\text{sq}}(\underline{q}, \underline{l}, R)$ is continuous[1] at R, then the theorem shows that $\lim_{n\to\infty} \bar{d}_{\text{bcq}}$ exists and $\lim_{n\to\infty} \bar{d}_{\text{bcq}}(\underline{q}, \underline{l}, n, L_n) = \delta_{\text{sq}}(\underline{q}, \underline{l}, R)$.

For the case of pe-BCQ with rate r, $L_n/n \to r$. Therefore, the performance of pe-BCQ is asymptotically the same as the performance of the scalar quantizer with the same levels and lengths and with optimized thresholds that give an average length $\bar{l}_{\text{sq}}$ no larger than r. Optimizing over $\underline{q}$ and $\underline{l}$ means that the asymptotic performance of pe-BCQ is exactly the same as the performance of pe-SQ.

The following lemma gives a key property of BCQ's that is used in the proof of Theorem 2.1. It establishes a close relationship between BCQ and scalar quantization. In particular, it states that BCQ essentially performs scalar quantization but using a set of thresholds $\underline{t}$ that depends on the source vector $\underline{x}$ being quantized. Another important application of the lemma is to simplify the BCQ quantization [**4**].

LEMMA 2.1. Given $\underline{q}, \underline{l}, n$ and L, let $\underline{x}$ be a source vector and $\underline{y} = Q_{\text{bcq}}^{(\underline{q},\underline{l},n,L)}(\underline{x})$. Then, there exists a threshold vector $\underline{t}$ such that $\|\underline{x} - \underline{y}\|^2 = \|\underline{x} - Q_{\underline{q},\underline{t}}(\underline{x})\|^2$ and $\ell(Q_{\underline{q},\underline{t}}(\underline{x})) \le \ell(\underline{y})$. Conversely, if $\underline{t}$ minimizes $\|\underline{x} - Q_{\underline{q},\underline{t}'}(\underline{x})\|^2$ over all $\underline{t}'$ such that $\ell(Q_{\underline{q},\underline{t}'}(\underline{x})) \le L$, then $\|\underline{x} - Q_{\underline{q},\underline{t}}(\underline{x})\|^2 = \|\underline{x} - Q_{\text{bcq}}^{(\underline{q},\underline{l},n,L)}(\underline{x})\|^2$.

3. Asymptotic Rate of BCQ

In this section, we consider the asymptotic behavior of the rate of BCQ with block encoding. In particular, we study the convergence of $R_{\text{bcq}}^{\text{be}}$ for different classes of BCQ's. This is of particular importance for the classes using binary encoding schemes other than block encoding, since it gives a measure on how suboptimal these methods are. The loss of a binary encoding scheme relative to block encoding is called the *code-space loss.* The asymptotic code-space loss will be considered in the next section.

The following theorem gives the asymptotic behavior of $R_{\text{bcq}}^{\text{be}}$ for the case $L_n/n \to R$ for some R. This case includes both pe-BCQ, block-encoded BCQ (be-BCQ) and arithmetic-encoded BCQ (ae-BCQ) [**6**].

[1] This is expected for continuous sources.

THEOREM 3.1. Let $\underline{l}$ and L_n be such that $L_n/n \geq l_{\min}$ and[2] $L_n/n \to R$. Then,

$$\lim_{n\to\infty} R^{\text{be}}_{\text{bcq}}(\underline{l}, n, L_n) = h_{\underline{l}}(R) \triangleq \max_{\substack{(p_1,p_2,\ldots,p_m):p_j\geq 0,\\ \sum_j p_j=1, \sum_j p_j l_j \leq R}} -\sum_{j=1}^{m} p_j \log p_j \ .$$

The function $h_{\underline{l}}$ can be explicitly written as

$$h_{\underline{l}}(R) = \begin{cases} \log n_{l_{\min}}, & R = l_{\min} \\ \alpha^* R + \log \sum_{j=1}^{m} 2^{-\alpha^* l_j}, & l_{\min} < R \leq \langle \underline{l} \rangle \\ \log m, & R > \langle \underline{l} \rangle \end{cases} ,$$

where $n_{l_{\min}}$ is the number of l_j's in $\underline{l}$ which are equal to $l_{\min}$, α^* is the solution to the following equation:

$$\sum_{j=1}^{m} l_j 2^{-\alpha^* l_j} \Bigg/ \sum_{j=1}^{m} 2^{-\alpha^* l_j} = R \ , \tag{3.1}$$

and $\langle \underline{l} \rangle \triangleq \sum_{j=1}^{m} l_j/m$. Hence, $h_{\underline{l}}(R)$ is uniformly continuous, non-decreasing and convex $\bigcap$ for $R \geq l_{\min}$. If $l_{\min} < l_{\max}$, then $h_{\underline{l}}^{-1}$ exists on $(\log n_{l_{\min}}, \log m)$.

4. Asymptotic Length Threshold for be-BCQ

In this section, we consider the asymptotic behavior of the length threshold of be-BCQ normalized by n. We consider a be-BCQ with fixed $m, \underline{q}$ and $\underline{l}$ and vary the length threshold L_n with n to get the desired rate[3] $r \in (\log n_{l_{\min}}, \log m)$. In this case, we have

$$\lim_{n\to\infty} \frac{L_n}{n} = h_{\underline{l}}^{-1}(r).$$

This means that L_n is asymptotically linear in n.

5. Asymptotic Code-Space Loss for Other Binary Encoding Schemes

Since block, binary encoding gives the minimum rate for a BCQ, a suboptimal binary encoding scheme, e.g. prefix and arithmetic coding, will usually have a higher rate. The increase in rate is called the *code-space loss.* In this section, we consider the asymptotic code-space loss for ae-BCQ and pe-BCQ for which $L_n/n \to r$, where r is the desired rate.

By Theorem 3.1, the asymptotic code-space loss is

$$r - h_{\underline{l}}(r).$$

By the properties of $h_{\underline{l}}$, we can show that

$$r - h_{\underline{l}}(r) \geq 0,$$

[2]Note that R need not be the rate of the BCQ.

[3]See [**5**, Section 6.5] for a more precise statement.

since $\sum_{j=1}^{m} 2^{-l_j} \le 1$ for pe-BCQ and ae-BCQ. Equality holds if, and only if, $r = R^*(\underline{l}) \triangleq \sum_{j=1}^{m} l_j 2^{-l_j} / \sum_{j=1}^{m} 2^{-l_j}$ and $\sum_{j=1}^{m} 2^{-l_j} = 1$.

Now, for pe-BCQ, $\sum_{j=1}^{m} 2^{-l_j} = 1$, but it is usually the case that $r \ne R^*(\underline{l})$. Thus, in most cases, the asymptotic code-space loss is nonzero. On the other hand, for ae-BCQ, usually $\underline{l}$ can be chosen so that $\sum_{j=1}^{m} 2^{-l_j} = 1$, $l_j = -\log f_j$ and $r \approx -\sum_{j=1}^{m} f_j \log f_j = R^*(\underline{l})$. Therefore, the asymptotic code-space loss is usually small. Alternatively, sometimes we can vary r, during the design process, to reduce the code-space loss. Thus, the final rate might be different from the target rate. This is usually acceptable if the final rate is smaller than the target rate. If not, we might want to keep to target rate and accept the code-space loss.

6. OPTA's for Different Classes of BCQ

In this section, we apply the above results to find the OPTA's of different classes of BCQ's.

6.1. OPTA for pe-BCQ. For pe-BCQ, the OPTA is defined as

$$\delta_{\mathrm{bcq}}^{\mathrm{pe}}(r) = \inf_{m,n,\underline{q},\underline{l} \in \mathcal{L}_m^{\mathrm{pe}}} \bar{d}_{\mathrm{bcq}}(\underline{q}, \underline{l}, n, nr),$$

where $\mathcal{L}_m^{\mathrm{pe}} = \{\underline{l} \in (Z_+)^m : \sum_{j=1}^{m} 2^{-l_j} \le 1\}$, and Z_+ is the set of positive integers. Therefore, using Theorem 2.1, we can easily see the following:

THEOREM 6.1.

$$\delta_{\mathrm{sq}}^{\mathrm{pe}}(r+) \le \delta_{\mathrm{bcq}}^{\mathrm{pe}}(r) \le \delta_{\mathrm{sq}}^{\mathrm{pe}}(r-),$$

where $\delta_{\mathrm{sq}}^{\mathrm{pe}}$ is the OPTA of pe-SQ given by

$$\delta_{\mathrm{sq}}^{\mathrm{pe}}(r) = \inf_{m,\underline{q},\underline{l} \in \mathcal{L}_m^{\mathrm{pe}}} \delta_{\mathrm{sq}}(\underline{q}, \underline{l}, r).$$

Now, if $\delta_{\mathrm{sq}}^{\mathrm{pe}}(r)$ is continuous at r, we see that $\delta_{\mathrm{bcq}}^{\mathrm{pe}}(r) = \delta_{\mathrm{sq}}^{\mathrm{pe}}(r)$, i.e. pe-BCQ can perform as well as, but not better than, pe-SQ. Moreover, pe-BCQ inherits the redundancy loss of pe-SQ and is, thus, bounded away from the performance of an optimum entropy-constrained scalar quantizer (ECSQ) by the amount of that loss, where ECSQ is the scalar quantizer having the minimum distortion subject to a constraint on its output entropy.

Similar results can be derived for ae-BCQ [**5**].

6.2. Asymptotic OPTA be-BCQ. We define the n-dimensional OPTA of a be-BCQ with m levels as

$$\delta_{\mathrm{bcq}}^{\mathrm{be}}(r, n, m) \triangleq \inf_{\underline{q},\underline{l},L : R_{\mathrm{bcq}}^{\mathrm{be}}(\underline{l}, n, L) \le r} \bar{d}_{\mathrm{bcq}}(\underline{q}, \underline{l}, n, L).$$

The asymptotic behavior of the OPTA is given by the following theorem:

THEOREM 6.2.

$$\delta_{\rm sq}^{\rm ent}(r+,m) \leq \liminf_{n\to\infty} \delta_{\rm bcq}^{\rm be}(r,n,m) \leq \limsup_{n\to\infty} \delta_{\rm bcq}^{\rm be}(r,n,m) \leq \delta_{\rm sq}^{\rm ent}(r-,m),$$

where $\delta_{\rm sq}^{\rm ent}(r,m)$ is the OPTA of ECSQ, i.e. $\delta_{\rm sq}^{\rm ent}(r,m)$ is the minimum distortion of any scalar quantizer with m levels and output entropy less than or equal to r.

From the above theorem, we see that, asymptotically, be-BCQ performs as well as ECSQ and cannot perform better.

The block-constrained quantizer (lf-BCQ) proposed by Laroia and Farvardin [**1**] is a block-encoded BCQ with rational lengths. They proposed this restriction of lengths to simplify the BCQ quantization and the block binary encoding. For a rational $\underline{l} \in \boldsymbol{Q}^m$, where $\boldsymbol{Q}$ is the set of rational numbers, we define the *denominator* of $\underline{l}$ as the least-common denominator (lcd) of its components. Now, we consider different classes of lf-BCQ's according to the denominator of $\underline{l}$. We denote the set of m-dimensional, rational $\underline{l}$ having denominator b by $\mathcal{L}_m^b$.

Now, the n-dimensional OPTA $\delta_{\rm bcq}^{{\rm be},b}(r,n,m)$ for the class of lf-BCQ's with m levels and lengths having denominator b can be defined the same as $\delta_{\rm bcq}^{\rm be}(r,n,m)$ above with the inf taken over all $\underline{l} \in \mathcal{L}_m^b$. The asymptotic behavior of $\delta_{\rm bcq}^{{\rm be},b}$ is given by Theorem 6.2 if we replace $\delta_{\rm bcq}^{\rm be}$ by $\delta_{\rm bcq}^{{\rm be},b}$ and $\delta_{\rm sq}^{\rm ent}$ by $\delta_{\rm sq}^{{\rm be},b}$, where

$$\delta_{\rm sq}^{{\rm be},b}(r,m) \triangleq \inf_{\underline{q},\underline{l}\in\mathcal{L}_m^b, R:h_{\underline{l}}(R)\leq r} \delta_{\rm sq}(\underline{q},\underline{l}).$$

Thus, $\delta_{\rm sq}^{{\rm be},b}$ is an achievable bound for lf-BCQ's with denominator b. This result is a more general version of a result given by Laroia and Farvardin [**2**]. In particular, our result includes the effect of b. It can be easily seen the $\delta_{\rm sq}^{{\rm be},b} \geq \delta_{\rm sq}^{\rm ent}$. Moreover, we conjecture that $\delta_{\rm sq}^{\rm ent}(r,m) = \inf_b \delta_{\rm sq}^{{\rm be},b}(r,m) = \lim_{b\to\infty} \delta_{\rm sq}^{{\rm be},b}(r,m)$.

An interesting question is whether $\delta_{\rm bcq}^{\rm be}(r,n,m)$ or $\delta_{\rm bcq}^{{\rm be},b}(r,n,m)$ can be less than $\delta_{\rm sq}^{\rm ent}(r,m)$ for some finite n. Laroia and Farvardin [**2**] conjectured that $\delta_{\rm sq}^{\rm ent}(r,m) \leq \delta_{\rm bcq}^{{\rm be},b}(r,n,m)$ for all n and b. However, in [**5**], we give a counterexample to their conjecture. In particular, we find a be-BCQ with $b = 1$ that performs better than $\delta_{\rm sq}^{\rm ent}$ for a discrete source. The case of continuous sources is still open, although we conjecture that there exists a continuous source for which the same situation occurs. However, we still think that their conjecture will be approximately true for most sources of interest such as Gaussian and Laplacian sources. A more plausible conjecture is obtained by replacing $\delta_{\rm sq}^{\rm ent}$ by its lower convex hull $\underline{\delta}_{\rm sq}^{\rm ent}$.

7. Conclusion

In this paper, we have summarized the asymptotic behavior of the rate and distortion of a BCQ. We gave explicit functions for the asymptotic rate and distortion.

For be-BCQ, we presented an asymptotic formula for the asymptotic length threshold. In particular, we show that L_n is asymptotically linear in n.

Also, we have considered the asymptotic code-space loss for BCQ's using prefix and arithmetic binary encodings. We derived the necessary and sufficient conditions for the code-space loss to vanish asymptotically.

Finally, we have used the derived results to study the OPTA's for different classes of BCQ's. We have given the OPTA's for pe-BCQ. For the cases of be-BCQ and lf-BCQ, we have presented asymptotic OPTA's, i.e. OPTA's for sufficiently high dimensions.

References

1. R. Laroia and N. Farvardin, "A structured fixed-rate vector quantizer derived from a variable-length encoded scalar quantizer," *Proc. of the Twenty-Fourth Annual Conference on Information Sciences and Systems,* pp. 796-801, Princeton, NJ, Mar. 1990.
2. R. Laroia and N. Farvardin, "A structured fixed-rate vector quantizer derived from a variable-length encoded scalar quantizer," *IEEE Trans. Inform. Theory,* to appear.
3. R. Laroia and N. Farvardin, "Extension of of the fixed-rate structured vector quantizer to vector sources," *Proc. of the Twenty-Fifth Annual Conference on Information Sciences and Systems,* pp. 576-581, Johns Hopkins, Baltimore, MD, Mar. 1991.
4. A. S. Balamesh and D. L. Neuhoff, "Block-constrained methods of fixed-rate, entropy-coded, scalar quantization," *submitted to IEEE Trans. Inform. Theory.*
5. A. S. Balamesh, *Block-Constrained Methods of Fixed-Rate, Entropy-Coded Quantization,* Ph.D. Dissertation, The University of Michigan, Ann Arbor, 1993.
6. A. S. Balamesh and D. L. Neuhoff, "A new fixed-rate quantization scheme based on arithmetic coding," *Proc. 1993 Int. Symposium on Inform. Theory,* p. 435, San Antonio, TX, Jan. 1993.

Department of Electrical Engineering, King Abdul-Aziz University, Jeddah, Saudi Arabia

E-mail address: CCP3017@SAKAAU03.BITNET

Department of Electrical Engineering and Computer Science, The University of Michigan, Ann Arbor, Michigan 48109

E-mail address: neuhoff@eecs.umich.edu

DIMACS Series in Discrete Mathematics
and Theoretical Computer Science
Volume **14**, 1993

Syndrome-Based VQ Codebooks

PETER F. SWASZEK

November 30, 1993

ABSTRACT. Low rate vector quantization (VQ) codebooks constructed from binary linear block codes are examined under the mean square error criterion. Assuming a stationary, independent source and implementing the vector quantizer using syndromes, a performance expression is developed. A bound on performance and examples using quasi-perfect and other good channel codes are presented.

1. Introduction

One approach to source coder design that has enjoyed some success is to exploit the duality of the problems of source coding and modulation over the Gaussian channel. Examples include lattice constellation codebooks, trellis coded modulation and quantization, and permutation codes. Here we consider the use of linear block codes as vector quantizer (VQ) codebooks. Specifically, we use syndrome decoding of block codes to generate the quantization regions and their codevectors. Previously, block codes have been used to derive rate-distortion theoretic results and in several full-search vector quantizers. This paper consists of two parts: first, a survey of our prior results on syndrome-based VQ codebooks from binary, perfect codes [**6**] and second, the extension of these results to a bound on performance and specific examples of binary code based VQs. We begin with a brief review of the material on VQ needed for our approach.

Let the source data be a vector of n real values, $\mathbf{x} \epsilon \mathbf{R}^n$, and let the VQ have resolution (rate) of r bits per dimension. The VQ consists of two operations: an encoder which maps each $\mathbf{x}$ onto the index set $\{1, 2, \ldots, 2^{nr} = N\}$ and a decoder which recreates one of 2^{nr} codevectors $\hat{\mathbf{x}}$ (from the VQ's codebook). The encoder is a partition of the input space into disjoint quantization regions $\mathcal{Q}_i$ which cover $\mathbf{R}^n$ and the decoder is the assignment of a codevector $\hat{\mathbf{x}}_i = [\hat{x}_{i,1}, \ldots, \hat{x}_{i,n}]$ to all

1991 *Mathematics Subject Classification.* Primary 94A29, 94A34.

Presented at the 1992 DIMACS/IEEE Workshop on Coding and Quantization, Oct. 1992

$\mathbf{x}\epsilon\mathcal{Q}_i$. A common measure of source coder performance is the mean squared error per dimension

$$\text{MSE} = \frac{1}{n}\int_{\mathbf{R}^n} |\mathbf{x}-\hat{\mathbf{x}}|^2 \, f_n(\mathbf{x})\, d\mathbf{x} = \frac{1}{n}\sum_{i=1}^{N}\int_{\mathcal{Q}_i} |\mathbf{x}-\hat{\mathbf{x}}_i|^2 \, f_n(\mathbf{x})\, d\mathbf{x}$$

where $f_n(\mathbf{x})$ is the source's probability density function.

A large body of literature has developed on the VQ problem (see [**2**]). For example, it is well known that for minimum MSE each $\mathcal{Q}_i$ should be the nearest neighbor region about $\hat{\mathbf{x}}_i$ and that each codevector should be the centroid (conditional mean) of its corresponding region

$$\hat{\mathbf{x}}_i = E\{\mathbf{x}|\mathbf{x}\epsilon\mathcal{Q}_i\} = \frac{\int_{\mathcal{Q}_i} \mathbf{x} f_n(\mathbf{x}) d\mathbf{x}}{\int_{\mathcal{Q}_i} f_n(\mathbf{x}) d\mathbf{x}} \tag{1.1}$$

If the codevectors are the centroids (but the $\mathcal{Q}_i$ need not be nearest neighbor regions), then the MSE expression reduces to the difference between the input and output variances. For unit variance marginals this is

$$\text{MSE} = 1 - \frac{1}{n}\sum_{i=1}^{N} p_i \, |\hat{\mathbf{x}}_i|^2$$

where p_i is the ith region's probability, $p_i = \int_{\mathcal{Q}_i} f_n(\mathbf{x}) d\mathbf{x}$.

Two general approaches have been followed in the study of VQ: unstructured VQs resulting from the generalized Lloyd algorithm and VQs with specific codebook structures. Our approach below falls into the structured VQ category.

2. Block Codes in VQ

For the modulation problem, block codes are employed to add redundancy to data sequences before transmission. An (n, k) binary linear code consists of 2^k codewords each of length n. In antipodal signaling the codewords' zeroes and ones are mapped to amplitudes of $-a$ and $+a$, respectively, on some orthonormal basis set to generate a continuous time signal. As such, each signal can be represented as a point in a signal constellation of dimension n at distance $\sqrt{na^2}$ from the origin. Further, for maximum likelihood decoding (assuming equiprobable messages), the resulting nearest-neighbor decision regions are congruent; the signal set is completely symmetric. A signal constellation from a linear binary block code could be used to specify a VQ codebook (of rate $r = \frac{k}{n}$) whose codevectors all fall on a single sphere in $\mathbf{R}^n$ [**1**]. Since $n > k$ the resulting bit rates are less than unity. For higher rates we could implement multiple sphere, block code based VQs [**6**].

There are two computational issues in using codes as VQ codebooks, locating the centroid of each region to determine performance and implementing soft decoding for the VQ encoder, both of which may be undesirable. In the modulation problem "soft decoding" refers to mapping the received vector $\mathbf{x}$ to that signal vector closest in an Euclidean sense. A second, more computationally efficient option, "syndrome decoding," refers to first thresholding the elements of $\mathbf{x}$ (with threshold zero) producing a sequence of zeroes and ones and then using the parity check matrix H of the code to compute a syndrome. The syndrome selects the error pattern to map the binary sequence back to a codeword. For source encoding we turn this system around. Specifically, encoding with a *syndrome-based VQ* consists of thresholding the source vector, computing the syndrome to map to a codevector, and using the k information bits as the VQ index (an example of such a source encoding scheme for a binary symmetric source and Hamming distortion appears in [**4**, p. 81]; here we are interested in continuous amplitude sources and mean square distortion). The VQ's decoder regenerates a codevector equal to the centroid of the "syndrome encoded" region.

For the analysis below we assume that the input $\mathbf{x}$ consists of iid random variables (zero mean and unit variance) with marginal pdf $f(x)$ symmetric about the origin. Let $\mathbf{e}_l = [e_{l,1}, \dots, e_{l,n}]$, $l = 1, 2, \dots 2^{n-k} = M$, be the coset leaders from the standard array of the (n, k) code. We emphasize that the $N = 2^k$ quantization regions are congruent due to the linear nature of the code; hence, the symmetry condition on the source is sufficient for the overall MSE to equal the MSE conditioned on the source vector being in any one quantization region. We evaluate the MSE for the region $\mathcal{Q}_1$ associated with the all zero codeword. Further, the symmetry results in equi-probable regions, $p_i = 2^{-nr}$, which requires no additional entropy coding of the VQ index.

As defined, region $\mathcal{Q}_1$ consists of all $\mathbf{x}$ such that the thresholding operation produces either the all-zero vector itself or one of the coset leaders

$$\mathcal{Q}_1 = \bigcup_{l=1}^{M} \left\{ \mathbf{x} : \frac{1}{2}(1 + \operatorname{sgn}(x_j)) = e_{l,j};\ j = 1, 2, \dots n \right\}$$

Since the signum function breaks the real line at zero, $\mathcal{Q}_1$ can be decomposed as

$$\mathcal{Q}_1 = \bigcup_{l=1}^{M} \mathcal{Q}_{1,l}$$

where $\mathcal{Q}_{1,l}$ is the n-dimensional orthant corresponding to the coset leader $\mathbf{e}_l$. Noting that the $\mathcal{Q}_{1,l}$ are disjoint, the ith element of the centroid in (1.1) is

$$\hat{x}_{1,i} = \frac{\displaystyle\sum_{l=1}^{M} \int_{\mathcal{Q}_{1,l}} x_i f_n(\mathbf{x}) d\mathbf{x}}{\displaystyle\sum_{l=1}^{M} \int_{\mathcal{Q}_{1,l}} f_n(\mathbf{x}) d\mathbf{x}}$$

Since the elements of $\mathbf{x}$ are assumed iid, each individual integral in the numerator factors

$$\int_{\mathcal{Q}_{1,l}} x_i f_n(\mathbf{x}) d\mathbf{x} = \int x_i f(x_i) dx_i \prod_{j=1, j\neq i}^{n} \int f(x_j) dx_j$$

where the limits are either $(-\infty, 0)$ or $(0, \infty)$ depending upon whether $e_{l,j}$ equals zero or one, respectively. Since the pdfs are symmetric about zero the first integral is either $-\gamma/2$ or $+\gamma/2$

$$\gamma = \int_{-\infty}^{\infty} |x| \, f(x) \, dx$$

For the integrals over x_j, $j \neq i$, both sets of limits yield the value one-half. Similarly, the denominator factors into the product of n terms, each equal to one-half. The resulting centroid has components

$$\hat{x}_{1,i} = \frac{\sum_{l=1}^{M} (2e_{l,i} - 1) \frac{\gamma}{2} (0.5)^{n-1}}{\sum_{l=1}^{M} (0.5)^n} = \left(\frac{2}{M} \sum_{l=1}^{M} e_{l,i} - 1 \right) \gamma \tag{2.1}$$

Recalling the symmetry assumption on the source, the MSE per dimension is

$$\text{MSE} = 1 - \frac{1}{n} \sum_{i=1}^{n} \hat{x}_{1,i}^2 \tag{2.2}$$

As an example, consider a t-error correcting perfect code as the basis for the VQ. Such codes satisfy the Hamming bound

$$\sum_{i=0}^{t} \binom{n}{i} \leq M$$

with equality; the coset leaders correspond to all vectors with t or fewer ones and no others. Summing over the M cosets yields

$$\hat{x}_{1,i} = \left(\frac{2}{M} \sum_{j=0}^{t-1} \binom{n-1}{j} - 1 \right) \gamma$$

which we note is independent of i; i.e. the centroid of $\mathcal{Q}_1$ is along the all zero codeword's orientation. The obvious examples for this case include the $(2^m - 1, 2^m - 1 - m)$ single error correcting Hamming codes $(m \geq 3)$ and the (23,12) triple error correcting Golay code which have performance

$$\text{MSE}_{\text{Hamming}} = 1 - \left(2^{1-m} - 1\right)^2 \gamma^2 \qquad \text{and} \qquad \text{MSE}_{\text{Golay}} = 1 - \left(\frac{770}{1024}\right)^2 \gamma^2$$

For comparison, the time-shared rate $r = \frac{k}{n}$ scalar quantizer (k uses of a one-bit quantizer and $n - k$ uses of a zero bit quantizer) has performance

$$\mathrm{MSE}_{\mathrm{scalar}} = 1 - r\,\gamma^2$$

Comparing the coefficients of γ^2 we see that the Hamming code ($m \geq 4$) and Golay code VQs outperform low rate scalar quantization for all sources. We note that γ^2 takes on values in the range $[0, 1]$ (for example, for the Gaussian and Laplacian sources γ^2 equals $\frac{2}{\pi}$ and $\frac{1}{2}$, respectively); hence, sources with larger γ are more impacted by increases in the coefficient.

3. A bound and examples of performance

For any t-error correcting code, the centroid expression (2.1) can be written as

$$\hat{x}_{1,i} = \left(\frac{2}{M} \sum_{j=0}^{t-1} \binom{n-1}{j} + \frac{2}{M} \sum_{l} e_{l,i} - 1 \right) \gamma \tag{3.1}$$

where l in the second summation ranges over those coset leaders with $t + 1$ or more ones. Since we know that $\hat{x}_{1,i} < 0$ ignoring these cosets yields a more negative result for $\hat{x}_{1,i}$, an upper bound on $\hat{x}_{1,i}^2$, and a lower bound on the MSE in (2.2)

$$\mathrm{MSE} \geq 1 - \left(\frac{2}{M} \sum_{j=0}^{t-1} \binom{n-1}{j} - 1 \right)^2 \gamma^2$$

For large n, the Hamming bound [**3**, p.558] is

$$\sum_{i=0}^{t} \binom{n}{i} \approx 2^{nH_2(t/n)} \qquad \text{and} \qquad r \approx 1 - H_2\left(\frac{d}{2n}\right)$$

where $H_2(x)$ is the binary entropy function and d is the minimum distance of the code. Equating t to $\frac{d}{2}$, the second relationship yields $t \approx n\,H_2^{-1}(1 - r)$. Using the first relationship in our MSE expression above yields

$$\mathrm{MSE} \geq 1 - \left[\frac{2}{M}\, 2^{(n-1)H_2((t-1)/(n-1))} - 1 \right]^2 \gamma^2$$

Replacing H_2 in this expression by the first two terms in a Taylor series expansion

$$\mathrm{MSE} \geq 1 - \left(2^{r + H_2'(H_2^{-1}(1-r))\left[H_2^{-1}(1-r) - 1\right]} - 1 \right)^2 \gamma^2$$

Figures 1a and 1b show this bound on MSE (dashed line) for the Gaussian source and on the coefficient of γ^2 in the general MSE expression, respectively, versus rate r. Also included are the scalar result (solid line), the distortion-rate function for the Gaussian case (dotted line), and actual code performance (circles) as described below.

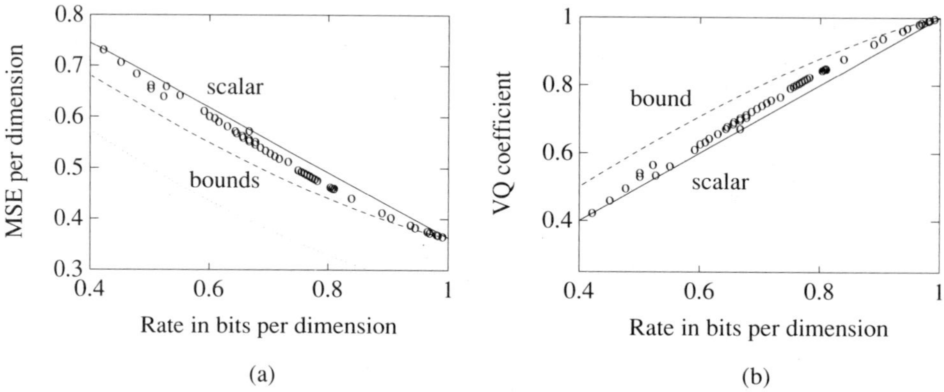

FIGURE 1. Performance of example syndrome-based VQs versus bit rate r; included are scalar performance and the developed bound: (a) MSE for the iid Gaussian source, (b) coefficient of γ^2.

To see if we can get performance close to this bound, we examined VQs from a variety of good channel codes. Remembering that the evaluation of the region centroids and the MSE require summations over the M coset leaders, we make the following conjecture:

CONJECTURE 3.1. For given values for k and n the best VQ performance is achieved by the (n, k) code whose coset leaders minimize

$$T = \sum_{i=1}^{n} \sum_{l=1}^{M} e_{l,i}$$

i.e., perfect codes are best, followed by quasi-perfect codes.

Discussion: recall that each VQ region consists of M orthants and that the larger the distance to the centroid, the smaller the MSE. Since the centroid's magnitude decreases as the orthants are more widely spread, compact regions (i.e. coset leaders "close to" the codeword) have smallest MSE for given values of n and k.

Recalling expression (3.1) above we note that knowledge of the M coset leaders is necessary to compute performance. For a given code there are restrictions on the possible coset leaders. For example, consider the (10,5) single-error correcting code from [**5**]. The 32 coset leaders consist of the zero-error pattern, the ten single-error patterns, and 21 of the 45 possible double-error patterns. Since 12 of the 21 double-error cosets contain two double-error patterns our VQ regions are not unique; the leaders can be chosen to optimize the VQ's performance. (Note that this is significantly different from choosing coset leaders for signal demodulation on the BSC for which only the number of errors is important, the actual error positions are irrelevant). Such an optimization requires specific knowledge of the coset structure of the code. In this example, fully searching over all possible choices of the coset leaders yields that

$$0.6946 \leq \text{MSE} \leq 0.7016$$

unfortunately above that of scalar quantization for the same rate. While important for the actual MSE value, the actual assignment of the $t+1$ error cosets seems to be a second order effect.

As examples of code based VQ we examined quasi-perfect codes and some optimum channel codes (up to dimension 60) [**5, 8, 9, 10**] as well as the double error correcting BCH codes (and the Hamming and Golay codes above). Rather than searching for the best choice of $\geq t+1$ error cosets, we evaluated performance for one choice. Their performance for the iid Gaussian source appears in Figure 1a. Figure 1b shows the coefficient of γ^2 of these VQs.

4. Comments

The bound in the binary case suggests that additional gain is available for syndrome-based VQs with rate less than 1 bit/dimension. To date we have examined only small to moderate dimension codes in detail and have seen modest improvements in performance. For low rates there is still a significant gap to the bound. Current work includes non-binary, non-linear, and Lee metric codes [**7**].

References

1. J. P. Adoul & C. Lamblin, "A comparison of some algebraic structures for CELP coding of speech," *Proc. IEEE Int'l. Conf. Acoustics, Speech, & Signal Processing*, 1987, pp.1953–1956.
2. H. Abut, editor, *Vector Quantization*, New York: IEEE Press, 1990.
3. F. J. MacWilliams & N. J. A. Sloane, *The Theory of Error-Correcting Codes*, Amsterdam: North-Holland, 1977.
4. R. J. McEliece, *The Theory of Information and Coding*, Reading: Addison-Wesley, 1977.
5. D. Slepian, "A class of binary signaling alphabets," *Bell Sys. Tech. Jour.*, vol. 35, pp.203–234, Jan. 1956.
6. P. F. Swaszek, "Vector quantization based on block and spherical codes," *Proc. Conf. Information Science & Systems*, pp.570–575, Mar. 1991.
7. P. F. Swaszek, "Vector quantization codebooks from the Nordstrom-Robinson code and Berlekamp's negacyclic codes," *Proc. IEEE Int'l. Symp. Information Theory*, pp.175, Jan. 1993.
8. N. Tokura, K. Taniguchi, & T. Kasami, "A search procedure for finding optimum group codes for the binary symmetric channel," *IEEE Trans. Inform. Theory*, vol. IT-13, pp.587–595, Oct. 1967.
9. T. J. Wagner, "A search technique for quasi-perfect codes," *Information and Control*, 9, pp.94–99, 1966.
10. T. J. Wagner, "Some additional quasi-perfect codes," *Information and Control*, 10, pp.334, 1967.

Department of Electrical Engineering, University of Rhode Island, Kingston, RI 02881

E-mail address: swaszek@ele.uri.edu

DIMACS Series in Discrete Mathematics
and Theoretical Computer Science
Volume 14, 1993

Decoding Under Integer Metric Constraints

EPHRAIM ZEHAVI AND JACK SALZ

January 14, 1993

ABSTRACT. We investigate the problem of decoding digital data when soft decisions are constrained to take on values from a finite set. We propose a physically reasonable objective function for selecting the desired assignment of metrics to the received analog signals. We develop a search algorithm for designing a table look-up that is used by the decoder to select the appropriate intermediate metrics and show that an optimum solution exists. We provide a number of illuminating examples to elucidate our ideas and work out in detail some practical cases.

1. Introduction

In this paper, we examine the problem of decoding coded digital data when soft decisions are constrained to take on values from a finite set of possible metrics (integer values). This is an important practical consideration since actual decoders must inherently use finite-precision arithmetic, while optimum decision rules require the evaluation of likelihood functions, which for real transmission channels assume a continuum of values.

In order to circumvent these nonphysical specifications, ad-hoc approaches are usually proposed such as, for example, quantizing the received signals or quantizing the continuous decision functions themselves. While these solutions often appear reasonable, the concomitant consequences in terms of performance degradations are extremely difficult to assess. More importantly, the trade-offs between finite computational resources and performance penalties are generally ill understood and a design theory based on finite precision would appear to be very desirable and useful.

Here we address some aspects of this general problem. We restrict attention to the design of decoders of digital data transmitted over analog channels. We insist right from the start that decision functions associated with the decoding

1991 *Mathematics Subject Classification.* Primary 94A05; Secondary 94A13.

process must assume only integer[1] values from a given finite set. How to assign (select) these integer-valued decision functions, or metrics, based on reasonable algorithms and how to assess the consequences of the various choices, are the central themes of this paper.

Specifically, our approach is the following. Given the requirement that soft decisions in decoding block or convolutionally coded signals must be assigned values from a finite set of integers, we propose and develop algorithms for making such assignments which are based on maximizing a mathematically tractable and physically reasonable cost function. As we shall elucidate in the sequel, the proposed cost function is referred to in the literature as the generalized cut-off rate of the channel [**1**]. While this channel rate may not be the largest achievable rate, it possesses the important property of guaranteeing that as long as the actual data rate is less than this rate, the probability of error can be made as small as desired by increasing the code length.

Wozencraft and Kennedy [**2**] were first to suggest that a reasonable modulation system design criterion is the "cutoff rate," R_0, of the discrete memoryless channel (DMC). Since, R_0 is the upper limit of code rates for which the average decoding computation per digit is finite when sequential decoding is used. Massey [**3**] argued that the appropriate modulation criterion is R_0 and introduced an iterative procedure for finding the optimum quantization boundaries that maximize R_0, for the binary case. His result was generalized by Lee [**4**] for L-ary modulation. While this approach induces a partition of the likelihood space, the decoder still has to assign optimal metrics with infinite precision for the quantization regions. However, in most practical coded systems the decoder must use a finite set of metrics which are fixed for all channel conditions. In this case the designer task is to find a "good" partition and metric assignment for the likelihood space. Biederman, Omura and Jain [**1**] considered the error performance of a coded system where channel statistics can only be approximated. Because of this mismatch, they were led to introduce the "Generalized R_0" criterion. In particular, when the decoder is using an integer set of metrics, their results reduce to polynomial equations for which Viterbi and Omura [**5**] derived an upper bound on the error performance of a coded system employing a convolutional code.

In Section 2, we introduce the channel model and formulate our problem. In Section 3, we develop the design algorithm and prove the existence of the optimum metric. Section 4 analyzes some special illuminating cases and has some numerical examples. Section 5 contains our conclusions.

2. Channel Model Motivation and Problem Formulation

For simplicity of presentation, we treat block coded systems, but the general ideas apply to convolutionally coded systems as well. A general block coded

[1] The derivation in the paper holds for any finite and bounded set of metrics.

digital data communications system is depicted in Fig. 1. A buffer accepts

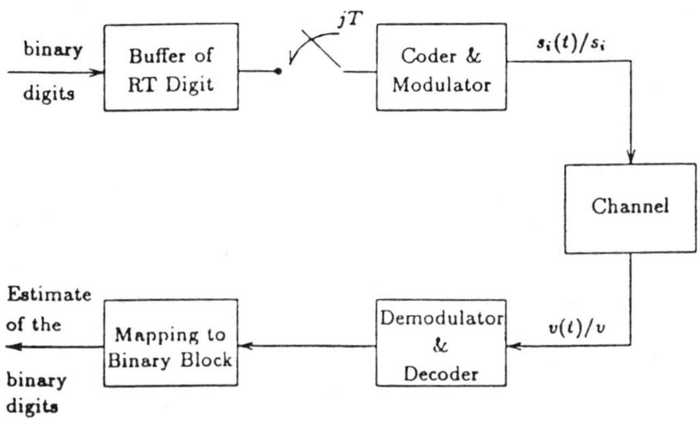

FIGURE 1. A general block coded digital data communications system.

blocks of $B = RT$ binary digits where R is the input rate in bits/s, and T is the block duration in seconds. For each block, the coder-modulator combination selects one of $M = 2^{RT}$ suitable signals, $s_i(t)$, $i = 1, \dots, M$, $0 \leq t \leq T$, for transmission over the channel. We presume that it is possible to represent these time functions by vectors, s_i, $i = 1, \dots, M$ in N'-dimensional space. Usually, N' depends on the time-bandwidth product, or on other suitable signal parameters. The association of the binary data blocks with the signal vectors, $\{s\}$, is the function of the coder.

The channel corrupts the input signal, yielding an output waveform, $v(t)$, which will also be represented by a vector v in N-dimensional space where $N \geq N'$. We presume that we are given the vector-valued probability density function of the channel output vector conditioned on each of the M input vectors, i.e., $p(v|s_i)$, $i = 1, \dots, M$.

At the receiver, the demodulator-decoder combination partitions the entire N-dimensional space into M nonintersecting sets, A_i, $i = 1, \dots, M$, corresponding to the M input signals. If the received vector v falls in A_i the decoder, which knows the encoding rule of the coder, provides the output buffer with the binary block corresponding to the signal s_i. If the output binary digits do not correspond exactly to the digits in the input buffer, a "block error" is committed.

As is well known, the optimum selection criterion for the partition set, A_i, $i = 1, \dots, M$, which maximizes the probability of correct decoding, P_c, is given by the maximum-likelihood detection rule:

$$v \in A_i, \text{ if } p(v|s_i) = \max_j \ p(v|s_j) \tag{2.1}$$

where it is assumed that the M possible signals are equally probable. Clearly, this is the optimum metric, but its computation requires infinite precision. To motivate the use of our objective function, we consider the resulting probability of error when the optimum decision rule is employed.

Let $G_i(v) = 1$ when $v \in A_i$, and 0 otherwise. The probability of error is then,

$$P_e = 1 - P_c = \frac{1}{M}\sum_{j=1}^{M}\sum_{\substack{i=1\\ i\neq j}}^{M}\int p(v|s_j)G_i(v)dv \ . \tag{2.2}$$

Of course for any code consisting of a set of M vectors $\{s_i\}$ it is very difficult to evaluate the probability of error exactly; therefore, it is necessary to upper bound (2.2) and then to assume that the codes are selected at random.

Returning to the problem at hand, suppose that for some reason instead of decoding with the optimum decision function (metric) $\log p(v|s_i)$, we must decode with a mismatched metric, $\tilde{m}(v|s_i)$. We clearly would like to choose such assignments in such a way as to minimize the probability of error and yet not violate the constraints. So, our goal is to determine a metric assignment for v from a given set of metrics, which minimize a tight upper bound on the probability of error, where these metrics are used to decide on signal s_i when

$$\tilde{m}(v|s_i) \geq \tilde{m}(v|s_j), \text{ for all } i \neq j \ , \tag{2.3}$$

while $\tilde{m}(v|s_i)$ can assume values only from the set of integers $1, 2, \ldots, Q'$, (or any other finite set of metrics), which will be called a metric set. When equality results, a fair coin is tossed to resolve the tie.

To proceed toward the objective function, the constrained integer metrics $\tilde{m}(v|s_i)$ are used in a standard Chernoff bound applied to (2.2):

$$P_e(\lambda) \leq \frac{1}{M}\sum_{j=1}^{M}\sum_{\substack{i=1\\ i\neq j}}^{M}\int P(v|s_j)e^{\lambda[\tilde{m}(v|s_i)-\tilde{m}(v|s_j)]}dv, \ \lambda > 0 \ . \tag{2.4}$$

This holds since for all v and $\lambda > 0$,

$$G_i(v) \leq e^{\lambda[\tilde{m}(v|s_i)-\tilde{m}(v|s_j)]} \ . \tag{2.5}$$

As is standard in this approach, the positive constant λ may be optimized to yield the tightest bound. To make further progress, we apply a standard random coding argument and average (2.5) with respect to all sets of code vectors, s_i; it then follows that there must be at least one signal set that achieves a probability of error less than the average.

Toward this end, let $s_1, s_2, \ldots, s_M$ be selected independently from a population characterized by a probability density function, $q(s)$. Averaging (2.4) yields an upper bound on the average probability of error $\tilde{P}_e$,

$$\tilde{P}_e \leq e^{RT}\int \left[E_{q(s)}P(v|s)e^{-\tilde{m}(v|s)}E_{q(s)}e^{\lambda\tilde{m}(v|s)}\right] dv \ , \tag{2.6}$$

where,

$$E_{q(s)}f(\cdot) = \int q(s)f(\cdot)ds, \text{ and } R = \frac{\ln M}{T} . \tag{2.7}$$

The next stage in our model simplification is to restrict treatment to the "memoryless" channel. This assumption implies that each component in the vectors s_i is picked independently using an identical probability distribution. This gives rise to the product

$$P(v|s_i) = \prod_{n=1}^{N} p(v_n|s_{ni}) , \tag{2.8}$$

where the v_n's and s_{ni}'s are the nth components of the vectors v and s_i respectively and $p(v_n|s_{ni})$ is the nth component probability density. Hence the following also holds;

$$E_{q(s)}P(v|s_i) = \prod_{n=1}^{N} Eq(s_{ni})p(v_n|s_{ni}) = [q(s)p(v_n|s)]^N , \tag{2.9}$$

where, $p(v|s)$ and $q(s)$ are now one-dimensional probability densities in case of baseband transmission and two-dimensional, or complex-valued, when passband transmission (QAM or L-ary PSK) is used. We also make the reasonable assumption that the metrics $\tilde{m}(v|s_i)$, $i = 1, \ldots, M$ are additive, i.e.,

$$\tilde{m}(v|s_i) = \sum_{n=1}^{N} m(v_n|s_{ni}) . \tag{2.10}$$

The integer values assumed by the metrics $m(v_n|s_{ni})$ are now taken from the finite set of integers $1, 2, \ldots, Q$. In this "memoryless" notation, the signal length becomes,

$$T = N\tau , \tag{2.11}$$

where τ is the duration of the basic signaling interval.

Substituting (2.8)–(2.11) into (2.6) we obtain an upper bound in the form,

$$\overline{P}_e \leq e^{-N\tau(\tilde{R}(\lambda)-R)} , \tag{2.12}$$

where

$$\tilde{R}(\lambda) = -\frac{1}{\tau}\ln \int dv[E_{q(s)}p(v|s)e^{-\lambda m(v|s)}E_{q(s)}e^{\lambda m(v|s)}] . \tag{2.13}$$

Since λ is an arbitrary positive number, we may optimize the parameter λ to yield a tighter upper bound:

$$\overline{P}_e \leq e^{-N\tau(\tilde{R}(\lambda^*)-R)}, \text{ where } \tilde{R}(\lambda^*) = \max_{\lambda>0} \tilde{R}(\lambda) .$$

It is easy to verify that the objective function $\tilde{R}(\lambda^*)$ is invariant to scaling and shifting of the metric set, and that $\tilde{R}(\lambda^*)$ is greater than zero for at least one metric assignment for any memoryless communication system for which the mutual information $I(v : s) > 0$.

Returning to (2.13) we observe that for any set of mismatched metrics $\{m(v|s_i)\}$ the generalized cutoff rate is defined as [**1**]

$$\tilde{R}(\lambda^*, q^*) = \max_{\lambda>0, q>0} \tilde{R}(\lambda, q) \tag{2.14}$$

where $\int q(s)ds = 1$.

Invoking the fact that in most practical systems the signal points in a constellation are drawn from a discrete ensemble; a reasonable assumption to make is that, if there are L points in the constellation, the probability of drawing such a point in a random code is $q(s) = 1/L$. When these assumptions are applied in (2.13) we obtain the simplified and workable objective function.

$$\begin{aligned} e^{-\tau\tilde{R}(\lambda)} &= W(m(v), \lambda) \\ &= \int dv \left[\frac{1}{L}\sum_{i=1}^{L} p(v|s_i)e^{-\lambda m(v|s_i)}\right]\left[\frac{1}{L}\sum_{i=1}^{L} e^{\lambda m(v|s_i)}\right] \end{aligned} \tag{2.15}$$

where $m(v) = (m(v|s_1), m(v|s_2), \ldots, m(v|s_L))$ is the metric L-tuple. Since each $m(v|s_i) \in \{1, 2, \ldots, Q\}$, one of Q^L L-tuples is associated with each point v.

Our central problem can now be stated as follows. Find $\lambda^* > 0$ and metric assignment $m^*(v)$ for all v such that

$$W(m^*(v), \lambda^*) = \min_{m(v), \lambda>0} W(m(v), \lambda) \tag{2.16}$$

where each entry in the L-tuple assumes values in the set of integers, $\{1, 2, \ldots, Q\}$.

In the next section, we develop an algorithm which provides a solution to this problem and prove its optimality.

3. The Optimum Algorithm

Before deriving the optimum design algorithm and proving the existence of a solution, we examine in some detail feasible and reasonable metric assignments in some limiting situations. We hope that these examples will provide some intuition as to the nature of the optimum assignments in general.

To fix ideas, consider a situation where the channel-characterizing probability densities, $p(v|s_i)$, $i = 1, 2, \ldots, L$, are sharply peaked at the signal points s_i. These points are the elementary alphabet from which code words are composed and can be on either the real line, a plane, or some higher dimensional fixed space. The general ideas illustrated here are independent of the dimensionality of the basic alphabet subspace.

To see the rationale for this solution, consider the Voronoi regions of the space of the basic alphabet vectors v. These regions c_n, form a partition of the subspace and are defined as follows:

$$C_n = \{v : v \in \mathcal{R} \text{ (or } \mathcal{R}^2),\ p(v|s_n) \geq p(v|s_i) \text{ for all } i\} . \tag{3.1}$$

Now suppose that the metric set is $\mathcal{Q} = \{0, 1\}$, and make the following metric assignments:

$$m(v|s_n) = \begin{cases} 1 & v \in C_n \\ 0 & v \notin C_n \end{cases} , \quad n = 1, \ldots, L . \tag{3.2}$$

For this assignment we obtain explicitly

$$W(\lambda^*) = \frac{1}{L}\left[\sqrt{P_c} + \sqrt{(L-1)(1-P_c)}\right]^2 . \tag{3.3}$$

Here,

$$P_c = \frac{1}{L}\sum_{n=1}^{L}\int_{C_n} p(v|s_n)dv , \tag{3.4}$$

can be thought of as the uncoded probability of making correct decisions. It can be easily shown that $\tilde{R}(\lambda^*)$ is equal to the computation cutoff rate of a symmetric discrete memory channel with input $s \in \{s_1, s_2, \ldots, s_L\}$ and output $y \in \{y_1, y_2, \ldots, y_L\}$, with transition probability

$$p(y_i|s_j) = \begin{cases} P_c & i = j \\ \frac{1-P_c}{L-1} & i \neq j \end{cases} . \tag{3.5}$$

Now, let us assign the metrics $\{0, 1\}$ in a more efficient way with respect to the objective function (2.15). It is clear that the right side of (2.15) can only take on L different values, i.e.

$$\sum_{i=1}^{L} e^{\lambda m(v|s_i)} = re^{\lambda} + (L-r),\ r \in \{0, 1, \ldots, L-1\} . \tag{3.6}$$

Here we exclude the all-one metric, since it is equivalent to the all-zero metric. We also can conclude that if $p(v|s_i) > p(v|s_j)$ then $m(v|s_i) \geq m(v|s_j)$, since otherwise we can reduce the objective function by exchanging the metrics. Thus, the received signal space ν is partitioned into subsets. Now, let us denote by $B_r(v)$ the set of r most likely signals, i.e.

$$B_r(v) = \{s_i | p(v|s_i) > p(v|s_j) \text{ for at least } L - r \text{ distinct } s_j\} . \tag{3.7}$$

For a fixed value of λ, we have to assign a metric vector with r^* ones that minimizes the function

$$\left[e^{-\lambda}\sum_{i \in B_r(v)} p(v|s_i) + \sum_{i \notin B_r(v)} p(v|s_i)\right][re^{\lambda} + (L-r)] . \tag{3.8}$$

The required optimal metric assignment is to find λ^*, that minimizes equation (2.15), where the metric assignment is according to equations (3.7) and (3.8).

It becomes evident that explicit solution of the optimum assignment even in the simplest of situations is not tractable and can be done only by the use of a search algorithm.

We now return to the objective function (2.15). We wish to determine a $\lambda > 0$ and a metric vector $m(v) = (m(v|s_1), m(v|s_2), \dots, m(v|s_L))$ among all Q^L tuples that minimizes (2.15). Since the integrand is positive, the minimization can be carried out for each point v. Thus our problem reduces to the following integer programming minimization problem:

$$\min_{\lambda>0, m(v)\in Q^L} \sum_{i,j}^{L} p(v|s_i)e^{-\lambda[m(v|s_i)-m(v|s_j)]} \tag{3.9}$$

for a given set of metric assignment $\{m^*(v|s_i)_1^L\}$ when

$$\sum_{i,j}^{L} p(v|s_i)e^{-\lambda[m^*(v|s_i)-m^*(v|s_j)]} \leq \sum_{i,j}^{L} p(v|s_i)e^{-\lambda[m(v|s_i)-m(v|s_j)]} \tag{3.10}$$

for all $v \in \mathcal{R}$ (or $\mathcal{R}^2$).

This induces, for each λ, a complete partition of the v space into Q^L disjoint sets, $\{A_n\}_1^{Q^L}$. Having once performed this partition for a given λ, we repeat it for all positive λ. To complete the optimum assignment, we choose the $m(v|s_i)$ and the λ that satisfy (3.10) and yield the smallest value of (2.15).

While the foregoing description of the design algorithm is straightforward, two fundamental questions must be answered. First, how complex is the search algorithm, and second, are we guaranteed to find it. We now discuss the first question. We envision a decoder that will have a table look-up consisting of a list of the metric vectors to be assigned to each received point v. Since v is assumed to be continuous, the table look-up will provide metrics to a finely quantized version of the v space. Thus the complexity of the decoder will consist only of adding integer values from the set $\{1, 2, \dots, Q\}$ after looking up corresponding values in the table look-up. Thus the design task is to construct the table look-up which will be done, off-line, once and for all. As to the second question, we have actually answered it in the affirmative by the example we have presented earlier. There we have demonstrated that there exist acceptable metric assignments for a unique $\lambda > 0$ and in fact have calculated the resulting generalized cutoff rates for such assignments.

4. Special Cases and Numerical Examples

In this section we will examine few examples where our approach can be easily used to find a good metric assignment. We will start with the simple binary case for which the problem is reduced to finding a minimum value of a polynomial.

4.1. The binary case — $L = 2$. Henceforth the analysis will be restricted to a binary channel with continuous channel output random variables, v, characterized by some symmetric conditional probability density functions $f_{v|\pm a}(v)$, $v \in (-\infty, \infty)$. Eq. (2.15) can be now written as

$$W(m(v), \lambda) = 1 + \frac{1}{2}\int dv[f(v|a)e^{-\Delta(v)} + f(v|-a)e^{\Delta(v)}] \tag{4.1}$$

where the difference metric $\Delta(v) = m(v|a) - m(v|-a)$ takes values in the set $Q = \{0, \pm 1, \ldots \pm 2Q\}$. Let us fix λ; then for any value of v we have to assign a pair of metrics k or $-k$, which corresponds to an estimate that the signal a or $-a$ was transmitted, respectively. In order to minimize our objective function we would select Δ that minimizes the integrand in (2.15). In other words, the metric k will be assigned to the vector v, if k is the solution to the inequality

$$f(v|a)\zeta^{-k} + f(v|-a)\zeta^{k} \leq f(v|a)\zeta^{-j} + f(v|-a)\zeta^{j}, \text{ for all } j \in Q\ , \tag{4.2}$$

where $\zeta = e^{\lambda}$. This inequality an be expressed as a function of the likelihood function $\Lambda(v) = \frac{f_{v|a}(v)}{f_{v|-a}(v)}$, i.e.,

$$\Lambda(v)(\zeta^{-k} - \zeta^{-j}) \leq \zeta^{j} - \zeta^{k}\ , \text{ for all } j \in Q\ .$$

Thus, the optimal metric assignment is to assign the metric k for all received signals v that satisfy the inequality

$$\zeta^{2k-1} < \Lambda(v) \leq \zeta^{2k+1}\ . \tag{4.3}$$

We note that any value of λ induces a unique partition of the received signal space into $(4Q + 1)$, nonoverlapped distinct subsets of the real line. The minimization of the objective function is reduced to finding the optimal parameter $\lambda^* = \ln(\zeta^*)$.

For example let us find the optimal quantization for a BPSK coded system over a Gaussian channel. In this case $\Lambda(v) = \exp(2va)$ and $a^2 = \frac{2E_s}{N_0}$. The optimal quantizer, in the sense of (2.15), will assign a metric k or $-k$ to v according to

$$m(v) = \operatorname{sgn}(v)k,\ |2v| \in ((2k-1)\delta,\ (2k+1)\delta]\ , \tag{4.4}$$

where $\delta = \ln(\zeta)/a$, and $\zeta = e^{\lambda}$.

For $E_s/N_0 = 0.5$ dB, and the metric set $\{0, \pm 1, \pm 2, \pm 3, \pm 4\}$ the optimal spacing of the quantizer is $\delta = 0.55$. Hence, the uniform quantizer is optimal under an integer metric constraint for BPSK modulation and a Gaussian channel. This results agrees with the upper bounds on the error performance of a coded system which are obtained by generating function techniques, and the simulation results of Heller and Jacobs [**6**].

4.2. 2 L-ary PSK modulation over a Gaussian channel. Let us assume a Gaussian channel, and that the received signal is a two-dimensional vector $v = (x, y)$, with a conditional probability density function

$$(4.5)\quad p((x,y)|(a,b)) = \frac{1}{2\pi}\exp\left(-\frac{(x-a)^2}{2} - \frac{(x-b)^2}{2}\right),\ a^2+b^2 = 2E_s/N_0$$

where (a, b) are the coordinates of the signals in the 2-D signal space. For L-ary PSK modulation the signal constellation is symmetric with respect to rotation of $2\pi/L$ and reflection. Thus, it is sufficient to find the optimal metric assignment for all vectors inside an angle of π/L. Clearly for a fixed value of v, one has to sort the conditional probabilities $p(v|s_i)$ in decreasing order (i.e., sorting the signal points by increasing angular distance), and to assign their metric in decreasing order. For example for $\phi \in [0, \pi/L)$, and the signal set $s_i = \sqrt{a^2+b^2}e^{2ji\pi/L}$, $i = 1, \ldots, M$, the metrics satisfy the inequality

$$(4.6)\qquad m(v|s_1) \geq m(v|s_2) \geq m(v|s_L) \geq m(v|s_3) \geq \cdots \geq m(v|s_{L/2+1})\ .$$

The vector $m(v)$ takes $f_L(Q)$ different values, for $\phi \in [0, \pi/L)$, where the function $f_L(Q)$ is expressed in a recursive form,

$$(4.7)\qquad f_L(Q) + \sum_{i=1}^{Q} f_{L-1}(Q+1-i);\ f_2(j) = j,\ j \geq 0\ .$$

The function $f_L(Q)$ is given in Table 1 for different values of L. For QPSK,

L	$f_L(Q)$	$m(v)$, for $Q = 2$
1	1	(0)
2	Q	(00), (10)
3	$\frac{Q(Q+1)}{2}$	(000), (110), (100)
4	$\frac{Q(Q+1)(Q+2)}{2}$	(0000), (1101), (1100), (1000)
8	$Q(1+Q)(2+Q)(5021280- 7516422Q + 1704521Q^2+ 1076532 \times Q^3- 285491 \times Q^4))/2520$	(00000000), (11110111), (11100111), (11100011), (11000011), (11000001), (11000000), (10000000)

TABLE 1. Some values of $f_L(Q)$ for different values of L.

$E_s/N_0 = 0.5$ dB, the partition of the signal space is shown in Figure 2. Note that our objective function induces a partition of the signal space that is different from the eight Voronoi regions.

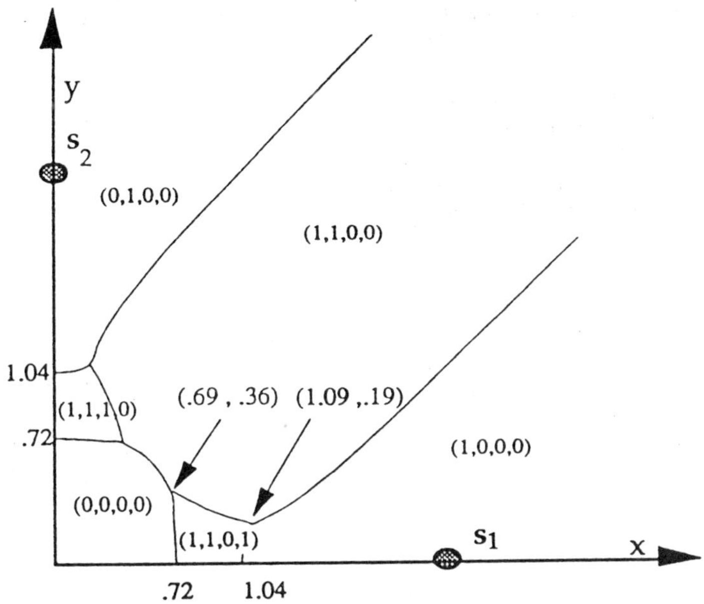

FIGURE 2. Partition of the first quadrant for QPSK, $Q = 2$.

5. Summary and Conclusions

In this paper we propose a physically reasonable objective function for selecting the desired assignment of metrics to the received analog signals. We have presented a simple and intuitive search algorithm for designing a table look-up that is used by the decoder to select the appropriate intermediate metrics and have shown that an optimum solution exists. However, for a decoder with a large set of metrics, this algorithm would not be practical, and other alternatives need to be introduced. We have provided a number of illuminating examples to elucidate our ideas and have worked out in detail some practical cases. The analysis in this paper is applicable to the evaluation of the error performance of a particular trellis code, that satisfies some conditions.

REFERENCES

1. L. Biederman, J. K. Omura, and P. C. Jain, "Decoding with approximate channel statistics for band-limited nonlinear satellite channels," *IEEE Trans. on Inform. Theory*, Vol. IT-22, pp. 697–707, Nov. 1981.
2. J. M. Wozencraft and R. S. Kennedy, "Modulation and demodulation for probabilistic coding," *IEEE Trans. Inform. Theory*, Vol. IT-12, pp. 291–297, July 1966.
3. J. L. Massey, "Coding and modulation in digital communication," Proc. Int. Seminar on Digital Commun., Switzerland, Mar. 1974.
4. Lin-Nan Lee, "On optimal soft-decision demodulation," *IEEE Trans. on Inform. Theory*, Vol. IT-22, pp. 437–444, July 1976.
5. A. J. Viterbi and J. K. Omura, *Principles of Digital Communication and Coding*, McGraw-Hill, 1979.

6. J. A. Heller and I. M. Jacobs, "Viterbi decoding for satellite space communication," *IEEE Trans. Commun. Technology*, Vol. COM-19, pp. 835–848, 1971.

QUALCOMM INC., SAN DIEGO, CA 10555
E-mail address: zehavi@qualcomm.com

AT&T BELL LABORATORIES, HOLMDEL, NJ 07733
E-mail address: jack2@vax135.att.com

DIMACS Series in Discrete Mathematics
and Theoretical Computer Science
Volume **14**, 1993

The Optimality of the Natural Binary Code

S. W. MCLAUGHLIN, J. ASHLEY AND D. L. NEUHOFF

January 6, 1993

ABSTRACT. We consider the problem of quantization in conjunction with a noisy binary symmetric channel. In the design of quantizers for noisy channels, one is concerned with the assignment of channel codewords to quantization cells, or *index assignment* to minimize the distortion introduced by the channel errors. In general, finding the best index assignment is an $N!$ search, which, becomes prohibitive for even relatively small N. In this paper, we show that for a uniform source and uniform scalar quantizer, the best index assignment (that which minimizes the expected distortion due to channel errors) is the natural binary code. This result is extended to the vector case in other work.

1. Introduction

We consider a class of source codes called *noisy channel quantizers (NCQ)*, which are effectively, quantizers designed with the channel in mind. A noisy channel quantizer consists of an encoder and decoder, whose principal characteristics derive from its length L, size N, quantizing partition $\mathbf{S}$, codebook $\mathbf{C}$, index assignment $\mathcal{A}$, and decoding rule d. The length L is the number of binary channel symbols that are used to represent a source sample. The partition $\mathbf{S} = \{S_i\}_{i=1}^{N}$ divides $\mathbb{R}$ into N quantization cells. The index assignment $\mathcal{A} = \{c_i\}_{i=0}^{N-1}$ is a set of L bits that are transmitted across the noisy channel, and where c_i is the channel codeword associated with cell S_i. The codebook $\mathbf{C} = \{y_i : 1 \leq i \leq 2^L\}$ contains a reproduction vector from $\mathbb{R}$ for every possible L-bit channel sequence. The decoding rule d is a one-to-one mapping from $\{0,1\}^L$ into $\{1, ..., 2^L\}$.

The NCQ operates as follows: Given a source sample u, the encoder determines the cell S_i in which the source sample lies and produces the L channel symbols in $\mathcal{A}$ corresponding to S_i (i.e. c_i), which are transmitted across the noisy channel. If the output of the channel is the L-tuple c_j (which happens

1991 *Mathematics Subject Classification.* Primary 94A05, 94A29.

with probability $q_L(c_j|c_i)$), then the decoder produces $y_{d(c_j)}$ as the reproduction of u.

The performance of an NCQ is measured by its rate R and distortion D. The rate R is defined to be L, the number of channel symbols per source symbol. The distortion D is defined to be the mean squared error

$$\begin{aligned} D &= E||U-Y||^2 \\ &= \sum_{i=1}^{N}\sum_{j=1}^{Q^L} q_L(c_j|c_i)\int_{S_i}||u-y_{d(c_j)}||^2 p(u)du \end{aligned} \tag{1.1}$$

where U denotes a source sample, Y denotes the reproduction produced by the decoder, $p(u)$ is the probability density function of the source, and where the expectation is with respect to the randomness in both the source and channel. We have adopted mean squared error as the distortion measure because of its tractability and because it is a commonly used fidelity measure.

In this paper, we consider only the problem of the index assignment. In particular, we assume that the partition $\mathbf{S}$ and codebook $\mathbf{C}$ are given, and that we are to find the best index assignment $\mathcal{A}$.

There are a variety of references [**1**]-[**3**] that state that the natural binary code is a good index assignment for a uniform source and a uniform scalar quantizer. In [**1**]-[**3**] it was assumed that the channel was nearly noiseless, which leads to the assumption that only single channel errors occur. In this paper we make no simplifying assumptions, and show that for the uniform source and a uniform scalar quantizer and show that the best nonredundant channel code is the natural binary code. This result is generalized in [**4**] to a class of vector quantizers and sources.

2. Uniform Source/Uniform Scalar Quantizer

We are given a uniform source (without loss of generality on $[-\frac{1}{2},\frac{1}{2}]$) and a uniform $N(=2^L)$-level scalar quantizer. The quantizer is used in conjunction with a noisy binary symmetric channel with crossover probability $q < .5$. Specifically, we are given a set of N uniform quantization points that form the uniform codebook $\mathbf{C}_u = \{y_i\}_{i=0}^{N-1}$ where $y_i = -\frac{1}{2}+(2i+1)/2N$ and we are given a uniform partition $\mathbf{S}_u = \{S_i\}_{i=0}^{N-1}$ where $S_i = \left[-\frac{1}{2}+\frac{i}{N}, -\frac{1}{2}+\frac{i+1}{N}\right)$. It is easy to see that y_i is the probabilistic centroid of S_i. We look to find the best nonredundant index assignment. That is, we seek an index assignment $\mathcal{A} = \{c_i\}_{i=0}^{N-1}$ where $c_i \in \{0,1\}^L$ is the codeword assigned to y_i, that they minimize distortion. This code is *nonredundant* in that each binary L-tuple in $\{0,1\}^L$ is assigned to a distinct quantization point. One such nonredundant code, known as the *natural binary code* (NBC), is one where if $y_0 < y_1 < \ldots < y_{N-1}$, then the codeword assigned to y_i is the L-bit binary expansion of i.

Recall that since the codebook is the set of probabilistic centroids, the expression for distortion can be written as

$$\begin{aligned} D &= \sum_{i=0}^{N-1} \int_{S_i} (u-y_i)^2 p(u)du + \sum_{i=0}^{N-1} P(U \in S_i) \sum_{j=0}^{N-1} q_{ij}(y_i - y_j)^2 \\ &= D_S + D_C \end{aligned} \tag{2.1}$$

where $q_{ij} = q^{d_H(c_i,c_j)}(1-q)^{L-d_H(c_i,c_j)}$ is the probability that the channel output is c_j given that its input was c_i and $d_H(c_i, c_j)$ is the Hamming distance between the channel codewords assigned to y_i and y_j. Since D_S is independent of the codeword assignment, we look to minimize D_C with respect to the index assignment. That is we perform

$$\min_{\mathcal{A}} D_C = \min_{\mathcal{A}} \sum_{i=0}^{N-1} P(U \in S_i) \sum_{j=0}^{N-1} q_{ij}(y_i - y_j)^2 \tag{2.2}$$

Since the source is uniform and the quantization points are uniformly distributed, $P(U \in S_i) = 1/N$. Thus D_C becomes

$$D_C = \frac{1}{N} \sum_{i=0}^{N-1} \sum_{j=0}^{N-1} q_{ij}(y_i - y_j)^2 \tag{2.3}$$

We can write D_C in vector/matrix form,

$$D_C = \frac{2}{N}\|\underline{y}\|^2 - \frac{2}{N}\underline{y}^T Q_N \underline{y} \tag{2.4}$$

where $\underline{y} = (y_0, \dots, y_{N-1})^T$ is a vector representation of the codebook $\mathbf{C}_u$, and $Q_N = [q_{ij}]$ is an $N \times N$ matrix of transition probabilities.

The code whose distortion is given in (2.4) is described by the set of quantization points $\mathbf{C}_u$ and the index assignment $\mathcal{A}$. To minimize D_C, one could fix the set $\mathbf{C}_u$ and find the best index assignment $\mathcal{A}$. All possible assignments $\mathcal{A}$ are just some permutation of a nominal assignment $\mathcal{A}_0$, i.e. two assignments $\{c_0, \dots, c_{N-1}\}$ and $\{c'_0, \dots, c'_{N-1}\}$ differ only in the ordering of the binary L-tuples. Choosing the best codeword assignment $\mathcal{A}$ corresponds to finding the best permutation of $\mathcal{A}_0$.

In what follows, we shall consider an alternate, more convenient description of the index assignment. We shall fix the ordering of the codewords in $\mathcal{A}_0$ and permute the ordering of the quantization points in $\mathbf{C}_u$ to obtain the best assignment. Without loss of generality, we choose the nominal set of codewords $\mathcal{A}_0 = \{c_0, \dots, c_{N-1}\}$ such that c_i is the binary expansion of i. With this, if $\mathbf{C}'_u = \{y'_0, \dots, y'_{N-1}\}$ is some permutation of $\mathbf{C}_u$, then the binary expansion of i is the codeword assigned to y'_i. We can describe any such permutation by a one-to-one mapping

$$\phi : \{0, \dots, N-1\} \longmapsto \{0, \dots, N-1\} \tag{2.5}$$

where $\phi(i) = j$ means that $y_i \in \mathbf{C}_u$ has been moved to the j'th position in $\mathbf{C}'_u$. implies the codeword assigned to quantization point $y_{\phi^{-1}(i)}$ is the binary expansion of i.

Next we look to incorporate the sets $\mathbf{C}'_u$ and $\mathcal{A}_0$ into (2.4). Recall we have fixed the set $\mathcal{A}_0 = \{c_0, \ldots, c_{N-1}\}$ such that c_i is the binary expansion of i. Let us define a vector $\underline{z} = (y_{\phi^{-1}(0)}, y_{\phi^{-1}(1)}, \ldots, y_{\phi^{-1}(N-1)})^T$ to be a permutation of $\underline{y}$ and call it the *codeword-normalized vector.* The vectors $\underline{y}$ and $\underline{z}$ correspond to the sets $\mathbf{C}_u$ and $\mathbf{C}'_u$, respectively. Since the ordering of the sets $\mathcal{A}_0$ and $\mathbf{C}'_u$ determines the codeword assignment, the codeword-normalized vector $\underline{z}$ has an implicit codeword interpretation, namely, the component z_i (i.e. quantization point $y_{\phi^{-1}(i)}$) has the binary expansion of i as its codeword. The codeword-normalized vector $\underline{z}$ is a function of the permutation mapping ϕ, but for notational convenience, let us instead define the mapping Φ, where $\Phi(\underline{y}) = \underline{z}$, to represent the permutation of $\underline{y}$, where it is understood, that it is really the mapping ϕ that is performing the permutation.

With these definitions of $\mathbf{C}_u, \mathcal{A}_0$, $\underline{z}$ and $\underline{y}$, then for any Φ we can rewrite (2.4) as

$$D_C = \frac{2}{N}\|\Phi(\underline{y})\|^2 - \frac{2}{N}(\Phi(\underline{y}))^T Q_N \Phi(\underline{y}) \tag{2.6}$$

or equivalently,

$$D_C = \frac{2}{N}||\underline{z}||^2 - \frac{2}{N}\underline{z}^T Q_N \underline{z} \tag{2.7}$$

where now

$$q_{ij} = q^{d_H(i,j)}(1-q)^{L-d_H(i,j)} \tag{2.8}$$

is the probability that the binary expansion of j is received given that the binary expansion of i was sent, and $d_H(i,j)$ is short for $d_H(c_i, c_j)$.

Given this formulation, we perform the following minimization:

$$\min_{\Phi} D_C = \min_{\Phi} \frac{2}{N}\|\Phi(\underline{y})\|^2 - \frac{2}{N}(\Phi(\underline{y}))^T Q_N \Phi(\underline{y}) \tag{2.9}$$

An equivalent minimization over the codeword-normalized vector $\underline{z}$ is

$$\min_{\Phi} D_C = \min_{\underline{z}} \frac{2}{N}||\underline{z}||^2 - \frac{2}{N}\underline{z}^T Q_N \underline{z} \tag{2.10}$$

$$\text{subject to: } z_i \in \mathbf{C}_u \text{ for all } i \text{ and } z_i \neq z_j,\ i \neq j \tag{2.11}$$

This is equivalent to finding the vector $\underline{z}$ which has as its components distinct elements of the uniform codebook.

For now we will relax the constraint on $\underline{z}$ and perform the minimization

$$\min_{\underline{z}} D_C = \min_{\underline{z}} \frac{2}{N}||\underline{z}||^2 - \frac{2}{N}\underline{z}^T Q_N \underline{z} \tag{2.12}$$

$$\text{subject to: } \sum_{i=0}^{N-1} z_i = 0 \text{ and } \sum_{i=0}^{N-1} z_i^2 = \sum_{i=0}^{N-1} y_i^2 \tag{2.13}$$

Otherwise $\underline{z}$ is unconstrained. Even though in (2.13) $\underline{z}$ is not constrained to be from $\mathbf{C}_u$, we shall see later that a solution to (2.12) and (2.13) exists such that $z_i \in \mathbf{C}_u$ for all i, and $z_i \neq z_j$, $i \neq j$.

It is possible to show ([**4**], Chapter 4) that D_C can be expressed as

$$D_C = \frac{2}{N}\|\underline{z}\|^2 - \frac{2}{N}\sum_{j=0}^{L}(1-2q)^j\|\mathrm{Proj}_j\underline{z}\|^2 \tag{2.14}$$

where $\|\mathrm{Proj}_j\underline{z}\|^2$ is the squared projection of $\underline{z}$ onto the subspace E_j spanned by the eigenvectors of Q_N corresponding to eigenvalue $(1-2q)^j$. It was also shown in [**4**] that there are only $L+1 (L = \log_2 N)$ eigenvalues of Q_N, each with a value of some integral power of $(1-2q)$.

Since we wish to minimize (2.14) over those $\underline{z}$'s such that $\sum_i z_i = 0$, it is straightforward to see that the projection of $\underline{z}$ onto the eigenspace E_0 corresponding to the eigenvalue $\lambda_0 = 1$ is zero. This gives the final desired form of D_C .

$$D_C = \frac{2}{N}\|\underline{z}\|^2 - \frac{2}{N}\sum_{j=1}^{L}(1-2q)^j\|\mathrm{Proj}_j\underline{z}\|^2 \tag{2.15}$$

Using (2.13) the minimization becomes

$$\min_{\underline{z}} D_C = \min_{\underline{z}} \frac{2}{N}\|\underline{z}\|^2 - \frac{2}{N}\sum_{j=1}^{L}(1-2q)^j\|\mathrm{Proj}_j\underline{z}\|^2$$

$$\text{subject to: } \sum_{i=0}^{N-1} z_i = 0 \text{ and } \sum_{i=0}^{N-1} z_i^2 = \sum_{i=0}^{N-1} y_i^2 \tag{2.16}$$

In what follows we shall state a number of lemmas, proofs of which are given in [**4**].

LEMMA 2.1. Given a uniform source, an $N(=2^L)$ point uniform scalar quantizer described by a codeword-normalized vector $\underline{z}$, and a codeword assignment $\mathcal{A}_0$, the channel distortion is lower bounded by $D_C \geq \frac{4q}{N}\sum_{i=0}^{N-1} y_i^2$ with equality if and only if $\underline{z} \in E_1$, where E_j is the eigenspace of Q_N spanned by the eigenvectors corresponding to the the eigenvalue $(1-2q)^j$.

LEMMA 2.2. The L eigenvectors of Q_N $(N = 2^L)$ which form a basis of E_1 can be expressed as

$$v^{(L,i)} = \left(x_{00\ldots0}^{(L,i)}, x_{0\ldots01}^{(L,i)}, \ldots, x_{11\ldots1}^{(L,i)}\right) \quad i = 0, \ldots, L-1 \tag{2.17}$$

with

$$x_w^{(L,i)} = (-1)^{<w,b_i>} = (-1)^{w_i} \text{ for all } w \in \{0,1\}^L \tag{2.18}$$

where $< w, b_i >$ is the inner product of the binary L-tuples w and b_i and

$$\begin{aligned} b_0 &= 00\ldots01 \\ b_1 &= 00\ldots10 \\ b_{L-1} &= 10\ldots00 \end{aligned} \tag{2.19}$$

We combine Lemma 2.1 and Lemma 2.2 to get a corollary that gives an explicit formula for the components of the codeword normalized vector $\underline{z}$ that minimize D_C.

COROLLARY 2.1. The codeword normalized vector $\underline{z}$ is an element of E_1 if and only if there exist real numbers $\alpha_0, \ldots, \alpha_{L-1}$ such that

$$z_w = \sum_{i=0}^{L-1} \alpha_i (-1)^{w_i} \text{ for all } w \in \{0,1\}^L \tag{2.20}$$

Finally we are able to state the main theorem regarding the optimality of the NBC. See [**4**] for a complete proof.

THEOREM 2.1. For a uniform source, a uniform $N(=2^L)$-level quantizer, and a binary symmetric channel with crossover probability $q < .5$, the optimum codeword assignment is the natural binary code. The resulting channel distortion is

$$D_C = \frac{4q}{N} \sum_{i=0}^{N-1} y_i^2 \tag{2.21}$$

PROOF. We show that the vector of quantization points $\underline{y} = (y_0, \ldots, y_{N-1})^T$ is an element of E_1. Recall that since a codeword-normalized vector $\underline{z} \in E_1$ has a codeword interpretation, namely that z_w is assigned the binary expansion of w as its codeword, then if $\underline{y} \in E_1$, it has the same codeword interpretation (which is the NBC) and it achieves the minimum D_C. □

By Corollary 2.1, $\underline{z}^* \in E_1$ if and only if $z_w^* = \sum_{i=0}^{L-1} \alpha_i (-1)^{w_i}$. To show that $\underline{y} = (y_0, \ldots, y_{N-1})^T$ is an element of E_1, we must show there exist real numbers α_i, $i = 0, \ldots, L-1$, such that

$$y_w = \sum_{i=0}^{L-1} \alpha_i (-1)^{w_i} \text{ for all } w \in \{0,1\}^L \tag{2.22}$$

If we choose

$$\alpha_i = -\frac{2^i}{2^{L+1}} \quad i = 0, \ldots, L-1 \tag{2.23}$$

then it can be shown [**4**] that the resulting points $y_w^* \triangleq \sum_{i=0}^{L-1} \alpha_i (-1)^{w_i} = y_w$

Since $\underline{y} \in E_1$ it achieves the minimum channel distortion by Lemma 2, and y_w has the codeword w assigned to it. This completes the proof of Theorem 1.□

Comments about Theorem 2.1. Two observations and comments about Theorem 1 can be made. First the assumption that the uniform source and scalar quantizer be zero mean is for convenience only and entails no loss of generality. The theorem is true for any uniform source/uniform scalar quantizer pair that have a nonzero mean. Second, the NBC is not a unique codeword assignment. Certainly any code which is obtained by adding (mod-2) a constant weight binary L-tuple to each codeword of the NBC is also an optimal code. Also any permutation of the positions in the NBC yields an optimal assignment.

References

1. Y. Yamaguchi and T. Huang, "Optimum fixed-length binary code," MIT Research Lab of Electronics, Cambridge, MA, Quarterly Progress Report 78, pp. 231-233, July 15, 1965.
2. T. Huang, et. al. "Optimum binary code," MIT Research Lab of Electronics, Cambridge, MA, Quarterly Progress Report 79, pp. 214-217, October 15, 1965.
3. N.S. Jayant and P. Noll, *Digital Coding of Waveforms*, Prentice Hall, Englewood Cliffs, NJ, pp. 175-184.
4. S.W. McLaughlin, *Source Channel Coding with Applications to Digital Magnetic Recording*, Ph.D. dissertation, EECS Department, University of Michigan, August 1992.

Department of Electrical Engineering, Rochester Institute of Technology, Rochester, NY 14623

E-mail address: SWMEEE@ritvax.isc.rit.edu

IBM Almaden Research Center, San Jose, CA 95120

E-mail address: jashley@almaden.ibm.com

Department of Electrical Engineering and Computer Science, University of Michigan, Ann Arbor, MI 48109

E-mail address: neuhoff@eecs.umich.edu

DIMACS Series in Discrete Mathematics
and Theoretical Computer Science
Volume **14**, 1993

Multiple Description Scalar Quantizer Design: Good Index Assignments

V. VAISHAMPAYAN

January 11, 1993

ABSTRACT. We consider the design of a multiple description scalar quantizer (MDSQ). An MDSQ is a scalar quantizer which is to be used over a two-channel diversity system. The encoder of the MDSQ maps a source sample to an index pair, each component of which takes values in a specified set of indices. The first and second components of this index pair are transmitted over the first and second channel of the diversity system, respectively. The objective of the design is to minimize the average distortion when both channels work subject to constraints on the average distortion when only one of the two channels works. It turns out that the assignment of the index pairs to the quantizer cells is of crucial importance in the design. Motivated by information theoretic results for the multiple descriptions problem, we develop a simple criterion for designing optimal index assignments. Two families of optimal index assignments are presented.

1. Introduction

We consider a diversity system that consists of two independent channels linking the source to the destination. The objective of the source encoder is to transmit different descriptions of the source output over each channel. Each description alone should result in an acceptable reproduction of the source output. Further, it should be possible to combine the two descriptions to obtain a higher fidelity reproduction of the source output. This problem is known as the multiple descriptions problem in the information theory literature.

1.1. Preliminaries. Assume that we wish to encode the output of a source which is represented by the stationary and ergodic random process $\{X_n,\ n \in \mathbb{Z}\}$ with zero mean and variance σ_X^2. We have available a diversity system consisting

---

1991 *Mathematics Subject Classification.* Primary 94A15.

This work was supported in part by NSF Grant Number NCR-9104566.

of two channels, each capable of transmitting information reliably at rates of R bits/source sample (bpss), respectively. Each channel may either be in an operational or non-operational state; this is not known to the encoder. The encoder sends a different description over each channel. Given the state of each channel, the source decoder forms the best estimate of the source output from the available data.

The encoder maps a source sample x to an index l which takes values in the set $\{1, 2, \ldots, N\}$, where $N \leq M$ and $M = 2^{2R}$. The encoder mapping is specified by a vector of thresholds $\mathbf{t} = (t_0, t_1, \ldots, t_N)^T$, where it is assumed that $t_0 \leq t_1 \leq \ldots \leq t_N$, and the interval $B_l = (t_{l-1}, t_l]$ is mapped to index l. Here, $(t_0, t_N]$ is the support of the source probability density function (pdf). The index l is then mapped to an index pair (i, j), $i, j \in \mathcal{I} = \{1, 2, \ldots, \sqrt{M}\}$, by the mapping $ij(\cdot)$. We refer to this mapping as the index assignment. Index i is transmitted over channel 1 and index j is transmitted over channel 2. We assume that the decoder knows whether each channel is in an operational or non-operational state. If both channels work, a central decoder maps the index pair (i, j) to the real number $\hat{x}^0$ which takes values in the central reconstruction codebook $\hat{\mathcal{X}}^0 = \{\hat{x}^0_{ij},\ i = 1, 2, \ldots, \sqrt{M}, j = 1, 2, \ldots, \sqrt{M}\}$. The central decoder is represented by the mapping g_0. If only channel 1 is operational, side decoder 1, represented by the mapping g_1, maps index i to real number $\hat{x}^1$ which takes values in the first side codebook $\hat{\mathcal{X}}^1 = \{\hat{x}^1_m,\ m = 1, 2, \ldots, \sqrt{M}\}$. If only channel 2 is operational, side decoder 2, represented by the mapping g_2, maps index j to real number $\hat{x}^2$ which takes values in the second side codebook $\hat{\mathcal{X}}^2 = \{\hat{x}^2_m,\ m = 1, 2, \ldots, \sqrt{M}\}$. Let the per-sample distortion between x and $\hat{x}^k$ be represented by $d_k(x, \hat{x}^k)$, $k = 0, 1, 2$. We assume that d_k, $k = 0, 1, 2$, are squared-error distortions and refer to $E[d_0]$ as the central mean squared-error (MSE) and to $E[d_k], k = 1, 2$ as the side MSE's.

The objective of multiple description scalar quantizer design is to select $\mathbf{t}$, $N \leq M$, the index assignment $ij(\cdot)$, $\hat{\mathcal{X}}^0$, $\hat{\mathcal{X}}^1$ and $\hat{\mathcal{X}}^2$ such that $E[d_0(X, \hat{X}^0)]$ is minimized, subject to $E[d_1(X, \hat{X}^1)] \leq D_1$ and $E[d_2(X, \hat{X}^2)] \leq D_2$.

For a given N and a fixed index assignment, the above constrained optimization problem can be solved by using the method of Lagrange multipliers [**1**]. Let us define $\mathbf{z} = (t_1, t_2, \ldots, t_{N-1}, \hat{x}^0_1, \hat{x}^0_2, \ldots, \hat{x}^0_N, \hat{x}^1_1, \hat{x}^1_2, \ldots, \hat{x}^1_M, \hat{x}^2_1, \hat{x}^2_2, \ldots, \hat{x}^2_M)^T$. Let $L(\mathbf{z}, \lambda_1, \lambda_2) = E[d_0(X, \hat{X}^0)] + \lambda_1(E[d_1(X, \hat{X}^1)] - D_1) + \lambda_2(E[d_2(X, \hat{X}^2)] - D_2)$ be the Lagrangian functional for the optimization problem. Let $\mathbf{z}^*$ locally minimize $E(d_0)$ subject to $E(d_1) \leq D_1$ and $E(d_2) \leq D_2$. Then there exist $\lambda_1 \geq 0$ and $\lambda_2 \geq 0$ such that $\nabla L(\mathbf{z}^*, \lambda_1, \lambda_2) = 0$, $\lambda_1(E(d_1) - D_1) = 0$ and $\lambda_2(E(d_2) - D_2) = 0$. These necessary conditions for optimality can be solved using a generalization of Lloyd's algorithm for quantizer design [**2**].

It turns out, however, that the index assignment plays a crucial role in the performance that can be achieved by solving the above necessary conditions for optimality and we address this issue here. In order to find good index assignments, we first study the multiple description rate distortion bound in Section 2.

In Section 3, we study the behavior of the side and central MSE's for a scalar quantizer and based upon this we develop good index assignments. The paper is summarized in Section 4.

2. Rate Distortion Bounds on MDSQ Performance

The multiple descriptions problem has been studied from an information theoretic perspective by several authors. El Gamal and Cover [**3**] assume that the source is memoryless and discrete and that the distortion measures are bounded. Their main result is as follows. Let a multiple description encoder transmit information at rates R_1 and R_2 bpss over each of the two channels. Let $p(x,\hat{x}^0,\hat{x}^1,\hat{x}^2) = p_t(\hat{x}^0,\hat{x}^1,\hat{x}^2|x)p_X(x)$ be a joint probability mass function and let

$$\begin{aligned}\mathcal{P} = \quad & \big\{p(x,\hat{x}^0,\hat{x}^1,\hat{x}^2) : E(d_1) \le D_1, E(d_2) \le D_2, \\ & \qquad I(X;\hat{X}^1) < R_1, I(X;\hat{X}^2) < R_2, \\ & \qquad I(X;\hat{X}^0,\hat{X}^1,\hat{X}^2) + I(\hat{X}^1;\hat{X}^2) < R_1 + R_2\big\}. \end{aligned} \tag{2.1}$$

Then there exists an encoder-decoder pair with average central distortion no greater than D_0, provided $D_0 > \inf_{p\in\mathcal{P}} E(d_0)$. This bound on the average central distortion has been evaluated for a memoryless Gaussian source and squared-error distortion measure [**3**], [**4**]. It is shown that given $D_1 \ge 2^{-2R_1}$, $D_2 \ge 2^{-2R_2}$, a multiple description encoder-decoder pair operating at rates R_1 and R_2 exists, with $E(d_1) \le D_1$, $E(d_2) \le D_2$ and with average central distortion no greater than D_0, for any

$$D_0 > \begin{cases} \dfrac{2^{-2(R_1+R_2)}}{1-(\sqrt{\Pi}-\sqrt{\Delta})^2}, & \text{if } \Pi \ge \Delta, \\ 2^{-2(R_1+R_2)}, & \text{otherwise,} \end{cases} \tag{2.2}$$

where $\Pi = (1-D_1)(1-D_2)$ and $\Delta = D_1D_2 - 2^{-2(R_1+R_2)}$. Conversely, in [**4**] it is shown that given $D_1 \ge 2^{-2R_1}$ and $D_2 \ge 2^{-2R_2}$ it is impossible for a multiple description encoder-decoder pair operating at rates R_1 and R_2 with average side distortions that satisfy $E(d_1) \le D_1$ and $E(d_2) \le D_2$, to have an average central distortion smaller than the right hand side of (2.2).

It will prove useful to interpret these results when the rates R_1 and R_2 are equal and high. Suppose that information is transmitted over channels 1 and 2 at the rate R bpss, but that the MSE's achieved by side decoders 1 and 2 decrease at the smaller exponential rate $2(1-a_1)R$ and $2(1-a_2)R$, $0 < a_2, a_1 \le 1$, In other words assume that[1] $E(d_p) \sim c_p 2^{-2(1-a_p)R}$, $p = 1, 2$. We assume, without loss of generality, that $a_1 \le a_2$. By making appropriate substitutions in (2.2), it follows that, for an optimum system, $E(d_0) \sim (1/c_2)2^{-2(1+a_2)R}$, if $a_1 < a_2$, and, $E(d_0) \sim (1/(\sqrt{c_1}+\sqrt{c_2})^2)2^{-2(1+a)R}$ if $a_1 = a_2 = a$. We would like the central

[1]By definition [**5**], $f(x) \sim g(x)$ if $\lim_{x\to\infty} f(x)/g(x) = 1$.

MSE to decrease at a faster exponential rate than either of the side MSE's. In order to do so, it follows from the above discussion that it only necessary to penalize the exponential rate of decrease of one of the side MSE's. However, penalizing both the side MSE's leads to a smaller coefficient for the exponential term in the expression for the central MSE. Note that in this case the sum of the exponents in the expressions for $E(d_0)$ and $E(d_1)$ (or $E(d_2)$) is always $-4R$. This is the essence of the tradeoff between the side and the central MSE's.

3. The Index Assignment Problem

The index assignment problem is addressed in this section. We study the behavior of the MDSQ at high rates and show that the performance of an index assignment is determined by a parameter, which we call the spread of the index assignment. We then present two families of index assignments. We will assume that $M_1 = M_2 = \sqrt{M}$ and that the encoded information is sent across the channels of the diversity system using fixed length codes.

In searching for a meaningful yet tractable criterion on which to base the index assignment, we study the exponential behavior of the central and side MSE's with the transmission rate. For the remainder of this section we assume that M is large.

We start by defining the *extent* of the cell of a quantizer as the maximum distance between any two points contained in that cell. The definition of extent generalizes the notion of length to include cells that are formed by the union of disjoint intervals (note that side quantizer cells have this structure). Let $lmin_p(n)$, $p = 1, 2$, be the minimum value of the interval index l which is mapped by $a(\cdot)$ to an index pair whose pth component is equal to n. Let $lmax_p(n)$, $p = 1, 2$, be the maximum value of the interval index l which is mapped by $a(\cdot)$ to an index pair whose pth component is equal to n. Also define the *spread* $s_p(n)$, $p = 1, 2$ as $lmax_p(n) - lmin_p(n) + 1$. Assume for simplicity that the source pdf has finite support[2] and that the source variance is unity. Let $N \leq M$ be the number of central cells in the MDSQ and let $\sqrt{M} = 2^R$. In the sequel, we will use the fact that if the extent of every cell in an encoder partition[3] is $\Theta(1/N^b)$, $0 \leq b \leq 1$, then the corresponding minimum MSE is $\Theta(1/N^{2b})$. This result is well-known [**6**] when each cell in a partition is an interval. However, it is also true, when each cell may be the union of several disjoint intervals, as is the case with the side cells of an MDSQ.

We have available a total of $M = 2^{2R}$ index pairs for transmission. If each of these index pairs is used (i.e., if the length of each central cell is $\Theta(2^{-2R})$), then $E(d_0)$ will be $\Theta(2^{-4R})$. It then follows from the rate distortion result, that either $E(d_1)$ or $E(d_2)$ must be $\Theta(1)$. This case is uninteresting for the problem

---

[2]It should be possible to generalize the results that follow to pdf's with infinite support by a suitable limiting argument.

[3]By definition [**5**], a function $g(N)$ is $\Theta(f(N))$ if there exist $c_1 > 0$, $c_2 > 0$ and N_0 such that for all $N > N_0$, $c_1|f(N))| < |g(N)| < c_2|f(N)|$.

of finding balanced descriptions since we are looking for quantizer designs that result in equal and positive exponential decay rates for $E(d_1)$ and $E(d_2)$.

Let us select a subset consisting of $N = 2^{(1+a)R}$ index pairs, $0 \leq a \leq 1$, out of the M available index pairs, and use these to encode the source. If we assume that the extent of every central cell is $\Theta(2^{-(1+a)R})$, then the minimum $E(d_0)$ will be $\Theta(2^{-2(1+a)R})$. From rate distortion theory it then follows that the side MSE's can go to zero no faster than $\Theta(2^{-2(1-a)R})$, assuming that the descriptions are balanced. However, the actual exponential rate at which $E(d_1)$ and $E(d_2)$ decrease is determined by the index pairs that are used for the transmission as well as the index assignment itself. The reason is that the exponential rate of decrease of the extent of each side cell is determined by the spread of its index, which in turn is determined by the index assignment. For each i and $p = 1, 2$, let the spread $s_p(i)$ be $\Theta(2^{2Rb})$ for some b, $0 \leq b \leq (1+a)/2$. Then the extent of every cell of the first side partition is $\Theta(2^{-R(1+a-2b)})$. This implies that the side MSE's can decrease at a rate no greater than $\Theta(2^{-2(1+a-2b)R})$. The rate distortion results imply that $1 + a - 2b \leq 1 - a$ which in turn implies that $b \geq a$. Thus rate distortion theory gives us the minimum rate of growth of the spread that any index assignment can achieve. Our objective, in searching for a good set of index pairs and an associated index assignment is to find one for which the spread[4] $s_p(i)$ is minimized, assuming that it is constant with respect to i and p.

We first address the issue of selecting a set $\mathcal{C}$ consisting of $N = 2^{2R(1+a)}$ index pairs. Assume that the index pairs $(1,1), (2,2), \ldots, (\sqrt{M}, \sqrt{M})$ are always among the index pairs that will be transmitted and that these index pairs will be assigned to central cells from the left to the right. Additional index pairs must first be selected so that their number is $\Theta(2^{2R(1+a)})$. Now, if we had a choice between adding $(1,2)$ and $(1, \sqrt{M})$ to the set of index pairs, we would prefer $(1,2)$ since by assigning index pairs to central cells in the order $(1,1), (1,2), (2,2), (3,3), \ldots, (\sqrt{M}, \sqrt{M})$ the maximum spread over all cells of each side partition would be 2. In contrast, if we had used the index pair $(1, \sqrt{M})$, the maximum spread could never be smaller than $\lceil \sqrt{M}/2 \rceil + 1$. If we think of an index pair as identifying an element in a $\sqrt{M} \times \sqrt{M}$ matrix, it becomes clear that we should exhaust all the elements that lie on a diagonal that lies closer[5] to the main diagonal before moving to a diagonal that lies further away from the main diagonal.

We now consider the index assignment problem. This can be thought of as a problem of finding a scanning sequence for a selected set of index pairs that results in a small spread of each cell of each side partition. We consider a set of index pairs constructed from those that lie on the main diagonal and on the $2k$ diagonals closest to the main diagonal. Two index assignments are first obtained, each of which is composed of two types of basic building blocks.

---

[4]Henceforth we will use "spread" to denote the common value of $s_p(i)$.

[5]A diagonal consisting of elements $(i, i+m)$, $i \in \mathbb{Z}$ is closer to the main diagonal than the diagonal consisting of index pairs $(i, i+n)$, $i \in \mathbb{Z}$ if $|m| < |n|$.

The first of the index assignments, referred to as the nested index assignment, is composed of two types of building blocks. We refer to these building blocks as the East scan (E) and the South scan (S). Each building block begins on a main diagonal element, say (i,i), visits every element of the ith row with column index no smaller than i and every element of the ith column with row index no smaller than i. More precisely, define E_i and S_i as, respectively, the sequence of index pairs $(i,i),(i,i+1),(i+1,i),(i,i+2),(i+2,i),\ldots,(i,i+k),(i+k,i)$ and $(i,i),(i+1,i),(i,i+1),(i+2,i),(i,i+2),\ldots,(i+k,i),(i,i+k)$. We use the notation $(E_i)_{i=l}^{m}$ for the sequence $E_lE_{l+1}\ldots E_m$ with the understanding that if $l>m$, then the scan is not performed. For $k>0$, define the nested index assignment to be the sequence

$$\left((E_i)_{i=(2p)k}^{(2p+1)k-1}(S_i)_{i=(2p+1)k}^{(2p+2)k-1}\right)_p. \tag{3.1}$$

The second index assignment, referred to as the linear assignment is composed of building blocks referred to as the U-scan and the D-scan. For $j=2i$, i an integer, define U_j and D_j as the sequence of index pairs $(i+\lfloor k/2\rfloor,i-\lfloor k/2\rfloor),(i+\lfloor k/2\rfloor-1,i-\lfloor k/2\rfloor+1),\ldots,(i-\lfloor k/2\rfloor,i+\lfloor k/2\rfloor)$ and $(i-\lfloor k/2\rfloor,i+\lfloor k/2\rfloor),(i-\lfloor k/2\rfloor+1,i+\lfloor k/2\rfloor-1),\ldots,(i+\lfloor k/2\rfloor,i-\lfloor k/2\rfloor)$, respectively. For $j=2i+1$, i an integer, define U_j and D_j by $(i+1+\lfloor(k-1)/2\rfloor,i-\lfloor(k-1)/2\rfloor),(i+\lfloor(k-1)/2\rfloor,i-\lfloor(k-1)/2\rfloor+1),\ldots,(i-\lfloor(k-1)/2\rfloor,i+1+\lfloor(k-1)/2\rfloor)$ and $(i-\lfloor(k-1)/2\rfloor,i+1+\lfloor(k-1)/2\rfloor),(i-\lfloor(k-1)/2\rfloor+1,i+\lfloor(k-1)/2\rfloor),\ldots,(i+1+\lfloor(k-1)/2\rfloor,i-\lfloor(k-1)/2\rfloor)$, respectively. For $k>0$, define the linear index assignment as the sequence of index pairs

$$\left((U_j)_{j=(2k)(2p)}^{(2k)(2p+1)-1}(D_j)_{j=(2k)(2p+1)}^{(2k)(2p+2)-1}\right)_p. \tag{3.2}$$

It is easily verified that both index assignments result in a spread for each side cell that is a constant and is given by $2k^2+k+1$. We now show that either of these index assignments can be used to achieve side and central MSE's that decay at the exponential rates that are predicted by the rate distortion results presented in Section 2. Note that $R_p=(\log_2 M)/2$, $p=1,2$. The number of central cells is given by $(2k+1)\sqrt{M}-k(k+1)$ and the spread of each side cell is $2k^2+k+1$. Assuming that each central cell is $\Theta(1/((2k+1)\sqrt{M}-k(k+1)))$ and setting $M=k^{2n}$, where $n\geq 1$ is an integer, it follows that $E(d_0)$ is $\Theta(2^{-2R(1+1/n)})$ and that $E(d_1)$ and $E(d_2)$ are $\Theta(2^{-2R(1-1/n)})$. For $n=1$, $E(d_0)$ will decrease at the maximum exponential rate of $2R$ whereas $E(d_1)$ and $E(d_2)$ exhibit zero decay rates. For $n=\infty$, $E(d_0)$, $E(d_1)$ and $E(d_2)$ all decay at the same exponential rate of R. Intermediate rates can be obtained by selecting a value of n greater that 1. Note that the sum of the rates at which $E(d_0)$ and $E(d_1)$ decay is always equal to $-4R$, hence the optimum decay rates predicted by rate distortion theory are obtained.

We have not found an index assignment that attains a spread smaller than $2k^2+k+1$. It remains to be shown whether $2k^2+k+1$ is the minimum attainable spread.

4. Summary

We have considered the design of multiple description scalar quantizers. It is shown that the solution of an index assignment problem is a critical part of the design. Motivated by results from information theory, we have studied the behavior of the MDSQ's at high rates and have developed a simple criterion for index assignment selection. Two index assignments have been presented.

References

1. D. G. Luenberger, *Linear and Nonlinear Programming.* Reading, Massachusetts: Addison Wesley, second ed., 1984.
2. V. A. Vaishampayan, "Design of multiple description scalar quantizers," *IEEE Trans. Inform. Theory*, to appear, May 1993.
3. A. A. El Gamal and T. M. Cover, "Achievable rates for multiple descriptions," *IEEE Trans. Inform. Th.*, vol. IT-28, pp. 851–857, November 1982.
4. L. Ozarow, "On a source coding problem with two channels and three receivers," *Bell Syst. Tech. J.*, vol. 59, pp. 1909–1921, December 1980.
5. H. S. Wilf, *Algorithms and Complexity.* Englewood Cliffs, New Jersey: Prentice Hall, 1986.
6. S. P. Lloyd, "Least squares quantization in PCM," *IEEE Trans. Inform. Theory*, vol. IT-28, pp. 129–137, March 1982.

Department of Electrical Engineering, Texas A&M University, College Station, TX 77843

E-mail address: vinay@ee.tamu.edu

DIMACS Series in Discrete Mathematics
and Theoretical Computer Science
Volume **14**, 1993

Structured Vector Quantizers as Generalized Product Codes

WAI-YIP CHAN AND ALLEN GERSHO

January 10, 1993

ABSTRACT. Structured vector quantization (VQ) can outperform unstructured VQ in terms of performance-complexity tradeoff. We explore the design of structured VQ under a *generalized product code* (GPC) model which subsumes and extends many existing VQ structures. Associated with the model are: (i) algorithms that enable the trading of encoding complexity and, independently, storage complexity with distortion; (ii) an algorithm paradigm for joint-codebook optimization. These are illustrated by the design of summation product codes.

Introduction

The exponential complexity of vector quantization (VQ) limits the performance achievable in practice. The poor performance-complexity tradeoff of optimal unstructured VQ can be improved by using structured but suboptimal VQ. This means that for a given complexity, better performance can be achieved with structured than unstructured VQ. Two approaches to structured VQ can be identified.

In the *assisted search* approach, the decoder uses the index received from the encoder to address a codebook and emits the code vector associated with the index as the reproduction. The encoder generates the index with the assistance of an auxiliary data structure thereby incurring greatly reduced computation complexity. In one scenario, the data structure enables the encoder to eliminate a large number of code vectors from consideration (see, e.g., [**1**]). In another scenario, the data structure is that of a product code vector quantizer (described

---

1991 *Mathematics Subject Classification.* Primary 94A29.
This work was supported in part by the National Science Foundation, the State of California MICRO program, Rockwell International Corporation, Compression Labs, Inc., Eastman Kodak Company, and the Natural Sciences and Research Council of Canada.

next) whose Cartesian-product indexes are mapped one-to-one or many-to-one to the decoder reproductions (see, e.g., [**2**]). The major drawback of the assisted search approach is that the storage complexity of the encoder is greater than that in unstructured VQ; this complexity may be intractable for sufficiently high rate or large vector dimension.

The *product code* VQ approach involves using multiple *feature codebooks*. The decoder computes or *synthesizes* a reproduction using the indexes supplied by the encoder to address the feature codebooks. The product code VQ resolves the storage complexity problem of the assisted search approach. We define product code VQ next and show how it can achieve a wide range of performance complexity tradeoff. Our product code model is a generalization of Sabin and Gray's [**3**] product code VQ.

Generalized Product Codes

Suppose a source of random vectors $\mathbf{X}$ of dimension k is to be encoded at a rate of r bits per vector component. In unstructured VQ, encoding is accomplished using a single codebook populated with 2^{kr} codewords. On the other hand, a product code (Figure 1) represents a source vector $\mathbf{x}$ by a set of $s > 1$

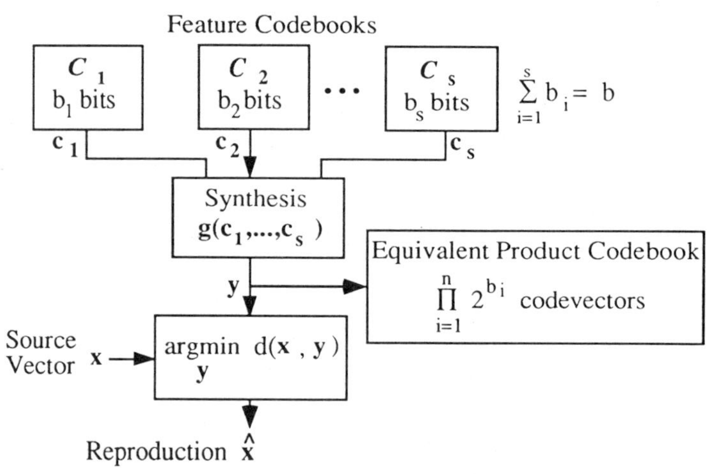

FIGURE 1. The Structure of a Product Code.

features $\mathbf{f}_1, \ldots, \mathbf{f}_s$, where feature $\mathbf{f}_i$, $i = 1, \ldots, s$, may be a scalar or a vector of dimension k_i. The $b = kr$ bits available to encode a source vector are allocated among the s features, with b_i bits for feature $\mathbf{f}_i$ such that $\sum_{i=1}^{s} b_i = b$. Feature $\mathbf{f}_i$ is encoded using a *feature codebook* C_i, containing 2^{b_i} *feature code vectors* $\mathbf{c}_{i,n}$, $n = 1, \ldots, 2^{b_i}$. With each feature $\mathbf{f}_i$ quantized to $\hat{\mathbf{f}}_i = \mathbf{c}_{i,n^*}$ (henceforth quantized entities are annotated with the "hat" symbol), a reproduction $\hat{\mathbf{x}}$ of $\mathbf{x}$ can be synthesized: $\hat{\mathbf{x}} = \mathbf{g}(\hat{\mathbf{f}}_1, \ldots \hat{\mathbf{f}}_s)$ where $\mathbf{g}$ is the *synthesis map*. The set of all 2^b Cartesian products of the feature code vectors can be used to synthesize

2^b reproductions to populate an *equivalent product codebook.* In a well-formed product code, the 2^b reproductions should be distinct from each other. For a given product code, distortion is minimized if the encoder searches over the entire equivalent product codebook to find a reproduction to minimize the *overall distortion measure* $d(\mathbf{x}, \hat{\mathbf{x}})$ of the product code; this is called a *full-search* or *joint-search product code.* (Unless otherwise noted, we assume d to be the mean squared error (MSE) distortion in the sequel.) In comparison with its unstructured VQ counterpart, a joint-search product code incurs the same order of encoding complexity, saves on codebook storage, and pays a penalty in rate-distortion performance. Not offering any reduction in the encoding complexity, joint-search product codes are not likely to be an attractive alternative to unstructured VQ in most realistic applications.

In a *sequential-search product code*, an ordering is imposed on the s features. Encoding of the features is performed in the prescribed order in s stages, using in the i-th stage a *feature extraction rule* or *feature analysis rule* $\mathbf{f}_i = h_i(\mathbf{x}, \hat{\mathbf{f}}_1, \ldots \hat{\mathbf{f}}_{i-1})$, and a *feature distortion measure* $d_i(\mathbf{f}_i, \hat{\mathbf{f}}_i)$, $i = 1, \ldots, s$. In general, the feature $\mathbf{f}_i$ of stage i depends on the input vector $\mathbf{x}$ as well as the quantized features from prior stages. With respect to the feature extraction rules, the synthesis map may have the *perfect reconstruction* property, $\mathbf{x} = \mathbf{g}(\mathbf{f}_1, \ldots \mathbf{f}_s)$ when the features are not quantized. A variation of the sequential minimization above involves using the overall distortion measure as the feature distortion measure in the last stage. The distortion $d(\mathbf{x}, \mathbf{g}(\hat{\mathbf{f}}_1, \ldots \hat{\mathbf{f}}_{s-1}, \mathbf{c}_{s,n}))$ is minimized over the last feature codebook $\mathcal{C}_s = \{\mathbf{c}_{s,n}, n = 1, \ldots, 2^{b_s}\}$. This variation allows the last stage to "compensate" somewhat for the suboptimality of sequential search with respect to the overall distortion.

A generalized product code (GPC) (Figure 2) is a sequential-search product code whose features $\mathbf{f}_i$, $i = 2, \ldots, s$ may each have multiple, say M_i, codebooks $\mathcal{C}_{i,1}, \ldots, \mathcal{C}_{i,M_i}$, all of the same size 2^{b_i}. The first feature $\mathbf{f}_1$ however has only one codebook, i.e. $M_1 = 1$. The number of codebooks in each stage is called the codebook *fanout.* Associated with every feature code vector, say the l-th code vector of codebook $\mathcal{C}_{i,j}$, $i = 1, \ldots, s-1$, $j = 1, \ldots, M_i$, is a *codebook pointer* $\mu_{i,j,l}$, $l = 1, \ldots, 2^{b_i}$ with a value equal to the index of one of the codebooks of feature $\mathbf{f}_{i+1}$, i.e. the pointer points to a codebook in the next stage. When the number of codebooks M_i for feature $\mathbf{f}_i$, $i = 2, \ldots, s$ is less than the total number of code vectors $M_{i-1} * 2^{b_{i-1}}$ for the preceding feature $\mathbf{f}_{i-1}$, some of the pointers $\mu_{i-1,j,l}$, $j = 1, \ldots, M_{i-1}$, $l = 1, \ldots, 2^{b_{i-1}}$ will have identical values; in this case, we say that the M_i codebooks of feature $\mathbf{f}_i$ are *shared* by the $M_{i-1} * 2^{b_{i-1}}$ *conditional feature sources* induced by the $M_{i-1} * 2^{b_{i-1}}$ decisions of the preceding stage. A stage in which no feature codebook is shared is said to have "maximum fanout."

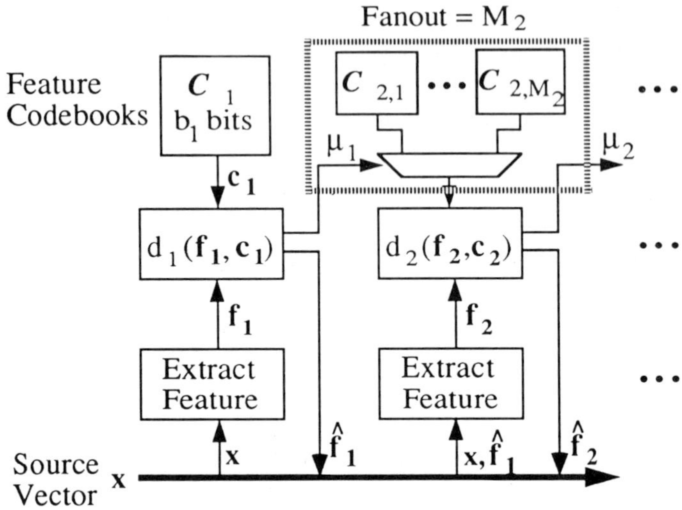

FIGURE 2. The Encoder Structure of a Generalized Product Code.

Trellis Structure and Complexity

By virtue of the above sequential search, fanout enhanced structure, the feature codebooks of a GPC can be laid out as a trellis in which the codebooks of each feature form the nodes in one stage and the codebook pointers form the directed links connecting the nodes between two successive stages. With the trellis structure, the recipe for achieving a range of tradeoff between distortion performance and encoding complexity follows naturally: the class of dynamic-programming tree search algorithms (e.g. the Viterbi algorithm [**4**] and the M-algorithm [**5**]). With the M-algorithm, for instance, the encoding complexity is determined by the number of *survivors* kept in the course of a sequential search. The storage complexity can also be traded with distortion performance by adjusting the codebook fanout. One means to designing the shared codebooks in a given stage for a given fanout is to perform *source clustering* using a generalized form of the generalized Lloyd algorithm, called the *constrained storage VQ* (CSVQ) algorithm [**6**]. For a given bit allocation among the features, distortion performance can be traded with either encoding and/or codebook storage complexity; the two complexity parameters can be varied independently. The range of variation is between approximately $\sum_{i=1}^{s} 2^{b_i}$ and $\prod_{i=1}^{s} 2^{b_i} = 2^b$.

In practice, the features derived from audio or visual signals are not likely to be independent. The trellis structure provides for the exploitation of the conditional information between the features as a function of codebook storage cost. In sequential search, the structure exploits the conditional or "predictive" information furnished by the features quantized thus far. Examples of the maximum fanout structure are Wilson's "unrestricted polar quantizer" [**7**] and the well known tree-structured VQ (TSVQ) [**8**]. TSVQ is equivalent to a multi-stage VQ (MSVQ) [**9**] with maximum fanout and "path-dependent" feature codebooks [**10**]; conversely, MSVQ is equivalent to a TSVQ with non-path-dependent feature codebooks in each stage so that the maximum fanout of the TSVQ can be reduced to unity. TSVQ and MSVQ can be unified by allowing a decoder which synthesizes a reproduction by summing together feature code vectors of the same dimension, i.e. TSVQ and MSVQ can be admitted into a family of *summation product codes* (SPC). Thus, coding structures with the same synthesis functional form may be grouped into one family. Structures within the same family can be compared on the basis of their relative restrictiveness or generality and hence their relative performance-complexity characteristics. For instance, the "split VQ" or *concatenation product code* can be admitted into the SPC family for the quantization of speech linear prediction parameters [**11**]. Both conventional TSVQ and MSVQ maintain only one survivor in the course of their sequential search. Significant performance improvements can be obtained with moderate number of survivors [**12**] and moderate codebook fanout [**13**]

Companded Codebook Sharing

From asymptotic quantization theory [**14**] [**15**] [**16**], it can be argued that when the first stage of an MSVQ is operating in a high-rate region, the probability distributions of the conditional residual sources in the second stage are all similar in shape but differing from each other by rotation and scaling (assuming that the first stage has no overload distortion). The CSVQ algorithm provides one means for these sources to share a given number of codebooks without directly measuring the similarity between their probability distributions. Makhoul *et al.* [**17**], on the other hand, suggested employing a linear transform tailored to each source. Lee *et al.* [**16**] demonstrated the asymptotic high-rate optimality of this procedure. It is possible that these methods, devised specifically for MSVQ and TSVQ and extendable to SPCs in general, may be more efficient than the CSVQ method for certain rate regions. Nevertheless, CSVQ is generally applicable to fanout control in the design of GPCs. We now extend the codebook sharing paradigm to incorporate simple companding schemes and thereby admitting the source transformation schemes of Makhoul *et al.* and Lee *et al.* into the GPC model.

Suppose that in a stage of a GPC, there are N conditional feature sources sharing M feature codebooks, $M < N$. Associated with the j-th source is a codebook pointer $\mu(j)$, $j \in \{1, \dots, N\}$, and a parametric *expandor function* $\mathbf{u}_j$ with T parameters $\rho_{j,1}, \dots, \rho_{j,T}$ which are not necessarily scalars. The term "expandor function" is borrowed from companding. The expanded code vectors $\{\mathbf{v}_n, n = 1, \dots, 2^{b_i}\}$ for encoding the j-th source are obtained as $\mathbf{v}_n = \mathbf{u}_j(\mathbf{c}_{i,\mu(j),n}, \rho_{j,1}, \dots, \rho_{j,T})$ where $\{\mathbf{c}_{i,\mu(j),n}, n = 1, \dots, 2^{b_i}\}$ constitute the feature codebook whose address is given by the value of pointer $\mu(j)$. The expandor function $\mathbf{u}_j$ can be regarded as the synthesis function of a degenerate product code that has only one feature. The desired benefit from using $\mathbf{u}_j$ is to enhance the matching between the j-th source and its feature codebook. We call the above codebook sharing arrangement *companding CSVQ*.

Simple expandor functions are scaling, translation, and rotation, whose parameters are respectively a scalar gain, a vector offset, and a unitary matrix. In the cases of scaling and translation, it is rather straightforward to modify the CSVQ algorithm to jointly design the shared codebooks, the pointers, and the expandor parameters [**18**]. The simplest case of a scaling expandor function has been applied to enhance the sharing of codebooks in multistage VQ; moderate improvement in storage efficiency was obtained [**10**]. A novel application of the scaling scheme: is the design of TSVQ codebooks entirely stripped of code vectors; instead, the tree nodes are populated with only gain parameters and residual-codebook pointers [**19**]. Residual codebooks are stored separately in a library for sharing between all levels of the tree. A $4:1$ storage saving has been obtained with virtually no loss in rate-distortion performance.

Joint Codebook Design

The term "product code VQ" is sometimes associated with the "shape-gain VQ" (SGVQ) of Sabin and Gray [**3**]. In SGVQ, the synthesis function plays a key role in the derivation of the feature extraction rules and feature distortion measures [**12**]. The original derivation in Sabin and Gray [**3**] is integral to the construction of their training algorithm for designing the feature codebooks. Given a training set and initial "shape" and "gain" feature codebooks, the algorithm iteratively and alternately updates the codebooks to minimize the overall MSE distortion. We call this codebook design approach the *sequential-update joint-codebook optimization method* or *sequential update method* for short. Inspired by this method, a joint design algorithm as an enhancement over the conventional stage-by-stage design for MSVQ was recently proposed [**20**].

We have explored a joint-codebook optimization paradigm that can be generally applied to the training of feature codebooks. To this end, we applied the equivalent product codebook concept to formulate a *joint-update joint-codebook optimization paradigm*, or *joint update paradigm* for short [**18**] [**21**]. The paradigm algorithm retains the basic framework of the generalized Lloyd algorithm (GLA): given a training set and initial feature codebooks, the feature codebooks are updated to alternately optimize the encoder and decoder until a convergence criterion is satisfied. The departure point from GLA is posed by the multiple-feature-codebook structure. An unstructured VQ codebook stores one code vector for each region of the encoder partition, resulting in a one-to-one correspondence between the encoder partition regions and the code vectors. The instrumentation of the nearest neighbor and centroid conditions in the GLA to respectively optimize the encoder and the decoder is very simple; each codeword is uniquely associated with one region and one centroid. For GPCs, such an association can be effected through the equivalent product codebook. Given any encoder partition, suboptimal or otherwise, the decoder can generate a reproduction for each partition region to minimize the overall distortion. The set of all such conditionally (for a given encoder partition) optimal reproductions, one for each of the 2^b regions, constitute a *reference product codebook* or *optimal synthesis codebook*, the best codebook the decoder could use. When the decoder is restricted to storing only the feature codebooks, however, these codebooks should have an equivalent product codebook which best approximates the reference codebook in the sense of minimizing the overall distortion (Figure 3). This provides the key to updating the feature codebooks in the decoder for a given encoder partition.

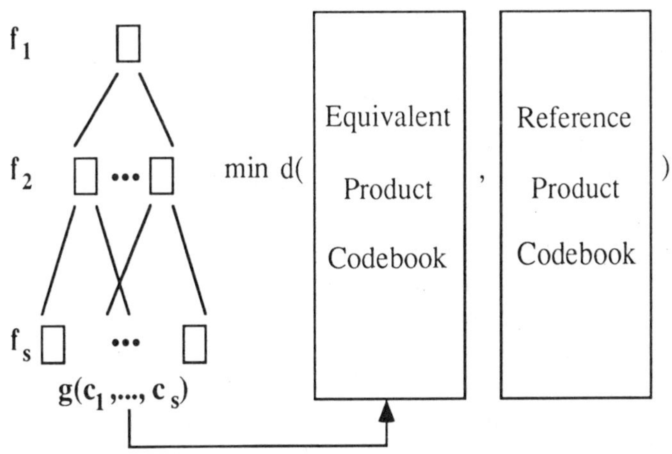

FIGURE 3. Solving for the feature code vectors by minimizing the distortion between the reference and equivalent product codebook.

It can be shown that the overall distortion for a given encoder partition can be written as a sum of two terms [**18**], a minimum distortion term incurred when the decoder uses the reference product codebook, and an *excess distortion* term incurred when the decoder synthesizes the reproductions from the feature codebooks. The excess distortion is a penalty paid for the savings in storage obtained by storing feature codebooks instead of the reference product codebook in the decoder. The key to the joint update paradigm is in setting up a system of 2^b *synthesis equations* to solve for the feature (vector) variables to minimize the excess distortion. This is in general difficult if not infeasible for large b, more so if the synthesis function is non-linear. However, for MSVQ and other SPC variants, the linear synthesis function together with the MSE criterion can be exploited to greatly reduce the system size [**18**]. For MSVQ with s stages and unity fanout, joint codebook update involves solving k weighted linear least-square systems, each with $\sum_{i=1}^{s} 2^{b_i}$ scalar variables, i.e. the k components of the feature code vectors are decoupled by virtue of the unweighted MSE criterion.

The reference product codebook embodies a notion of "optimal synthesis." Once the encoder has identified the regions $\{\mathcal{R}_1, \ldots, \mathcal{R}_s\}$ in the respective feature vector spaces into which the features of a given source vector $\mathbf{x}$ fall, the best reproduction $\hat{\mathbf{x}}$ the decoder can emit to minimize the MSE distortion is the mean of the source vector $\mathbf{X}$ conditioned on the feature regions: $\hat{\mathbf{x}} = E\{\mathbf{X} \mid \mathcal{R}_1, \ldots, \mathcal{R}_s\}$ [**22**]. Since a joint distribution between the source vector and its features is usually not available analytically, the conditional means may be stored as a table with 2^b entries. When the overall distortion is MSE, the conditional means constitute the reference product codebook in the joint codebook update paradigm. It follows that if the decoder could afford the storage space, the decoder should store the reference codebook instead of the feature codebooks.

Conclusion

The GPC model was spurred by the need to codify and extend the seemingly great varieties of VQ structures. The GPC model admits most of the existing structured VQ schemes and can guide the development of novel VQ structures. The efficacy of the GPC structure hinges on the exploitation of conditional information accumulated during the course of a sequential search. The cost of the exploitation is in terms of time and space complexity.

We have compiled and devised various general tools for the design of GPC vector quantizers. These tools are: tree/trellis search algorithms, source clustering algorithms, simple companding functions, and codebook training algorithm paradigms. Within the SPC family, we have obtained experimental performance results for the quantization of audio/visual data that attest to the utility and versatility of the GPC model and its tools. The advantage of GPC design is readily extended to the design of structured vector quantizers and signal coders in general.

References

1. D. Y. Cheng and A. Gersho, "A Fast Codebook Search Algorithm for Nearest-Neighbor Pattern Matching," *Proc. Int. Conf. Acoust., Sp., & Sig. Proc.*, pp. 265-268, Tokyo, April 1986.
2. N. Moayeri, D. L. Neuhoff and W. E. Stark, "Fine-Coarse Vector Quantization," *IEEE Trans. Acoust., Sp., & Sig. Proc.*, pp. 1503-1515, July 1991.
3. M. J. Sabin and R. M. Gray, "Product Code Vector Quantizers for Waveform and Voice Coding," *IEEE Trans. Acoust., Sp., & Sig. Proc.*, vol. ASSP-32, pp. 474-488, June 1984.
4. A. J. Viterbi and J. K. Omura, *Principles of Digital Communication and Coding*, McGraw-Hill, 1979.
5. J. B. Anderson and S. Mohan, "Sequential Coding Algorithms: A Survey and Cost Analysis," *IEEE Trans. Comm.*, vol. COM-32, no. 2, pp. 169-176, February 1984.
6. W. Y. Chan and A. Gersho, "Constrained Storage Quantization of Multiple Vector Sources by Codebook Sharing," *IEEE Trans. Comm.*, vol. COM-39, no. 1, pp. 11-13,

Jan. 1991.

7. S. G. Wilson, "Magnitude/Phase Quantization of Independent Gaussian Variates," *IEEE Trans. Comm.*, pp. 1924-1929, Nov. 1980.
8. A. Buzo, A. H. Gray, Jr., R. M. Gray and J. D. Markel, "Speech Coding Based Upon Vector Quantization," *IEEE Trans. Acoust., Sp., & Sig. Proc.*, vol. ASSP-28, pp. 562-574, Oct. 1980.
9. B. H. Juang and A. H. Gray, Jr., "Multiple Stage Vector Quantization for Speech Coding," *Proc. Int. Conf. Acoust., Sp., & Sig. Proc.*, pp. 597-600, Paris, April 1982.
10. W. Y. Chan and A. Gersho, "Enhanced Multistage Vector Quantization with Constrained Storage," *Proc. 24th Asilomar Conf. Cir., Sys., & Comp.*, pp. 659-663, Nov. 1990.
11. E. Paksoy, W. Y. Chan and A. Gersho, "Vector Quantization of Speech LSF Parameters with Generalized Product Codes," *Proc. Intl. Conf. Spoken Language Processing*, pp. 33-36, Banff, Canada, Oct. 1992.
12. W. Y. Chan, "The Design of Generalized Product Code Vector Quantizers," *Proc. Int. Conf. Acoust., Sp., & Sig. Proc.*, pp. III-389-392, San Francisco, March 1992.
13. W. Y. Chan and A. Gersho, "Constrained-Storage Vector Quantization in High Fidelity Audio Transform Coding," *Proc. Int. Conf. Acoust., Sp., & Sig. Proc.*, pp. 3597-3600, Toronto, May 1991.
14. A. Gersho, "Asymptotically Optimal Block Quantization," *IEEE Trans. Info. Th.*, vol. IT-25, pp. 373-380, July 1979.
15. R. M. Gray, *Source Coding Theory*, Kluwer Academic Publishers, 1990.
16. D. H. Lee, D. L. Neuhoff and K. K. Paliwal, "Cell-Conditioned Multistage Vector Quantization," *Proc. Int. Conf. Acoust., Sp., & Sig. Proc.*, pp. 653-656, Toronto, May 1991.
17. J. Makhoul, S. Roucos and H. Gish, "Vector Quantization in Speech Coding," *Proc. IEEE*, vol. 73, no. 11, pp. 1551-1587, November 1985.
18. W. Y. Chan and A. Gersho, "Generalized Product Code Vector Quantization," in preparation.
19. W. Y. Chan and A. Gersho, "Source Clustering for Codebook Compression," *Proc. Int. Symp. Info. Th.*, San Antonio, Texas, January 1993.
20. W. Y. Chan, S. Gupta and A. Gersho, "Enhanced Multistage Vector Quantization by Joint Codebook Design," *IEEE Trans. Comm.*, vol. COM-40, no. 11, pp. 1693-1697, Nov. 1992.
21. W. Y. Chan, "Product Code Vector Quantization Methods with Application to High Fidelity Audio Coding," PhD thesis, University of California, Santa Barbara, Dec. 1991.
22. A. Gersho, "Optimal Nonlinear Interpolative Vector Quantization," *IEEE Trans. Comm.*, vol. COM-38, no. 9, pp. 1285-1287, Sep. 1990.

Department of Electrical Engineering, McGill University, Montreal, Canada H3A 2A7

E-mail address: chan@polaris.ee.mcgill.ca

Department of Electrical and Computer Engineering, University of California, Santa Barbara, CA 93106

E-mail address: gersho@ece.ucsb.edu

DIMACS Series in Discrete Mathematics
and Theoretical Computer Science
Volume **14**, 1993

A New Construction of Trellis-Coded Quantizers

RENÉ J. VAN DER VLEUTEN AND JOS H. WEBER

November 18, 1992

ABSTRACT. A new construction of trellis-coded quantizers (TCQs) is proposed and the performance of the new TCQs is determined for the uniform, Gaussian, and Laplacian probability density functions (PDFs).

For the Gaussian and Laplacian PDFs, the new TCQs at 1, 2, and 3 b/symbol improve upon all previously published results (including those of Marcellin and Fischer [**1**]). For the uniform PDF, the performances of the new TCQs equal those of [**1**].

1. Introduction

Vector quantization in its basic form is a straightforward extension of the one-dimensional scalar quantization or PCM. The main disadvantage of this form of vector quantization is that its complexity increases exponentially with increasing vector dimension. Therefore, variations of vector quantization which try to reduce the amount of computation have been developed. They are based on a limited search of the codebook and corresponding codebook design algorithms.

One of these variations is known as *trellis waveform coding* [**2**], a proven technique for source coding with a long history. The encoder is based upon a codebook and a finite-state machine, the state of which specifies the codebook element which is used to represent the input symbol. Investigating all allowed sequences of codebook elements, the encoder finds the sequence that minimizes the reconstruction error variance. The optimal algorithm for this search is the Viterbi algorithm [**3**].

Marcellin and Fischer [**1**] recognized that trellis waveform coding can be improved by a technique which they call *trellis-coded quantization.* It is similar to trellis waveform coding, but, instead of a single codebook element, the finite-state machine in this case specifies a **set** of codebook elements. The encoder now

1991 *Mathematics Subject Classification.* Primary 94A29.

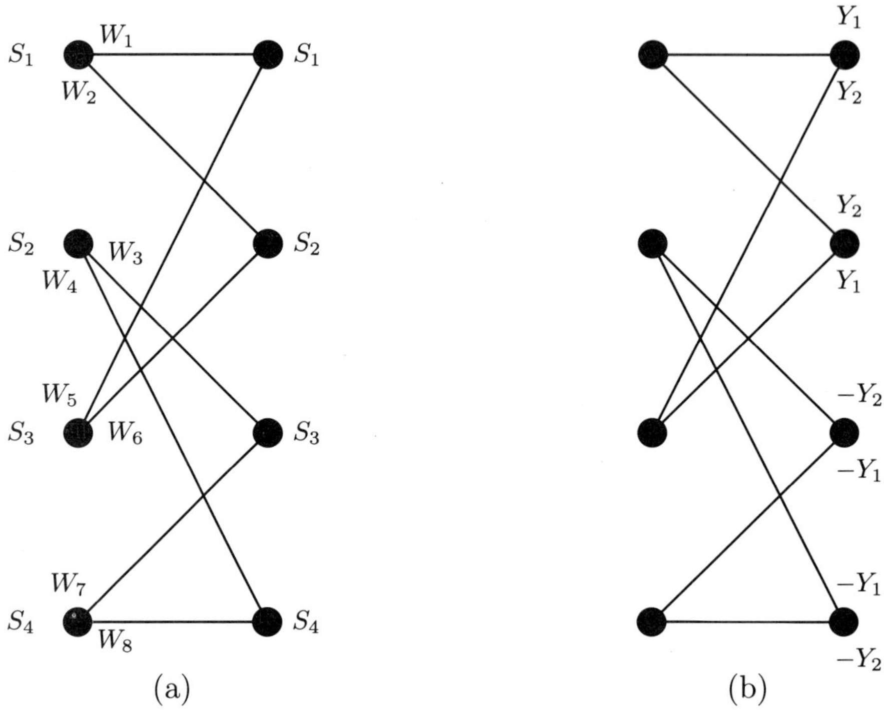

FIGURE 1. Trellis diagram of a four-state TCQ with two branches entering and leaving each state: (a) the states are numbered S_l, $1 \leq l \leq 4$; the branches have sets of representation symbols W_k, $1 \leq k \leq 8$, and (b) example of the proposed construction.

investigates all allowed sequences of sets of codebook elements, selecting from each set the codebook element that minimizes the reconstruction error variance.

Recently, we proposed a new construction of trellis-waveform coders for the rate of 1 b/symbol [**4, 5**]. Here we extend the construction to trellis-coded quantization. The new construction produces trellis-coded quantizers (TCQs) which have performances equal or superior to the TCQs designed in [**1**]. It is also simpler and more general than that of [**1**], because it does not make use of convolutional codes.

2. The new construction

Consider a TCQ having 2^ν states S_k, $1 \leq k \leq 2^\nu$, with two branches entering and leaving each state. The branch from state $S_{\lceil \frac{k}{2} \rceil}$ to state S_k is assigned the set W_k and the branch from state $S_{\lceil \frac{k}{2} \rceil + 2^{\nu-1}}$ to state S_k is assigned the set W_{k+2^ν}, where $\lceil x \rceil$ denotes the smallest integer not less than x. For quantizing at R b/symbol ($R = 1, 2, \dots$), each set contains 2^{R-1} representation symbols. As an example, in Figure 1(a) a four-state trellis is shown with its branch values

W_k and states S_l.

For the proposed construction, the mapping of the sets of representation symbols onto the branches follows a regular and simple rule, which can formally be specified as follows. For the 2^ν-state TCQ ($\nu > 1$) using 2^ν sets of representation symbols Y_m and $-Y_m$ for $1 \leq m \leq 2^{\nu-1}$, the sets are mapped onto the trellis according to

(2.1)
$$W_m = W_{m-1+2(m \bmod 2)+2^\nu} = -W_{m+3\cdot 2^{\nu-1}} = -W_{m-1+2(m \bmod 2)+2^{\nu-1}} = Y_m,$$

where W_m denotes the set $\{w_{m,1}; w_{m,2}; \ldots; w_{m,2^{R-1}}\}$ and $-W_m$ is used to denote the set $\{-w_{m,1}; -w_{m,2}; \ldots; -w_{m,2^{R-1}}\}$. Figure 1(b) shows an example of the construction.

To be able to compare the performances of the new TCQs with those of other quantizers, experiments have been performed for the uniform ($\sigma^2 = 4/3$), Gaussian ($\sigma^2 = 1$), and Laplacian ($\sigma^2 = 1$) probability density functions (PDFs).

For the experiments, as in [**1**], a training set of 100 sequences, each consisting of 1000 independent random samples, was used. To optimize the codebook, 100 iterations were performed using an algorithm based on that described in [**6**], but extended for TCQ and adapted to maintain the structure prescribed by (2.1). Representation symbols onto which no input symbols are mapped are updated to zero (the average input value). The initial trellis codebook was chosen deterministically using uniformly spaced levels from the interval $\langle -2, 2 \rangle$. Specifically, the sets Y_m were initialized as:

(2.2)
$$y_{m,i} = \begin{cases} 2 + 2^{2-\nu-R} - m \cdot 2^{3-\nu-R} - (i-1) \cdot 2^{3-R} & \text{if } m \text{ is odd and} \\ 2 + 3 \cdot 2^{2-\nu-R} + 2^{2-R} - m \cdot 2^{3-\nu-R} - i \cdot 2^{3-R} & \text{if } m \text{ is even.} \end{cases}$$

This initialization, contrary to a random initialization, guarantees a certain minimal distance both inside each set and between the sets of the two branches entering or leaving each state. The same initial codebook was used for all PDFs.

The performances of the new TCQs for the Gaussian and Laplacian PDFs are listed in Table 1, Table 2, and Table 3 for $R = 1$, $R = 2$, and $R = 3$, respectively, together with the best results obtained in [**1**] (MF), the Lloyd-Max quantizer performance (LM), and the rate-distortion bound (RD). The results obtained for the uniform PDF are not listed since they are equal to those of [**1**]. For the new TCQs, the 95% confidence intervals of the SNR values correspond to tolerances of no more than 0.01 dB for the Gaussian and 0.02 dB for the Laplacian PDF.

It can be observed that the gains of the new TCQs over those of [**1**] steadily increase as the TCQs get larger. Furthermore, the new TCQs improve upon all previous results found in the literature (as listed in [**1**]). For the Laplacian PDF, the previous best SNRs at $R = 1$, $R = 2$, and $R = 3$ were 5.76 dB, 11.45 dB,

PDF	Quant.	States							LM	RD
		8	16	32	64	128	256	512		
Lapl.	New	4.82	5.16	5.39	5.54	5.69	5.85	5.95	3.01	6.62
Lapl.	MF	4.47	4.92	5.13	5.35	5.49	5.54	—	3.01	6.62
Gauss.	New	5.16	5.30	5.39	5.49	5.56	5.63	5.68	4.40	6.02
Gauss.	MF	5.19	5.27	5.34	5.43	5.52	5.56	—	4.40	6.02

TABLE 1. SNRs (in dB) of the new TCQs compared with the TCQs of [**1**] (MF), the Lloyd-Max quantizer performance (LM), and the rate-distortion bound (RD), at $R = 1$.

PDF	Quant.	States							LM	RD
		8	16	32	64	128	256	512		
Lapl.	New	10.18	10.64	10.98	11.27	11.44	11.65	11.81	7.54	12.66
Lapl.	MF	9.56	10.47	10.73	10.98	11.16	11.22	—	7.54	12.66
Gauss.	New	10.83	11.01	11.14	11.30	11.41	11.50	11.57	9.30	12.04
Gauss.	MF	10.70	10.78	10.85	10.94	10.99	11.04	—	9.30	12.04

TABLE 2. SNRs (in dB) of the new TCQs compared with the TCQs of [**1**] (MF), the Lloyd-Max quantizer performance (LM), and the rate-distortion bound (RD), at $R = 2$.

PDF	Quant.	States						LM	RD
		8	16	32	64	128	256		
Lapl.	New	15.87	16.48	16.90	17.19	17.43	17.57	12.64	18.68
Lapl.	MF	15.00	16.20	16.43	16.79	16.84	16.96	12.64	18.68
Gauss.	New	16.64	16.90	17.11	17.25	17.39	17.43	14.62	18.06
Gauss.	MF	16.33	16.40	16.47	16.56	16.61	16.64	14.62	18.06

TABLE 3. SNRs (in dB) of the new TCQs compared with the TCQs of [**1**] (MF), the Lloyd-Max quantizer performance (LM), and the rate-distortion bound (RD), at $R = 3$.

and 17.20 dB, respectively. For the Gaussian PDF they were 5.56 dB, 11.04 dB, and 16.78 dB.

3. Conclusions

The proposed construction is more general and simpler than that of [**1**] and results in TCQs which have a better performance.

For the Gaussian and Laplacian PDFs, the new TCQs at 1, 2, and 3 b/symbol improve upon all previously published results. For the uniform PDF, the performances of the new TCQs equal those of [**1**].

References

1. M. W. Marcellin and T. R. Fischer, "Trellis coded quantization of memoryless and Gauss-Markov sources," *IEEE Trans. Commun.*, vol. COM-38, pp. 82–93, Jan. 1990.
2. A. Gersho and R. M. Gray, *Vector Quantization and Signal Compression.* Boston: Kluwer Acad. Pub., 1992.
3. G. D. Forney, Jr., "The Viterbi algorithm," *Proc. IEEE*, vol. 61, pp. 268–278, Mar. 1973.
4. R. J. van der Vleuten and J. H. Weber, "A new constructive design method for trellis waveform coders," in *Thirteenth Symp. Inform. Theory in the Benelux*, (Enschede, The Netherlands), pp. 15–22, June 1–2, 1992.
5. R. J. van der Vleuten and J. H. Weber, "A new construction of trellis waveform coders," in *Signal Processing VI: Theories and Applications (EUSIPCO-92)*, (Brussels, Belgium), pp. 1477–1480, Elsevier Sci. Pub., Aug. 24–27, 1992.
6. L. C. Stewart, R. M. Gray, and Y. Linde, "The design of trellis waveform coders," *IEEE Trans. Commun.*, vol. COM-30, pp. 702–710, Apr. 1982.

Delft University of Technology, Department of Electrical Engineering, Information Theory Group, P.O. Box 5031, 2600 GA Delft, The Netherlands

E-mail address: vleuten@et.tudelft.nl, weber@et.tudelft.nl

DIMACS Series in Discrete Mathematics
and Theoretical Computer Science
Volume **14**, 1993

Trellis-Based Scalar-Vector Quantizer for Memoryless Sources

RAJIV LAROIA AND NARIMAN FARVARDIN

March 7, 1993

ABSTRACT. This paper describes a structured vector quantization approach for stationary memoryless sources that combines scalar-vector quantizer (SVQ) ideas (Laroia and Farvardin) with trellis coded quantization (Marcellin and Fischer). The resulting quantizer is called the trellis-based scalar-vector quantizer (TB-SVQ). The SVQ structure allows the TB-SVQ to realize a large boundary gain, while the underlying trellis code enables it to achieve a significant portion of the total granular gain. For large block-lengths and powerful (possibly complex) trellis codes, the TB-SVQ can, in principle, achieve the rate-distortion bound. As indicated by the results obtained here, even for reasonable block-lengths and relatively simple trellis codes, the TB-SVQ outperforms all other reasonable complexity fixed-rate quantizers.

1. Introduction

Vector quantizers represent m-vectors of source samples, enabling the placement of codevectors (reconstruction vectors) in high probability density regions of m-space. For memoryless sources there are three different gains that vector quantizers can realize over uniform scalar quantizers. The first is the *boundary gain* [**1**], [**2**] which, as the name suggests, is realized by selecting an appropriate codebook boundary which ensures that most of the codevectors are placed in the high probability region $\mathcal{R}_m$ as dictated by the asymptotic equipartition principle AEP. In contrast, the uniform scalar quantizer output (in m-dimensions) lies on a cubic lattice bounded by an m-cube. A quantizer that has all its codevectors uniformly distributed in $\mathcal{R}_m$ asymptotically achieves the optimal boundary gain as $m \to \infty$. The second type of gain over uniform scalar quantization is

1991 *Mathematics Subject Classification.* Primary 94A29.

This work was supported in part by National Science Foundation grants NSFD MIP-9109109 and NSFD CDR-85-00108.

the *granular gain* [**1**], [**2**], [**3**] (called the space-filling advantage in [**3**]) that is achieved by having more spherical (assuming squared-error distortion measure) Voronoi regions of codevectors than the m-cubes for uniform scalar quantizers. The boundary and granular gains are realized only by vector quantizers. As noted in [**1**], quantization and transmission are dual problems. The granular gain in quantization is related to the shaping gain [**4**] in transmission and the boundary gain is related to the coding gain in transmission. Finally, there is the *non-uniform density gain* which results from having the codevectors closely spaced in higher probability density regions and farther apart in lower probability density regions of $\mathbb{R}^m$. Note that due to the uniform density nature of the region $\mathcal{R}_m$, this gain disappears in optimally shaped codebooks for a large m.

For 'uniform' (lattice or trellis code based) vector quantizers the granular gain is upper-bounded by 1.423 (1.53 dB) for the squared-error distortion and is independent of the source probability density. The boundary gain is usually larger for most non-uniform sources and is dependent on the source density.

A structured fixed-rate vector quantizer, called the scalar-vector quantizer, was introduced by Laroia and Farvardin in [**5**]. This scalar-vector quantizer (denoted by SVQ) is a vector quantizer derived from a variable-length scalar quantizer and, for a class of useful sources, can (asymptotically in m) achieve optimal boundary gains by placing the codevectors on and inside the region $\mathcal{R}_m$. In addition, the SVQ allows non-uniformly spaced codevectors and hence the possibility of achieving some non-uniform density gain. No granular gain is realized by the SVQ as the underlying grid is rectangular.

The trellis coded quantizer (TCQ) introduced by Marcellin and Fischer in [**6**] is also derived from a scalar quantizer and uses Ungerboeck's idea of coding by set partitioning [**7**] to realize a significant portion of the maximum granular gain of 1.53 dB. This quantizer also realizes some non-uniform density gain by allowing the underlying scalar quantizer to have non-uniformly spaced levels, but makes no explicit attempt to exploit the boundary gain.

In this paper we combine the SVQ idea [**5**] with that of trellis coded quantization [**6**] and propose a new fixed-rate quantizer which we call the trellis-based scalar-vector quantizer (TB-SVQ). The SVQ structure allows the TB-SVQ to achieve a large boundary gain while the underlying trellis code enables it to realize a significant granular gain. In addition, the TB-SVQ could be derived for a non-uniform scalar quantizer resulting in some non-uniform density gain. The TB-SVQ is hence capable of achieving all the three gains described above and performs better than both SVQ and TCQ. For Gaussian and Laplacian sources it also performs better than all (implementable) schemes considered here.

2. The Scalar-Vector Quantizer

The scalar-vector quantizer (SVQ) is a specific kind of vector quantizer in which the codebook structure is derived from a variable-length scalar quantizer

[**5**]. Consider an n-level scalar quantizer $\mathcal{S}$ described in terms of the set of quantization levels $\mathcal{Q} = \{q_1, q_2, \dots, q_n\}$ and the corresponding set of positive integer lengths $\mathcal{L} = \{\ell_1, \ell_2, \dots, \ell_n\}$, where ℓ_i is the length associated with the level q_i, $i \in J_n \equiv \{1, 2, ..., n\}$. These lengths are not required to be the codeword lengths of a uniquely decodable code such as the Huffman code. If each component of an input m-vector (block of m input samples) is separately quantized using $\mathcal{S}$, the quantized vector is in $\mathcal{Q}^m$ which is an m-dimensional grid of n^m points. The codebook $\mathcal{Z}$ of the SVQ $\mathcal{V}$ derived from $\mathcal{S} \equiv (\mathcal{Q}, \mathcal{L})$ is a subset of $\mathcal{Q}^m$. Specifically, if $\mathcal{V}$ is a rate r bits/sample SVQ, a vector in $\mathcal{Q}^m$ is a codevector of $\mathcal{V}$ only if its total length (defined as the sum of the lengths of its components) is no greater than a threshold L, where L is chosen such that the codebook contains no more than 2^{mr} codevectors. A formal definition of the SVQ now follows.

DEFINITION 2.1. An m-dimensional SVQ $\mathcal{V}$ derived from a the variable-length scalar quantizer $\mathcal{S} = (\mathcal{Q}, \mathcal{L})$ is a vector quantizer with a codebook $\mathcal{Z}$ given as,

(2.1)
$$\mathcal{Z} = \{\mathbf{z} \equiv (z_1, z_2, \dots, z_m) \in \mathcal{Q}^m \ : \ \ell_{f(z_1)} + \ell_{f(z_2)} + \cdots + \ell_{f(z_m)} \leq L\} ,$$

where the index function $f(\cdot) : \mathcal{Q} \to J_n$ is defined by,

(2.2)
$$f(q_i) = i, \ i \in J_n .$$

For a rate r bits/sample SVQ, the threshold L is selected as the largest integer such that $card(\mathcal{Z}) \leq 2^{mr}$.

An m-dimensional SVQ $\mathcal{V}$ is completely defined in terms of the triple $(\mathcal{Q}, \mathcal{L}, L)$, i.e., the quantization levels of the scalar quantizer $\mathcal{S}$, the set of lengths associated with these levels and a threshold. It is shown in [**5**] that this simple structure of the SVQ codebook results in fast and efficient algorithms for codebook search and codevector encoding/decoding. Several algorithms for the design of the SVQ are also given in [**5**]. Next we show that by choosing an appropriate set of lengths the SVQ can realize boundary gain.

The AEP dictates that for a Gaussian source an m-sphere bounded codebook asymptotically realizes the optimal boundary gain as m increases. Also, for a given dimension m and rate r, an m-sphere codebook boundary minimizes the overload probability and maximizes the boundary gain [**1**]. An m-sphere bounded cubic lattice based codebook can be expressed as an SVQ codebook by choosing the underlying scalar quantizer $\mathcal{S}$ as a uniform scalar quantizer and defining the length ℓ_i associated with the level q_i as $\ell_i = |q_i|^2$. Similarly, the asymptotically optimal codebook boundary for a Laplacian source is an m-pyramid. The SVQ can accomplish this if the level q_i is assigned a length $\ell_i = |q_i|$.

3. Trellis Coded Quantization (TCQ)

Marcellin and Fischer were the first to apply Ungerboeck's trellis coding ideas to quantization [**6**]. They showed that trellis coded quantization of uniform sources results in higher granular gains for a given complexity than lattice quantization. Trellis coded quantization has also been applied to some non-uniform sources such as Gaussian and Laplacian sources [**6**]. For these sources, the quantization levels are not restricted to (scaled) integers but can have non-uniform spacing, permitting the TCQ to realize some non-uniform density gain. The underlying 'trellis code' hence is no longer a geometrically uniform code [**8**] and we shall call it a non-uniform trellis code. In spite of the fact that no explicit attempt is made to realize the boundary gain, the TCQ performs remarkably well for both Gaussian and Laplacian sources at rates of 3 bits/sample and less [**6**].

4. Trellis-Based Structured Vector Quantizer (TB-SVQ)

Having described the boundary gain property of the SVQ and the granular gain property of the TCQ, the most logical next step is to try and combine these two into a single quantizer that realizes both these gains. We call this quantizer the trellis-based scalar-vector quantizer (TB-SVQ). The TB-SVQ uses the SVQ idea to shape the 'codebook' boundary, but unlike the SVQ the 'codevectors' of the TB-SVQ referred to as code-sequences, do not lie on a rectangular grid but are sequences from a (non-uniform) trellis code[1]. Note that the SVQ as defined in Section II has a finite block-length m while the TB-SVQ code-sequences are vectors in an infinite dimensional sequence space. We will use the term TB-SVQ block-length (or dimension) to refer to the block-length of the underlying SVQ. The TB-SVQ is now defined as follows.

An m-dimensional TB-SVQ is specified by an alphabet (set of quantization levels) $\mathcal{Q} \equiv \{q_1, q_2, \dots, q_{2n}\}$, a corresponding set of lengths $\mathcal{L} \equiv \{\ell_1, \ell_2, \dots, \ell_{2n}\}$ (where ℓ_i is the length of q_i), a threshold L and a trellis code $\mathcal{T}(\mathcal{Q})$ whose branches are labeled with elements in $\mathcal{Q}$. The TB-SVQ 'codebook' is a collection of code-sequences such that every code-sequence $\{c_i\}$ is a sequence from the trellis code $\mathcal{T}(\mathcal{Q})$ with the additional constraint that when $\{c_i\}$ is partitioned into m-vectors (each in $\mathcal{Q}^m$), the total length of each vector is no greater than the threshold L. As before, the total length of a vector is the sum of the lengths of its components.

Unlike a TCQ, the number of quantization levels ($2n$) of a TB-SVQ is not restricted to 2^{r+1}, where r is the quantizer rate in bits/sample. In general, the TB-SVQ has more than 2^{r+1} levels ($n > 2^r$). This additional alphabet expansion is similar to the shaping constellation expansion in transmission [**4**]. If there is no additional alphabet expansion ($n = 2^r$), the TB-SVQ effectively reduces to a

[1] Unless stated otherwise, for the rest of this paper we will assume that the trellis code is one dimensional and has a redundancy of 1 bit/dimension.

TCQ which is analogous to an unshaped trellis-coded constellation.

Given a sequence $\{x_i\}$ of source samples, the quantization operation of the TB-SVQ consists of searching for the code-sequence that is closest to $\{x_i\}$ in some given distortion metric — usually squared error. Later in this section we will describe an algorithm to do the code-sequence search but first we address the problem of encoding and decoding these sequences. It is shown next that by imposing some minor constraints on the TB-SVQ the corresponding algorithms of the SVQ can be used for this purpose. The encoding and decoding algorithms described here are respectively similar to the decoding and encoding algorithms for the SVQ-shaped trellis-coded constellations given in [**9**].

4.1. Encoding and decoding algorithms for the TB-SVQ. A convolutional code based implementation of a trellis code provides a natural mapping from a bit sequence to a trellis sequence and vice versa. This leads to simple encoding and decoding algorithms for the TCQ. Since in general, all trellis sequences are not code-sequences of the TB-SVQ, the task of encoding and decoding for the TB-SVQ is not as straightforward. However, by placing the following two constraints on the TB-SVQ we will show that the corresponding SVQ algorithms can be used for this purpose.

(i) The trellis code $\mathcal{T}(\mathcal{Q})$ must partition the alphabet $\mathcal{Q}$ (containing $2n$ quantization levels) into two subsets $\mathcal{Q}_A$ and $\mathcal{Q}_B$ such that both $\mathcal{Q}_A$ and $\mathcal{Q}_B$ have n levels each and all outgoing transitions from every trellis state are either associated with levels in $\mathcal{Q}_A$ or $\mathcal{Q}_B$ but not both. In other words, the set of allowed outputs in any trellis state is either $\mathcal{Q}_A$ or $\mathcal{Q}_B$. This constraint is satisfied by all of Ungerboeck's trellis codes.

(ii) It should be possible to pair every level a_i in $\mathcal{Q}_A$ with a distinct level b_i in $\mathcal{Q}_B$, such that a_i and b_i have the same length. Let the set of pairs be denoted by $\mathcal{P} \equiv \{\mathbf{P}_1, \mathbf{P}_2, \ldots, \mathbf{P}_n\}$, where $\mathbf{P}_i \equiv (a_i, b_i)$. To every pair $\mathbf{P}_i$, $i \in J_n$, assign a length l_i equal to the length of the level a_i (or b_i). Note that according to the first constraint, given an initial trellis state s_0, any sequence of pairs $\mathbf{X}_0, \mathbf{X}_1, \mathbf{X}_2, \ldots$, where $\mathbf{X}_i \in \mathcal{P}$, can be converted into a unique trellis sequence as follows. The pair $\mathbf{X}_0$ consists of two quantization levels from which we choose the one allowed in state s_0. This changes the state to s_1. From the pair $\mathbf{X}_1$ we choose the level allowed in state s_1 and so on, resulting in a unique trellis sequence.

The m-dimensional SVQ defined by the alphabet $\mathcal{P} = \{\mathbf{P}_1, \mathbf{P}_2, \ldots, \mathbf{P}_n\}$, the corresponding set of lengths $\{l_1, l_2, \ldots, l_n\}$ and a threshold L is called the primary SVQ associated with the TB-SVQ. The codebook of the primary SVQ consists of codevectors in $\mathcal{P}^m$ called primary codevectors. As described above, given an initial trellis state, each primary codevector can be converted into a unique trellis sequence. Having defined the primary SVQ, we now show that the encoding and decoding algorithms of the primary SVQ given in [**5**] can respectively be used to encode and decode the TB-SVQ code-sequences.

The encoding algorithm. This algorithm maps code-sequences to binary bit sequences for the purpose of transmission. Given a code-sequence $\{c_i\}$, partition this sequence into a sequence $\{\mathbf{v}_i\}$ of m-vectors in $\mathcal{Q}^m$. Since $\{c_i\}$ is a code-sequence, each m-vector will have a total length no greater than the threshold L. Because every component of an m-vector $\mathbf{v}_i$ belongs to a unique pair in $\mathcal{P}$, the vector $\mathbf{v}_i$ can be converted into a unique primary codevector. Hence, the given code-sequence $\{c_i\}$ uniquely corresponds to a sequence of primary codevectors. Each primary codevector in this sequence is encoded into mr-bit codewords using the SVQ encoding algorithm given in [**5**], [**9**].

The decoding algorithm. The decoding algorithm maps a sequence of binary bits into a code-sequence. The bit sequence is first partitioned into mr-bit codewords and converted into a sequence of primary codevectors using the SVQ decoding algorithm [**5**], [**9**]. Given that the quantizer started in a known trellis state, this sequence of primary codevectors is converted into a unique code-sequence as already described above.

These encoder and decoder maps along with the set of code-sequences completely specify the TB-SVQ. To quantize a sequence of source samples using this quantizer we need to search through the set of all code-sequences to determine which one best represents the given source sequence. An algorithm to do this follows.

4.2. The code-sequence search algorithm. This is a dynamic programming algorithm that is a generalization of both the codebook search algorithm of SVQ [**5**], and the Viterbi trellis search algorithm of the TCQ [**6**]. Before describing the algorithm we introduce some notation that will be helpful for this purpose.

Consider a ν-state trellis code $\mathcal{T}(\mathcal{Q})$ defined on an alphabet $\mathcal{Q}$ with $2n$ quantization levels. The trellis diagram for this code can be thought of as a ν-state finite-state machine (FSM). In the kth sample interval, the input $\theta_k \in \Theta \equiv \{0, 1, 2, \ldots, n-1\}$ to the FSM chooses its output o_k from one of n quantization levels allowed in the current state $s_k \in \Sigma \equiv \{0, 1, 2, \ldots, \nu - 1\}$ and also determines the state s_{k+1} for the next sample interval. The FSM can be completely described by two functions, the next-state function η and the output function $\mathcal{O}$. The next-state function $\eta(\cdot,\cdot) : \Sigma \times \Theta \to \Sigma$, with $s_{k+1} = \eta(s_k, \theta_k)$ and the output function $\mathcal{O}(\cdot,\cdot) : \Sigma \times \Theta \to \mathcal{Q}$, with $o_k = \mathcal{O}(s_k, \theta_k)$. For all trellis codes of interest, the next-state function η is invertible for a given input θ_i and hence we can define a previous-state function $\mu(\cdot,\cdot) : \Sigma \times \Theta \to \Sigma$, with $s_k = \mu(s_{k+1}, \theta_k)$. The above notation will simplify the presentation of the search algorithm as the details of the trellis code are now captured by the two functions $\mathcal{O}$ and η (or $\mathcal{O}$ and μ).

Let $d(x, y)$ denote the distortion between a source sample x and its reproduction y. We wish to quantize the given source output sequence to the code-sequence that minimizes the average distortion. Partition the source sequence into blocks of m samples (m-vectors) and let $\{\mathbf{x}_k\}$ denote the sequence of source m-vectors, where $\mathbf{x}_k \equiv (x_{1k}, x_{2k}, \dots, x_{mk})$.

Denote by Δ_k^s the minimum distortion that results when the first k source vectors are quantized to a code-sequence such that the final trellis state is s, where $s \in \Sigma$. Now consider the quantization of the kth source vector. Denote by $D_{i,k}^{j,s}$ the minimum cumulative distortion (sum of the distortions of all source samples up to the ith sample of the kth source vector) that results when the first i components of the kth quantized vector have a total length j and the final trellis state is s. To make the notation simpler, we shall suppress the dependence on k and write this distortion as $D_i^{j,s}$.

The distortion $D_{i+1}^{j,s}$ can recursively be obtained as,

$$(4.1)\quad D_{i+1}^{j,s} = \min_{\theta \in \Theta} [D_i^{j-\ell(\theta),s'} + d(x_{(i+1)k} - q(\theta))],\ i = 0, 1, 2, \dots, m-1\ ,$$

where $s' = \mu(s, \theta)$, $q(\theta) = \mathcal{O}(s', \theta)$ and $\ell(\theta)$ is the length of the quantization level $q(\theta)$, i.e., $\ell(\theta) = \ell_{f_{q(\theta)}}$, f being the index function of (2.2). Also, define $D_i^{j,s} = \infty$ for $j < 0$, $i \leq 0$ and $D_0^{0,s} = \Delta_{k-1}^s$.

By using a dynamic programming algorithm similar to the one in [**5**], the equations in (4.1) can be solved for $D_m^{j,s}$, $\forall j \in J_L = \{1, 2, \dots, L\}$ and $\forall s \in \Sigma$. From the $D_m^{j,s}$ we can obtain Δ_k^s as,

$$(4.2)\qquad \Delta_k^s = \min_{j \in J_L} D_m^{j,s},\ s \in \Sigma\ .$$

If in the dynamic programming algorithm for solving (4.1), we track not only the distortion of the survivor path, but also the path itself, then we can easily obtain the code-sequence that resulted in the distortion Δ_k^s, $s \in \Sigma$.

It is impractical in any system to wait for the entire source sequence (possibly very long) before deciding the code-sequence to which it should be quantized. Such a system would have very large quantization delays. In practice little is lost by making these decisions after a fixed delay of d source m-vectors. Hence, decision about the kth quantized vector $\mathbf{v}_k$ of the desired code-sequence can be made after determining Δ_{k+d}^s, $\forall s \in \Sigma$.

The complexity of the search algorithm presented above is higher than the complexity of the SVQ codebook search algorithm. This is because the $D_i^{j,s}$ must be determined not only for all $i \in J_m$ and $j \in J_L$ but also for $s \in \Sigma$. Hence the complexity of the TB-SVQ search increases approximately linearly with the number of trellis states. For Ungerboeck's 4-state one-dimensional trellis code, the complexity is approximately four times that of the equivalent SVQ search complexity. The SVQ however realizes no granular gain while the TB-SVQ can easily realize up to 1 dB granular gain. Because of the granular gain advantage, the TB-SVQ complexity can be reduced significantly while maintaining a performance better than the SVQ. This can be done by assigning smaller lengths to quantization levels (coarser length quantization as described in [**5**]) and hence reducing the threshold L.

5. Design and Performance

The TB-SVQ is first derived from an ECSQ designed for the source probability distribution; its quantization levels are then optimized using an algorithm similar to the Step A of the SVQ design algorithm [**5**]. In practice, a uniform-threshold scalar quantizer (UTSQ) is used in place of the optimal ECSQ. The UTSQ is considerably simpler to design and its performance is very close to the performance of the optimal ECSQ for most sources [**10**], [**11**]. The spacing β between the quantization thresholds of the (symmetric) UTSQ is determined such that its output entropy is equal to the desired rate r (bits/sample) of the TB-SVQ. Since all trellis codes considered here have a redundancy of 1 bit/sample, we actually start with a symmetric UTSQ that has a spacing of $\beta/2$ between its thresholds and has an even number of levels. The quantization levels are placed between the thresholds at the center of the probability mass. As in the SVQ design, the length ℓ_i of the quantization level q_i is determined as $\ell_i = [b \log 1/p_i]$, where p_i is the probability of the quantization region of q_i, square brackets indicate rounding off to the nearest integer and b is a scalar factor that determines the effective round-off error [**5**] (for all results obtained here, we have taken $b = 1$). For this length assignment, the second constraint in Section 4.1 will automatically be satisfied for sources with symmetric *pdf*s provided the trellis code $\mathcal{T}(\mathcal{Q})$ partitions the quantization levels as shown in Fig. 1. This is because if there is a quantization level at q with length ℓ that belongs to the set $\mathcal{Q}_A$ (or $\mathcal{Q}_B$), there will be a quantization level at $-q$ also with length ℓ that belongs to $\mathcal{Q}_B$ (or $\mathcal{Q}_A$). The quantization levels are paired as described in Section 4.1 and the threshold L is determined such that the primary SVQ has 2^{mr} codevectors in its codebook. The algorithm to determine L is described in [**5**]. Starting with the initial TB-SVQ defined by the levels $\mathcal{Q}$, the lengths $\mathcal{L}$, the threshold L and a given trellis code $\mathcal{T}(\mathcal{Q})$, we quantize a large training sequence of source samples and iteratively update the quantization levels using an algorithm similar to the Step A of the SVQ design algorithm. The updating essentially amounts to replacing each quantization level by the mean of all source samples that are quantized to it. Since each such iteration reduces the squared-error distortion, convergence to a locally optimal set of quantization levels is guaranteed. The overall design however is still suboptimal because the lengths are not optimally assigned. Unlike the SVQ design algorithm, in the present case the lengths $\mathcal{L}$ and the threshold L are not updated (no Step B). They are determined once and kept fixed. It was found that this did not significantly affect the performance.

Performance results for the TB-SVQs designed using this method are given in Tables 1 and 2 for Gaussian and Laplacian sources. The quantizers were designed using a training sequence of 100,000 source samples. Results for four different trellis codes were obtained on out-of-training data. They are the one-dimensional 4, 8, 16 and 32-state codes of [**6**]. The block-length m of the TB-SVQ is 32. For comparison, we have also included the results for the 32-dimensional SVQ [**5**].

Rate	SVQ	TB-SVQ (States)				TCQ	ECSQ	R(D)
		4	8	16	32			
1	4.63	5.14	5.27	5.29	5.32	5.56	4.64	6.02
2	10.40	11.11	11.19	11.25	11.31	11.04	10.55	12.04
3	15.97	16.77 (2.98)	16.86 (2.98)	16.92 (2.98)	16.95 (2.98)	16.64	16.56	18.06

TABLE 1. Performance (SNR in dB) of the TB-SVQ for four different trellis codes (4, 8, 16 and 32-state) and three different rates (1, 2 and 3 bits/sample). The source is Gaussian, the block-length of the SVQ and the TB-SVQ is 32 and the TCQ has 256 states [6]. The numbers in parentheses indicate the actual rate if different from the desired rate.

These results indicate that at least for Gaussian and Laplacian sources, a rate 3 bits/sample TB-SVQ with a simple 4-state trellis code can perform about 0.8 to 1 dB better than the 32-dimensional SVQ. A 32-state trellis code results in an additional gain of about 0.2 dB over the 4-state trellis but at the cost of a substantially higher complexity. At lower rates the gains are reduced. In these tables, we have also included (where available) the 256-state TCQ results of Marcellin and Fischer [**6**]. Except for the Gaussian case at rate 1 bit/sample, the 4-state TB-SVQ also performs up to 0.3 dB better than the 256-state TCQ.

Rate	SVQ	TB-SVQ (States)				TCQ	ECSQ	R(D)
		4	8	16	32			
1	5.59	5.85	5.91	5.95	5.96	5.54	5.76	6.62
2	10.87	11.52 (1.99)	11.62 (1.99)	11.67 (1.99)	11.72 (1.99)	11.22	11.31	12.66
3	16.14	17.08	17.15	17.23	17.30	16.96	17.20	18.68

TABLE 2. Performance (SNR in dB) of the TB-SVQ for four different trellis codes (4, 8, 16 and 32-state) and three different rates (1, 2 and 3 bits/sample). The source is Laplacian, the block-length of the SVQ and the TB-SVQ is 32 and the TCQ has 256 states [6]. The numbers in parentheses indicate the actual rate if different from the desired rate.

6. Conclusions

In this paper we have combined the scalar-vector quantizer of [**5**] with the trellis coded quantizer of [**6**] and proposed a new quantizer called the trellis-based scalar-vector quantizer. The SVQ structure enables the TB-SVQ to realize a significant boundary gain while the trellis code allows it to realize granular gain. In addition, by having non-uniformly spaced quantization levels in the TB-SVQ alphabet, some non-uniform density gain can also be attained. The TB-SVQ is hence capable of realizing all three gains over the baseline uniform scalar quantizer. It can, in principle, approach the rate-distortion bound at large block-lengths and with powerful (possibly complex) trellis codes while maintaining a fixed rate. Even with the Ungerboeck's relatively simple one-dimensional 4-state trellis code, it can realize a significant portion of the total granular gain and performs better than all other reasonable complexity fixed-rate quantizers.

References

1. M. V. Eyuboglu and G. D. Forney, Jr., "Lattice and Trellis Quantization with Lattice- and Trellis-Bounded Codebooks: High-Rate Theory for Memoryless Sources," *IEEE Trans. Inform. Theory*, vol. 39, pp. 46–59, Jan. 1993.
2. M. V. Eyuboglu and A. S. Balamesh, "Lattice and Trellis Quantization with Lattice- and Trellis-Bounded Codebooks: Construction and Implementation for Memoryless Sources," submitted to *IEEE Trans. Inform. Theory*, Oct. 1991.
3. T. D. Lookabaugh and R. M. Gray, "High-Resolution Quantization Theory and the Vector Quantizer Advantage," *IEEE Trans. Inform. Theory*, Vol. 35, pp. 1020–1033, Sept. 1989.
4. G. D. Forney, Jr. and L. F. Wei, "Multidimensional Constellations – Part I: Introduction, Figures of Merit, and Generalized Cross Constellations," *IEEE J. Select. Areas Commun.*, Vol. 7, pp. 877–892, Aug. 1989.
5. R. Laroia and N. Farvardin, "A Structured Fixed-Rate Vector Quantizer Derived from a Variable-Length Scalar Quantizer," *IEEE Trans. Inform. Theory*, to appear May 1993.
6. M. W. Marcellin and T. R. Fischer, "Trellis Coded Quantization of Memoryless and Gauss-Markov sources," *IEEE Trans. Commun.*, Vol. 38, pp. 82–93, Jan. 1990.
7. G. Ungerboeck, "Channel Coding with Multilevel/Phase Signals," *IEEE Trans. Inform. Theory*, Vol. IT-28, pp. 55–67, Jan. 1982.
8. G. D. Forney, Jr., "Geometrically Uniform Codes," *IEEE Trans. Inform. Theory*, Vol. 37, pp. 1241–1260, Sept. 1991.
9. R. Laroia, N. Farvardin and S. Tretter, "On Optimal Shaping of Multidimensional Constellations," submitted to *IEEE Trans. Inform. Theory*, Jan. 1992.
10. N. Farvardin and J. W. Modestino, "Optimum Quantizer Performance for a Class of Non-Gaussian Memoryless Sources," *IEEE Trans. Inform. Theory*, Vol. IT-30, pp. 485–497, May 1984.
11. T. Berger, "Optimum Quantizers and Permutation Codes," *IEEE Trans. Inform. Theory*, Vol. IT-18, pp. 759–765, Nov. 1972.

AT&T Bell Laboratories, 600 Mountain Avenue, Murray Hill, NJ 07974
E-mail address: laroia@research.att.com

Electrical Engineering Department and Systems Research Center, University of Maryland, College Park, Maryland 20742
E-mail address: farvar@src.umd.edu

DIMACS Series in Discrete Mathematics
and Theoretical Computer Science
Volume **14**, 1993

Lattice-Structured Codebooks—Construction and Implementation for Memoryless Sources

M. VEDAT EYUBOĞLU AND AHMED S. BALAMESH

February 22, 1993

ABSTRACT. Nonuniform lattice-structured codebooks are constructed from mod-2 binary lattices. Explicit encoding and reconstruction methods are given, including a method for quantizing overloads. A special case of lattice-structured codebooks is the family of lattice-bounded lattice codebooks whose code vectors lie on a translate of a granular lattice and whose support region corresponds to a generalized fundamental Voronoi region of a boundary lattice.

1. Introduction

The support region of an n-dimensional lattice-based codebook should be chosen to minimize the average distortion. But for large n, codebooks with optimal support regions are generally difficult to implement, because they require large tables or complex enumeration algorithms for indexing. Recently, Laroia and Farvardin [**1**] have described a class of structured codebooks with near-optimal support regions, which can be implemented efficiently with reduced complexity.

In this paper we investigate an alternative class of codebooks, called lattice-structured codebooks, whose support regions are also nearly optimal. These codebooks are based on concepts that were recently developed for constellation shaping in data transmission [**2**], [**3**]. A mod-2 lattice-structured codebook is constructed from a scalar codebook by restricting its least and most significant bits using two linear binary block codes of length n. The block code that controls the least significant bit is called the granular block code, and it determines, together with the distortion measure, the shape of the granular cells. The block code that controls the most significant bit is called the boundary block code; together with a cost metric, it determines the shape of the support region. By

1991 *Mathematics Subject Classification.* Primary 94A29.

optimizing the scalar codebook and the cost metric of the boundary code, good and efficiently implementable codebooks can be designed.

In these codebooks, the codebook search in the encoder requires a 'soft-decision decoder' for the granular block code. The indexing can be implemented algorithmically (without having to store the codebook), with the most complex operations involving a soft-decision decoder for the boundary block code in the reconstruction. Since occasional overloads complicate the search, in the encoder an alternate codebook is used to quantize the overloads.

When their scalar component codebooks are uniform, lattice-structured codebooks become lattice-bounded lattice codebooks [**4**]. A lattice-bounded lattice codebook can be described by a translate of an n-dimensional granular lattice, which determines the granular cells, and a boundary lattice which determines the support region. Depending on the cost metric used, the support region can take the shape of any generalized fundamental Voronoi region of the boundary lattice.

Lattice-bounded lattice codebooks were first proposed by Conway and Sloane who showed how to construct such codebooks for Gaussian sources in the special case where the boundary lattice is a scaled version of the granular lattice [**5**]. Later, in the context of data transmission over Gaussian channels, a more general development was given by Forney in [**2**] for arbitrary lattices (Voronoi constellations).

A lattice-bounded lattice codebook that is designed for data transmission over a Gaussian channel can be used to quantize a Gaussian source, provided that we interchange the granular and boundary lattices. For non-Gaussian sources, it is also necessary to use a cost metric other than the standard Euclidean distance to obtain a support region that corresponds to some generalized Voronoi region of the boundary lattice, instead of the standard Euclidean-distance Voronoi region.

One criticism often raised against lattice codebooks is that, for small-to-moderate n, they are inferior to optimum vector quantizers for nonuniform sources. To overcome a similar limitation of lattice-based trellis codes, in [**6**] Marcellin and Fischer introduced trellis-coded quantization (TCQ). In TCQ, trellis codebooks are designed using nonuniform scalar component codebooks, which are optimized to better match the trellis codebook to the source probability density. Since binary lattices can also be described by trellis diagrams [**7**], their scalar component codebooks can be optimized in a similar fashion to obtain nonuniform codebooks with improved performance (for small-to-moderate n). These codebooks are no longer lattice codebooks, but they can be implemented with approximately the same complexity as the underlying lattice codebooks.

2. Mod-2 Lattice-Structured Codebooks

In this paper, most of our lattice terminology is adopted from [**8**], where an excellent treatise on binary lattices can be found. Throughout the paper, for simplicity, we shall restrict our attention to mod-2 binary lattices. The elements of an n-dimensional mod-2 lattice $\Lambda_{(n,k)}$ are the integer n-tuples that are congruent (mod 2) to the codewords of an (n, k) binary block code B. The best lattices in 4- and 8-dimensions, namely D_4 and E_8, are mod-2 lattices.

2.1. Codebook construction. We assume that the source can be modelled by a memoryless random n-vector $\mathbf{x}$ with one-dimensional nonuniform probability density $p_x(x)$. We also assume that the distortion measure is mean squared error (mse).

The construction that follows is based on the sign-bit shaping technique described by Forney in [**3**] in the context of data transmission. We start with a μ-bit scalar (component) codebook U which is labeled according to a two's-complement labeling, as illustrated in Figure 1. Let $\mathbf{q} = [q_1, q_2, \dots, q_n]$ be an n-vector in the n-dimensional codebook U^n, and represent its samples $q_j = q(a_j, \mathbf{i}_j, z_j)$, $j = 1, 2, \dots, n$, by the triplet $(a_j, \mathbf{i}_j, z_j)$, where a_j is the most significant (sign) bit, z_j is the least significant (parity) bit, and $\mathbf{i}_j = [i_{j,2}, i_{j,2}, \dots, i_{j,\mu-1}]$ is a $(\mu - 2)$-tuple that represents the remaining bits $i_{j,p}$, $2 \leq p \leq \mu - 1$. It follows that any n-vector $\mathbf{q} = \mathbf{q}(\mathbf{a}, \mathbf{i}, \mathbf{z}) \in U^n$ can be represented by the triplet $(\mathbf{a}, \mathbf{i}, \mathbf{z})$, where $\mathbf{a} = [a_1, a_2, \dots, a_n]$ is an n-tuple of sign bits, $\mathbf{z} = [z_1, z_2, \dots, z_n]$ is an n-tuple of parity bits, and $\mathbf{i} = [\mathbf{i}_1, \mathbf{i}_2, \dots, \mathbf{i}_n]$ is an n-vector with elements $\mathbf{i}_j$.

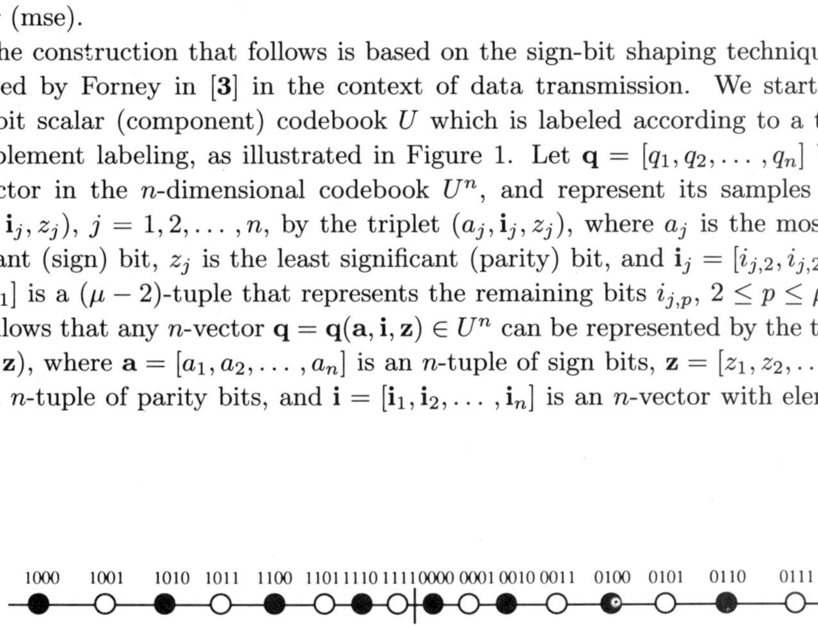

FIGURE 1. Two's-complement labelling for a μ-bit scalar codebook $U(\mu = 4)$.

We now define a lattice-structured codebook C, where $C \subseteq U^n$, by restricting the binary vectors $\mathbf{z}$ and $\mathbf{a}$ using an (n, k_g) granular block code B_g and an (n, k_b) boundary block code B_b, respectively.

We say $\mathbf{q}(\mathbf{a}, \mathbf{i}, \mathbf{z})$ is in C only if $\mathbf{z}$ is a codeword in B_g. That is, $\mathbf{q}(\mathbf{a}, \mathbf{i}, \mathbf{z})$ is a code vector only if $\mathbf{z}$ can be represented as $\mathbf{z} = \mathbf{v}G_g$, where $\mathbf{v}$ is a binary k_g-tuple and G_g is a $k_g \times n$ generator matrix for B_g. The set of code vectors in U^n that satisfy this condition is denoted as Ω, and $\Omega \subseteq U^n$. The block code B_g determines the shape of the granular cells of C. If B_g is a trivial (n, n) block code that consists of all binary n-tuples, then $\Omega = U^n$, and no granular gain will be obtained.

The sign vector $\mathbf{a}$ is restricted to form a support region for C that is suitable for the probability density $p_x(x)$. We start by noting that the boundary code B_b has 2^{n-k_b} distinct cosets $T(\mathbf{s}) = B_b \oplus \mathbf{t}(\mathbf{s})$, where $\mathbf{t}(\mathbf{s})$ is a binary n-tuple coset representative. Each coset $T(\mathbf{s})$ can also be identified by its $(n - k_b)$-bit syndrome $\mathbf{s} = \mathbf{a}H_b^T$, where $\mathbf{a}$ can be any element in $T(\mathbf{s})$, H_b is an $(n - k_b) \times n$ parity-check matrix for B_b, and H_b^T is a syndrome-former.

Suppose for each value of the indices $\mathbf{i}$ and $\mathbf{z} = \mathbf{v}G_g$, we partition the 2^n possible values of the n-vectors $\mathbf{q}(\mathbf{a}, \mathbf{i}, \mathbf{z})$, corresponding to different sign vectors $\mathbf{a}$, into 2^{n-k_b} equivalence classes

$$S(\mathbf{s}, \mathbf{i}, \mathbf{v}) = \{\mathbf{q}(\mathbf{a}, \mathbf{i}, \mathbf{z}) : \ \mathbf{a} \in T(\mathbf{s})\} \ .$$

Each equivalence class $S(\mathbf{s}, \mathbf{i}, \mathbf{v})$ includes 2^{k_b} vectors $\mathbf{q}(\mathbf{a}, \mathbf{i}, \mathbf{z})$, as $\mathbf{a}$ ranges through the coset $T(\mathbf{s}) = B_b \oplus \mathbf{t}(\mathbf{s})$ of B_b. Codebook C will contain *one and only one* code vector $\mathbf{y} = \mathbf{y}(\mathbf{s}, \mathbf{i}, \mathbf{v}) = \mathbf{q}[\mathbf{a}(\mathbf{s}, \mathbf{i}, \mathbf{v}), \mathbf{i}, \mathbf{z}]$ from each such equivalence class. That is, for each value of the triplet $(\mathbf{s}, \mathbf{i}, \mathbf{v})$, the sign vector $\mathbf{a}$ can take only one value from the coset $T(\mathbf{s})$; i.e., $\mathbf{a}(\mathbf{s}, \mathbf{i}, \mathbf{v}) = \mathbf{b}(\mathbf{s}, \mathbf{i}, \mathbf{v}) \oplus \mathbf{t}(\mathbf{s})$, where $\mathbf{b}(\mathbf{s}, \mathbf{i}, \mathbf{v})$ is some codeword in B_b. It follows that $C \subseteq \Omega \subseteq U^n$.

If B_b is a trivial $(n, 0)$ block code that consists only of the zero codeword, the sign vector $\mathbf{a}$ will be unrestricted, and therefore the codebook C will have a cubic boundary (i.e., $C = \Omega \subseteq U^n$), and no boundary gain will be obtained. If B_b and B_g are both trivial, then C will be a uniform scalar codebook (i.e., $C = \Omega = U^n$).

Since B_b has only 2^{n-k_b} cosets, and B_g has 2^{k_g} codewords, the size $|C|$ of the codebook C is smaller than that of U^n by a factor of $2^{k_b+(n-k_g)}$, or its rate r is smaller by $k_b/n + (n - k_g)/n$ bits per dimension; i.e.,

$$\begin{aligned} r &= (\log_2 |C|)/n = \mu - k_b/n - (n - k_g)/n \\ &= \mu - 2 + (n - k_b)/n + k_g/n \ . \end{aligned}$$

2.2. Codebook design. To complete the design of a mod-2 lattice-structured codebook, we need to determine the scalar component codebook U and select the set of code vectors $\mathbf{y}(\mathbf{s}, \mathbf{i}, \mathbf{v})$ from the equivalence classes $S(\mathbf{s}, \mathbf{i}, \mathbf{v})$ such that the average distortion is minimized. Here we give an approximate, iterative procedure to accomplish this. Using a set of training vectors $\{\mathbf{x}_1, \mathbf{x}_2, \ldots, \mathbf{x}_J\}$, where $\mathbf{x}_j = (x_{j1}, x_{j2}, \ldots, x_{jn})$, $j = 1, 2, \ldots, J$, in each step of the iteration, we first optimize the scalar codebook U using a generalized Linde-Buzo-Gray (LBG) algorithm, and then try to select the code vectors $\mathbf{y}(\mathbf{s}, \mathbf{i}, \mathbf{v}) \in S(\mathbf{s}, \mathbf{i}, \mathbf{v})$ to minimize the probability of overload.

First, we discuss the optimization of the scalar codebook U. At the i'th iteration, we use the current codebook C_i to quantize each training vector $\mathbf{x}_j$ to the nearest code vector $\mathbf{y}_j = (y_{j1}, y_{j2}, \ldots, y_{jn}) \in C_i$. Then, for each output value u_l of the scalar codebook U_i, we determine the set $\Gamma(u_l)$ of all training samples x_{ji} for which $y_{ji} = u_l$, and then replace u_l by the centroid of $\Gamma(u_l)$. We repeat this procedure until the scalar codebook converges to a local optimum, which we denote as U_{i+1}. (If the scalar codebook is restricted to be uniform, then a simpler procedure can be used to optimize its step size.)

Once U_{i+1} is determined, the code vectors $\mathbf{y}_{i+1}(\mathbf{s}, \mathbf{i}, \mathbf{v})$ are chosen from the equivalence classes $S(\mathbf{s}, \mathbf{i}, \mathbf{v})$ to minimize the probability of overload. This can be done approximately as follows. First, we quantize each training vector $\mathbf{x}_j$ using the scalar component codebook U_{i+1} and record the probability $p(u_l)$ of each output value u_l. Then, we assign the costs $c(u_l) = -\log\, p(u_l)$, and for each value of $\mathbf{s}$, $\mathbf{i}$ and $\mathbf{v}$, we select from the equivalence class $S(\mathbf{s},\mathbf{i},\mathbf{v}) = \{\mathbf{q}(\mathbf{a},\mathbf{i},\mathbf{z}) : \mathbf{a} \in T(\mathbf{s})\}$, the vector $\mathbf{y}_{i+1}(\mathbf{s},\mathbf{i},\mathbf{v}) = \mathbf{q}(\mathbf{a},\mathbf{i},\mathbf{z})$ with the least total cost. In other words, we minimize

$$-\sum_{0\leq j\leq n} c[q(a_j,\mathbf{i}_j,z_j)]$$

over all $\mathbf{a} \in B \oplus \mathbf{t}(\mathbf{s})$, where $c[q(a_j,\mathbf{i}_j,z_j)]$ represents the cost of the scalar output value of $q(a_j,\mathbf{i}_j,z_j)$, and $\mathbf{q}(\mathbf{a},\mathbf{i},\mathbf{z}) = [q(a_1,\mathbf{i}_1,z_1),\ldots,q(a_n,\mathbf{i}_n,z_n)]$. The vectors $\{\mathbf{y}_{i+1}(\mathbf{s},\mathbf{i},\mathbf{v})\}$ form the new codebook C_{i+1}.

2.3. Mod-2 lattice-bounded codebooks. When the scalar component codebook U is uniform, the lattice-structured codebook C becomes a lattice-bounded lattice codebook, and therefore can be characterized by its granular lattice Λ_g and boundary lattice Λ_b. Assuming that U has a step size of α, it can be shown that $\Lambda_g = \alpha\Lambda_{(n,k_g)}$, where $\Lambda_{(n,k_g)}$ is the mod-2 lattice corresponding to the block code B_g, and $\Lambda_b = \alpha L\Lambda_{(n,k_b)}$, where $\Lambda_{(n,k_g)}$ is the mod-2 lattice corresponding to the block code B_b, and $L = 2^{\mu-1}$.

Thus, the codebook C can be viewed as a collection of n-vectors of $\Lambda_g + (\alpha/2)^n$ which consists of one and only one code vector $\mathbf{y}(\mathbf{s},\mathbf{i},\mathbf{v}) = \mathbf{q}[\mathbf{t}(\mathbf{s}),\mathbf{i},\mathbf{z}] - \alpha L\mathbf{c}(\mathbf{s},\mathbf{i},\mathbf{v})$ from each coset $\Lambda_b + \mathbf{q}[\mathbf{t}(\mathbf{s}),\mathbf{i},\mathbf{z}]$ of Λ_b. When these code vectors are chosen to minimize the probability of overload, the codebook support region will become a generalized fundamental Voronoi region of Λ_b.

3. Implementation of Mod-2 Lattice-Structured Codebooks

As illustrated in Figure 2, in the encoder we first use a nearest-neighbor quantizer to find the n-vector $\mathbf{q} = \mathbf{q}(\mathbf{a},\mathbf{i},\mathbf{z})$ in Ω that is closest to the source vector $\mathbf{x}$. When U is uniform, this can be implemented using known lattice quantization algorithms for the granular lattice Λ_g [**7**], [**9**]. When U is nonuniform, a soft-decision decoder for the granular block code can be used. For example, it is always possible to represent all points in Ω using a trellis diagram for the block code B_g [**7**], and search this trellis to minimize the mse using the Viterbi algorithm. The complexity of this search depends primarily on the complexity of the trellis of B_g, and is only slightly affected by the nonuniform spacing in U.

Since the codebook C is a subset of Ω, occasionally, when the magnitude of $\mathbf{x}$ is too large, $\mathbf{q}(\mathbf{a},\mathbf{i},\mathbf{z})$ may not be a valid code vector; this is called an overload. Overloads must be detected and special procedures must be followed to correct them, as will be discussed in the next section. For the moment, we consider only the case of no overload; i.e., $\mathbf{q}(\mathbf{a},\mathbf{i},\mathbf{z}) \in C$.

To map $\mathbf{q}(\mathbf{a},\mathbf{i},\mathbf{z})$ into bits, we first extract the triplet $(\mathbf{a},\mathbf{i},\mathbf{z})$. The n-bit parity vector $\mathbf{z}$ is then 'compressed' to a k_g-bit granular index $\mathbf{v}$ by passing it through G_g^{-1}, an $n \times k_g$ right inverse of the generator matrix G_g for the block code B_g.

The n-bit sign vector $\mathbf{a}$ is 'compressed' to an $(n - k_b)$-bit 'boundary' index $\mathbf{s}$, by passing it through an $n \times (n - k_b)$ syndrome-former H_b^T for the block code B_b. The indices $\mathbf{s}$, $\mathbf{i}$ and $\mathbf{v}$ are then transmitted over a binary channel.

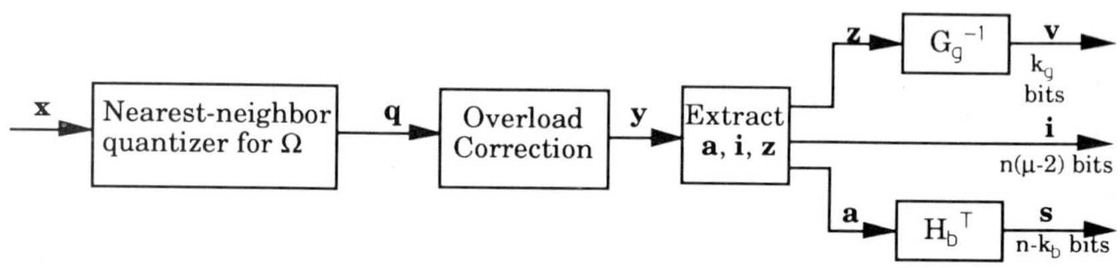

FIGURE 2. Encoder for mod-2 lattice-structured codebooks.

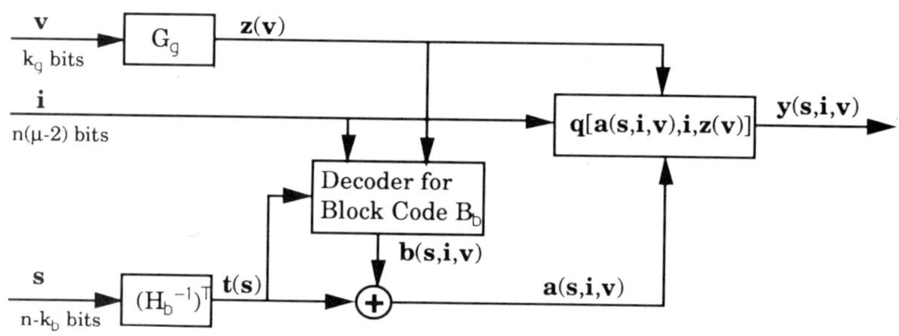

FIGURE 3. Reconstruction circuit for mod-2 lattice-structured codebooks.

In the reconstruction circuit, shown in Figure 3, the codeword $\mathbf{z}$ is recovered simply by passing the 'granular' index $\mathbf{v}$ through the generator matrix G_g; i.e., $\mathbf{z}(\mathbf{v}) = \mathbf{v}G_g$. The recovery of the sign vector $\mathbf{a}(\mathbf{s}, \mathbf{i}, \mathbf{v})$ from the indices $\mathbf{s}$, $\mathbf{i}$ and $\mathbf{v}$ is more complicated. In principle, $\mathbf{a}(\mathbf{s}, \mathbf{i}, \mathbf{v})$ can be determined from the received indices $\mathbf{s}$, $\mathbf{i}$ and $\mathbf{v}$ with a table look-up, but such a table would require $|C| = 2^{nr}$ binary entries. This is not feasible, except for very small values of n and r, and therefore the following algorithmic reconstruction will be preferred.

As illustrated in Figure 3, first the $(n - k_b)$-bit syndrome $\mathbf{s}$ is mapped to an n-bit coset representative vector $\mathbf{t}(\mathbf{s}) = \mathbf{s}(H_b^{-1})^T$. Since $\mathbf{s} = \mathbf{a}H_b^T$ is the syndrome representing the coset of B_b in which the original sign vector $\mathbf{a}(\mathbf{s}, \mathbf{i}, \mathbf{v})$ lies, the coset representative $\mathbf{t}(\mathbf{s}) = \mathbf{s}(H_b^{-1})^T$ must belong to the same coset, because $\mathbf{t}(\mathbf{s})H_b^T = \mathbf{s}$. Therefore, using a soft-decision decoder for B_b, we can find the sign vector $\mathbf{a}(\mathbf{s}, \mathbf{i}, \mathbf{v})$ which minimizes the total cost (determined during codebook training) over all $\mathbf{a} \in B \oplus \mathbf{t}(\mathbf{s})$. The code vector $\mathbf{y}(\mathbf{s}, \mathbf{i}, \mathbf{v}) = \mathbf{q}(\mathbf{a}, \mathbf{i}, \mathbf{z})$ is then perfectly recovered.

It can be observed that the primary complexity in the encoder lies in the soft-decision decoder for the granular block code, and the primary complexity in the reconstruction circuit lies in the soft-decision decoder for the boundary block code, which is typically more complex than the granular block code. The linear maps $\mathbf{s} = \mathbf{a}H_b^T$, $\mathbf{t} = \mathbf{s}(H_b^{-1})^T$, $\mathbf{v} = \mathbf{z}G_g^{-1}$ and $\mathbf{z} = \mathbf{v}G_g$ can be implemented using table look-up or by direct computation, and their complexity is very modest.

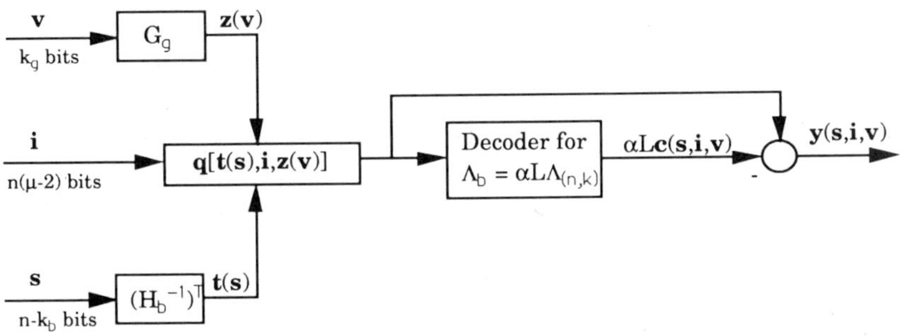

FIGURE 4. Reconstruction circuit for a lattice-bounded codebook.

If U is uniform, using the boundary-lattice formulation of Section 2.3, we can redraw the reconstruction circuit of Figure 3 as in Figure 4. Here we first form the coset representative $\mathbf{q}[\mathbf{t}(\mathbf{s}), \mathbf{i}, \mathbf{z}(\mathbf{v})]$, where $\mathbf{t}(\mathbf{s}) = \mathbf{s}(H_b^{-1})^T$ is an initial sign vector, and then use a generalized minimum-distance decoder for the boundary lattice $\Lambda_b = \alpha L \Lambda_{(n,k_b)}$ to find the 'nearest' lattice point $\alpha L\mathbf{c}(\mathbf{s}, \mathbf{i}, \mathbf{v}) \in \Lambda_b$; the difference $\mathbf{q}[\mathbf{t}(\mathbf{s}), \mathbf{i}, \mathbf{z}(\mathbf{v})] - \alpha L\mathbf{c}(\mathbf{s}, \mathbf{i}, \mathbf{v})$ is then the original code vector $\mathbf{y}(\mathbf{s}, \mathbf{i}, \mathbf{v})$, provided that we use a tie-breaking rule that is consistent with the codebook assumed in the encoder.

It was shown in [4] that, under certain conditions, the boundary gain of a lattice for quantization of a memoryless source is the same as the coding gain of the same lattice for data transmission over an additive memoryless channel, and similarly the granular gain of a lattice in quantization is the same as the shaping gain of the same lattice in data transmission. Note that operationally the relationship is reversed: the boundary operations in quantization are similar to shaping operations (both deal with large-scale support regions), and the granular operations are similar to coding operations (both deal with small-scale granular cells).

4. Overload Events

In Section 3, we assumed that the n-vector $\mathbf{q}$ chosen by the nearest-neighbor quantizer for Ω is a valid code vector in C; i.e., $\mathbf{q} = \mathbf{y} \in C$. Of course, occasionally there may be overloads; then $\mathbf{q} \notin \Omega$, and it should be mapped to the nearest valid code vector, or at least to a near code vector in C.

An overload condition can always be detected in the encoder, for example by reconstructing the code vector $\mathbf{y} = \mathbf{y}(\mathbf{s}, \mathbf{i}, \mathbf{v})$ from the encoded indices $\mathbf{s}$, $\mathbf{i}$ and $\mathbf{v}$, and then checking whether $\mathbf{q} = \mathbf{y}$. In what follows we assume that the overload is already detected.

Consider now the case where the scalar component codebook U is uniform. Then in case of an overload, if no special measures are taken, the decoder will reconstruct a code vector $\mathbf{y}$ that lies in the same coset of the boundary lattice Λ_b as $\mathbf{q}$. At high rates, the quantization error $\mathbf{x} - \mathbf{y} \cong \mathbf{q} - \mathbf{y} = \alpha L\mathbf{c}$ will be a non-zero point in Λ_b, with magnitude equal to at least the minimum distance $d_{\min}(\Lambda_b)$ between points in Λ_b, which is twice the packing radius of the support region. Thus with no special measures, the overload will cause a large 'wrap-around', and the overload mse will increase significantly. This is illustrated in Figure 5 using a two-dimensional cubic codebook. Similar problems will occur when U is nonuniform, although we expect overloads to occur less frequently in that case.

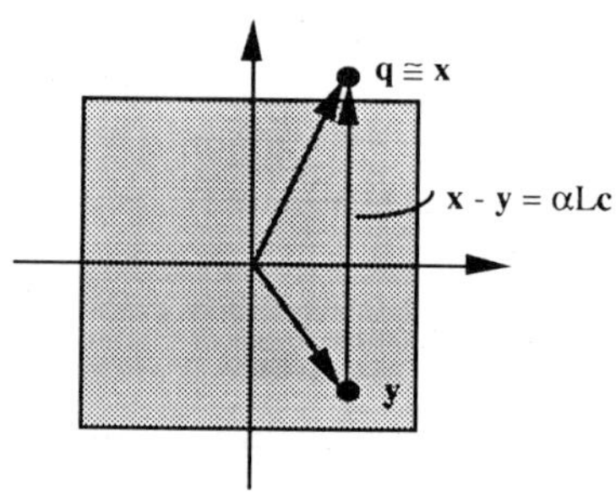

FIGURE 5. Wrap-around effect for untreated overloads.

Now we describe a somewhat indirect but very effective and general method for dealing with overloads. Here two codebooks are used: an n-dimensional lattice-structured codebook C for quantizing the source vectors that fall within the support region of C and an n-dimensional overload codebook C' for quantizing the overloads. The overload codebook can be the n-fold Cartesian product of a uniform scalar codebook, or it can be any n-dimensional lattice codebook with a cubic support region. Ideally, the support regions of C and C' should overlap as little as possible.

To avoid ambiguity in the reconstruction, one extra bit must be transmitted per n dimensions to identify which codebook is being used. We assume that C and C' both have the same rate r', so that the overall rate is $r = r' + 1/n$. It is possible to use codebooks of different rate, but then the overall rate will be probabilistic, which may require buffering for fixed-rate channels.

This method was simulated for a Gaussian source using an 8-dimensional lattice-bounded codebook C based on the granular lattice $\Lambda_g = \alpha \mathbf{Z}^8$ and a mod-2 boundary lattice $\Lambda_b = \alpha L E_8$, whose nominal boundary gain is 0.5 bit per dimension (3.01 dB). The overload codebook C' was another lattice codebook whose granular lattice is $\Lambda_g = \alpha' E_8$ and whose boundary lattice is the scaled integer lattice; i.e., $\Lambda_b = \alpha' L \mathbf{Z}^8$. Both C and C' are of rate $r' = \mu - 0.5$, so that the overall rate is $r = r' + 0.125 = \mu - 0.375$.

The code vectors in C' are more sparse, but this is acceptable since overloads are relatively infrequent. Tests were run for $\mu = 3$, 5 and 7. For each simulation point, at least 100,000 source vectors and 100 overloads were simulated. The scale factors α and α' were selected empirically to obtain the minimum mse. The set of test vectors that were used to optimize the scale factors was independent from the set of test vectors used in final simulations.

In Figure 6 we show the performance of this method along with that of a uniform scalar quantizer. Note that the SNR of the lattice-bounded codebook improves with rate more rapidly than that of the uniform scalar quantizer. At around $r = 7$, the gain over the uniform scalar codebook is about 0.5 bit per dimension, which is the nominal boundary gain of E_8. At lower rates, the gain is smaller, presumably because of the effect of the nearest neighbors.

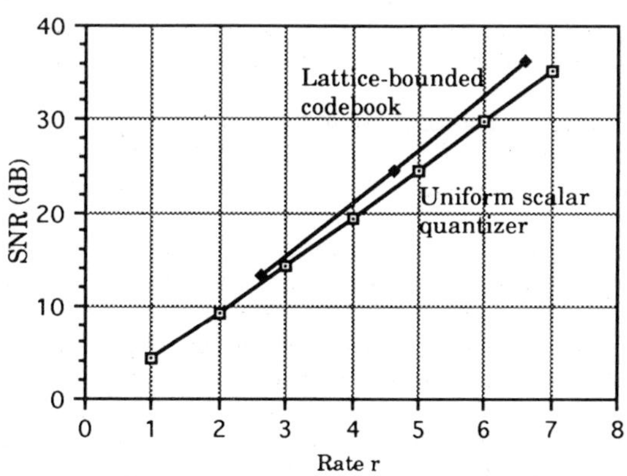

FIGURE 6. SNR vs. rate for a lattice-bounded codebook C with $\Lambda_g = \alpha \mathbf{Z}^8$ and $\Lambda_b = \alpha L E_8$, and an overload codebook C' with $\Lambda_g = \alpha' E_8$ and $\Lambda_b = \alpha' L \mathbf{Z}^8$.

5. Conclusions

We have discussed the construction and implementation of lattice-structured codebooks, which include lattice-bounded lattice codebooks as a special case.

For Gaussian sources, the boundary gain of mod-2 lattice-bounded lattice codebooks over a uniform scalar quantizer is at most 1 bit per dimension (6.02 dB). As examples, the well-known lattices D_4 and E_8 correspond to (4,1) and (8,4) block codes which can be represented by simple 2- and 4-state trellises, respectively. At high rates, these codes can provide a nominal boundary gain of about 0.25 and 0.5 bit per dimension (1.50 and 3.01 dB), respectively.

The granular gains of D_4 and E_8 are 0.06 and 0.11 bit per dimension (0.36 dB and 0.66 dB), respectively, and the mod-2 24-dimensional lattice $X_{24}^{\perp}$ has a granular gain of 0.14 (0.84 dB) bit per dimension [**4**]. These lattices have 2-, 4- and 8-state trellis diagrams, respectively [**7**], and a nearest-neighbor quantizer for them can be implemented with a simple Viterbi algorithm. Larger gains can be obtained using nonuniform optimized scalar codebooks.

The ideas described in this paper were extended to mod-2^m lattices in [**10**]. It is also possible to apply these concepts to trellis codebooks thereby extending the techniques of Marcellin and Fischer to codebooks with non-cubic support regions [**10**].

Much work remains to improve our understanding of lattice-structured quantizers, and to assess their potential for use in practical applications. In particular, a detailed simulation study is required to compare their performance and complexity against those of other structured vector quantizers.

References

1. R. Laroia and N. Farvardin, "A structured fixed-rate vector quantizer derived from variable-length encoded scalar quantizer," submitted to *IEEE Trans. Inform. Theory*, August 1991.
2. G. D. Forney, Jr., "Multidimensional constellations— Part II: Voronoi constellations," *J. Select. Areas in Commun.*, vol. 7, pp. 941-958, 1989.
3. G. D. Forney, Jr., "Trellis shaping," *IEEE Trans. Inform. Theory*, vol. IT-38, pp. 281-300, March 1992.
4. M. V. Eyuboğlu and G. D. Forney, Jr., "Lattice and trellis quantization using lattice- and trellis-bounded codebooks: High-rate theory for memoryless sources," *IEEE Inform. Theory*, vol. IT-39, pp. 46-59, January 1993.
5. J. H. Conway and N.J.A. Sloane, "A fast encoding method for lattice codes and quantizers," *IEEE Trans. Inform. Theory*, vol. IT-29, pp. 820-824, 1983.
6. M. W. Marcellin and T. R. Fischer, "Trellis-coded quantization of memoryless and Gauss-Markov sources," *IEEE Trans. Commun.*, vol. COM-38, pp. 82-93, 1990.
7. G. D. Forney, Jr., "Coset codes—Part II: Binary codes and lattices," *IEEE Trans. Inform. Theory*, vol. IT-34, pp. 1151-1187, 1988.
8. G. D. Forney, Jr., "Coset codes—Part I: Introduction and geometrical classification," *IEEE Trans. Inform. Theory*, vol. IT-34, pp. 1123-1151, 1988.
9. J. H. Conway and N.J.A. Sloane, "Fast quantizing and decoding algorithms for lattice quantizers and codes," *IEEE Trans. Inform. Theory*, vol. IT-28, pp. 227-232, 1982.
10. M. V. Eyuboğlu and A. Balamesh, "Lattice- and trellis-structured codebooks—Construction and implementation for memoryless codebooks," submitted to *IEEE*

Trans. Inform. Theory, October 1991.

Motorola Codex, 20 Cabot Blvd. MS: C2-135, Mansfield, MA 02048
E-mail address: vedat_eyuboglu@mcimail.com

Department of Electrical Engineering, King Abdul-Aziz University, Jeddah, Saudi Arabia
E-mail address: CCP3017@SAKKAU03.BITNET

DIMACS Series in Discrete Mathematics
and Theoretical Computer Science
Volume **14**, 1993

Decoding on a Finite State Transition Diagram While Avoiding a Sub-Diagram

LYLE FREDRICKSON, RAZMIK KARABED, PAUL SIEGEL AND

HEMANT THAPAR

October 19, 1992

ABSTRACT. In this paper, we address and motivate the problem of decoding on a finite state transition diagram while avoiding a sub-diagram. The solution is to modify the iterative process of Viterbi decoding.

Summary

A Finite State Transition Diagram (FSTD) F is an edge labeled digraph with state set $S = \{s_0, \ldots, s_p\}$ and label set $H = \{h_0, \ldots, h_q\}$. Without loss of generality, we can assume there is at most one arc from s_i to s_j for any "i" and "j".

Decoding Problem: Given a metric M, a FSTD F, a state s' and a sequence $\underline{r} = (r_0, r_1, r_2, \ldots)$, for every state s_i and length l, among all paths of length $l+1$ in F starting from s' and ending on s_i, find a path of arcs $\underline{p} = (p_0, \ldots, p_l)$ with corresponding label sequence $\underline{h} = (h_0, \ldots, h_{l-1})$, such that $\underline{h}$ is closest to $(r_0, \ldots, r_l)$ in metric M.

Solution: The celebrated Viterbi decoder.

Now, suppose we are given a FSTD F, a state s' and a sequence $\underline{r}$, but in the decoding problem, we additionally require that $\underline{p} = (p_0, \ldots p_l)$ does not belong to a fixed subdiagram G of F. A subdiagram G of a FSTD F is a labeled digraph obtained from F by erasing arcs and states. We say a path $\underline{p}$ does not belong to G if it uses at least one arc not in G. For simplicity, we assume that G is irreducible.

1991 *Mathematics Subject Classification.* Primary 94B35.

With this assumption, if the starting state s' is not in G, then any path $\underline{p}$ starting from s' will be outside G. Therefore, the two decoding problems become equivalent, and the same Viterbi decoder works on both cases. Therefore in this paper, we focus on the case in which the initial state s' is in sub-diagram G.

To motivate this problem, we consider a certain rate 8/10 Matched Spectral Null (MSN) trellis code [**1, 2**] having a null at DC designed for the $1-D$ partial response channel. This code is to provide a 3 dB coding gain. It will be illustrated that if a simplified Viterbi decoder in the sense of [**1**] is used for the given code, then the path memory will be infinite. However, if a specific sub-diagram G is avoided in the decoder FSTD F, then the path memory becomes 24 bits (a very attractive length).

Briefly, our result is that the Viterbi decoder can be modified to solve the new decoding problem. The main modifications are:

(i) For each state s, keep two survivor paths $sp_1(s)$ and $sp_2(s)$. The survivor path $sp_1(s)$ is the best path in F starting from s' and ending on s at the current time, and the survivor path $sp_2(s)$ is the best path in F having at least one arc not in G starting from s' and ending on s at the current time. Note that if s is not in G, then clearly $sp_2(s) = sp_1(s)$, and one survivor suffices.

(ii) For each state s, keep two metrics $m_1(s)$ and $m_2(s)$. The metric $m_1(s)$ corresponds to $sp_1(s)$ and $m_2(s)$ to $sp_2(s)$. Note that as in the above, if s is not in G, then $m_1(s) = m_2(s)$, and only one metric is needed.

(iii) Updating rules. Let states $s_1, s_2, \ldots$, and s_n be the predecessor states to the state s. And let h_i be the label on the arc e_i from s_i to s. Further, let r be the current value of the received sequence. Now, the updating rules are:

- Update $m_1(s)$
  $m_1(s) = \min\{m_1(s_1) + (r-h_1)^2, \ldots, m_1(s_n) + (r-h_n)^2\}$.
- Update $sp_1(s)$
  If the ith state, s_i, produces the minimum above, then $sp_1(s) = \{sp_1(s_i), e_i\}$.
- Update $m_2(s)$
  For i in the set $\{1, 2, \ldots, n\}$, let

$$\begin{aligned} m(s_i) &= m_1(s_i), && \text{if the arc } e_i \text{ is not in } G, \\ &= m_2(s_i), && \text{if the arc } e_i \text{ is in } G. \\ sp(s_i) &= sp_1(s_i), && \text{if the arc } e_i \text{ is not in } G, \\ &= sp_2(s_i), && \text{if the arc } e_i \text{ is in } G. \end{aligned}$$

  Then, $m_2(s) = \min\{m(s_1) + (r-h_1)^2, \ldots, m(s_n) + (r-h_n)^2\}$.
- Update $sp_2(s)$
  If the ith state, s_i, produces the minimum above, then $sp_2(s) = \{sp(s_i), e_i\}$.

We conclude that although Viterbi decoding is traditionally used to decode on a finite state transition diagram F, it can be modified to decode on F while avoiding a fixed sub-diagram G of F. To motivate this problem we give an example, where avoiding a sub-diagram in the decoder trellis (or FSTD) reduces the path memory length from infinity to 24 bits.

References

1. R. Karabed and P. Siegel, "Matched spectral null codes for partial response channels," *IEEE Tran. Info. Th.*, vol. 37, no. 3, pt. II, pp. 818–855, May 1991.
2. L. Fredrickson, R. Karabed, J. Rae, P. Siegel, H. Thapar, R. Wood, "Time-Varying Detector for Control of Error Event Length," patent pending.

IBM Corporation, 5600 Cottle Rd. F84/0281, San Jose, CA 95193

IBM Corporation, 650 Harry Rd. K65/802, San Jose, CA 95120
E-mail address: karabed@almaden.ibm.com, siegelph@almaden.ibm.com, hthapar@vnet.ibm.com

DIMACS Series in Discrete Mathematics
and Theoretical Computer Science
Volume **14**, 1993

Covering Properties of Binary Convolutional Codes and Lattice Quantization of Uniform Sources

A. R. CALDERBANK, P. C. FISHBURN AND A. RABINOVICH

May 25, 1993

ABSTRACT. This paper describes methods for analyzing the expected and worst-case performance of sequence-based methods of quantization. We suppose that the quantization algorithm is dynamic programming, where the current step depends on a vector of path metrics, which we call a metric function. Our principal objective is a concise representation of these metric functions and the possible trajectories of the dynamic programming algorithm.

1. Lattice Quantization of Uniform Sources

In this section we are concerned with representing a source sequence x as the sum of a lattice point c and an error sequence $e = (e_i)$. In quantization the objective is the lattice point c, and the expected value $E(e_i^2)$ is the mean squared error (normalized per dimension).

A *lattice* is an additive subgroup of $\mathbb{R}^N$. If C is an $[N, k]$ binary linear code, then the *binary lattice* $\Lambda(C)$ is defined by

$$\Lambda(C) = \{x \in \mathbb{Z}^N | x \equiv c \pmod 2 \text{ for some } c \in C\} \ .$$

It is easy to verify that $\Lambda(C)$ is closed under addition so that it is indeed a lattice. The lattice $\Lambda(C)$ lies between $2\mathbb{Z}^N$ and $\mathbb{Z}^N$; the index of $2\mathbb{Z}^N$ in $\Lambda(C)$ is 2^k, and the index of $\Lambda(C)$ in $\mathbb{Z}^N$ is 2^{N-k}. A binary convolutional code C determines an infinite binary lattice $\Lambda(C)$ consisting of all sequences with integer entries that are congruent to some codeword modulo 2.

If $\Lambda_s \subseteq \mathbb{R}^N$ is a lattice, and $y \in \Lambda_s$ is a lattice point, then the *Voronoi region* $\mathcal{R}(y)$ consists of those points in $\mathbb{R}^N$ that are at least as close to y as to any other

---

1991 *Mathematics Subject Classification.* Primary 94A29; Secondary 94B10.

$y' \in \Lambda_s$. Thus

$$\mathcal{R}(y) = \{x \in \mathbb{R}^N \mid \|x - y\| \le \|x - y'\| \text{ for all } y' \in \Lambda_s\} .$$

The interiors of different Voronoi regions are disjoint though two neighboring Voronoi regions may share a face. These faces lie in the hyperplanes midway between two neighboring lattice points. Translation by $y \in \Lambda_s$ maps the Voronoi region $\mathcal{R}(w)$ to the Voronoi region $\mathcal{R}(w + y)$. Thus all Voronoi regions are congruent, and we may speak of the Voronoi region $\mathcal{R}(\Lambda_s) = \mathcal{R}(0) = \mathcal{R}$, say.

The second moment $G(\mathcal{R})$ results from taking the average squared distance from a point in $\mathcal{R}$ to the centroid 0, and normalizing to obtain a dimensionless quantity. Formally

$$G(\mathcal{R}) = \frac{\int_{\mathcal{R}} \|x\|^2 dv}{NV(\mathcal{R})^{1+2/N}} ,$$

where

$$V(\mathcal{R}) = \int_{\mathcal{R}} dv$$

is the volume of the region $\mathcal{R}$. The *shape gain* $\gamma(\Lambda_s)$ is the ratio of the second moment of the cube $[-1/2, 1/2]^N$, which is 1/12, to $G(R(\Lambda_s))$. The shape gain in N-dimensional space is bounded above by the shape gain of the N-sphere. The limiting gain is $\pi e/6 = 1.53$ dB.

In the theory of quantization, this ratio of second moments measures the reduction in mean squared error (compared with uniform scalar quantization) that comes from the shape of the quantization cell (the *cell shape gain*).

For binary lattices $\Lambda(C)$ the problem of calculating the second moment of the Voronoi region $\mathcal{R}$ simplifies considerably. For simplicity let C be an $[N, k]$ binary linear code. Then the map $\varphi : [0, 2)^N \to \mathcal{R}$ given by $\varphi(\omega) = \omega - Q(\omega)$ produces a uniform covering of $\mathcal{R}$ in which every vector is covered 2^k times. Thus a uniform distribution on $[0, 2)$ will produce a uniform distribution on $\mathcal{R}$.

EXAMPLE 1.1. Here $C = \{(00), (11)\}$ and $\Lambda(C)$ is the checkerboard lattice D_2. Figure 1 shows the Voronoi regions. The square $[0, 2)^2$ covers $\mathcal{R}$ twice.

To simplify further, we need the observation that if $r = (r_1, \ldots, r_N) \in [0, 1]^N$, then the closest point to r in the lattice $\Lambda(C)$ is just the closest codeword in C. This is evident in the example given above, and we leave the general proof to the reader. Hence we may create a random variable uniformly distributed over the Voronoi region $\mathcal{R}$ by passing an iid source uniformly distributed over $[0, 1]$ through a maximum likelihood decoder for C, and then changing signs by tossing a fair coin. In particular, to calculate the second moment $G(\mathcal{R})$ it suffices to consider an iid source uniformly distributed over $[0, 1]$.

We define the *normalized second moment* μ of a binary lattice $\Lambda(C)$ to be the mean squared error per dimension when an iid source S uniformly distributed over $[0, 1]$ is quantized by a maximum likelihood decoder for C. Quantization of S at rate 1 using the points 0 and 1 gives mse equal to 1/12. The binary code reduces the rate from 1 to R, and interpolation predicts that mse will increase by

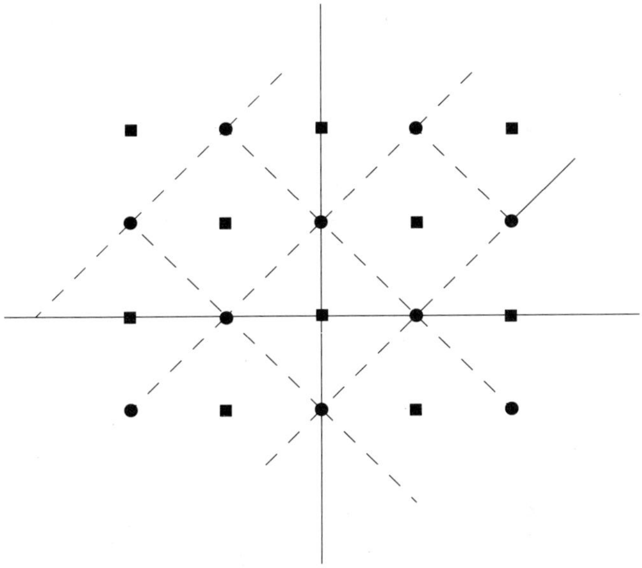

FIGURE 1. The checkerboard lattice D_2.

a factor $4^{(1-R)}$. The *cell shape gain* $\gamma(\Lambda(C))$ is given by $\gamma(\Lambda(C)) = [4^{(1-R)}/12]/\mu$ and is expressed in dB.

Table 1, given below, is taken from Calderbank, Fishburn and Rabinovich [**2**], and provides normalized second moments for certain convolutional codes (those listed in Lin and Costello [**4**]). It would be of interest to have a more extensive table.

We conclude this section by observing that these methods might be useful in implementing the dithered lattice quantization schemes proposed by Zamir and Feder [**5, 6**] which require a random variable distributed uniformly over a Voronoi region.

2. Quantization of a Binary Symmetric Source using Convolutional Codes

In Section 1 we related quantization of a uniform source by a binary lattice to decoding a sequence of samples uniformly distributed over $[0, 1]$ by a soft decision decoder for the binary code. In this section we shall consider hard decision decoding of a binary symmetric source using convolutional codes. We are given an arbitrarily long binary sequence, and we wish to calculate the expected and worst case Hamming distortion per dimension. This normalization gives the fraction of bits that we need to change in order to reach a codeword in the convolutional code.

An elementary but fundamental observation is that a convolutional code with 2^v states gives 2^v approximations to a given source sequence, and that these

Rate	# States	Generator Matrix (octal)	Normalized Second Moment μ	Shape Gain (dB)
1/4	4	[5,7,7,7]	.198	0.7570
	8	[54,64,64,74]	.189	0.9596
1/3	4	[5,7,7]	.1717	0.8742
	8	[54,64,75]	.1623	1.118
1/2	2	[2,6]	.14661	0.5569
	4	[5,7]	.1332	0.9734
	8	[64,74]	.1304	1.066
	16	[46,72]	.1287	1.123
	32	[65,57]	.1273	1.170
	64	[554,744]	.126	1.215

TABLE 1. Normalized Second Moments of Convolutional Codes.

approximations do not differ very much. If we subtract the smallest path metric from the others, then we obtain a vector with bounded entries. These vectors determine the evolution of the Viterbi algorithm. For a finite source, such as a source with output alphabet $\{0,1\}$, there will be finitely many vectors, and the possible one-step trajectories of the Viterbi algorithm determine a directed graph on these vectors. (For continuous sources the vectors live in a compact region of 2^v-dimensional space.) This directed graph is dual to the usual encoder state diagram; it describes covering properties of the convolutional code, whereas the encoder state diagram describes distance properties. The authors are interested in whether the duality between packing and covering can be expressed as a mathematical relation between these two directed graphs.

We shall describe our new graphical methods for analyzing the covering properties of binary convolutional codes by means of the simplest possible example: the convolutional code with generator matrix $[1, 1+D]$ (for more information see [**1**]). Part of the reason for this choice is to provide background information for the contribution by Levy, Costello, and Calderbank [**3**]. The trellis diagram for this 2-state convolutional code is shown in Figure 2, where time evolves from left to right following the arrows.

Let R^N be a sequence of N binary source pairs ($2N$ binary digits). Let $C_\gamma^N(R^N)$, $\gamma = 0$ or 1, be the maximum likelihood path terminating in state γ, conditioned on reception of the source sequence R^N. Let $D_\gamma^N = d_H(C_\gamma^N(R^N), R^N)$ be the Hamming distance between $C_\gamma^N(R^N)$ and R^N, let the relative distance

$$\overline{D}_\gamma^N = D_\gamma^N - \min(D_0^N, D_1^N) ,$$

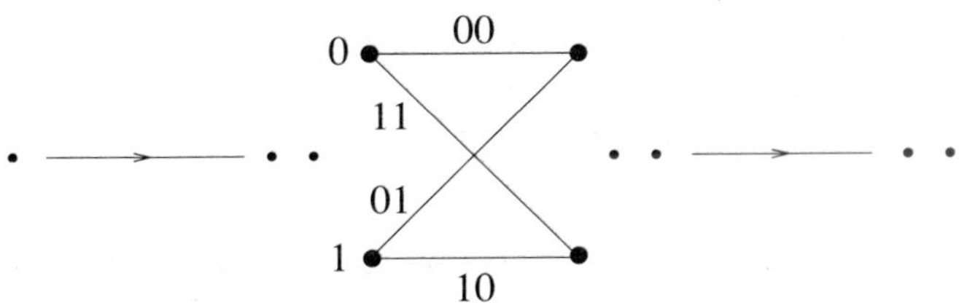

FIGURE 2. The trellis diagram of the 2-state convolutional code with generator matrix $[1, 1+D]$.

and let $\overline{D}^N = (\overline{D}_0^N, \overline{D}_1^N)$.

Calderbank, Fishburn and Rabinovich [**2**] refer to the vectors $\overline{D}^N$ as *metric states.* For any convolutional code we shall see that there are only finitely many metric states. The number of metric states grows exponentially with the total memory of the code, but many interesting convolutional codes are quite tractable. For the convolutional code $[1, 1+D]$, the difference between a branch label and a source pair is at most 2 so that the possible metric states are $(2,0)$, $(1,0)$, $(0,0)$, $(0,1)$ and $(0,2)$. To see that the number of metric states is finite for an arbitrary convolutional code, we use linearity of the code and the triangle inequality to prove

$$\left|d_H(R^N, C_\gamma^N) - d_H(R^N, C_\delta^N)\right| \le d_H(C_\gamma^N, C_\delta^N) ,$$

where C_γ^N is the set of convolutional codewords terminating in state γ.

The one-step Viterbi trajectories determine the directed graph on metric states shown in Figure 3. A thick line signifies transition probability 1/2 and a thin line probability 1/4. If the source pair t causes a metric state transition

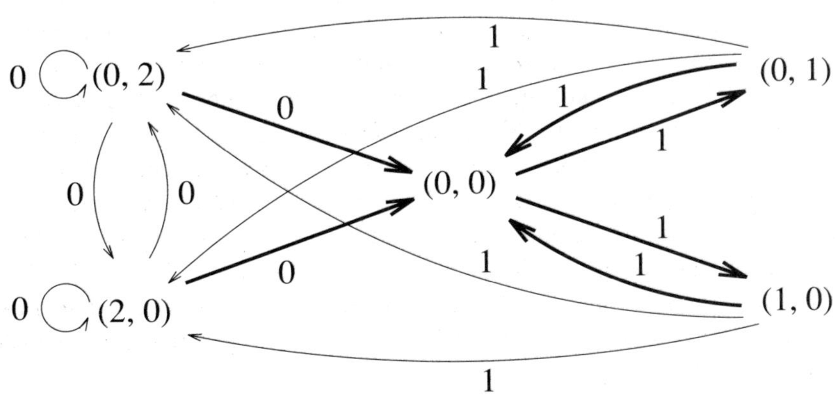

FIGURE 3. The directed graph of one-step Viterbi trajectories.

from $\overline{D}$ to D', then the one-step aggregate distortion $g(t, \overline{D})$ is given by

$$g(t, \overline{D}) = \sum_{\gamma} (D'_{\gamma} - \overline{D}_{\gamma}) ,$$

where the index γ ranges over the states of the convolutional code (in this case $\gamma = 0$ or 1). Edges in Figure 3 are labelled by the corresponding one-step aggregate distortions.

Next we collapse the directed graph shown in Figure 3 by amalgamating metric states into what Calderbank, Fishburn and Rabinovich call *m-states*, as shown in Figure 4. A vertex labelled $[a, b]$ in the collapsed graph represents the metric

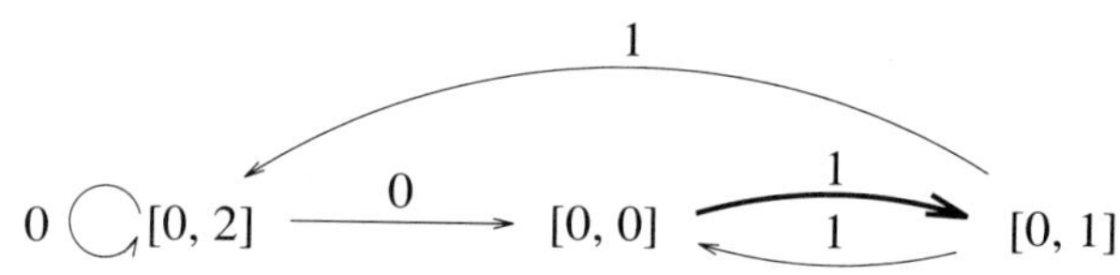

FIGURE 4. The directed graph on m-states.

states (a, b), (b, a). An edge in the collapsed graph represents many edges in the original graph, but all these edges have the same one-step aggregate Hamming distortion. Thick lines in Figure 4 represent transitions with probability 1, and thin lines represent transitions with probability 0.5.

For a general convolutional code, there is an algebraic method for amalgamating metric states. We observe that addition of a codeword from the convolutional code may be viewed as a symmetry of the infinite encoder trellis. At time i this symmetry permutes encoder states by adding some fixed binary vector to each state label. For example, addition of the codeword $c = \ldots 101010 \ldots$ reflects all paths about the center of Figure 1. The reflection of the maximum likelihood path corresponding to the source sequence R is the maximum likelihood path corresponding to $R + c$. This reflection interchanges metric states (a, b) and (b, a). Note that for a binary symmetric source the sequences R and $R + c$ are equiprobable (*cf.* Levy et al. [**3**]). Thus paths in Figure 3 that correspond to approximations of source vectors from the *same* coset of the convolutional code C collapse to a single path in Figure 4. For a general convolutional code, the permutations of encoder states obtained by adding convolutional codewords form an elementary abelian group of order 2^v where v is the memory of the code. The m-states are the orbits of metric states under the action of this group. The directed graph on m-states gives a picture of how the coset space of the convolutional code evolves with time.

Figure 4 makes it very easy to calculate expected and worst-case performance. If $\pi_{[\overline{D}]}$ is the steady-state probability of the m-state containing the metric state

$\overline{D}$, then the expected Hamming distortion ρ per dimension is given by

$$\mu = \frac{1}{(2 \times 2)} \sum_{t,[\overline{D}]} \pi_{[\overline{D}]} q_t g(t, \overline{D})$$

where $q_t = 1/4$ is the probability of source pair t. The factor (2×2) that appears in the denominator is the product of the number of encoder states with the number of dimensions per trellis stage. For the convolutional code $[1, 1+D]$, the expected Hamming distortion ρ equals $1/6$ (for comparison, this quantity is $11/64$ for the $[8, 4, 4]$ Hamming code).

The worst-case Hamming distortion per dimension among all arbitrarily long source sequences is determined by the cycles in Figure 4. For the convolutional code $[1, 1 + D]$, the worst-case Hamming distortion per dimension equals $1/4$, corresponding to the cycle $[0, 0] \to [0, 1] \to [1, 0]$. The $[8, 4, 4]$ Hamming code gives this same value, since it has covering radius 2.

References

1. A. R. Calderbank and P. C. Fishburn, "The normalized second moment of the binary lattice determined by a convolutional code," to appear, *IEEE Trans. Inform. Theory.*
2. A. R. Calderbank, P. C. Fishburn, and A. Rabinovich, "Covering properties of convolutional codes and associated lattices," preprint, 1992.
3. Y. Levy, D. J. Costello, Jr., and A. R. Calderbank, "A Markovian Method Common to Both Quantization and Decoding using Convolutional Codes," these Proceedings.
4. S. Lin and D. J. Costello, Jr., *Error Control Coding*, Prentice-Hall, Englewood Cliffs, NJ, 1983.
5. R. Zamir and M. Feder, "On universal quantization by randomized uniform/lattice quantizers," *IEEE Trans. Inform. Theory*, vol. IT-38, pp. 428–436, 1992.
6. R. Zamir and M. Feder, "Rate distortion performance in coding band-limited sources by sampling and dithered quantization," preprint, 1992.

Mathematical Sciences Research Center, AT&T Bell Laboratories, Murray Hill, NJ 07974

E-mail address: rc@research.att.com

Mathematical Sciences Research Center, AT&T Bell Laboratories, Murray Hill, NJ 07974

Statistics Department, Stanford University, Palo Alto, CA 94305

E-mail address: asya@playfair.stanford.edu

DIMACS Series in Discrete Mathematics
and Theoretical Computer Science
Volume **14**, 1993

A Markovian Method Common to Both Quantization and Decoding Using Convolutional Codes

Y. LEVY, D. J. COSTELLO, JR. AND A. R. CALDERBANK

April 29, 1993

ABSTRACT. This paper considers Markovian methods for the performance analysis of the Viterbi search algorithm when applied to both data transmission and source compression. In the decoding of convolutional codes, we evaluate the exact bit error probability associated with decoding an information sequence. In the encoding of binary sources, we evaluate the expected Hamming distortion per dimension associated with quantizing a source sequence. The decoder can be modeled as a Markov chain whose states are vectors of path metrics calculated by the Viterbi algorithm. Since the Viterbi algorithm is common to both transmission and compression, the same Markov chain appears in both problems.

1. Introduction

This paper considers Markovian methods for the performance analysis of sequence based techniques for data transmission and source compression. The set of symbol sequences or codewords is generated by a finite state machine. The set can then be searched efficiently to find the optimum codeword with respect to any measure that can be calculated on a symbol-by-symbol basis. The search algorithm is the Viterbi algorithm.

The original application of the Viterbi algorithm is the decoding of convolutional codes. Here one is interested in evaluating the exact probability of error $P_e(u)$ associated with Viterbi decoding of an information sequence u. Calculating the exact probability of error is difficult, and so simulation or upper bounds are usually used to estimate this quantity. However in 1969, Morrissey [**1**] described

1991 *Mathematics Subject Classification.* Primary 94A29, 94A05; Secondary 94B35.
This work was supported in part by NSF Grant NCR89-03429 and by NASA Grant NAG5-557.

Markovian methods for calculating the exact probability of error for binary rate $1/n$ convolutional codes with short constraint lengths, and suggested extending these methods to general rate k/n codes.

The same Markov chain introduced by Morrissey appears in more recent work by Calderbank, Fishburn, and Rabinovich [**2**] concerning the covering properties of binary convolutional codes and associated lattices. At that time these authors were unaware of the methods described by Morrissey. Calderbank, Fishburn and Rabinovich consider quantization of equiprobable binary data using a Viterbi decoder for a convolutional code. Here one is given an arbitrarily long binary sequence and one wishes to calculate the expected and worst-case Hamming distortion per dimension. The per-dimension normalization gives the fraction of bits that need to be changed in order to reach a codeword in the convolutional code.

The observation that unites these two problems is that a convolutional code with 2^ν states gives 2^ν approximations to a given sequence and that these approximations do not differ very much. Subtracting the smallest path metric gives finitely many possible metric vectors. The one-step trajectories of the Viterbi algorithm determine a Markov chain with these vectors as states. The states of this Markov chain should be viewed as the internal states of the convolutional decoder. Viterbi decoding is common to both transmission and quantization, which is why the same Markov chain appears in both problems. In the sequel we shall make this introductory discussion more concrete by considering the 2-state convolutional code with generator matrix $[1, 1 + D]$.

As an aside, we note that there is one difference between the problem of calculating the exact bit error rate for a binary symmetric channel with crossover probability p, and the problem of calculating expected Hamming distortion when quantizing a binary source, where a 1 occurs with probability p, and a 0 with probability $1 - p$. Quantization is concerned with approximating the source sequence by *some* convolutional codeword. Probability of decoder error is concerned with approximating the sequence of errors introduced by the channel by a *particular* codeword (the zero codeword). This difference has important consequences for the complexity of the two problems. In the quantization problem, complexity can sometimes be reduced through amalgamating states of the Markov chain by averaging over the full ensemble of convolutional codewords (for more details in the case $p = 1/2$, see [**3**]). In the calculation of bit error rate it is not possible to reduce complexity in this way, because there is no ensemble to average over.

2. Calculating the Probability of Decoder Error

Figure 1 shows the trellis diagram of the 2-state convolutional code with generator matrix $[1, 1 + D]$ where time evolves from left to right following the arrows.

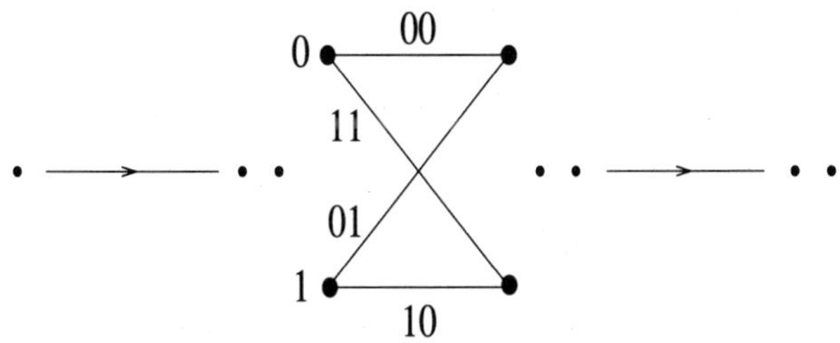

FIGURE 1. The trellis diagram of the 2-state convolutional code with generator matrix $[1, 1 + D]$.

An information sequence corresponds to a path U^N of length N through the trellis. Let $A_\gamma(U^N)$ be the maximum likelihood path from the origin of the trellis to state γ after N time units, conditioned upon reception of an output sequence R^N from a binary symmetric channel with crossover probability p. Let $D_\gamma^N = d_H(A_\gamma(U^N), R^N)$ be the Hamming distance between $A_\gamma(U^N)$ and R^N, let the *relative distance*

$$\overline{D}_\gamma^N = D_\gamma^N - \min_\delta(D_\delta^N) \tag{2.1}$$

and let

$$\overline{D}^N = (\overline{D}_0^N, \overline{D}_1^N). \tag{2.2}$$

Calderbank, Fishburn and Rabinovich [**2**] refer to the vectors $\overline{D}^N$ as *metric states*; they are the internal states of the convolutional decoder. For this code, the difference between a branch label and a channel output is at most 2, so that the possible metric states are $(2,0), (1,0), (0,0), (0,1), (0,2)$. If we set $z = \overline{D}_1^N - \overline{D}_0^N$, the one-step trajectories of the Viterbi algorithm determine a Markov chain with the following state transition probabilities from z to z':

	z': 2	1	0	-1	-2
z = 2	$(1-p)^2$	0	$2p(1-p)$	0	p^2
1	$(1-p)^2$	0	$2p(1-p)$	0	p^2
0	0	$1-p$	0	p	0
-1	$p(1-p)$	0	$p^2+(1-p)^2$	0	$p(1-p)$
-2	$p(1-p)$	0	$p^2+(1-p)^2$	0	$p(1-p)$

Each combination of a metric state $\overline{D}$ and received pair t is associated with a probability of error $P_{t,\overline{D}}$, defined as the probability [1] that, given $\overline{D}^N = \overline{D}$, it is impossible to decode the correct bit at time N upon reception of the received

[1]We assume that ties are broken by choosing the surviving path which is more favorable to a "hard decision". The metrics for competing paths are listed in reverse order and the lexicographically least vector of path metrics is chosen. If the metrics at the previous state are different, then the surviving path with the smallest metric at the previous state is chosen.

pair t. The bit error probability is then given by

$$P_e = \sum_{\overline{D},t} \pi_{\overline{D}}\, q_t\, P_{t,\overline{D}}, \tag{2.3}$$

where $\pi_{\overline{D}}$ is the steady state probability of state $\overline{D}$, and q_t is the probability of received pair t.

For this example, assuming that the all-zero sequence was sent, the probability of error associated with each metric can be computed by noting that there will be an error if and only if (i) the correct node has a nonzero relative distance, or (ii) if both nodes have zero relative distance and channel errors of the type $(0,1)$ or $(1,0)$ occur. The state transitions and corresponding probabilities of error are shown below:

	$q_t = (1-p)^2$, $t = (0,0)$				$q_t = p(1-p)$, $t = (0,1)$				$q_t = p(1-p)$, $t = (1,0)$				$q_t = p^2$, $t = (1,1)$			
z	$\overline{D}'_0$	$\overline{D}'_1$	z'	$P_{t,\overline{D}}$	$\overline{D}'_0$	$\overline{D}'_1$	z'	$P_{t,\overline{D}}$	$\overline{D}'_0$	$\overline{D}'_1$	z'	$P_{t,\overline{D}}$	$\overline{D}'_0$	$\overline{D}'_1$	z'	$P_{t,\overline{D}}$
2	0	2	2	0	1	1	0	0	1	1	0	0	2	0	-2	0
1	0	2	2	0	1	1	0	0	1	1	0	0	2	0	-2	0
0	0	1	1	0	0	1	1	1	1	0	-1	1	1	0	-1	0
-1	1	1	0	1	0	2	2	1	2	0	-2	1	1	1	0	1
-2	1	1	0	1	0	2	2	1	2	0	-2	1	1	1	0	1

This yields

$$P_e = \frac{7p^2 - 12p^3 + 10p^4 - 4p^5}{1 + 3p^2 - 2p^3}, \tag{2.4}$$

after calculation of the steady-state probabilities and substitution in (2.3).

3. Calculating Expected Hamming Distortion

Calderbank, Fishburn and Rabinovich [**2**] describe an algebraic method for amalgamating metric states into $m-$states. It is based on the observation that adding a convolutional codeword may be viewed as a symmetry of the infinite trellis. For example, addition of $\ldots 101010 \ldots$ corresponds to a reflection about the center of the trellis. At time N this symmetry permutes encoder states by adding a fixed binary symbol to each state label. The *m-states* are the orbits of metric states under this very simple group of order 2; namely $\{(0,2),(2,0)\}, \{(0,1),(1,0)\}$, and $\{(0,0)\}$. For amalgamation to work it is necessary that the source sequence $s + c$ (where c is a convolutional codeword) be equiprobable. For $p \neq 1/2$ this is not the case, and reduction in complexity will require new amalgamation techniques.

In this problem the received vector R^N becomes a sequence of binary source samples where 1 occurs with probability p and 0 with probability $1-p$. Quantization amounts to decoding R^N to the closest convolutional codeword U^N. Here again the one-step trajectories of the Viterbi decoding algorithm determine the Markov chain described in Section 2.

For every decoder state $\overline{D}$, and every source pair t, we calculate the one-step aggregate distortion $g(t,\overline{D})$. If the source pair t causes a transition from $\overline{D}$ to

(D_0', D_1'), then the one-step aggregate distortion $g(t, \overline{D})$is given by

$$g(t, \overline{D}) = (D_0' - \overline{D}_0) + (D_1' - \overline{D}_1) \ . \tag{3.1}$$

The expected Hamming distortion μ per dimension (cf. (2.3)) is then given by

$$\mu = \frac{1}{4} \sum_{\overline{D},t} \pi_{\overline{D}}\, q_t\, g(t, \overline{D}), \tag{3.2}$$

where q_t is the probability of source pair t. The number 4 appearing in the denominator of (3.2) is the product of the number of states with the number of dimensions per trellis stage.

For this example, the state transitions are described in Section 2, and the one-step aggregate distortions can be computed as $g(t, 2) = g(t, -2) = 0$ and $g(t, 1) = g(t, 0) = g(t, -1) = 1$ for all possible source pairs t.

Since $g(z) = 1$ for $z \in \{1, 0, -1\}$,

$$\mu = \frac{1}{4}(\pi_1 + \pi_0 + \pi_{-1}). \tag{3.3}$$

Solving for the steady-state probabilities, we find

$$\mu = \pi_0/2, \tag{3.4}$$

and

$$\pi_0 = \frac{2p - 3p^2 + 2p^3}{1 + 3p^2 - 2p^3} \,. \tag{3.5}$$

4. Non-Binary Source Distributions

In this section we briefly consider drawing source samples from the interval $[0, 1]$ rather than the discrete set $\{0, 1\}$.

For the decoding problem, the mathematical objective is now the bit error probability under full soft decision decoding. We can also change the problem slightly by replacing $\{0, 1\}$ with a larger discrete alphabet, for example $\{0, 1/3, 2/3, 1\}$ or $\{0, 1/2, 1\}$. The solution to this more complicated discrete problem gives the bit error probability of non-binary receiver quantization followed by soft decision decoding.

For the uniform source on $[0, 1]$, the solution to the quantization problem is the second moment of the Voronoi region of an infinite dimensional lattice (see [**3**] for more details). This infinite lattice is the set of all integer valued sequences that are congruent modulo 2 to some convolutional codeword. In source compression the Voronoi regions are the quantization cells and the second moment gives the expected mean squared error per symbol.

5. More Complicated Convolutional Codes

As the memory of the convolutional code grows, the Markovian method outlined in this paper becomes less tractable. However if we are content with approximating the bit error probability or the expected mean squared error, then an approximation to the steady-state probability of the decoder states would be very useful.

References

1. T. N. Morrissey, Jr. A Markovian analysis of Viterbi decoders for convolutional codes. In *Proceedings of the National Electronics Conference*, pages 303–307, October 1969.
2. A. R. Calderbank, P. C. Fishburn, and A. Rabinovich. Covering properties of convolutional codes and associated lattices, preprint 1992.
3. A. R. Calderbank and P. C. Fishburn. The normalized second moment of the binary lattice determined by a convolutional code, to appear, *IEEE Trans. Inform. Theory*.

Department of Electrical Engineering, University of Notre Dame, Notre Dame, IN 46556

E-mail address: ylevy@bach.helios.nd.edu, costello.2@nd.edu

Mathematical Sciences Research Center, AT&T Bell Laboratories, Murray Hill, NJ 07974

E-mail address: rc@research.att.com

DIMACS Series in Discrete Mathematics
and Theoretical Computer Science
Volume **14**, 1993

Trellis Codes, Symbolic Dynamics, and Isometries

CHRIS HEEGARD AND ERIC J. ROSSIN

May 20, 1993

ABSTRACT. We define a trellis group code over $\mathbb{R}^n$ by taking the orbit of a bi-infinite "seed sequence", $x_0 \in (\mathbb{R}^n)^{\mathbb{Z}}$, under an infinite defining group of transformations, Λ. The code is described by combining a geometrically uniform signal set and a non-trivial extension of the notion of an isometric labeling, with results from the theory of symbolic dynamic systems over groups. The isometric labeling describes a group isomorphism between a finite abstract label group, $\mathbb{G}$, and a group acting on cosets of isometries of $\mathbb{R}^n$. The defining group of the trellis code, $\Lambda \subset \mathbb{G}^{\mathbb{Z}}$, is described algebraically as a subgroup of the direct-product label group, ($\mathbb{G}^{\mathbb{Z}}$ as an infinite group) and in terms of symbolic dynamics as a subshift of the fullshift $\mathbb{G}^{\mathbb{Z}}$. Since the theory does not assume either the label group, $\mathbb{G}$, nor the defining group, Λ, to be abelian groups, it is particularly useful for describing the theory of rotationally invariant (RI) trellis codes. As an example, a class of RI trellis codes for QAM modulation is presented, which includes the 8-state RI trellis code used in the V.32 modem standard.

1. Introduction

In this paper, we define a trellis group code over $\mathbb{R}^n$ by taking the orbit of a bi-infinite "seed sequence", $x_0 \in (\mathbb{R}^n)^{\mathbb{Z}}$, under an infinite defining group of transformations, Λ. The code is described by combining a geometrically uniform signal set and a non-trivial extension of the notion of an isometric labeling with results from the theory of symbolic dynamic systems over groups [**7**]. The isometric labeling describes a group isomorphism between a finite abstract group, $\mathbb{G}$, called the label group, and a group acting on cosets of isometries of $\mathbb{R}^n$. The defining group of the trellis code, $\Lambda \subset \mathbb{G}^{\mathbb{Z}}$, is described *algebraically* as a subgroup of the direct-product label group, ($\mathbb{G}^{\mathbb{Z}}$ as an infinite group) and in terms

1991 *Mathematics Subject Classification.* Primary 94B12.
This work was supported in part by NSF grant NCR-8903931 and NCR-9207331.

of *symbolic dynamics* as a subshift (a subset closed both topologically and under a shift operator) of the *fullshift* $\mathbb{G}^{\mathbb{Z}}$ (as a full $|\mathbb{G}|$-shift). Such a group can always be presented by a deterministic, finite-state, directed graph labeled with elements of the label group $\mathbb{G}$. Furthermore, the defining group is a "shift of finite type" (SFT), conjugate (as a symbolic dynamic system) to a fullshift $\mathbb{H}^{\mathbb{Z}}$, where $\mathbb{H} \lhd \mathbb{G}$ is a normal subgroup (however, this conjugacy will not be a group isomorphism, in general). Finally, the code itself, as an orbit of the defining group of transformations, is described as an SFT, conjugate to the fullshift $\mathbb{H}^{\mathbb{Z}}$, with both a corresponding finite state machine encoder and a finite state trellis suitable for describing a decoder.

The theory of trellis codes does not assume either the label group, $\mathbb{G}$, nor the defining group, Λ, to be abelian groups. This is particularly important for the application of the theory to rotationally invariant (RI) trellis codes. A class of RI trellis codes for QAM modulation based on a non-abelian label group is presented. Interestingly, the 8-state RI trellis code of Wei [**5**], used in the V.32 modem standard, belongs to this class.

2. Group codes

Group codes were first described by Slepian [**1, 2**]. A group code is constructed from a finite group of linear transformations over $\mathbb{R}^n$, Λ ($|\Lambda| \equiv N$), and a "seed" vector x_0, also in $\mathbb{R}^n$. The group code, $C(\Lambda, x_0)$, is the orbit of x_0 under Λ; $C(\Lambda, x_0) = \{\lambda(x_0) \in \mathbb{R}^n | \lambda \in \Lambda\}$. Since Slepian's defining group, Λ, is finite, every transformation $\lambda \in \Lambda$ must be *orthogonal* (i.e., if M is the matrix representing $\lambda \in \Lambda$, then $MM^{tr} = I$) of *finite order* (i.e., $\lambda^m = \mathbb{I}$, for some integer m, where $\mathbb{I}$ is the identity transformation). Thus each transformation is either a simple rotation ($\det M = +1$) or a rotation composed with a reflection ($\det M = -1$). Hence, $C(\Lambda, x_0)$ is a block code consisting of points on the surface of an n-sphere of radius $\|x_0\|$. When n is small, and the group code is considered as a signal constellation, such a code is also called a *Slepian signal set*. A *generator set*, Λ_0, for the code is a minimal set of transformations that generates $C(\Lambda, x_0)$ (i.e., $C(\Lambda_0, x_0) = C(\Lambda, x_0), N_0 = |\Lambda_0| = |C(\Lambda, x_0)|$). Note that the generator set may or may not be (i) a subset of the defining group, Λ, (ii) a group.

A group code has several important properties. First, it is invariant under Λ, i.e., $\Lambda(C(\Lambda, x_0)) = C(\Lambda, x_0)$. Also, if $x_1 \in C(\Lambda, x_0)$ ($x_1 = \lambda_1(x_0)$ for some $\lambda_1 \in \Lambda$), then $C(\Lambda, x_1) = C(\Lambda, x_0)$. The code is "geometrically uniform", which in part implies that the set of distances (using the Euclidean metric) from one codeword to all others (i.e., the distance profile) is independent of the "reference" codeword. This also implies that

$$d_{min}{}^2 = \min_{\lambda \in \Lambda, \lambda(x_0) \neq x_0} \|\lambda(x_0) - x_0\|^2,$$

where $d_{min}{}^2$ is the minimum squared Euclidean distance. Finally, the generating set is obtained as representatives of the right (or left) cosets of the stabilizer subgroup of x_0, $S(x_0) = \{\lambda \in \Lambda | \lambda(x_0) = x_0\}$. When Λ is presented as a matrix group, that is, for all x, $\lambda(x) = Mx$, where $\lambda \in \Lambda$ and $x \in \mathbb{R}^n$, then the stabilizer $S(x_0) = \{M | Mx_0 = x_0\}$, and we work with right cosets. Note that $S(x_0)$ is in general not normal (i.e., self-conjugate), hence Λ_0 may not be a group. However, one often can choose a system of coset representatives that do form a group. In fact, such a choice of Λ_0 is often normal in Λ ($\Lambda_0 \lhd \Lambda$), whence one can write Λ as the *semi-direct* product, $\Lambda = \Lambda_0 \rtimes S(x_0)$ [**11**].

For example, consider the signal set generated by the group D_4, the symmetries of the square. As a group of isometries in $\mathbb{R}^2$, D_4 can be generated as $< R, S >$, where R is a counter-clockwise rotation by 90° and S is a reflection about the 45° line. The group D_4 has 8 elements, $\{I, R, R^2, R^3, S, SR, SR^2, SR^3\}$, and is non-commutative. To generate a signal set from this group, choose an initial seed $x_0 \in \mathbb{R}^2$ and apply x_0 to each matrix $M \in D_4$. The size of the signal set is dependent on the choice of x_0, and can be 8-PSK or QPSK (the latter if x_0 is chosen to lie on the axis of reflection). In this case there is a non-trivial stabilizer, $S(x_0) = \{I, S\}$, and a generating set can be chosen as either $\Lambda_0 =< R >$ or $\Lambda_1 =< SR, R^2 >$. Note that both Λ_0 and Λ_1 are normal subgroups of D_4 (since they are of index 2), and yet are not isomorphic, since $\Lambda_0 \cong \mathbb{Z}_4$ while $\Lambda_1 \cong \mathbb{Z}_2 \times \mathbb{Z}_2$.

3. Geometrically uniform codes

The matrices used to generate group codes are examples of isometries. An isometry, λ, is a distance-preserving map, i.e., $\lambda : \mathbb{R}^n \to \mathbb{R}^n$, $\|\lambda(x)\| = \|x\|$. The set of isometries in Euclidean space that map a finite set of points (e.g., a signal set) onto itself define a finite (non-abelian) group under composition. For example, if $\mathcal{S}$ is a signal set in $\mathbb{R}^n$, and Λ is a group of isometries in $\mathbb{R}^n$ such that $\Lambda(\mathcal{S}) = \mathcal{S}$, then Λ is a group that fixes $\mathcal{S}$. Note that if $\mathcal{S}$ is a Slepian signal set, Λ consists of reflections and rotations in $\mathbb{R}^n$. Forney extended Slepian's idea to groups other than matrices [**3**] by considering translations and extending the signal sets to infinite sets such as lattices. The code (or signal set), $C(\Lambda; x_0)$, is now infinite; a finite set is obtained by intersection with a boundary region, $B \subset \mathbb{R}^n$, that is, $C_B(\Lambda; x_0) = C(\Lambda; x_0) \cap B$. Note that $C_B(\Lambda; x_0)$ is no longer geometrically uniform, due to this boundary. For example, a signal set could be constructed as follows (note this is presented for demonstration purposes only, and not as a practical signal set). Take the orbit of the point $x_0 = (\frac{1}{2}, \frac{1}{2}) \in \mathbb{R}^2$ under the action of the group of isometries $\Lambda =< S, R, T_x T_y, T_x {T_y}^{-1} >$. Here T_x is a translation by $(2, 0)$ and T_y by $(0, 2)$. The signal set, $C(\Lambda; x_0)$, is not a lattice since it is not closed under addition in $\mathbb{R}^2$. However, the distance spectrum is the same for every point, and it is geometrically uniform (such a set is called a regular array).

Forney also introduced the idea of an "isometric labeling." An isometric labeling of a geometrically uniform signal set is an abstract group, together with a set of labels, and a correspondence between this group and the signal set, such that isometries on the signal set correspond to a group action on the labels. Note that in [**3**], the labeling was itself the (abelian) abstract group, where the group action was addition of labels. We consider the more general case of isometries between (possibly non-abelian) label groups and cosets of the defining group of isometries. In principle, an isometric labeling implies a "nice" choice of the label set to allow an efficient encoder structure.

Given an isometric labeling, the "code" can then be viewed as the orbit of G acting on the label set L, or, in some cases, over G itself, as in [**3**]. One can now construct sequence codes over L. For example, Forney showed that if the label group is binary, then it follows that when a linear convolutional code chooses points from a lattice (which is a geometrically uniform signal set as described above) the result is a geometrically uniform trellis code. All the ideas from geometrically uniform signal sets carry over to such trellis codes, e.g., uniformity of the distance spectrum, etc. This is particularly important in helping to reduce the computational complexity of searching for good trellis codes. What also carries over is the notion that the code (as sequences) is the orbit of a group acting on the label set, only now the group is itself an infinite set of sequences. Geometrically uniform trellis codes are then the orbits of special groups of sequences (symbolic systems over the group G). This idea will be made precise in the following sections.

4. Symbolic dynamics over groups

This section reviews some basic ideas from the field of symbolic dynamics, and then summarizes some results of Kitchens [**7**] on symbolic systems over groups. For a more complete introduction to symbolic dynamics as applied to coding, see [**10, 12, 6, 13**].

Symbolic dynamics is the study of shift invariant sets of sequences over a finite alphabet, A. The basic objects of study are subsets of $A^{\mathbb{Z}}$, the set of all bi-infinite sequences over A. A finite length sequence of elements from A is called a *word* (or *block*) over A. (Sometimes the term *strings* will be used for sequences, and finite strings for words or blocks.) Let x be a *point* in $A^{\mathbb{Z}}$ (i.e., x is a bi-infinite sequence over A). We define the left-shift map $\sigma : A^{\mathbb{Z}} \to A^{\mathbb{Z}}$ by $[\sigma x]_i = x_{i+1}\ \forall i$. The map σ is clearly invertible and $\{\sigma^n | n \in \mathbb{Z}\}$ establishes a group-action of the infinite cyclic group $\mathbb{Z}$ on the set $A^{\mathbb{Z}}$. We can also endow $A^{\mathbb{Z}}$ with a topology, thus turning the set $A^{\mathbb{Z}}$ into a topological space. The pair $(A^{\mathbb{Z}}, \sigma)$ is said to be a *symbolic dynamical system* (or simply a *symbolic system*) commonly known as the *fullshift* over A.

The objects of most interest are shift-invariant subsets of the fullshift, e.g., $\mathcal{S} \subset A^{\mathbb{Z}}$, $\sigma(\mathcal{S}) = \mathcal{S}$. The shift operator σ restricted to $\mathcal{S}$ is well defined. The pair $(\mathcal{S}, \sigma)$ is said to be a *subshift* of $(A^{\mathbb{Z}}, \sigma)$ or simply a *subshift over A*. We will usually drop the notation $(\mathcal{S}, \sigma)$, and instead write $\mathcal{S}$.

The subshift $\mathcal{S}$ is assumed to be *closed* under the topology of $A^{\mathbb{Z}}$. A closed subset $\mathcal{S}$ is characterized by the property that any sequence $x \in A^{\mathbb{Z}}$ belongs to $\mathcal{S}$ iff every finite substring of x is contained in some sequence belonging to $\mathcal{S}$. The requirement that the shifts of interest be closed eliminates "pathological" shift-invariant subsets from consideration. For an example of a subset that is not closed, consider the following "unobservable" code, due to Loeliger [**14**]. Let $\mathcal{C}_{even}$ be the subset of $(\mathbb{Z}_2)^{\mathbb{Z}}$ with even Hamming weight. The code $\mathcal{C}_{even}$ is clearly shift-invariant. However, every finite string of 0's is contained in some $x \in \mathcal{C}_{even}$, yet the all 0's sequence is not in $\mathcal{C}_{even}$. Therefore $\mathcal{C}_{even}$ is not closed.

For trellis codes, one is interested in studying maps between full-shifts (the "uncoded" data) and subshifts (the "codes") that have a particular Euclidean distance characteristic. In symbolic dynamics, the maps of interest are called *block maps*, and the subshifts they induce are called *sliding block codes.* Fix integers m and a and a subshift X. A block map Φ, maps a "window" of coordinates of $x \in X$ from $i-m$ to $i+a$ to the ith coordinate y_i of $y \in Y$. That is, if X is a subshift over A_1, and Y is a subshift over A_2, then $\Phi : \mathcal{B}_{m+a+1}(X) \to A_2$ (where $\mathcal{B}_N(\mathcal{S})$is the collection of all allowed words of length N in $\mathcal{S}$ over A_1). Now define the map $\phi : X \to {A_2}^{\mathbb{Z}}$, where y_i is given by

$$y_i = \Phi(x_{i-m}, x_{i-m+1}, \cdots, x_{i+a}).$$

The map ϕ is called a sliding block code with memory m and anticipation a.

If a sliding block code $\phi : X \to Y$ is onto, then ϕ is called a *factoring of X onto Y*, and Y is called a *factor* of X. More generally, a *factor map* between two systems $(\mathcal{S}, \sigma)$ and $(\mathcal{T}, \tau)$ is a continuous map $\phi : \mathcal{S} \to \mathcal{T}$ such that $\phi\sigma = \tau\phi$. If ϕ is one-to-one, then ϕ is called an *embedding of X into Y.* If ϕ has an inverse that is also a sliding block map, i.e., $\exists \psi : Y \to X$ such that $\psi(\phi(x)) = x \ \forall x \in X$, then ϕ is *invertible* with unique inverse ψ. In this case, we say X and Y are *conjugate*, and write $X \cong Y$.

The subshifts of interest for coding are *sophic shifts* and *shifts of finite type* (SFT) [**12, 6**]. A sophic shift is a subshift that can be generated by a finite state machine, that is, all bi-infinite walks on a labeled, directed graph with a finite number of states. An SFT is a sophic shift for which there exists a finite word length (i.e., memory) after which all future behavior is specified. An SFT can also be characterized by an integer m such that for any word w of length at least m, left semi-infinite sequences x, x', and right semi-infinite sequences y, y',

$$xwy \in \mathcal{S} \text{ and } x'wy' \in \mathcal{S} \Rightarrow xwy' \in \mathcal{S}(x'wy \in \mathcal{S}).$$

Clearly every full-shift is an SFT (with memory $m = 0$).

A subshift $\mathcal{S}$ is said to be *irreducible* if whenever x and y are in the subshift, there exists an admissible word $w \in \mathcal{S}$ such that the sequence obtained by concatenating $x|_{-\infty}^{-1}$, w and $y|_0^{\infty}$ is also in the subshift. A subshift is it strongly controllable if w can always be chosen to be the same length. Every sophic system (and hence SFT) can be presented by a minimal, deterministic, finite-state, directed graph, whose edges are labeled over the alphabet, A [**15**]. This minimal graph is unique, up to graph isomorphism, and is called the Shannon (or Fischer) cover.

An SFT is important for coding, since any shift that is conjugate to an SFT is itself an SFT. Given a conjugacy between a full-shift, say $A^{\mathbb{Z}}$ and an SFT $\mathcal{S}$, then there exist both an *encoder* (i.e., $\phi : A^{\mathbb{Z}} \to \mathcal{S}$) and an *uncoder* (i.e., $\psi : \mathcal{S} \to A^{\mathbb{Z}}$) that can be described as sliding-window maps. Thus, if ϕ is used to encode data to be transmitted over a noisy channel, a finite number of errors cannot cause ψ to make an unbounded number of errors while inverting ϕ.

In this paper, we consider the case when the finite alphabet is $\mathbb{G}$, a finite group. The full shift $\mathbb{G}^{\mathbb{Z}}$ is then a group under the Cartesian product of $\mathbb{G}$. The subshifts of interest are subgroups S of $G^{\mathbb{Z}}$. The shift operator is then an automorphism; it is also continuous under the topology of $\mathbb{G}^{\mathbb{Z}}$. The ith coordinate of the product of $x, y \in \mathcal{S}$, $(x * y)_i$, can be determined with bounded memory and anticipation. Kitchens [**7**] determined that if a subshift $\mathcal{S}$ is a group, then $\mathcal{S}$ is in fact an SFT which is conjugate to some full shift. The states of the graph which generate $\mathcal{S}$ form a group (as well as the state sequences); the outgoing edges from the "identity" state form a normal subgroup of the label group, H, (called the "input group" in [**9**]) and the subshift is in fact conjugate to the fullshift $H^{\mathbb{Z}}$ (but not isomorphic as groups). The parallel transitions also form a normal subgroup called the "parallel edge group".

5. Trellis codes from symbolic systems of isometries

To describe a geometrically uniform trellis code $\mathcal{C}$, begin with the set of isometries, U, that map cosets of a particular constellation partition onto itself. Note that these are cosets of a group of isometries over $\mathbb{R}^n$. This set forms a finite (non-abelian) group under composition. Describe a symbolic dynamic group, $\mathcal{S}$, over U; $\mathcal{S}$ is generated by a graph that is referred to as an isometry graph of the code. The trellis code, $\mathcal{C}$, is then the orbit of an initial sequence $x_0 \in (\mathbb{R}^n)^{\mathbb{Z}}$ under the action of $\mathcal{S}$. The code $\mathcal{C}$ is a *trellis group code*, since it is a generalization of a Slepian group code as defined in Section 2. Note that if x_0 is a constant sequence, the encoder can be obtained by taking the action of each edge label of the graph of $\mathcal{S}$ on the "point" x_0. However, the resulting graph will in general not be minimal, (i.e., the graph that generates C may be smaller than the graph that generates $\mathcal{S}$).

Recently, work has been done to describe convolutional codes over groups via linear system theory (LST) [**9, 8**]. There is naturally a strong correspondence between the concepts in symbolic dynamics and LST. Hence, we include the following table which summarizes the related concepts in the two disciplines. The table also lists the specific concepts for subshifts that are sophic systems.

Symbolic Dynamics	LST	Sofic System
• Topologically Closed	• Observable Complete	• Always True
• SFT	• Strongly Observable	• Unique label sequences
• Irreducible	• Controllable	• Each state leads to all others
• Aperiodic	• Strongly controllable	• GCD of cycle lengths is 1

TABLE 1. Symbolic Dynamics/Linear System Theory Dictionary

6. Application: rotationally invariant trellis codes for QAM

Rotationally invariant (RI) trellis codes are important whenever the modulation signal set has a rotational symmetry and the transmission system can introduce a phase rotation. Rotational invariance means that a trellis code is closed under rotation of the individual elements of the signal set that it labels. For a geometrically uniform trellis code to be RI within the framework of this paper, it is now clear that a necessary and sufficient condition is that the symbolic system, $\mathcal{S}$, that generates it must include the "all rotations" sequence.

We demonstrate these ideas by considering a set of maps U of the form $u(x) = Ax + b$, where $A \in \left\{ \begin{bmatrix} 1 & 0 \\ 0 & 1 \end{bmatrix}, \begin{bmatrix} 1 & 1 \\ 0 & 1 \end{bmatrix}, \begin{bmatrix} 1 & 0 \\ 0 & -1 \end{bmatrix}, \begin{bmatrix} 1 & 1 \\ 0 & -1 \end{bmatrix} \right\}$ is an invertible matrix and $x, b \in \mathbb{Z}_2 \times \mathbb{Z}_4$. These maps, which operate on the labels of a QAM constellation, form a group of 32 elements, U. Each map in U induces an isometry on the QAM signal set (the standard 8-way partition of $\mathbb{Z}^2$ under an isometric labeling [4]). The code $\mathcal{C}$ is then the orbit of an isometry graph over U. This implies that the graph of the encoder is embedded in the isometry graph, since all codewords can be generated as the action of the isometries on the "all zero" sequence. In other words, if the isometry graph is only labeled with the b's (i.e., let A be the identity map), the resulting graph must be reducible to the graph of the encoder for $\mathcal{C}$.

For example, consider the following class of RI trellis codes: let the generator G be the rate 1/2 convolutional code over $\mathbb{Z}_4$ (the integers modulo 4) given by $[1 - D, G_p(D)]$. The input sequence is also over $\mathbb{Z}_4$, but the output is taken as $(m, p) \in \mathbb{Z}_2 \times \mathbb{Z}_4$, where m is the most significant bit generated by the $1 - D$ term, and p is the output from $G_p(D)$. The outputs of the code are then mapped to the 8 cosets. Two examples of codes in this class are a 4-state code with generator $[1 - D, 2 - D]$, that has a free Euclidean distance of 3 and an 8-state isometry graph, and an 8-state code with generator $[1 - D, 2 + D + 2D^2]$, that has a free Euclidean distance of 5 and which also has an 8-state isometry graph. The latter code is equivalent to the 8-state RI trellis code used in the V.32 standard [**5**], while the first is an example where the isometry graph is larger than the graph of the encoder.

References

1. D. Slepian, *Group codes for the Gaussian channel*, Bell System Technical Journal **47** (April, 1968), 575–602.
2. I. Ingemarsson, *Group codes for the Gaussian channel*, Topics in coding theory (in honour of Lars H. Zetterberg) (1989), Springer-Verlag, 73–108.
3. G. D. Forney, Jr., *Geometrically uniform codes*, IEEE Transactions on Information Theory **37** (Sep., 1991), 1241–1260.
4. E. Rossin and C. Heegard, *Rotationally invariant trellis codes with a linear structure*, Proceedings 26th Conference on Information Sciences and Systems (Mar. 18–20, 1992).
5. L. F. Wei, *Rotationally invariant convolutional channel coding with expanded signal space — Parts I and II*, IEEE Journal on Selected Areas of Communication **SAC-2** (Sep., 1984), 659–686.
6. B. Marcus, *Sofic systems and encoding data*, IEEE Transactions on Information Theory **IT-31** (May, 1985), 366–377.
7. B. Kitchens, *Expansive dynamics on zero-dimensional groups*, Ergodic Theory and Dynamical Systems **7** (1987), 249–261.
8. H.-A. Loeliger and T. Mittelholzer, *Convolutional codes over groups*, to be published.
9. G. D. Forney, Jr. and M. D. Trott, *The dynamics of codes over groups*, to be published.
10. N. T. Sindhushayana, *Symbolic dynamics, automata theory and the theory of coding: a comparative study and applications*, M.S. Thesis (1992).
11. M. Hall, Jr., The theory of groups, Chelsea Publishing Company (1976).
12. R. L. Adler, D. Coppersmith, and M. Hassner, *Algorithms for sliding block codes: An application of symbolic dynamics to information theory*, IEEE Transactions on Information Theory **IT-29** (January, 1983), 5–22.
13. C. Heegard, B. Marcus, and P. H. Siegel, *Variable-length state splitting with applications to average runlength-constrained (ARC) codes*, IEEE Transactions on Information Theory **37** (May, 1991), 759–777.
14. H.-A. Loeliger, *On convolutional codes over groups*, in Proc. 5th Tirennia Workshop on Digital Communications (September, 1991).
15. R. Fischer, *Graphs and symbolic dynamics*, in Topics in Information Theory, Colloquia Mathematica Societatis János Bolyai (Hungary) **16** (1975), 229–244.

School of Electrical Engineering, Cornell University, Ithaca, NY 14853
E-mail address: heegard@ee.cornell.edu; ejr@ee.cornell.edu

DIMACS Series in Discrete Mathematics
and Theoretical Computer Science
Volume **14**, 1993

The Design of Finite-State Machines for Quantization Using Simulated Annealing

ERCAN ENGİN KURUOĞLU AND ENDER AYANOĞLU

January 23, 1993

ABSTRACT. In this paper, the combinatorial optimization algorithm known as *simulated annealing* is used for the optimization of the trellis structure or the next-state map of the decoder finite-state machine in scalar and vector trellis waveform coding, finite-state vector quantization, and trellis coded quantization. The generalized Lloyd algorithm is incorporated into simulated annealing to design the codebook or the output map. Comparison of simulation results with previous work in the literature shows that this method yields better coding systems than those published in the literature in general.

1. Introduction

Source coding, one of the main concerns of information theory, is the study of coding of information-bearing signals or data, so that they can be transmitted through finite transmission rate and noiseless communication channels to be recovered at the decoder with little or no distortion. When a waveform is encoded in a way to only approximately recover the transmitted data at the decoder, without any source modeling, the source coding technique is known as waveform coding. A high-performance waveform coding technique is known as trellis waveform coding or trellis quantization, and belongs to the more general class of lookahead or delayed decision source or waveform coding [**1**], [**2**]. Trellis waveform coding uses a finite-state machine as the decoder. This machine is defined by an output map, corresponding to the codebook, and a next-state map, corresponding to the trellis structure, both being functions of the channel symbol and the current state. The extension of the next-state map or the state transition diagram in time yields the trellis structure, a weighted directed graph consisting of identical stages. The branches of the trellis are labeled by members

1991 *Mathematics Subject Classification.* Primary 94A29.

of the codebook, i.e., the reproduction symbols or the codewords. Each stage of the graph corresponds to a time instant. The encoder is matched to the decoder in the sense that it examines the trellis and finds the channel sequence that leads to minimum distortion between the input and the reproduction symbols. This can be accomplished by a trellis search algorithm, i.e., the encoder in a trellis waveform coding system is simply a trellis search algorithm matched to the decoder finite-state machine. One such search algorithm is the Viterbi Algorithm (VA) [**3**]. VA solves the shortest path problem in an efficient manner in weighted directed graphs such as those encountered in trellis waveform coding. Therefore, the design problem for the trellis waveform coding system reduces to the design of the decoder finite-state machine. This problem has been addressed by several authors in the literature. For example, for fixed next-state maps, Stewart et al. applied the generalized Lloyd algorithm (GLA) to the optimization of codewords [**2**]. Freeman et al. used a conjugate gradient method for the optimization of codewords [**4**], keeping the trellis structure fixed as in [**2**]. Foster et al. developed a finite-state vector quantizer, codewords designed by GLA, and the finite-state machine structure designed by a heuristic approach [**5**]. In this work, we optimize both the codewords and the finite-state machine structure, but use a different approach than [**5**]. We will present simulation results for four different quantization systems with finite-state decoders, all of which can be considered as special cases or extensions of the trellis waveform coding system as described above.

As noted above, in trellis waveform coding, the decoder is equivalent to the state transition diagram of the finite-state machine, or the trellis structure. Then, for a given set of codewords, or quantization levels, and a given input sequence, it is clear that finding the optimum decoder is equivalent to finding the trellis structure that will generate a channel sequence with minimum distortion at the decoder output. This is a combinatorial optimization problem and in this paper, for the solution of this problem we propose the *simulated annealing* algorithm [**6**].

2. Simulated Annealing

Simulated annealing (SA) is an optimization algorithm which takes its motivation from condensed matter physics. Annealing is a term borrowed from condensed matter physics and there is an analogy between the annealing of solids and the problem of solving large scale combinatorial optimization problems. The annealing of solids is a process in which a solid is heated up to a high temperature where virtually all electrons are free. Then the temperature is decreased slightly, and kept at that value long enough so that the solid reaches equilibrium. That is, the electrons align themselves in the minimum energy configuration. The process is continued in this way until the temperature is very low, so that virtually there are no free electrons in the solid. At the end of the process, one obtains a minimum energy configuration in the solid. But, to reach such a configuration, cooling should be very slow, so that exact equilibrium is reached and no electrons are captured in the vacancies with high energies. In simulated annealing, the problem is specified with the function to be optimized and the state space of the function parameters. The function to be optimized corresponds to the system energy in the annealing of the solids, and the state space to the configuration of electrons on different energy levels. The algorithm is initiated by choosing an arbitrary initial state. The function is evaluated at this state. Then, a neighboring state is chosen and the function value evaluated at this state is compared with the previous one. If the second value evaluated is "better" than the first one, this state is chosen as the new state of the function. It is obvious that the function will evolve to be "optimized" in this process, but it may get stuck in one of the local optima. Simulated annealing prevents this phenomenon by accepting some "worse" neighboring states as the new state of the function. This is performed according to the Metropolis criterion which generates an approximate Boltzmann distribution for the state probabilities when the equilibrium is reached [**7**]. For a detailed analysis and various applications of the simulated annealing algorithm, the reader is referred to [**8**], [**9**], [**10**].

3. Next-State Map Design

In this paper we propose using SA for the optimization of the next-state map. The state space is chosen to be all the possible state transitions in a single stage of the trellis. We are interested in trellis waveform coders with rate 1 bit/sample. This imposes a constraint on the encoder structure: from each node, there are two outgoing branches which correspond to values of 0 and 1 for the binary channel code. The move set has been chosen to be just the moving of one of the branches from its current position to another, so that the output of a move is again in the state space. The energy or the cost function to be minimized is simply the minimum distortion calculated by the Viterbi algorithm. The initial value of the control parameter or the temperature is calculated as suggested by Johnson et al. [**11**]. Geometric improvement [**9**] is used as the cooling schedule. The length of Metropolis loops, i.e., the number of perturbations (flipping of the branches) at each temperature (at each value of the control parameter), is determined experimentally and heuristically. For example, for fast cooling schedules one needs longer Metropolis loops, or as the number of nodes in the trellis is increased, the size of the state space increases and longer Metropolis loops are needed to reach equilibrium.

4. Output Map Design

A second issue in trellis waveform coding is the design of the output map or the codebook. We propose GLA [**1**] for this purpose. GLA takes the output of the encoder and computes the centroids of the source symbols coded with the same codeword. Then these centroids are assigned as the new codeword values.

The source is encoded again using the new codebook and the process is repeated until there is negligible improvement.

In this work, GLA and SA are run together. For a given codebook, the trellis structure is optimized using SA, and for this structure, the codebook is modified using GLA. Then for the new codebook, the trellis structure is reoptimized. The process is continued until the system reaches an equilibrium, with respect to the SA criteria.

5. Simulation Results

To evaluate the performance of the system, several different sources are encoded and the performance results are compared with the results obtained by other researchers.

5.1. Scalar Trellis Waveform Coding. A zero-mean, unit-variance memoryless Gaussian source was coded with SA and GLA, in order to compare with GLA with the fixed finite-state decoder structure [**2**], and also, with the methods Freeman et al. used for the optimization of codewords [**4**], keeping the trellis structure fixed as in [**2**]. In Table 1, the SQNR values for SA+GLA are given

	SA+GLA		PA64		CGA		GLA
K	train	test	train	test	train	test	test
2	4.59	4.58	4.70	4.70	4.85	4.70	4.40
3	5.04	5.04	5.05	4.85	5.13	5.07	4.70
4	5.20	5.11	5.20	5.03	5.35	5.18	4.92
5	5.38	5.24	5.40	5.05	5.47	5.30	5.07
6	5.50	5.26	5.70	5.15	5.55	5.42	5.12

TABLE 1. SQNR [dB] results for the memoryless Gaussian source. K: constraint length, SA+GLA: trellis waveform coder with simulated annealing and generalized Lloyd algorithm, PA64: Powell's 1964 algorithm, CGA: conjugate gradient algorithm, GLA: generalized Lloyd algorithm only.

together with the results of Freeman et al. [**4**] and Stewart et al. [**2**], for a trellis of 10,000 samples with unit rate and a memoryless Gaussian process $\{X_n\}$ that has the distortion-rate theory bound ($D(R)$ bound) equal to 6.02 dB where SQNR is defined as

$$\text{SQNR} = 10\ \log_{10} \frac{\sum_k X_k^2}{\sum_k (X_k - \widehat{X}_k)^2}$$

and $\widehat{X}_k$ is the quantized form of X_k. First, note the improvement from GLA to SA+GLA. This improvement is due to the optimization of the trellis structure, and it is bigger for sources with memory, as will be seen in the sequel.

To judge the improvement possible with codebook design algorithms other than GLA, we listed the trellis waveform coding system results from [**4**]. Freeman et al. viewed the encoder simulation as the evaluation of an objective function of the code assignment variables. They used two optimization methods due to Powell. The first one is a nonderivative descent method called Powell's 1964 algorithm (PA64) [**12**] and the second is a gradient descent method called Powell's conjugate gradient algorithm (CGA) [**13**], [**14**]. Each of these methods performs a series of line searches in conjugate search directions. A line search is in effect the minimization with respect to one parameter, that gives the position along a straight line in the space of independent variables [**4**].

As can be seen from Table 1, when test results are compared, SA+GLA outperforms Powell's 1964 algorithm PA64. On the other hand, conjugate gradient algorithm CGA gives the best results among the four. Noting the improvement from the GLA results to the SA+GLA results, and noting the improvement from the GLA results to the CGA results, one can speculate that using the conjugate gradient algorithm instead of GLA for codebook design and employing SA for trellis structure optimization, i.e., SA+CGA, better performance can be obtained.

The advantage of a waveform coding system with memory, such as the trellis waveform coder, is in getting high performance in encoding sources with memory. To this end, in this work, trellis waveform coding systems of different constraint lengths and of rate one were trained using SA and GLA by a first order Gauss-Markov source $\{X_n\}$ defined by

$$X_n = aX_{n-1} + W_n \qquad n = 1, 2, \ldots$$

where W_n is a white and zero-mean Gaussian time series, and $a = 0.9$. This source was chosen since it is a common model of real data and it is widely used in comparing data compression systems [**1**]. The $D(R)$ bound for this source is 13.2 dB. For constraint lengths of 2–8, signal-to-quantization-noise ratios (SQNR) were computed. Then the system was tested using a test sequence with the same statistics. In Table 2, the SQNR values are given (SA+GLA) together with the results of Stewart et al. (GLA) [**2**], and of Ayanoğlu and Gray (PTWC) [**15**]. Results obtained using SA are better than those of [**2**], especially for structures with small constraint lengths. This is expected since in [**2**] the trellis structure was fixed, not optimized. The results obtained via the predictive system [**15**] are better than our results for structures with small constraint lengths. Again, this is expected since the predictive system has a higher system complexity. However, our results are close to those of [**15**], so that the nonpredictive system once again becomes attractive. Alternatively, SA can be incorporated into the predictive system design with possibly better performance.

An important practical problem in using the Viterbi algorithm is that the algorithm does not make a decision on the optimum path until it reaches the final node. This requires the storage of all survivor paths until the algorithm

	SA+GLA		GLA		PTWC	
K	train	test	train	test	train	test
2	7.03	6.81	6.92	6.86	11.08	10.73
3	9.81	9.45	8.77	8.59	11.53	11.18
4	11.24	11.13	10.13	9.87	11.84	11.47
5	11.90	11.77	11.05	10.67	12.18	11.83
6	12.00	11.90	11.56	11.09	12.38	11.96
7	12.29	11.98	11.87	11.70	12.52	12.52
8	12.32	11.97	12.13	11.91	12.64	12.58

TABLE 2. SQNR [dB] results for the first order Gauss-Markov source. K: constraint length, SA+GLA: simulated annealing and generalized Lloyd algorithm, GLA: generalized Lloyd algorithm only, PTWC: predictive trellis waveform coder.

execution is completed. It is possible to get around this difficulty with the following observation. Most of the time, at least some of the survivor paths at time k have a common root some l stages back at time $k - l$. If all the survivor paths at time k have the same common root l stages back, we can safely make a decision about the optimum path up to time $k - l$ without waiting any further. One way of performing truncated search is to stop the normal execution of VA periodically and perform a back search to find the root where the survivor paths have a common root. If a common root is found, a decision can be made for the optimal path before the root and the cursor of the storage array is moved to the root. Even if a root cannot be found at truncation depth l, by considering the path with the lowest metric up to this node, one can force a decision for the optimum path. If the search period (the truncation depth) is kept sufficiently large, the probability of making errors in the truncation process will be low. In the literature a truncation depth of 5 times the constraint length is suggested for decoding convolutional codes [**16**]. Since performing VA with truncated search reduces the storage requirements as well as the coding delay, it is desirable. To check the validity of our hypothesis that for large enough truncation depths, the performance of the full search VA and truncated search VA are very similar, we tested a trellis trained by full search standard VA and the first order Gauss-Markov source, using truncated search VA and with the same source. The results are given in Table 3. As can be seen, there is no performance loss for VAs with truncation depth of 10 times the constraint length and above. But for truncation depths shorter than 5 times the constraint length, the performance difference becomes significant.

5.2. Finite-State Vector Quantization. For the first-order Gauss-Markov source, we obtained simulation results for finite-state vector quantization (FSVQ), where the trellis search is reduced to a depth of one stage, designed using

K	TD=∞	$100K$	$50K$	$10K$	$5K$	$3K$	$2K$
2	5.482	5.482	5.482	5.476	5.448	5.358	5.122
3	8.709	8.709	8.709	8.683	8.592	8.449	8.235
4	11.304	11.304	11.304	11.294	11.153	10.706	10.183
5	11.550	11.550	11.550	11.539	11.315	10.821	10.359
6	12.103	12.103	12.103	12.057	11.732	11.194	10.805

TABLE 3. SQNR [dB] results for the first order Gauss-Markov source with different truncation depths. K: constraint length, TD: truncation depth.

SA+GLA. Our results are given in Table 4, together with the results obtained

	SA+GLA		VQ		OLT	
k	train	test	train	test	train	test
1	9.46	9.50	4.42	4.40	9.21	9.14
2	10.65	10.81	7.90	7.86	11.04	10.90
3	11.17	11.26	9.24	9.17	11.22	11.08
4	11.53	11.38	10.15	10.07	11.34	11.12

TABLE 4. SQNR [dB] results for 8-state FSVQ and VQ for the first order Gauss-Markov source. k: vector length, SA+GLA: FSVQ with simulated annealing and generalized Lloyd algorithm, VQ: memoryless vector quantizer, OLT : FSVQ with omniscient labeled transition design method.

by Foster et al. [**5**] and memoryless vector quantization results. Foster et al. used a method based on a heuristic approach called Omniscient Labeled Transition (OLT) for the design of the next-state map and GLA for the codebook design. Our results show that SA+GLA performs much better than VQ and generally better than OLT although not much better. OLT is known to yield the best results obtained in FSVQ so far [**1**]. Our results show that SA+GLA is a contender for performing better, and we believe the performance improvement may be more significant for more complicated sources, such as speech samples.

5.3. Vector Trellis Waveform Coding. Coding symbols in blocks rather than one by one may be expected to yield higher performance since there is a higher degree of freedom in choosing decision regions for quantization in block coding and since this enables exploitation of the correlation between samples. Simulation results for coding symbols in pairs are given along with the results for scalar coding using simulated annealing and the generalized Lloyd algorithm in Table 5. Although there exists a significantly large difference between training and test sequence results, indicating the insufficient size of the training sequence,

	SA+GLA				LSVTE			
	$k=1$		$k=2$		$k=3$		$k=4$	
N	train	test	train	test	train	test	train	test
4	9.83	9.53	10.62	10.44				
8	11.59	11.44	11.74	11.54				
16	11.95	11.90	12.04	11.72				
32	12.00	11.90	12.30	11.84	11.4	11.4		
64	12.25	11.97	12.54	11.93			11.7	11.6

TABLE 5. SQNR [dB] results for scalar and vector trellis waveform coding where the systems with $k = 1$ and $k = 2$ are designed using SA+GLA and results for $k = 3$ and $k = 4$ are those of the labeled state vector trellis encoding system. N: number of states, k: vector length, LSVTE: labeled state vector trellis encoding system.

it can still be concluded from this table that vector coding results are better than scalar coding results. However, the difference is not significantly large. This observation can be interpreted to suggest that scalar trellis waveform or delayed-decision coding by itself exploits the correlation between samples quite well, and there is not much left for improvement by vector trellis waveform coding. A comparison of our results with those of Bei and Gray's labeled state vector trellis encoding system [**17**] (for which two related data points are shown in Table 5) indicate *(i)* the observation that the performance improvement while increasing the vector length for this source is limited is shared in [**17**], and *(ii)* the system and the design technique proposed here outperform that in [**17**].

5.4. Trellis Coded Quantization. A new approach in trellis source coding is the technique called *Trellis Coded Quantization* (TCQ) [**18**]. The technique is motivated by *Trellis Coded Modulation* (TCM) [**19**], which is superior to the conventional modulation techniques since the convolutional code and set partition are chosen in such a manner as to increase the Euclidean distance between sequences of channel symbols. The difference of TCQ from regular trellis waveform coding is that in TCQ the trellis branches are labeled with properly formed subsets instead of individual reproduction symbols. These subsets are formed from a supercodebook following Ungerboeck's set partitioning rules in TCM. For a trellis coding system of rate R bits per sample, the codewords in the supercodebook are the $R+1$ bits per sample Lloyd-Max quantizer output points.

Marcellin and Fischer [**18**] obtained simulation results for TCQ on memoryless sources, with an Ungerboeck trellis, codebooks of which are designed as described above. We simulated TCQ systems on first order Gauss-Markov sources, starting with the Ungerboeck trellis in [**18**] and then moving to other trellis structures through SA algorithm. For this source, we have reached trellis structures with slightly higher performance over the Ungerboeck trellis [**19**]. Finally, by applying simulated annealing and the generalized Lloyd algorithm for a trellis waveform coder with the same rate, we obtained substantial performance gains. We remark that these gains are obtained by an increase in complexity, however, considering the degree of improvement, this increase may be tolerable. The results are summarized in Table 6.

R	TCQ-UT	TCQ-SA	SA+GLA
1	4.55	4.79	11.44
2	7.58	7.65	14.42

TABLE 6. SQNR [dB] with trellis coded quantization. R: transmission rate, TCQ-UT: TCQ with the Ungerboeck trellis, TCQ-SA: SA applied to the Ungerboeck trellis, SA+GLA: trellis waveform coding with SA+GLA. The $D(R)$ bound for $R = 1$ bit/sample is 13.2 dB, for $R = 2$ bits/sample it is 19.3 dB.

6. Conclusions

In this paper, we studied the next-state map optimization for finite-state quantizers using simulated annealing. Our results indicate performance gains against *(i)* scalar trellis waveform coding, *(ii)* labeled state vector trellis waveform coding, *(iii)* omniscient labeled transition finite-state vector quantization, and *(iv)* trellis coded quantization. For the first order Gauss-Markov source with correlation coefficient 0.9, the performance improvement in *(i)* is significant, and in *(ii)* and *(iii)* is moderate. While the improvement due to the trellis structure optimization in *(iv)* is moderate, additional improvement for the trellis waveform coder of the same rate designed using the proposed algorithm is substantial.

REFERENCES

1. A. Gersho, R. M. Gray, *Vector Quantization and Signal Compression,* Kluwer Academic Publishers, 1991.
2. L. C. Stewart, R. M. Gray, Y. Linde, "The design of trellis waveform coders," *IEEE Trans. Comm.,* Vol. COM-30, pp. 702–711, April 1982.
3. G. D. Forney, "The Viterbi algorithm," *Proc. IEEE,* Vol. 61, pp. 268–278, March 1973.
4. G. H. Freeman, J. W. Mark, I. F. Blake, "Trellis source codes designed by conjugate gradient optimization," *IEEE Trans. Comm.,* Vol. COM-36, pp. 1–12, January 1988.
5. J. Foster, R. M. Gray, M. O. Dunham, "Finite-state vector quantization for waveform coding," *IEEE Trans. Info. Theory,* Vol. IT-31, pp. 348–359, May 1985.
6. S. Kirkpatrick, C. D. Gelatt, M. P. Vecchi, "Optimization by simulated annealing," *Science,* Vol. 220, pp. 671–680, May 1983.
7. N. Metropolis, A. Rosenbluth, M. Rosenbluth, A. Teller, E. Teller, "Equation of state calculations by fast computing machines," *J. of Chem. Physics,* Vol. 21, pp. 1087–1092, 1953.
8. N. E. Collins, R. W. Eglese, B. L. Golden, "Simulated annealing—an annotated bibliography," *Amer. J. of Math. and Man. Sci.,* Vol. 8, pp. 205–307, 1988.

9. P. J. M. van Laarhoven, E. H. L. Aarts, *Simulated Annealing: Theory and Applications,* MIA D. Reidel Publishing Company, 1988.
10. R. H. J. M. Otten, L. P. P. P. van Ginneken, *The Annealing Algorithm,* Kluwer Academic Publishers, 1989.
11. D. S. Johnson, C. R. Aragon, L. A. McGeoch, C. Shevon, "Optimization by simulated annealing: an experimental evaluation, Parts I and II," *Oper. Res.,* Vol. 37, pp. 865–892, December 1989, and Vol. 39, pp. 378–406, June 1991.
12. M. J. D. Powell, "An efficient method for finding the minimum of a function of several variables without calculating derivatives," *Comp. J.,* Vol.7, pp. 155-162, May 1964.
13. M. J. D. Powell, "Restart procedures for the conjugate gradient method," *Math. Prog.,* Vol. 12, pp. 241-254, 1977.
14. P. E. Gill, W. Murray, and M. H. Wright, *Practical Optimization,* Academic Press, London, 1981.
15. E. Ayanoğlu, R. M. Gray, "The design of predictive trellis waveform coders using the generalized Lloyd algorithm," *IEEE Trans. Comm.,* Vol. Com-34, pp. 1073–1081, November 1986.
16. A. J. Viterbi, J. K. Omura, *Principles of Digital Communication and Coding,* McGraw-Hill, 1979.
17. C.-D. Bei, R. M. Gray, "Simulation of vector trellis encoding systems," *IEEE Trans. Comm.,* Vol. COM-34, pp. 214–218, March 1986.
18. M. W. Marcellin, T. R. Fischer, "Trellis coded quantization of memoryless and Gauss-Markov sources," *IEEE Trans. Comm.*, vol. 38, pp.82-93, Januanry 1990.
19. G. Ungerboeck, "Trellis coded modulation with redundant signal sets," *IEEE Comm. Mag.*, vol. 25, pp. 5-21, February 1987.

Electrical and Electronics Engineering Department, Bilkent University, Ankara, 06533, Turkey
E-mail address: eengin@trbilun.bitnet

AT&T Bell Laboratories, 101 Crawfords Corner Road, Room 4F-507, Holmdel, NJ 07733-3030, USA
E-mail address: ender@boole.att.com

DIMACS Series in Discrete Mathematics
and Theoretical Computer Science
Volume **14**, 1993

The M-Algorithm, the Failure of Reduced-State Sequence Detection with Good Convolutional Codes, and Some Implications for Trellis Coding

J. B. ANDERSON AND E. OFFER

June 10, 1992

ABSTRACT. Reduced-state sequence detection is a method of reducing the state trellis of a channel code to a smaller structure. We show that it does not reduce the complexity of decoding for good convolutional codes, although it can very nicely repair the failings of bad codes. Conclusions like these probably apply to many trellis codes. For any trellis code, we çan show that the reduced-state method cannot perform more efficiently than the M-algorithm.

Various authors, including Duel-Hallen and Heegard, Eyuboglu, Qureshi, Chevillat, Eleftheriou, Svensson, Aulin and Larsson [**1**]–[**5**], have introduced the reduced-state sequence detector, or RSSD. Since there is no precise agreement on what an RSSD is, we will briefly review the procedure here. First we define some ground rules for the decoder design. The purpose of the decoder is to search through a code trellis and look for a path close to the received channel outputs, in order to decide the transmitted data symbols. We consider only decoders that never backtrack, as does, e.g., the stack algorithm; furthermore, they retain a fixed number of survivors at each trellis level, as do the Viterbi and M-algorithms; finally, the decoding is bounded-distance decoding, which means that channel error correction is guaranteed so long as the error sequence is of some size d or less. With these assumptions, the RSSD may be described as follows. Code trellis states at level n are grouped into *classes*, defined by the condition that no code words leading into states in a class are closer than $2d$ to any other code words leading into other states in the class. When the decoder

1991 *Mathematics Subject Classification*. Primary 94B35.
This work was supported in full by the Humboldt Foundation (Bonn) and by German Aerospace Research, Oberpfaffenhofen, Germany.

search moves on to the next trellis level, only one survivor leading into each class is kept. This contrasts with the usual state trellis decoding, in which one survivor is kept into each state. RSSD works because if the noisy received word satisfies the d condition, the transmitted path has to be among the survivors. The full bounded-distance potential of the code may be obtained if the d parameter is set equal to the code free distance divided by 2.

RSSDs should not be confused with reduced-search decoders, which search only a small part of the original, large trellis; in an RSSD, the trellis is reduced a priori and all of it is searched.

We now give a new algorithm that forms the reduced trellis for a convolutional code and a given d, and investigate what happens when the algorithm is applied to good codes. The class-forming algorithm depends on the linear code symmetries of convolutional codes and falls into three parts. The first two parts act to form the class that contains trellis state 0. The procedure reduces to a dynamic program (i.e., the Viterbi algorithm), run on the code trellis until the distance into each state in the trellis reaches a steady state. If the least-weight path into state i in this steady-state condition is heavier than $2d$, then state i may be added to the class containing state 0; otherwise, it may not. Part II tests whether a state that may be classed with state 0 may be combined with other states $j, k, \ldots$ that already have been classed with state 0. Part III forms the other classes, based on the class that contains state 0.

If the algorithm just described cannot find any state that may be classed with state 0, then by code linearity, no states in the code trellis may be classed with any other states, and the RSSD idea fails to produce a smaller trellis structure than the original state trellis. We have applied the algorithm to a large number of good codes of rates 1/3, 1/2, 2/3 and 3/4, and have found no code that admits of any RSSD trellis reduction. The details are in Ref. [**6**]. Only when the class-finding algorithm is applied to codes with much poorer free distance, such as QLI codes and feed-forward systematic codes, do non-trivial classes get formed. Then an interesting phenomenon occurs: The number of classes so formed is invariably close to the number of states in the best-free-distance code with free distance equal twice the parameter in the class formation. In this way, the RSSD idea seems to convert bad codes into good ones, so far as the trellis size needed to attain a d is concerned.

In conclusion, RSSD seems to point to some interesting structural properties of codes, but it does not create a simpler decoder for codes that are already good. It can happen that "bad" codes, i.e., codes with low free distance compared to their memory, are employed because they offer an advantage in a practical system. Examples are the QLI and systematic codes, whose structure makes the encoder state easy to estimate roughly. Now RSSD provides a simpler decoder than the Viterbi algorithm: it reduces the trellis size to that of the best free distance code at the lower distance.

It is also of interest to compare RSSD to the M-algorithm, which obeys the same ground rules. It is not hard to show that the M-algorithm is the optimal non-backtracking decoder that keeps a fixed number of survivors. A somewhat more subtle proof shows that RSSD cannot keep fewer survivors while attaining the same bounded-distance d parameter. Calculations with actual codes show that the M-algorithm actually retains many fewer survivors for the same d. For rate 1/2 coding, RSSD must retain about 4^d survivors, while the M-algorithm needs only 2.414^d. The difference is much more extreme in intersymbol interference problems. These facts make sense when one considers that RSSD makes its trellis reduction *a priori*, while the M-algorithm and other reduced-search decoders make their reductions only after viewing the received channel sequence.

References

1. A. Duel-Hallen and C. Heegard, "Delayed Decision Feedback Sequence Estimation," *IEEE Trans. Communications*, Vol. COM-37, pp. 428–436, May 1989.
2. M. V. Eyuboglu and S. Qureshi, "Reduced-state sequence estimation for coded modulation on interference channels," *IEEE J. Sel. Areas Commun.*, Vol. SAC-7, pp. 989–995, Aug. 1989.
3. P. R. Chevillat and E. Eleftheriou, "Decoding of trellis-encoded signals in the presence of intersymbol interference and noise," *IEEE Trans. Communications*, Vol. COM-37, pp. 669–676, July 1989.
4. T. Larsson, "A state-space partitioning approach to trellis decoding," Ph.D. Thesis, Dept. Computer Eng., Chalmers Tech. Univ., Gothenburg, Sweden, Dec. 1991.
5. A. Svensson, "Reduced state sequence detection of partial response continuous phase modulation," *IEE Proceedings*, Part I, Vol. 138, No. 4, pp. 256–268, Aug. 1991.
6. J. B. Anderson and E. Offer, "Reduced-state sequence detection with convolutional codes," submitted to *IEEE Trans. Information Theory*, Aug. 1992.

ECSE Department, Rensselaer Polytechnic Institute, Troy, New York 12180-3590 USA
E-mail address: anderson@ecse.rpi.edu

Inst. Communications Engin., German Aerospace Research, D-8031 Oberpfaffenhofen Germany
E-mail address: offer@holmes.nt.op.dlr.de

DIMACS Series in Discrete Mathematics
and Theoretical Computer Science
Volume **14**, 1993

An Algebraic Approach to Constructing Convolutional Codes from Quasi-Cyclic Codes

Y. LEVY AND D. J. COSTELLO, JR.

November 12, 1992

ABSTRACT. An algebraic approach to constructing convolutional codes from quasi-cyclic codes is investigated. The problem of minimizing the constraint length of the constructed convolutional codes is studied, and an algorithm to find an equivalent convolutional code with reduced constraint length is presented. A number of codes with minimum constraint length are found and a lower bound on their free distance is obtained. However, there remain some open problems. For one, the actual free distance of some of the convolutional codes appears to be much higher than the lower bound indicates. Also, the rate of the constructed convolutional codes is lower than the rate of the original quasi-cyclic codes and may lead to lower rate convolutional codes than expected.

1. Introduction

Binary convolutional codes are employed in many communication systems because they provide efficient error correction and allow simple decoding algorithms. However, since no simple algebraic approach allows us to construct the generators of a convolutional code directly, one idea is to start from existing block codes and transform them into convolutional codes. Massey, Costello, and Justesen [**1**] used this approach in relating the generator of cyclic block codes to the n generators of rate $1/n$ convolutional codes. Then, Justesen [**2**] generalized this approach to the construction of q-ary rate l/n convolutional codes. However, the main problem in relating cyclic codes to convolutional codes is to construct from one cyclic code generator polynomial the ln generator polynomials of a rate l/n convolutional code. Thus, the idea of multiple generators for convolutional codes leads to the use of quasi-cyclic block codes, for which the structure is

1991 *Mathematics Subject Classification.* Primary 94B05, 94B10.
This work was supported by NSF Grant NCR89-03429 and by NASA Grant NAG5-557.

more similar to the structure of convolutional codes, thereby allowing us to use a larger subclass of block codes than the class of cyclic codes. Forney [**4**] and Solomon and Van Tilborg [**5**] have looked at different connections between these two classes of codes.

Tanner [**3**] extended the work of these researchers by relating the syndrome matrix of a convolutional code to the syndrome matrix of a quasi-cyclic code. His main result was that the convolutional code constructed from the quasi-cyclic code has a free distance lower bounded by the minimum distance of the quasi-cyclic code. The main problem with this approach, however, is finding the convolutional code with the minimum constraint length. In this paper, we investigate the different possibilities that exist in order to reduce the constraint length of the convolutional code, and we give an algorithm to convert a cyclic code into a convolutional code by using quasi-cyclic codes as an intermediary. A table of the best codes constructed from BCH codes [**6**], [**8**] is given, and the results are compared to optimal codes found by computer search [**6**], [**7**].

2. Preliminaries

We will first describe the syndrome matrix of quasi-cyclic codes. Then, we will show how the syndrome matrix of a convolutional code can be related to the syndrome matrix of a quasi-cyclic code in a particular form.

2.1. Quasi-Cyclic Codes. Quasi-cyclic codes are a subclass of block codes [**8**] which include cyclic codes [**6**] as a subclass. The defining property of quasi-cyclic codes is that one codeword can be obtained from any other codeword by cyclic shifts of n positions, which allows us to decompose a codeword into n blocks of m symbols, or m blocks of n symbols. Note that if $n = 1$, the quasi-cyclic code is cyclic.

A linear quasi-cyclic (N,K) code C_q, where $N = nm$ is the codeword length, n is the number of blocks in the codeword, and m is the length of each block, is the set of all n-tuples having the property defined above. That is, if

$$\mathbf{v} = (v_0, v_1, ..., v_{N-1}) \tag{2.1}$$

is a codeword in C_q, $\mathbf{v}$ shifted cyclically by n positions is also a codeword. In order to decompose the generator matrix into circulant blocks, we can reorder the indices of $\mathbf{v}$ to obtain

(2.2)
$$\mathbf{V} = (\underbrace{v_0, v_m, v_{2m}, ..., v_{(n-1)m}}_{1^{st} block}, \underbrace{v_1, v_{m+1}, ..., v_{(n-1)m+1}}_{2^{nd} block}, ..., \underbrace{v_{m-1}, v_{2m-1}, ..., v_{nm-1}}_{m^{th} block}).$$

Thus, a cyclic shift of $\mathbf{V}$ by n positions consists of moving the mth block of n bits to the first block position, and the other blocks to the right by n positions. This yields

$$\mathbf{V} = (v_{im+j}), \tag{2.3}$$

for $i = 0$ to $n-1$ and $j = 0$ to $m-1$. A shift of n elements in $\mathbf{V}$ consists of adding 1 to j $mod\, m$. Such a shift takes any codeword to another codeword. It follows from this notation that we can rearrange the vectors into the row space of a block matrix $\mathbf{G}$ consisting of kn circulant blocks $\mathbf{G}_j^{(i)}$ of size $m \times m$:

$$\mathbf{G} = \begin{bmatrix} G_0^{(0)} & G_0^{(1)} & \cdots & G_0^{(n-1)} \\ G_1^{(0)} & G_1^{(1)} & \cdots & G_1^{(n-1)} \\ \vdots & \vdots & \cdots & \vdots \\ G_{k-1}^{(0)} & G_{k-1}^{(1)} & \cdots & G_{k-1}^{(n-1)} \end{bmatrix}, \tag{2.4}$$

where $k = \lfloor \frac{K}{m} \rfloor$, $\lfloor\ \rfloor$ denotes the floor function, and for all i, $0 \le i \le n-1$, and all j, $0 \le j \le k-1$, $G_j^{(i)}$ is an $m \times m$ circulant matrix; that is

$$G_j^{(i)} = \begin{bmatrix} g_{j0}^{(i)} & g_{j1}^{(i)} & \cdots & g_{jl}^{(i)} & 0 & \cdots & 0 \\ 0 & g_{j0}^{(i)} & g_{j1}^{(i)} & \cdots & g_{jl}^{(i)} & 0 & \\ & \ddots & \ddots & & & \ddots & \ddots \\ \ddots & & \ddots & \ddots & & & \ddots \\ & & & & & & \\ & \ddots & & & \ddots & \ddots & \\ g_{j1}^{(i)} & \cdots & g_{jl}^{(i)} & 0 & \cdots & 0 & g_{j0}^{(i)} \end{bmatrix}. \tag{2.5}$$

The polynomial

$$g_j^{(i)}(X) = g_{j0}^{(i)} + g_{j1}^{(i)}X + \ldots + g_{jl}^{(i)}X^l \tag{2.6}$$

of degree l is called the generator polynomial of the circulant matrix; note $l \le m-1$.

The syndrome matrix $\mathbf{H}$ of the quasi-cyclic code $\mathbf{C}_q$ is defined by $\mathbf{GH}^T = \mathbf{0}$ and is an $r \times n$ block matrix of $m \times m$ circulants, with $rm \ge N - K$. ($\mathbf{H}$ may contain linearly dependent rows.) In order to express the generator and syndrome matrices in a simpler manner, it is possible to use the polynomial form of (2.6). Therefore, the syndrome matrix $\mathbf{H}(X)$ can be written as:

$$\mathbf{H}(X) = \begin{bmatrix} h_0^{(0)}(X) & h_0^{(1)}(X) & \cdots & h_0^{(n-1)}(X) \\ h_1^{(0)}(X) & h_1^{(1)}(X) & \cdots & h_1^{(n-1)}(X) \\ \vdots & \vdots & \cdots & \vdots \\ h_{r-1}^{(0)}(X) & h_{r-1}^{(1)}(X) & \cdots & h_{r-1}^{(n-1)}(X) \end{bmatrix}. \tag{2.7}$$

In the next section, we will see how the syndrome matrix of a convolutional code can be related to the syndrome matrix of the quasi-cyclic code shown in (2.7).

2.2. Convolutional Codes. Let C_v be a rate l/n convolutional code [**6**]. Then, by defining

$$\mathbf{u}(X) = (u^{(1)}(X), u^{(2)}(X), \dots, u^{(l)}(X)), \tag{2.8}$$

as the information sequence and

$$\mathbf{v}(X) = (v^{(1)}(X), v^{(2)}(X), \dots, v^{(n)}(X)), \tag{2.9}$$

as the code sequence, we can write

$$\mathbf{u}(X) = \mathbf{G}(X)\mathbf{u}(X), \tag{2.10}$$

where $\mathbf{G}(X)$ is an $l \times n$ matrix of generator polynomials of the following form:

$$\mathbf{G}(X) = \begin{bmatrix} g_0^{(0)}(X) & g_0^{(1)}(X) & \cdots & g_0^{(n-1)}(X) \\ g_1^{(0)}(X) & g_1^{(1)}(X) & \cdots & g_1^{(n-1)}(X) \\ \vdots & \vdots & \cdots & \vdots \\ g_{l-1}^{(0)}(X) & g_{l-1}^{(1)}(X) & \cdots & g_{l-1}^{(n-1)}(X) \end{bmatrix}. \tag{2.11}$$

As in quasi-cyclic codes, the syndrome matrix $\mathbf{H}(X)$ is defined by $\mathbf{G}(X)\,\mathbf{H}^T(X) = \mathbf{0}$, and has the following form:

$$\mathbf{H}(X) = \begin{bmatrix} h_0^{(0)}(X) & h_0^{(1)}(X) & \cdots & h_0^{(n-1)}(X) \\ h_1^{(0)}(X) & h_1^{(1)}(X) & \cdots & h_1^{(n-1)}(X) \\ \vdots & \vdots & \cdots & \vdots \\ h_{r-1}^{(0)}(X) & h_{r-1}^{(1)}(X) & \cdots & h_{r-1}^{(n-1)}(X) \end{bmatrix}, \tag{2.12}$$

where $r = n - l$.

Note that the structure of $\mathbf{H}(X)$ in (2.7) and (2.12) is identical. This suggests a connection between the two classes of codes. However, the number of rows r in both matrices is not defined in the same way, which will affect the rate of the convolutional code constructed from a quasi-cyclic code, and the degree of each polynomial $h_j^{(i)}(X)$, for $0 \le j \le r-1$ and $0 \le i \le n-1$, is less than m in the quasi-cyclic code syndrome matrix, whereas it can be of any degree in the convolutional code syndrome matrix.

3. Connection between Convolutional Codes, Quasi-Cyclic Codes, and Cyclic Codes

Tanner [**3**] showed that the similarity of structure between the syndrome matrices of quasi-cyclic and convolutional codes could be used to construct convolutional codes from quasi-cyclic codes and vice versa. The goal of this section is to summarize his results and explain some of the remaining difficulties.

3.1. The Syndrome Matrix Connection between Quasi-Cyclic Codes and Convolutional Codes. Tanner's approach to relating the syndrome matrices of quasi-cyclic codes and convolutional codes is to eliminate the problem that polynomials in a convolutional code syndrome matrix may be of any finite degree by reducing these polynomials modulo $X^m + 1$; that is by taking the remainder after the division of each polynomial by $X^m + 1$. The first transformation consists in constructing a quasi-cyclic code from a convolutional code by this modular reduction, which allows one to derive theorems relating to the minimum distance and the rate of the quasi-cyclic code. Then, by applying the reverse transformation from a quasi-cyclic code to a convolutional code, it is possible to lower bound the free distance of the convolutional code. Since this second transformation is our major interest in this paper, we will only present the construction of convolutional codes from quasi-cyclic codes.

It is indeed possible to construct a convolutional code for which the modular reduction of the syndrome matrix is the syndrome matrix of a quasi-cyclic code with known minimum distance, and therefore the free distance of that convolutional code is lower bounded by the minimum distance of the quasi-cyclic code. This leads to the following lemma:

LEMMA 3.1. Let $\mathbf{C}_q$ be an (nm, K) quasi-cyclic code with minimum distance d_{min} defined by an $r \times n$ syndrome matrix $\mathbf{H}_q(X)$ of polynomials of degree at most $m-1$. Let $\mathbf{C}_v$ be the convolutional code defined by the $r \times n$ syndrome matrix $\mathbf{H}_v(X)$ such that

$$\mathbf{H}_v(X) = \mathbf{H}_q(X). \tag{3.1}$$

If $n - l$ is the rank of $\mathbf{H}_v(X)$, then C_v is a rate l/n convolutional code with $d_{free} \geq d_{min}$.

This lemma provides a very helpful method of constructing convolutional codes from quasi-cyclic codes. However, the problem of the constraint length ν has not been studied yet. In fact, the only information on the constraint length of the resulting convolutional codes come from the size of the quasi-cyclic code circulants m. Indeed,

$$\nu \leq l\,(m-1), \tag{3.2}$$

since the maximum degree of the polynomials of $\mathbf{H}_q(X)$ is $m-1$, and the number of information sequences is l.

In order to minimize the constraint length of the resulting convolutional codes, Tanner [**3**] suggested constructing quasi-cyclic codes for the purpose of finding convolutional codes. Indeed, numerous lists of quasi-cyclic codes have already been published, and they could easily be used in the construction described by Lemma 3.1. However, by converting block cyclic codes into quasi-cyclic codes, it is possible to find the quasi-cyclic code realization that gives the convolutional code with the highest rate and the smallest constraint length. This leads to our construction algorithm.

3.2. Construction of quasi-cyclic codes from cyclic codes. Starting from a cyclic code of composite length $N = nm$, it is possible to construct a quasi-cyclic code as described in the following lemma.

LEMMA 3.2. *Any $nm \times nm$ circulant matrix is equivalent under row and column permutations to an $n \times n$ block matrix of $m \times m$ circulants.*

This lemma allows us to transform the syndrome matrix of a cyclic code into the syndrome matrix of a quasi-cyclic code.

LEMMA 3.3. *Any rate K/nm cyclic code is equivalent to a quasi- cyclic code defined by an $n \times n$ syndrome matrix of $m \times m$ circulants.*

Lemma 3.2 and Lemma 3.3 provide a way of transforming a cyclic code syndrome matrix into a quasi-cyclic code syndrome matrix. Indeed, the actual syndrome matrix of a cyclic code of rate K/nm is of size $(nm-K)\times nm$. By extending the circulation of the parity-check polynomial, it is possible to obtain an $nm\times nm$ syndrome matrix $\mathbf{H}_c$ of rank $nm-K$. Then, each $m\times m$ block $\mathbf{H}_{q_{(I,J)}}$ of the $nm \times nm$ quasi-cyclic code syndrome matrix $\mathbf{H}_q$, for $0 \le I, J \le n-1$, is obtained by letting $\mathbf{H}_{q_{(I,J)}}(i,j) = \mathbf{H}_c(I+in, J+jn)$ for $0 \le i,j \le m-1$. In order to obtain the syndrome matrix of a rate $(nm-rm)/nm$ quasi-cyclic code, it is necessary to remove $l = n-r$ row blocks of m rows each from the matrix $\mathbf{H}_q$, while keeping the rank equal to $nm-K$. This means that $l \le \lfloor \frac{K}{m} \rfloor$. (See Example 1.)

This last operation consisting of deleting blocks of rows is the most tedious, since it is not obvious which blocks can be deleted without decreasing the rank, or which blocks one should delete in order to construct the convolutional code with the smallest constraint length. One way of checking the rank of the matrix is to use Tanner's transform theory developed in [**9**], which involves Galois field algebra that is not simple to implement. Another way is to transform $\mathbf{H}_q$ into systematic form

$$\mathbf{H}_q^s = \begin{bmatrix} \mathbf{I}_s : \mathbf{A} \\ \cdots\cdots \\ \mathbf{D} \end{bmatrix}, \tag{3.3}$$

where s is the rank of $\mathbf{H}_q^s$, $\mathbf{I}_s$ is the identity matrix of size $s\times s$, $\mathbf{A}$ is of dimension $s \times (n-s)$, and $\mathbf{D}$ is of dimension $(n-s)\times n$. Linearly dependent rows of $\mathbf{H}_q$ can appear only in the last rows of the matrix, denoted by $\mathbf{D}$.

Once the syndrome matrix of the quasi-cyclic code is constructed, it is also possible to permute rows and columns within blocks of circulants without changing the distance or the rate of the quasi-cyclic code. This operation is particularly useful for the purpose of constructing a convolutional code with low constraint length, since the degree of the polynomials in $\mathbf{H}_q(X)$ must be as low as possible in order to construct a convolutional code with minimal constraint length.

In the following section, we present an algorithm that combines all the operations needed in going from a cyclic code to a convolutional code using a quasi-cyclic code as an intermediary.

4. An Algorithm To Construct Convolutional Codes from Cyclic Codes

In this section, we study how to combine the operations discussed previously to construct the convolutional code with the smallest constraint length starting from a given cyclic code. The algorithm shown in Figure 1 describes the operations needed to transform the syndrome matrix of a cyclic code into the syndrome matrix of a quasi-cyclic code and then into a convolutional code generator matrix.

We now give an example of the construction of a convolutional code, starting from the (15,5) BCH code with minimum distance $d_{min} = 7$.

EXAMPLE 4.1. Let C_c be the (15,5) BCH code.

Step 1: $\mathbf{h}(X) = 1 + X + X^3 + X^5$; that is, $\mathbf{h} = [110101]$, $n = 3$, $m = 5$, and $K = 5$.

Step 2: $$\mathbf{H}_c = \begin{bmatrix} 1&1&0&1&0&1&0&0&0&0&0&0&0&0&0 \\ 0&1&1&0&1&0&1&0&0&0&0&0&0&0&0 \\ 0&0&1&1&0&1&0&1&0&0&0&0&0&0&0 \\ 0&0&0&1&1&0&1&0&1&0&0&0&0&0&0 \\ 0&0&0&0&1&1&0&1&0&1&0&0&0&0&0 \\ 0&0&0&0&0&1&1&0&1&0&1&0&0&0&0 \\ 0&0&0&0&0&0&1&1&0&1&0&1&0&0&0 \\ 0&0&0&0&0&0&0&1&1&0&1&0&1&0&0 \\ 0&0&0&0&0&0&0&0&1&1&0&1&0&1&0 \\ 0&0&0&0&0&0&0&0&0&1&1&0&1&0&1 \\ 1&0&0&0&0&0&0&0&0&0&1&1&0&1&0 \\ 0&1&0&0&0&0&0&0&0&0&0&1&1&0&1 \\ 1&0&1&0&0&0&0&0&0&0&0&0&1&1&0 \\ 0&1&0&1&0&0&0&0&0&0&0&0&0&1&1 \\ 1&0&1&0&1&0&0&0&0&0&0&0&0&0&1 \end{bmatrix}.$$

Step 3: $$\mathbf{H}_q = \left[\begin{array}{ccccc|ccccc|ccccc} 1&1&0&0&0&1&0&0&0&0&0&1&0&0&0 \\ 0&1&1&0&0&0&1&0&0&0&0&0&1&0&0 \\ 0&0&1&1&0&0&0&1&0&0&0&0&0&1&0 \\ 0&0&0&1&1&0&0&0&1&0&0&0&0&0&1 \\ 1&0&0&0&1&0&0&0&0&1&1&0&0&0&0 \\ \hline 0&0&1&0&0&1&1&0&0&0&1&0&0&0&0 \\ 0&0&0&1&0&0&1&1&0&0&0&1&0&0&0 \\ 0&0&0&0&1&0&0&1&1&0&0&0&1&0&0 \\ 1&0&0&0&0&0&0&0&1&1&0&0&0&1&0 \\ 0&1&0&0&0&1&0&0&0&1&0&0&0&0&1 \\ \hline 0&1&0&0&0&0&0&1&0&0&1&1&0&0&0 \\ 0&0&1&0&0&0&0&0&1&0&0&1&1&0&0 \\ 0&0&0&1&0&0&0&0&0&1&0&0&1&1&0 \\ 0&0&0&0&1&1&0&0&0&0&0&0&0&1&1 \\ 1&0&0&0&0&0&1&0&0&0&1&0&0&0&1 \end{array}\right].$$

Step 4: Permutations do not affect the maximum degree of $\mathbf{H}_q(X)$. (Note that in $\mathbf{H}_q$, the polynomials correspond to the first row of each circulant.)

Step 5: $t = \lfloor \frac{5}{5} \rfloor = 1$.

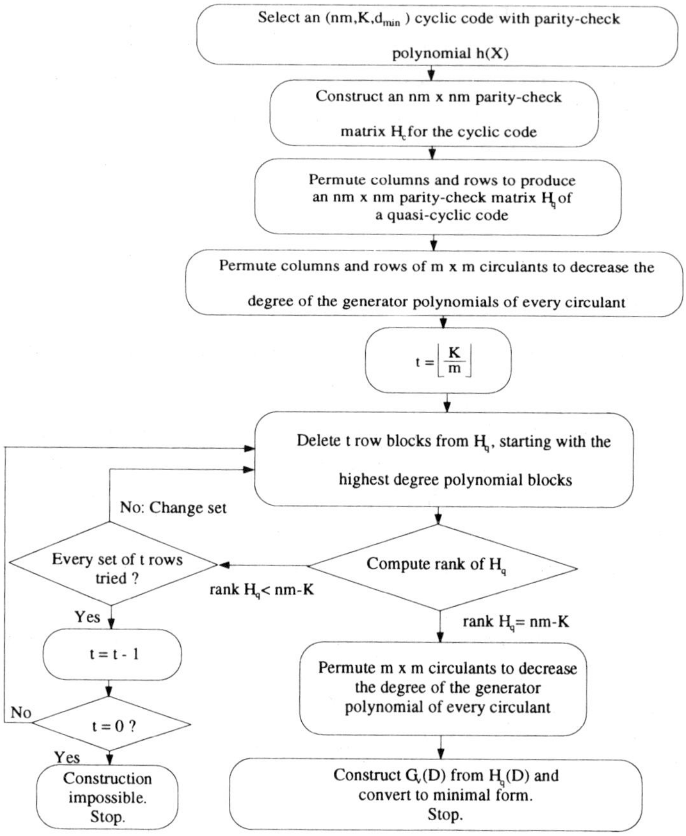

FIGURE 1. Algorithm flowchart.

Step 6: $$\mathbf{H}_q = \left[\begin{array}{ccccc|ccccc|ccccc} 1&1&0&0&0&1&0&0&0&0&0&1&0&0&0\\ 0&1&1&0&0&0&1&0&0&0&0&0&1&0&0\\ 0&0&1&1&0&0&0&1&0&0&0&0&0&1&0\\ 0&0&0&1&1&0&0&0&1&0&0&0&0&0&1\\ 1&0&0&0&1&0&0&0&0&1&1&0&0&0&0\\ \hline 0&0&1&0&0&1&1&0&0&0&1&0&0&0&0\\ 0&0&0&1&0&0&1&1&0&0&0&1&0&0&0\\ 0&0&0&0&1&0&0&1&1&0&0&0&1&0&0\\ 1&0&0&0&0&0&0&0&1&1&0&0&0&1&0\\ 0&1&0&0&0&1&0&0&0&1&0&0&0&0&1 \end{array}\right].$$

Step 7: rank $= 10 = nm - K$.

Step 8: No other permutations decrease the degree.

Step 9: $\mathbf{H}_v(D) = \mathbf{H}_q(X)|_{X=D} = \begin{bmatrix} 1+D & 1 & D \\ D^2 & 1+D & 1 \end{bmatrix}$.

Step 10: $\mathbf{G}_v(X) = \left[\, 1+D+D^2,\ 1,\ 1+D+D^3 \,\right]$.

Step 11: $\mathbf{G}_v(X)$ is already in minimal form.

The constraint length of the rate 1/3 convolutional code is 3, and $d_{free} \geq 7$. Actually, in this particular case, $d_{free} = 7$.

This example results in a constraint length of only 3, whereas the upper bound is 4 from (3.2). The free distance equals its lower bound, which is not the case in general, but the best rate 1/3 convolutional code with constraint length 3 has a free distance of 10 [**6**]. The algorithm was also applied to BCH codes of length 15, 63, and 255, since their lengths are composite. Specifically, $15 = 3 \times 5$, $63 = 3 \times 3 \times 7$, and $255 = 5 \times 3 \times 17$, which allows us to construct codes with rates k/3, k/5, k/7, and k/9. In the next section, we give a table of convolutional codes constructed from these classes of BCH codes.

5. Results and Comments on Construction of Convolutional Codes from BCH Codes

The following table of constructed codes shows the code rate, the generator matrix with polynomials in octal form (*e.g.*, 54 corresponds to 101100, or $1 + X^2 + X^3$), the constraint length, the memory order, the original BCH code, the lower bound on the free distance, the computed free distance (for some codes), and the best code found by exhaustive search. Not all constructed codes are shown. See [**11**] for the complete list.

Rate	Generator Matrix	Const. Length*	Mem. Order	BCH Code	Lower Bd on d_{free}	Comp. d_{free}	Best Code†
1/3	7 4 64	3	3	(15,5)	7	7	10 [**6**]
1/5	1 4 7 54 64	3	3	(15,5)	7	11	16 [**7**]
2/3	0 6 4 6 4 0	2	1	(15,11)	3	3	3 [**6**]
3/9	3 4 44 6 62 14 6 4 24 12 3 4 44 6 62 14 6 4 2 12 3 4 44 6 62 14 6	12	4	(63,24)	15	≤ 17	X††
1/7	44 0 66 76 52 74 62	4	4	(63,30)	13	21	28 [**7**]
4/7	02 3 1 32 64 56 6 51 4 04 04 4 43 1 36 26 7 74 62 72 14 74 64 4 34 0 6 04	16	5	(63,36)	11	11	X
6/7	4 0 0 0 0 2 4 4 0 2 0 0 4 0 6 4 2 0 0 2 0 0 4 4 0 0 4 4 6 2 0 4 0 0 0 4 0 4 0 4 4 0	4	1	(63,57)	3	3	X
1/3	62564 76204 3754	12	12	(255,215)	11	20	24 [**6**]
1/5	247 216 362 662 54	8	8	(255,239)	5	22	ν=5 [**7**]
4/5	22 0 42 24 76 2 6 0 1 6 4 7 7 5 3 54 0 1 34 6	11	4	(255,239)	5	≤ 6	X

* Constraint length ≡ total encoder memory

† Free distance of best known code with same constraint length, or ν equals the lowest constraint length of best known code with same free distance.

†† X ≡ unknown.

5.1. Comments on the Constructed Codes. Some conclusions can be drawn from the table above. On the one hand, this algebraic construction allows us to construct codes that are impossible to find by exhaustive search. On the other hand, the codes for which a comparable optimal code exists usually have a suboptimal ratio of free distance to constraint length, although for some constructed codes only the lower bound on the free distance is known, which may be weak compared to the actual free distance of the code.

Generally, it was observed that a large number of BCH codes do not lead to the construction of quasi-cyclic codes with lower cycle lengths m, and it is necessary to use BCH codes with much higher rates than the convolutional codes constructed. For example, the first rate 2/3 convolutional code constructed from GF(256) was based on a (255,215) code, whereas it should theoretically be possible to start with the (255,171) BCH code, which would lead to a higher free distance.

6. Conclusions

We have proposed a construction algorithm for convolutional codes based on Tanner's connection between cyclic codes, quasi-cyclic codes and convolutional codes. This algebraic construction allows us to construct non-standard rate convolutional codes with large constraint length, but in general leads to suboptimal codes.

References

1. J.L. Massey, D.J. Costello, Jr., and J. Justesen, "Polynomial Weights and Code Constructions," *IEEE Trans. Inf. Theory,* IT-19, pp. 101-110, Jan. 1973.
2. J. Justesen, "New Convolutional Code Constructions and a Class of Asymptotically Good Time-Varying Codes," *IEEE Trans. Inf. Theory,* IT-19 Number 2, pp. 220-223, March 1973.
3. R.M. Tanner, "Convolutional Codes from Quasi-Cyclic Codes: A Link Between the Theories of Block and Convolutional Codes," *Computer Research Laboratory, Technical Report, USC-CRL-87-21*, November 1987.
4. G.D. Forney, Jr., "Why Quasi-Cyclic Codes are interesting," privately circulated unpublished note (circa 1970).
5. G. Solomon and H. C. A. Van Tilborg, "A Connection Between Block and Convolutional Codes," *SIAM J. Appl. Math.*, Vol. 37, No. 2, October, 1979.
6. S. Lin and D.J. Costello, Jr., *Error Control Coding: Fundamentals and Applications*, pp. 322-327, Prentice-Hall, 1983.
7. D.G. Daut, J.W. Modestino, and L.D. Wismer, "New Short Constraint Length Convolutional Code Constructions for Selected Rational Rates," *IEEE Trans. Inf. Theory*, IT-28, pp. 794-800, Sept. 1982.
8. C.L. Chen, W.W. Peterson, and E.J. Weldon, Jr., "Some Results on Quasi-Cyclic Codes," *Inform. Control*, 15, pp. 407-423, November 1969.
9. R.M. Tanner, "A Transform Theory for Group-Invariant Codes," *IEEE Trans. Inf. Theory*, IT-34, No. 4, pp. 752-775, July 1988.
10. G.D. Forney, Jr., "Convolutional Codes I: Algebraic Structure" *IEEE Trans. Inf. Theory*, IT-16, pp. 720-738, November 1970.
11. Y. Levy, "An Algebraic Approach for Constructing Convolutional Codes from Block Codes," *Master's Thesis*, Department of Electrical Engineering, University of Notre Dame, pp. 81-83, April 1992.

Department of Electrical Engineering, University of Notre Dame, Notre Dame, Indiana 46556

E-mail address: ylevy@bach.helios.nd.edu, costello.2@nd.edu

DIMACS Series in Discrete Mathematics
and Theoretical Computer Science
Volume **14**, 1993

Table-Driven Decoding of Convolutional Codes with Soft Decision

H. KOORAPATY, D. L. BITZER, A. DHOLAKIA, AND M. A. VOUK

December 1, 1992

ABSTRACT. The performance of convolutional decoding schemes can be improved by employing soft decision. We present a table-driven soft decision decoding technique for binary one-half rate nonsystematic convolutional coding. The table-driven decoding is based on a one-to-one mapping between uncoded and encoded data blocks of equal lengths. Q-level quantization is performed at the receiver. A hard quantized received sequence is also formed. Error correction is performed on this sequence. Error correction is achieved by computing a data-independent syndrome sequence and performing a table look-up. A limitation of table-driven decoding is syndrome indistinguishability. Soft decisions and precomputed correction table information can be used to resolve conflicts due to syndrome indistinguishability and choose the most probable correction pattern. The corrected received sequence is used to retrieve the original data using the one-to-one mapping principle.

1. Introduction

Commonly employed Viterbi decoders for convolutionally encoded data provide optimal decoding but have complexity and computational requirements which increase exponentially with the constraint length of the code. An alternative is offered by simple and fast, but often sub-optimal, table look-up based (feedback) decoding. Table look-up based decoding schemes have been designed for both block coding [**6**], and convolutional coding [**7, 3**]. However, in the latter case most of the work was done for systematic codes. A novel approach to table look-up based decoding was described in [**1, 2, 4, 5**]. It is aimed at nonsystematic convolutional codes and allows hardware simplicity comparable to that of majority-logic decoding [**8**] but error correcting capabilities comparable to

1991 *Mathematics Subject Classification.* Primary 94B10, 94B35.

the Viterbi and sequential decoding approaches. In this paper, we present soft decision decoding using the table-driven approach.

2. Table-Driven Error Correction

In table-driven error correction we store precomputed correction information corresponding to known combinations of errors in a table. The error correction is performed on the hard quantized received encoded sequence. For error correction, we form a data-independent syndrome sequence and use it to access the correction table to decide where to perform the correction.

Multiple error patterns can generate the same syndrome. It is not possible to eliminate all conflicts for finite syndrome lengths, but in general, the longer the syndrome length, the better are the error correcting capabilities of the table (and the longer is the table). However, the improvement diminishes for syndrome lengths larger than four to five times the code constraint length. Hard decision table-driven decoding uses the minimum Hamming weight criterion to choose, in advance, the error pattern to correct. This imposes a limitation on performance, especially when the conflicting error patterns are of similar weight. For a given syndrome length, the performance can be improved by resolving conflicts at run-time through soft decision.

3. Error Correction with Soft Decision

Hard quantization is performed by the decoder in addition to Q-level quantization to generate a binary received sequence. This sequence is used to generate the syndrome. Error correction is performed on this sequence using information on the quality of each received symbol. The quality information is provided by the demodulator through Q-level quantization (Q>2) of the received symbols. This allows selection of the best correction pattern from a set of syndrome indistinguishable patterns. The corrected received sequence is used to retrieve the original data using the one-to-one mapping between data and received sequence blocks of equal length [**2**].

We explain our approach using a one-half rate convolutional code with generator sequences 11110101 and 10011011, but the technique is applicable to other coding rates as well. The syndrome sequence is formed using a *parity check sequence* which is a column of the syndrome former matrix. The syndrome former matrix is described in [**8**] and the application of the parity check sequence to our method is described in [**4**]. Each syndrome bit is the dot product of the parity check sequence and a received bit block of the same length. The parity check sequence for the example code is 1101100111101011. Syndrome generation can be implemented using a shift-register with sixteen memory elements as shown in Figure 1. The pattern of connecting the memory elements to the modulo-2 adder is determined by the parity check sequence.

We generate a finite length syndrome, called the *s-address*, to access the correction table. The s-address length is 21 bits in our example. The first syndrome bit is generated by a block of sixteen received bits since the parity check sequence is sixteen bits long. Each additional syndrome bit is produced by shifting in two new received bits. We refer to successive pairs of received bits as *received pairs.* Hence, a syndrome of length 21 bits is completely determined by a window of 56 received bits, or 28 received pairs, where the most recent received pair is the $(2, 1)$ pair and the oldest received pair is $(56, 55)$. A non-zero s-address signifies some combination of errors within this 56-bit window called an *error pattern.* We refer to the received pairs in the 56 bit *correction window* which contain at least one error as *error pairs.* Error correction is performed on error pairs within the correction window, one pair at a time. There are two types of error pairs, one with errors in only one of the two bits and the other with errors in both bits. We refer to the correction that an error pair needs, i.e, the combination of errors in it as a *correction case.* Hence an error pair of the first type has two correction cases (01 and 10) while an error pair of the second type has only one correction case (11). Error correction is performed on the oldest error pair in the error pattern called the *correction pair* as shown in Figure 2. Hence every error pattern within the correction window has a corresponding correction pair and a correction case according to which error correction is performed.

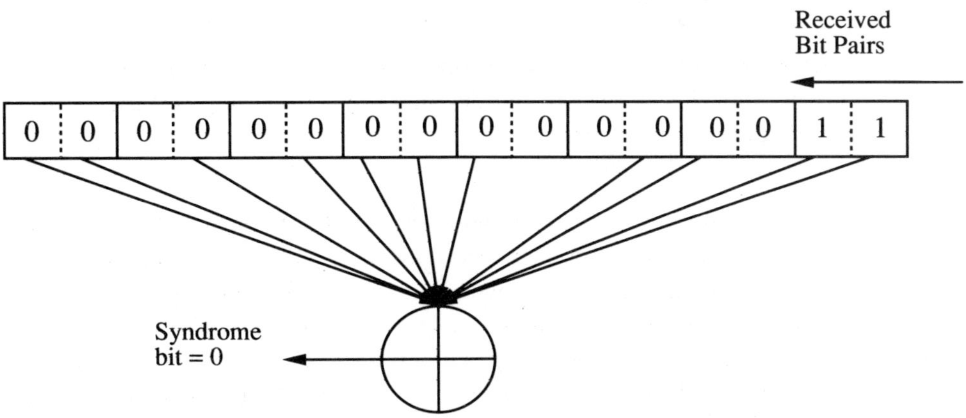

FIGURE 1. Leading s-address bit generation

Error correction is performed only when the leading bit of the s-address is a 1. The dot product of the parity check sequence and the oldest sixteen bits in the correction window determines the leading s-address bit. This restricts the possible locations of the correction pair to these sixteen bits, i.e, the oldest eight received pairs $(56, 55)$ through $(42, 41)$ as shown in Figure 2. The parity check sequence has a 11 as the right most pair. Therefore, the received pair $(42, 41)$ can be the correction pair only if it has a single bit in error (either bit 41 or bit 42, but not both). If both bits are in error, the leading syndrome bit produced would be 0 as shown in Figure 1. An s-address with a leading 1 would subsequently be produced after one or more new received pairs are shifted into the register. This implies that the correction pair is one of the oldest seven received pairs, $(56,55)$ through $(44,43)$, only if it has errors in both bits. Hence, an error pattern generating an s-address with a leading 1 has nine possible correction cases, one case (11) for each of the pairs $(56,55)$ through $(44,43)$, and two cases (01 and 10) for the pair $(42,41)$.

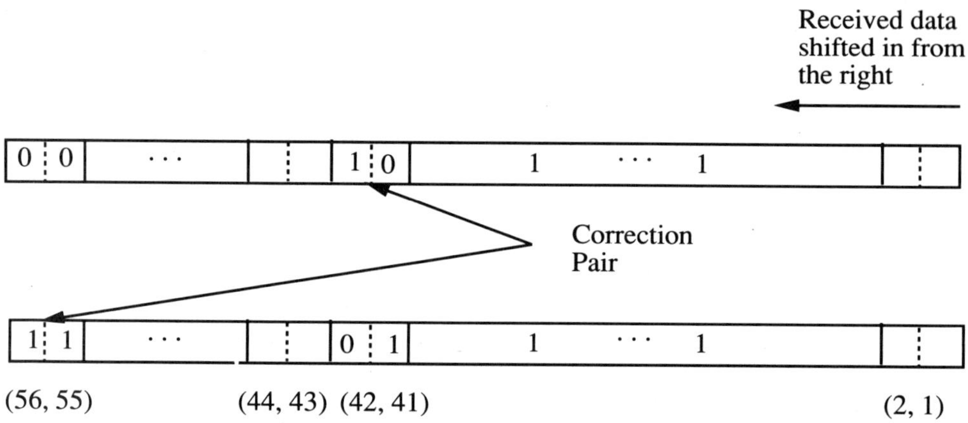

FIGURE 2. Correction pair locations corresponding to error patterns within the correction window (blank spaces in each pattern are 0's indicating no errors).

An s-address can be generated by different error patterns within the correction window. These conflicting error patterns may have different correction cases. We use soft decision in conjunction with precomputed information stored in the correction table to choose the most likely correction case. Each table entry has nine three bit fields corresponding to the nine possible correction cases for each s-address with a leading 1. Each field stores the Hamming weight of the corresponding error pattern. Since each field has three bits, we consider error patterns with Hamming weights seven or less. If a particular correction case corresponds to multiple error patterns of different weights, the minimum of all these weights is stored. An example of a table entry and the conflicting error patterns that generate the corresponding s-address is shown in Figure 3. The Q-level received symbols are used along with the precomputed table information described above to calculate a metric M for each correction case. The case with the highest metric is chosen for error correction.

Let $P(i,t)$ = Probability of receiving i bits in error in a block of t received bits, and $P_e(n)$ = Probability of receiving the nth bit in the correction window in error given the Q-level quantized received code symbol for bit n.

The metric M for a case requiring a correction in bit n of the correction pair

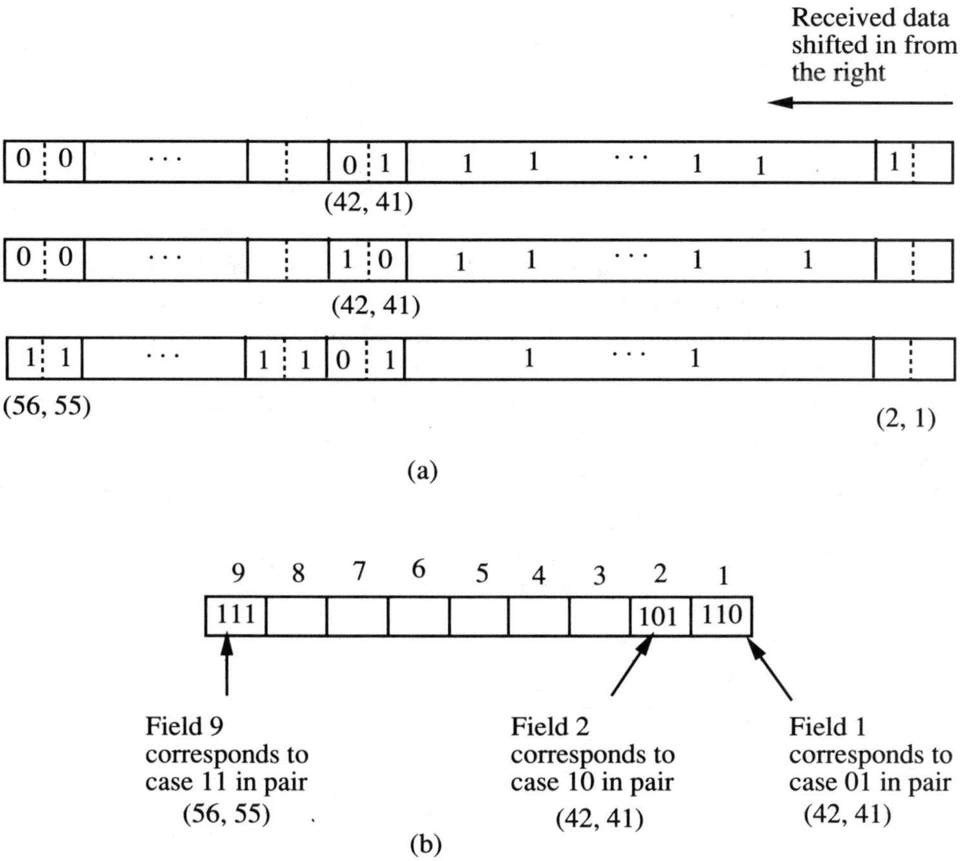

FIGURE 3. (a) Conflicting error patterns. (blank spaces in each pattern are 0's indicating no errors). (b) Corresponding correction table entry.

$(n+1, n)$ is

$$M = P(m-1, n-1) \times P_e(n), \tag{3.1}$$

where m is the weight of the error pattern corresponding to the case, retrieved from the correction table. The metric for a case requiring correction in bit $(n+1)$ of the correction pair $(n+1, n)$ is similarly calculated. The metric M for a case requiring corrections in bits n and $n+1$ of the correction pair $(n+1, n)$ is

$$M = P(m-2, n-1) \times \min(P_e(n), P_e(n+1)). \tag{3.2}$$

After performing the correction, received pairs are shifted into the correction window until another s-address with a leading 1 is generated. The error correction process described above is then repeated. This process results in error patterns with multiple error pairs being corrected over several correction iterations. The corrected received sequence is used to retrieve the original data using the one-to-one mapping between data and received sequence blocks of equal length [**2**].

4. Simulation and Performance

The performance of the soft decision technique presented in the previous sections has been studied through simulations and is illustrated in Figure 4. The example code of length eight was used with 8-level quantization. An improvement in performance of approximately 1 dB over a similar hard decision table-driven decoding method was observed at an input signal to noise ratio of 6 dB. Note that the ordinate represents the bit error probability of the corrected received sequence. Decoding is a separate step and our experience shows that after decoding, the information bit error probability is no worse than two times that of the corrected received sequence if the decoding method described in [**2**] is used.

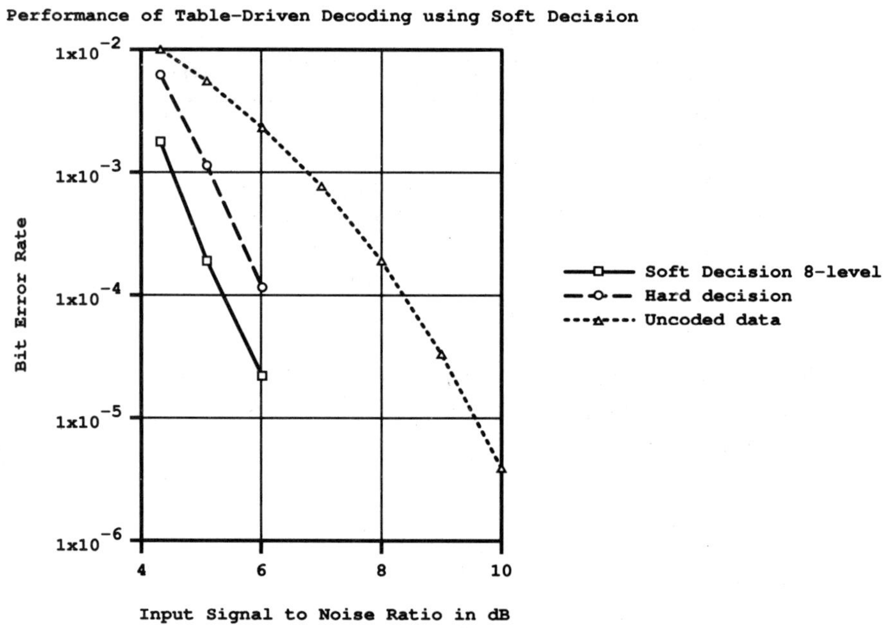

FIGURE 4. Performance of table-driven decoding with soft decision for a code with generator sequences 11110101 and 10011011.

5. Conclusions

A simple and fast table-driven decoding scheme for convolutionally encoded data is presented. This scheme uses soft decision information obtained by Q-level quantization of the received symbols. The table-driven nature of the decoding scheme reduces the computational complexity compared to the traditional Viterbi decoding method. This allows building decoders capable of handling higher data rates for nonsystematic codes. Further research is currently being carried out on the metrics used for selecting between conflicting error patterns and the decoding of data from the corrected received sequence.

REFERENCES

1. D.L. Bitzer, C.E. Alix, and K.M. Leuthold. System and method for decoding of convolutionally encoded data. United States Patent No. 5077743, December 1991 (US Patent for an improved decoder applied for.).
2. D.L. Bitzer and M.A. Vouk. A table-driven (feedback) decoder. In *Proceedings of the Tenth Annual International Phoenix Conference on Computers and Communications*, pages 385–392, Phoenix, AZ, March 1991.
3. G.C. Clark, Jr. and J.B. Cain. *Error-Correction Coding for Digital Communications.* Plenum Press, New York, 1981.
4. A. Dholakia, T.M. Lee, D.L. Bitzer, M.A. Vouk, L. Wang, and P.D. Franzon. An efficient table-driven decoder for one-half rate convolutional codes. In *Proceedings of the 30th Annual ACM Southeast Conference*, pages 116–123, Raleigh, NC, April 1992.
5. A. Dholakia, M.A. Vouk, and D.L. Bitzer. Table-driven decoding of binary one-half rate nonsystematic convolutional codes. To be presented at the 1993 IEEE International Symposium on Information Theory, January 1993.
6. R.G. Gallager. *Information Theory and Reliable Communication.* Wiley, New York, 1968.
7. J.A. Heller. Feedback decoding of convolutional codes. In A.J. Viterbi, editor, *Advances in Communication Systems, vol. 4*, pages 261–278. Academic Press, New York, 1975.
8. S. Lin and D.J. Costello, Jr. *Error Control Coding - Fundamentals and Applications.* Prentice-Hall, Englewood Cliffs,NJ 07632, 1983.

DEPARTMENT OF ELECTRICAL AND COMPUTER ENGINEERING, NORTH CAROLINA STATE UNIVERSITY, RALEIGH, NC 27695
E-mail address: havish@bvcd.csc.ncsu.edu

DEPARTMENT OF COMPUTER SCIENCE, NORTH CAROLINA STATE UNIVERSITY, RALEIGH, NC 27695

DEPARTMENT OF ELECTRICAL AND COMPUTER ENGINEERING, NORTH CAROLINA STATE UNIVERSITY, RALEIGH, NC 27695

DEPARTMENT OF COMPUTER SCIENCE, NORTH CAROLINA STATE UNIVERSITY, RALEIGH, NC 27695

DIMACS Series in Discrete Mathematics
and Theoretical Computer Science
Volume **14**, 1993

Rotationally Invariant Multilevel Codes

JAY N. LIVINGSTON

December 21, 1992

ABSTRACT. In this article, we describe a method for designing multilevel codes that are rotationally invariant. We further show that these codes can be linear, as well as demonstrating that suboptimal decoding can be used with these codes. The complexity of these codes provides a good performance/cost tradeoff.

1. Introduction

In trellis coded modulation (TCM), we are often concerned with encoding a sequence of symbols taken from either a finite lattice or an M-ary phase shift keying (MPSK) constellation. These constellations have what are known as *rotational symmetries*, which occur when the constellation is rotated through a fixed angle. If after rotation of the constellation we obtain the original constellation, then we call the angle of rotation a rotational symmetry. For example, a 16-QAM constellation with signal points drawn from the integer lattice exhibits four rotational symmetries, of 90, 180, 270, and 360 degrees. MPSK constellations have M symmetries, each at a multiple of $2\pi/M$ radians.

The effect of rotational symmetry is seen when considering the operation of the receiver. In real systems, synchronization and carrier recovery often lead to a phase offset relative to the original carrier. When this phase offset is equal to a rotational symmetry, the receiver is unable to detect it, since the rotated constellation is identical to the original. In this case, the receiver will make erroneous decisions, unless some corrective measures are taken.

The idea behind rotationally invariant codes is to find an encoder that ensures the following: given any coded sequence, if we rotate each symbol through a fixed rotational symmetry, then the new sequence of rotated symbols is also a valid

---

1991 *Mathematics Subject Classification.* Primary 94A05, 94B12.

code sequence. If this is the case, we may use differential encoding and decoding to overcome the effects of phase rotation.

Rotationally invariant codes have been an active area of research for the last decade (see [**1**]-[**3**]), since most practical TCM schemes are susceptible to phase ambiguities. Without rotational invariance, the receiver requires some means of determining absolute phase. If the encoder is rotationally invariant for every constellation symmetry, then the receiver can operate correctly with any constellation symmetry as a phase ambiguity. The need for rotationally invariant codes was seen early in the development of TCM. The pioneering work of Wei in [**1**]-[**3**] led to many practical and powerful codes that are rotationally invariant for QAM and MPSK constellations.

Separate from the investigation of rotational invariance has been the development of multilevel codes. This coding method offers a constructive approach to the design of codes for the Gaussian channel [**4**], [**5**], line codes [**6**], and codes for the fading channel [**7**]. The importance of this technique is the ability to design codes having, *a priori*, a specific performance level. Another advantage of multilevel codes is the ability to use a suboptimal decoding structure that is nearly optimal in performance, but with greatly simplified complexity.

In this article, we describe an approach to the design of rotationally invariant codes using multilevel coding. This technique allows the designer to achieve, *a priori*, a given performance level, as well as invariance to rotations through constellation symmetries.

In Section II, we give the problem statement and describe multilevel codes briefly. We also give examples of the design of some rotationally invariant codes, with design rules. Section III summarizes the paper.

2. Rotational Invariance as Seen by Multilevel Codes

We are concerned in this work with finding codes for two specific modulation schemes, namely QAM constellations and MPSK constellations. For the purposes of this article, we will restrict our comments to QAM constellations.

It has been argued (see e.g., [**8**]) that a "natural labeling" is best for achieving rotational invariance. In Figure 1, we illustrate natural labeling on a 16-QAM constellation and a 32-SQ constellation. Below each point is a binary label. Note that for the 16-QAM constellation, the two least significant bits are not rotationally invariant, while the two most significant bits are already invariant to rotations through multiples of $\pi/2$ radians. Also note that for the 32-SQ constellation, the least significant bit (LSB) is not rotationally invariant, while the four most significant bits again are already rotationally invariant. This leads us to the following observations:

Observation 1: *Only the least significant bit (for the 32-SQ constellation) needs to be encoded in such a way as to make it rotationally invariant.*

Observation 2: *Only the two least significant bits (for QAM) need to be*

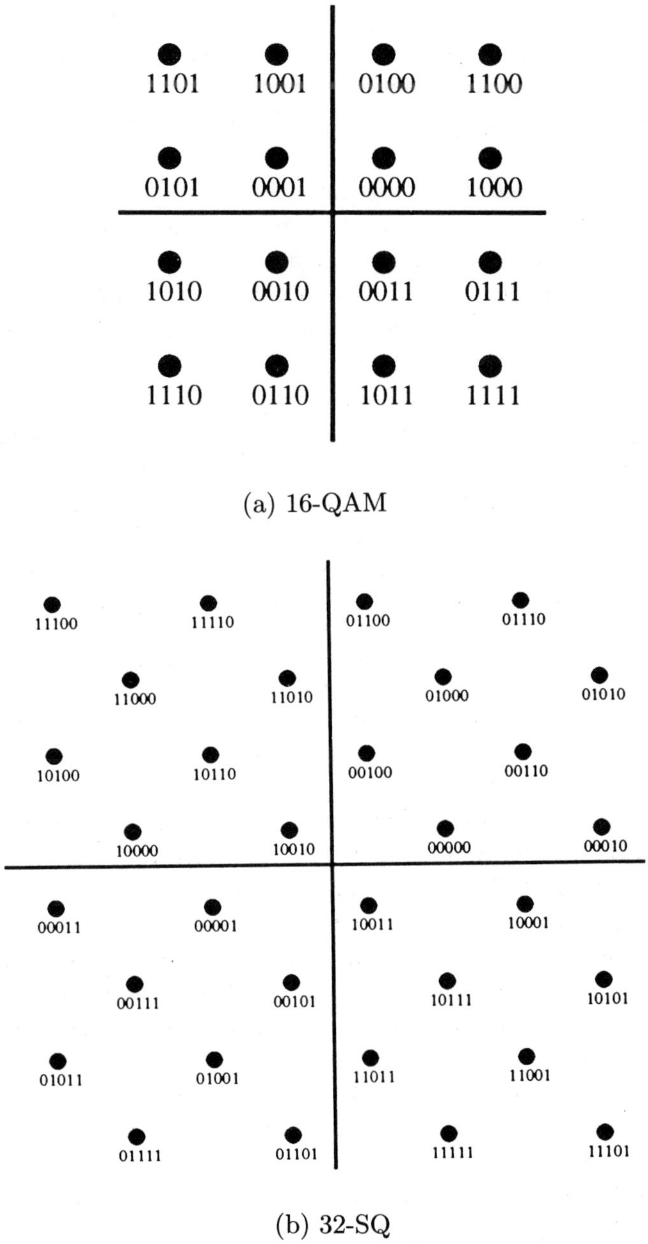

FIGURE 1. 16 QAM and 32-SQ constellations.

encoded in such a way as to make them rotationally invariant.

Since in this article we are concentrating on QAM constellations, we need to design codes that provide rotational invariance only for the two least significant bits. The problem facing the designer, then, is how to design a code that achieves this.

The theory behind multilevel codes involves partitioning the signal space into subsets. At each level of partitioning the constellation is further subdivided into smaller subsets. We label each edge at depth i with a binary variable, a_i. Then each subset in partition L is uniquely determined by the label $(a_1 a_2 \cdots a_L)$.

Associated with level i of the partition is a minimum intra-subset squared Euclidean distance, denoted δ_i. Obviously, if partitioning has been carried out correctly, $\delta_0 \leq \delta_1 \leq \cdots \leq \delta_L$.

The multilevel code employs an L-level code, $C = [C_1, \cdots, C_L]$, where the C_i are component codes. Each component code is responsible for selection of its corresponding label, a_i; i.e., C is the set of all sequences $\{(a_1^k, \cdots, a_L^k)\}$ of subsets in Γ_L that satisfy $(a_i^k) \in C_i$ for all $i = 1, 2, \ldots, L$ [**4**].

If each code has a minimum Hamming distance d_i, then it has been shown [**4**] that the minimum squared Euclidean distance for the multilevel code is given by

$$d_{free}^2 = \min\{d_1\delta_0, d_2\delta_1, \ldots, d_L\delta_{L-1}\}. \tag{2.1}$$

Thus it is simple to design a multilevel code with a given performance level. All that the designer needs are L binary codes and their associated minimum distances.

We will concentrate on two specific constellations to demonstrate the idea of rotational invariance and multilevel codes. They are given in Figure 1(a) and (b). Note that the first figure has four rotational symmetries, and the second has two. In Figure 1(b), we note that a rotation of π radians will result in the inversion of the least significant bit. Recall that for multilevel coding, we encode each bit with its own code. This leads to the following observation:

Observation 3: *Only the code for the LSB, code C_1, need be rotationally invariant for the 32-SQ constellation.*

In order in make code C_1 rotationally invariant, we again note that rotation involves simply inverting the LSB. This corresponds to adding the sequence $1 = \{1111\ldots\}$ to the output from code C_1. The requirement for rotational invariance is as follows (which, in the interest of brevity, we state without proof):

180 Degree Rotational Invariance: Given any output sequence from code C_1, say $a = \{a_1 a_2 \ldots\}$, then the sequence $a + \mathbf{1}$, where $\mathbf{1}$ represents the all-one sequence, must also be in the code.

The above condition is met very simply in the case of linear codes by requiring the sequence $\mathbf{1}$ be in the code C_1.

Example 1: We use the above technique on the 32-SQ constellation. After partitioning, we use a 2-level code, with each partition being binary. The first code C_1 must contain the sequence $\mathbf{1}$. We choose the code described by the trellis

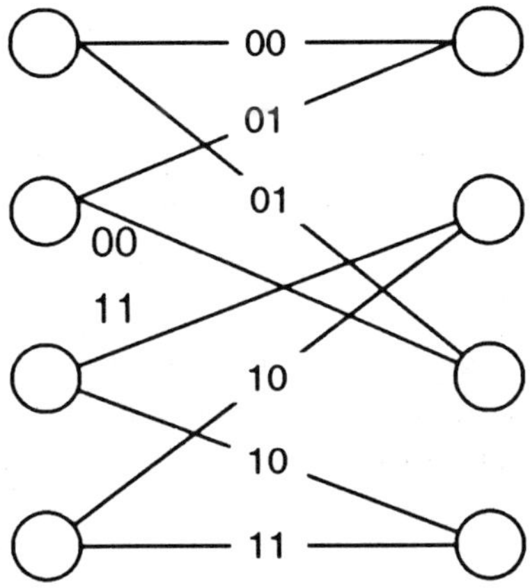

FIGURE 2. Code trellis for Example 1.

given in Figure 2. Here, the minimum Hamming distance of code C_1 is four. We choose code C_2 to be the simple even parity code of length 2, with minimum Hamming distance 2. Assuming the coded constellation has minimum distance between points of $\sqrt{2}$, then $d_f^2 = 8$ and $P_c = 10.5$, where d_f^2 is the free Euclidean distance of the code and P_c is the average power in the coded system. Similarly, using a 16-QAM constellation as the uncoded system and placing the points on an integer grid yields $P_u = 2.5$ and $d_u^2 = 1$, where P_u is the average power in the uncoded system and d_u^2 is the minimum squared Euclidean distance in the uncoded constellation. This gives us a coding gain of 2.8 dB, and the decoding complexity is essentially that of a 4-state code. This is the same gain as found by Wei in Example 1 of [**1**].

The case of four rotational symmetries is only slightly more difficult to deal with. We note that in Figure 1(a), that the two LSB's are affected by a rotation. This again yields an observation:

Observation 4: *Both code C_1 and C_2 must provide rotational invariance for a 16-QAM constellation.*

We can find a logical relationship between the two least significant bits and the rotation as follows:

(i) For the least significant bit, b_0, we have the same situation as with 180 degree rotational invariance, i.e., we require the all one's sequence to be in the linear code C_1 to provide rotational invariance.

(ii) For the next most significant bit, b_1, we find that the rotated bit b_1 is found from the unrotated bits using the following:

$$b_1(\textit{rotated}) = b_1 + b_0 \tag{2.2}$$

or

$$b_1(rotated) = b_1 + b_0 + 1 \tag{2.3}$$

where the addition is performed modulo 2.

The foregoing gives us the following conditions for rotational invariance with four symmetries:

90 Degree Rotational Invariance: 90 degree rotational invariance is guaranteed if the codes C_1 and C_2 (assumed linear) meet the following criteria:

(i) Code C_1 must contain the sequence **1**.

(ii) Code C_1 must be a *subcode* of code C_2 (i.e., all sequences in C_1 must be contained in C_2 as well).

Again, we omit the proof for brevity.

Condition (ii) above is fortunate, since it requires the rate of code C_1 to be less than or equal to the rate of code C_2. This is the proper relationship for the code rates to follow if we are to use multilevel codes that have good d_f^2, since we would like code C_1 to be more powerful than code C_2, code C_2 to be more powerful than code C_3, etc.

Example 2: A 2-level multilevel code using a constellation drawn from an integer lattice. Let C_1 be given by the trellis in Figure 3a. This code has a minimum Hamming distance of 4. Let C_2 be given by the trellis of Figure 3b. This code has minimum Hamming distance of 2, and contains the code of C_1 as a subcode. The coding gain can be found from:

$$G_c = 10\log(d_f^2) - 10\log(P_c/P_u), \tag{2.4}$$

where d_f^2 is the free Euclidean distance of the code, and P_c and P_u are the average power of the coded and uncoded constellations, respectively (note that $d_u^2 = 1$). We will use the continuous approximation to compute the average power. This yields:

$$P_c/P_u = 2^{B_c - B_u} \tag{2.5}$$

where B_c and B_u are the number of information bits in the coded and uncoded constellations, respectively.

For the code above, $d_f^2 = 4$, and since the rates of C_1 and C_2 are 1/4 and 1/2, respectively, $B_c - B_u = 1.25$. This gives an overall gain of 2.25 dB, with the decoding complexity of two 2-state codes.

As can be seen by these simple examples, the use of multilevel codes can simplify the design process, as well as yield immediate estimates of performance and coding gain.

An important fact to remember is that the multilevel coding scheme can be decoded using multistage decoding. This method can greatly reduce complexity, while losing little performance over maximum likelihood decoding.

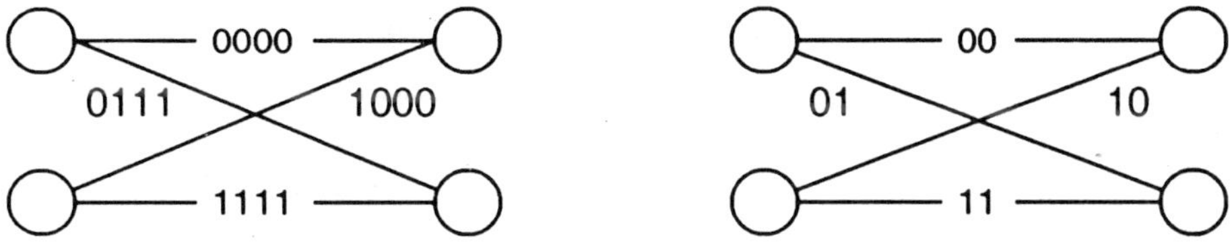

(a) Trellis for Code C_1 (b) Trellis for Code C_2

FIGURE 3. Code trellis for codes C_1 and C_2 of Example 2.

3. Summary

We have considered a new approach to the design of rotationally invariant codes, and have demonstrated the use of multilevel codes as a simple method of code design that offers good performance coupled with simple decoding strategies.

REFERENCES

1. L.-F. Wei, "Rotationally Invariant Convolutional Channel Coding with Expanded Signal Space–Part I: 180°," *IEEE Journal on Selected Areas in Communications,* vol. SAC-2, pp. 659–671, Sept. 1984.
2. L.-F. Wei, "Rotationally Invariant Convolutional Channel Coding with Expanded Signal Space–Part II: Nonlinear Codes," *IEEE Journal on Selected Areas in Communications,* vol. SAC-2, pp. 672–686, Sept. 1984.
3. L.-F. Wei, "Rotationally Invariant Trellis-Coded Modulations with Multidimensional M-PSK," *IEEE Journal on Selected Areas in Communications,* vol. SAC-7, pp. 1281-1295, Sept. 1989.
4. A. R. Calderbank, "Multilevel Codes and Multistage Decoding," *IEEE Transactions on Communications*, vol. 37, pp. 222–229, March 1989.
5. G. J. Pottie and D. P. Taylor, "Multilevel Codes Based on Partitioning," *IEEE Transactions on Information Theory*, vol. 35, no. 1, pp. 87–98, January 1989.
6. A. R. Calderbank, M. A. Herro, and V. Telang, "A Multilevel Approach to the Design of DC-Free Line Codes," *IEEE Transactions on Information Theory*, vol. 35, pp. 579–583, May 1989.
7. J. Livingston and M. Mulligan, "Multilevel Codes and Suboptimal Decoding for PSK Signaling on the Fading Channel," in *International Symposium on Information Theory and its Applications*, pp. 163–166, Honolulu, HI, 1990.
8. S. S. Pietrobon, G. Ungerboeck, and D. J. Costello, Jr., "Rotationally Invariant Nonlinear Trellis Codes for Two-Dimensional Modulation," submitted to *IEEE Trans. on Inform. Theory,* 1991.

DEPARTMENT OF ELECTRICAL ENGINEERING, TEXAS A&M UNIVERSITY, COLLEGE STATION, TX 77843

E-mail address: jnl@jeeves.tamu.edu

DIMACS Series in Discrete Mathematics
and Theoretical Computer Science
Volume **14**, 1993

Constellations for Diversity

KENNETH J. KERPEZ

May 24, 1993

ABSTRACT. Consider the case where there are several channels available for transmission, and the additive noise on each channel may have different power. This paper presents a signal constellation, called a "coordinated code," for the signal space formed by the different channels. The coordinated code has good performance when the noise powers are equal, while simultaneously providing diversity for good performance when the noise powers are unequal. The code is also relatively simple. The maximum likelihood receiver is presented; it extracts information from the coded signal in inverse proportion to each channel's noise power. The minimum distance of the code is found and the coding gain over a system that transmits independent bit streams on each channel is derived as a function of the noise statistics. The gain of the code is also found relative to symbol splitting diversity, which transmits a copy of the same message on each channel; this gain is as high as 9 dB.

1. Introduction

This paper considers the case where there is more than one channel available for transmission and each channel has additive noise with different power. The transmitter has no knowledge of the power of the noise on each channel. Also, the noise powers are constant or vary slowly so that the receiver may estimate the noise statistics. With "uncoordinated" transmission the total message is divided and each channel independently carries a part of it. Uncoordinated transmission has good performance when each channel has the same noise power, but if one channel is very noisy then the message is lost. Symbol splitting diversity transmits a copy of the entire message on each channel so that the message may still be fully recovered if some channels are very noisy [**1**]. However, symbol splitting has relatively poor performance if each channel has the same noise power. The scheme presented in this paper, called "coordinated coding,"

1991 *Mathematics Subject Classification.* Primary 94A05.

has the high performance of uncoordinated transmission when the noise powers are equal, and the high performance of symbol splitting when some channels are very noisy.

Suppose the number of channels available for transmission is L. The channels may either be used separately (uncoordinated), or the transmission on them may be coordinated. Uncoordinated transmission sends M level signals on each channel and carries a total of $L \log_2 M$ bits of information. Symbol splitting sends a copy of the same M^L-level signal on each channel and also carries $L \log_2 M$ bits of information. Coordinated coding sends M^L level signals on each channel. The coordinated code has a fixed, non-adaptive transmitter. Given the code signal sent on any one channel, the code signals sent on the other channels are uniquely determined by the coordinated code. Thus the coordinated code sends $L \log_2 M$ information bits, the same as uncoordinated transmission and symbol splitting. The codewords form an M^L-point L-dimensional constellation. The coded symbols that are closely spaced on one channel are widely spaced on the other channels. This allows the receiver to extract more information from the channel with less noise, thus providing diversity. It is shown that the coordinated code always performs at least as well as uncoordinated transmission or symbol splitting. For the calculations here, decreasing the received signal power on a channel has the same effect as increasing the noise power on that channel, so only the noise powers are varied.

Another method of implementing coordinated transmission is to use an adaptive transmitter, which was considered by Lechleider [**2**], and Falconer [**3**]. Adaptive transmitters have the disadvantage of requiring knowledge of the channel response at the transmitter, and they usually transmit different average powers on different channels. However, a fully adaptive transceiver can achieve better performance than the coordinated code presented here. Adaptive transmitters are not considered further in this paper.

High rate digital subscriber lines (HDSL) use two twisted pairs to carry 1.544 Mbit/sec bi-directional data over local copper telephone loops. The coordinated code was initially conceived to coordinate the transmission on the two pairs and achieve signal-to-noise ratio (SNR) gains for HDSL. The code can be used to improve the performance of an existing decision-feedback equalizer (DFE) by using the same adaptive filters and replacing only the DFE's decision block. Also, an HDSL with the coordinated code could operate on a short loop using just a single pair with almost no modification. Unlike trellis coding, the coordinated code does not use time as a variable, and is unaffected by intersymbol interference. The coordinated coding scheme is also relatively simple. In addition to HDSL, the code is applicable to variety of multi-channel and diversity systems, including digital radio and multi-tone transmission.

Section 2 of this paper describes the channel model. Section 3 describes the coordinated coding scheme in detail. The minimum distance of the coordinated code is given in Section 4. Section 4 also derives the coding gain over uncoordinated transmission. In Section 5 the coordinated code is compared to symbol splitting diversity. Section 6 compares the coordinated code to both uncoordinated transmission and symbol splitting diversity, by using the effective SNR.

2. The Channel Model

This paper primarily considers the transmission of M-ary pulse amplitude modulated (PAM) signals in the presence of additive Gaussian noise. However, the code is easily extended to QAM or PSK transmission [**4**].

On each of L separate channels, the receiver equalizes and amplifies the signal, then samples the signals each symbol period. The receiver then uses the L samples to estimate the transmitted message. At each symbol period the transmitter sends a message, $\underline{m} = [m_1, m_2, \ldots, m_L]$, where m_v is the transmitted voltage on channel v. There are M signaling levels for uncoordinated signals, so that

$$m_v \in \{-M+1, -M+3, \ldots, M-3, M-1\}$$

During transmission the message is corrupted by additive Gaussian noise, $\underline{n}$, and the received vector is $\underline{r} = \underline{m} + \underline{n}$. Here n_v and r_v are the noise and received signal on channel v, respectively, for $v = 1, 2, \ldots, L$. The vectors $\underline{r}$, $\underline{m}$, and $\underline{n}$ have length L. The noise, $\underline{n}$, has covariance matrix

$$K = E[\underline{n}^T \underline{n}] \tag{2.1}$$

and is zero-mean Gaussian so that [**5**]

(2.2)
$$Pr(n_1 \le N_1, \ldots, n_L \le N_L) = (2\pi)^{-n/2}(\det[K])^{-1/2} \int_{-\infty}^{N_1} \cdots \int_{-\infty}^{N_L} e^{-(\underline{n}K^{-1}\underline{n}^T)/2} .$$

The noise power on channel v is $E[n_v^2] = \sigma_v^2$. The ratio of the noise power on channel 1 to the noise power on channel v is defined as

$$\Delta_v = \frac{\sigma_1^2}{\sigma_v^2} . \tag{2.3}$$

If there are $L = 2$ channels, such as for HDSL, then the covariance matrix is

$$K = \begin{bmatrix} \sigma_1^2 & k\sigma_1\sigma_2 \\ k\sigma_1\sigma_2 & \sigma_2^2 \end{bmatrix} , \tag{2.4}$$

the correlation coefficient is $k = E[n_1 n_2]/(\sigma_1\sigma_2)$, and the subscript in (2.3) is dropped so the ratio of the noise powers on the two channels is simply $\Delta = \sigma_1^2/\sigma_2^2$.

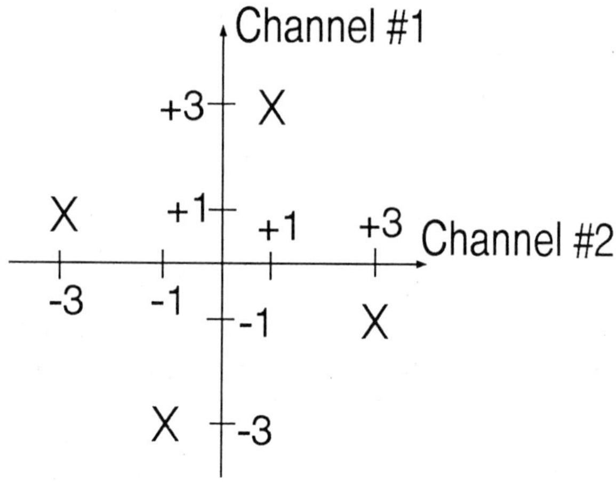

FIGURE 1. Coordinated code for 2 bits on two channels. $M = 2$, $L = 2$.

3. The Coordinated Code

In this section it is shown how to construct a coordinated code for an arbitrary number of channels and an arbitrary number of original signaling levels. The coordinated coding scheme may be used for any communication system where there is more than one channel and the channels may carry different signals.

For uncoordinated transmission, each channel transmits independent M-ary signals. The coordinated code transmits M^L-ary coded signals on each channel. The signals transmitted on one channel are a specific permutation of the signals transmitted on the other channel. The coded message on channel v is m_v, which is indexed by i_v, where

$$i_v = (M^L - 1 - m_v)/2 + 1$$

for $v = 1, 2, \ldots, L$ and $i_v = 1, 2, \ldots, M^L$. The indices of the message, i_1, i_2, are counting numbers and are convenient for enumerating the code and describing its minimum distance. Notice that the squared difference between messages is 4 times the squared difference between their indices. The received vector is $\underline{r} = \underline{m} + \underline{n}$, where vectors have length L.

Let i_1 be the index of the message transmitted on the first channel. Then the indices of all the other messages, i_v, $v = 2, 3, \ldots, L$, are uniquely determined by the code mapping

$$i_v = [(i_1 - 1)M^{L-v+1}] \; modulo \; M^L + M^{L-v+1} + 1 - \lceil \frac{i_1}{M^{v-1}} \rceil \tag{3.1}$$

where $\lceil j \rceil$ is the ceiling of j. There are M^L possible values of i_1 so the code transmits M^L information bits, the same as uncoordinated transmission. Figure 1 illustrates the code constellation for $M = 2$ and $L = 2$. Figure 2 illustrates the code constellation for $M = 4$ and $L = 2$, which is the original code proposed

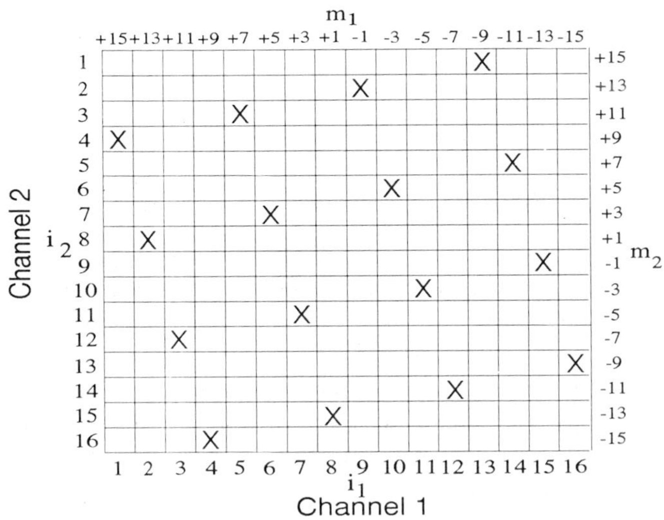

FIGURE 2. Coordinated code for 4 bits on two channels. $M = 4$, $L = 2$.

for HDSL. The code partitions the indices i_v into M^{v-1} subsets, and each subset has M^{L-v+1} indices. Relative to the index on channel 1, i_1, the distance between indices within each subset is maximized. Then adjacent elements in different subsets are arranged to have good spacing. The messages that are close on some channels are widely separated on other channels, which provides good diversity.

The code defines a signal constellation on the different channels. For $L = 2$ dimensions, the code constellation is a subset of a lattice. The lattice is a rotation of the square lattice Z^2 [**6**]. It is seen in Figures 1 and 2 that the rotation of Z^2 makes the projection of the lattice on either axis equally spaced, which maximizes the minimum distance of the projection and allows for effective diversity. The two-dimensional code constellation also defines a permutation matrix [**7**]. When M is large the code mapping may be shifted to have a symmetric permutation matrix (constellation), while maintaining its distance properties. This makes the set of transmitted signals $\{m_1, m_2\}$ equal the reversed set $\{m_2, m_1\}$, which facilitates decoding. This may be done for HDSL.

The maximum likelihood receiver estimates the message by minimizing the exponent in the multivariate Gaussian density of the received signal. From (2.1) and (2.2), given the received vector, $\underline{r}$, the maximum likelihood receiver outputs the codeword, $\widehat{\underline{m}}$, that minimizes the *metric* given by

$$metric\,(\underline{m}) = (\underline{r} - \underline{m})K^{-1}(\underline{r} - \underline{m})^T \,. \tag{3.2}$$

To make the analysis tractable, it is assumed in subsequent sections that the noise on different channels is independent, so the metric is

(3.3)

$$metric\,(m_1, m_2, \ldots, m_L) = \frac{(r_1 - m_1)^2}{\sigma_1^2} + \frac{(r_2 - m_2)^2}{\sigma_2^2} + \cdots + \frac{(r_L - m_L)^2}{\sigma_L^2} .$$

4. The Minimum Distance and Coding Gain Over Uncoordinated Transmission

It will be shown that when the noise on each channel has equal power and is independent, the coordinated code performs as well as transmitting independent, uncoordinated bit streams on each channel. If the noises have unequal power, then the coordinated code will perform better than uncoordinated transmission, if the noises on different channels are uncorrelated. For every case considered, the signal power, bit rate, and bandwidth are the same. The coding gain is defined as the increase in SNR needed by uncoordinated transmission to have the same error probability as coordinated coding. All coding gains presented here are for high SNR.

Now the coding gain is found for L channels transmitting a total of $L \log_2 M$ information bits per symbol. Let there be two different messages indexed by $j_1, j_2, \ldots, j_L$ and $i_1, i_2, \ldots, i_L$ respectively. Since they are different, from (3.1), $j_v \neq i_v$ for all $v = 1, 2, \ldots, L$. Define the distance $d_v = j_v - i_v$. Define the minimum distance vector, $[d_1, d_2, \ldots, d_L]_{\min}$, as the distance vector between the indices of two distinct codewords with the minimum Euclidean distance,

$$[d_1, d_2, \ldots, d_L]_{\min} = \min_{[j_1,\ldots,j_L] \neq [i_1,\ldots,i_L]} \sqrt{d_1^2 + d_2^2 + \ldots + d_L^2} .$$

THEOREM 4.1. The minimum distance vector of the coordinated code defined by (3.1) is a permutation of

$$[M^{L-1}, M^{L-2}, \ldots, M^2, M, 1] .$$

The proof of the theorem is complicated, so it is not presented here; it can be found in [**8**].

From Equation (3.1), since uncoordinated transmission has M signal levels and coordinated transmission has M^L levels, the increase in power for coding is

$$P^C_{avg}/P^U_{avg} = \frac{M^{2L} - 1}{(M^2 - 1)} . \tag{4.1}$$

From Theorem 1, the minimum squared Euclidean distance, $d^2_{\min}$, between two distinct codewords is

$$d^2_{\min} = \sum_{v=1}^{L} M^{v-1} = \frac{M^{2L} - 1}{(M^2 - 1)} . \tag{4.2}$$

The increase in the minimum squared Euclidean distance of the coordinated code (4.2) is the same as its increase in power (4.1). Thus the coordinated code performs at least as well as uncoordinated transmission when the noise on different channels is uncorrelated with the same power.

The coding gain is defined as the increase in SNR needed to have the same error probability if M-ary equal power signals are independently transmitted and received on each channel, compared to if coordinated code signals (3.1) are transmitted and received with (3.3). The noise on different channels is assumed to be independent. The actual transmitted message is indexed by $i_1, i_2, \ldots, i_L$, and a different possible message is indexed by $j_1, j_2, \ldots, j_L$. There is an error if the noise causes the message indexed by j to have a smaller metric than the correct message which is indexed by i; i.e., if

$$(4.3)\quad \frac{n_1^2}{\sigma_1^2} + \frac{n_2^2}{\sigma_2^2} + \cdots + \frac{n_L^2}{\sigma_L^2} \geq \frac{(n_1 - d_1)^2}{\sigma_1^2} + \frac{(n_2 - d_2)^2}{\sigma_2^2} + \cdots + \frac{(n_L - d_L)^2}{\sigma_L^2}\,.$$

Without loss of generality, order the channels so that $\sigma_1^2 \geq \sigma_2^2 \geq \ldots \geq \sigma_L^2$. This implies that for the ratios of noise powers defined in (2.3), $\Delta_2 \leq \ldots \leq \Delta_L$. A sum of independent Gaussian random variables is a Gaussian random variable with variance equal to the sum of the individual variances [**5**]. Equation (4.3) may be rearranged to show that the probability of making the error is the probability that a unit-variance Gaussian variable exceeds

$$(4.4)\qquad \frac{1}{2\sigma_1}\sqrt{d_1^2 + d_2^2\Delta_2 + \cdots + d_L^2\Delta_L}\,.$$

From Theorem 1, the minimum Euclidean distance occurs when $d_v^2 = M^{2(L-v)}$. From (4.1), the average power of coded signals is a factor of $M^{2(L-1)} + \cdots + M^2 + 1$ higher than uncoded. Uncoded signals have indices that differ by a minimum of 1. Combining these facts with (4.4) shows that when the noise is uncorrelated and the SNR is high, the coding gain over uncoordinated transmission is

$$(4.5)\quad gain = 10\log_{10}\left(\frac{M^{2(L-1)} + M^{2(L-2)}\Delta_2 + \cdots + M^2\Delta_{L-1} + \Delta_L}{M^{2(L-1)} + \cdots + M^2 + 1}\right)\,.$$

5. Coordinated Coding Compared to Symbol Splitting Diversity

Symbol splitting diversity sends the same M^L-level signal on each of L channels [**1**]. The permutation matrix, or constellation, of symbol splitting diversity has entries only on the main diagonal. Thus, when the noise power is about the same on each channel, the points of the symbol splitting diversity constellation are close together, which leads to relatively poor performance.

Assume that the noise on different channels is independent. Assume that the receiver uses the maximum likelihood detector (3.3). From Section 4, the minimum distance vector, $[d_1, d_2, \ldots, d_L]_{\min}$, of symbol splitting diversity equals $[1, 1, \ldots, 1]$. From Theorem 1, the minimum distance vector of the coordinated code is $[M^{L-1}, M^{L-2}, \ldots, 1]$. Both systems have the same average power. The SNR gain of the coordinated code over symbol splitting diversity was found, as in the derivation of (4.5), to be

$$(5.1)\qquad 10\log_{10}\left(\frac{M^{2(L-1)}+M^{2(L-2)}\Delta_2+\cdots+M^2\Delta_{L-1}+\Delta_L}{1+\Delta_2+\cdots+\Delta_{L-1}+\Delta_L}\right).$$

For $L=2$, $M=4$, and $\Delta=1$, the gain is 9 dB. The possibility of this gain is predicted by Shannon theory, since the bandwidth (number of channels) is large.

The analyses here are easily extended to fading channels, since fading causes the signal power to decrease on certain channels, which has the same effect on error rate as increasing the noise power on those channels. This paper assumes coherent detection. For non-coherent detection, the maximum likelihood receiver is a function of Rayleigh and Ricean densities [**1**], so the minimum distance and gain is different from that presented here. However, with sub-optimal square-law combining, the gain is still given by (5.1).

6. The Effective SNR

Define the effective SNR as the ratio, in decibels, of half the minimum distance of a given system to its error causing noise. The effective SNR is a way to simultaneously compare the three systems presented in this paper: uncoordinated, symbol splitting, and the coordinated code.

Define the effective SNR as

$$\min_{\underline{d}}\left[10\log_{10}\left((d_1/2\sigma_1)^2+(d_2/2\sigma_2)^2+\cdots+(d_L/2\sigma_L)^2\right)\right].$$

As previously, let $\sigma_1^2\geq\sigma_2^2\geq\cdots\geq\sigma_L^2$. Then the minimum distance of the coordinated code is given in Theorem 1.

The effective SNR of three different systems transmitting 2 bits per symbol period on $L=2$ channels was computed using the formulas above and is plotted in Figure 3 as Δ is varied while $\sigma_1^2+\sigma_2^2$ is held constant. The uncoordinated system sends 2 independent binary signals. The symbol splitting system sends the same quaternary symbol on both channels. The coordinated code is defined by (3.1) and is shown in Figure 1. It is seen that the coordinated code has a higher effective SNR than both of the other systems.

The effective SNR was also found for systems transmitting 4 bits per symbol period on $L=2$ channels, and is plotted in Figure 4. The uncoordinated system sends 2 independent quaternary signals. The symbol splitting system sends the same 16-level symbol on both channels. The coordinated code is defined by (3.1) and is shown in Figure 2. Again, the coordinated code has a higher effective SNR than both of the other systems.

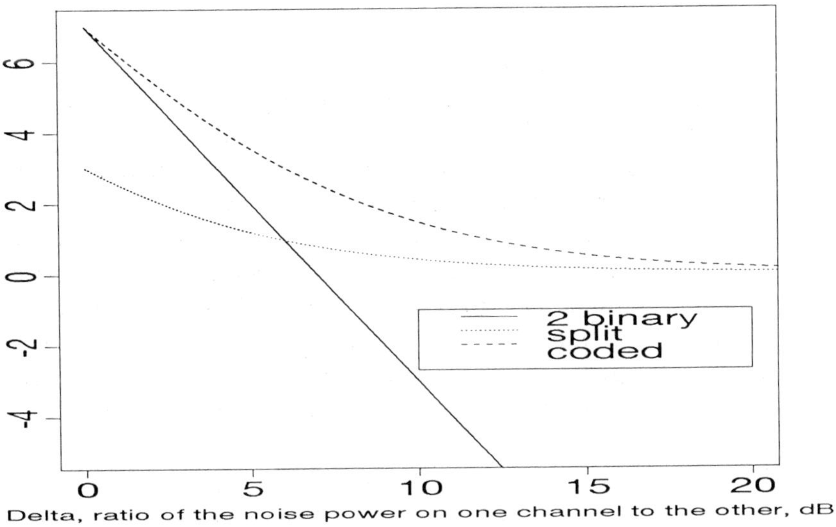

FIGURE 3. Effective SNR of systems transmitting 2 bits on 2 channels. $M = 2$, $L = 2$.

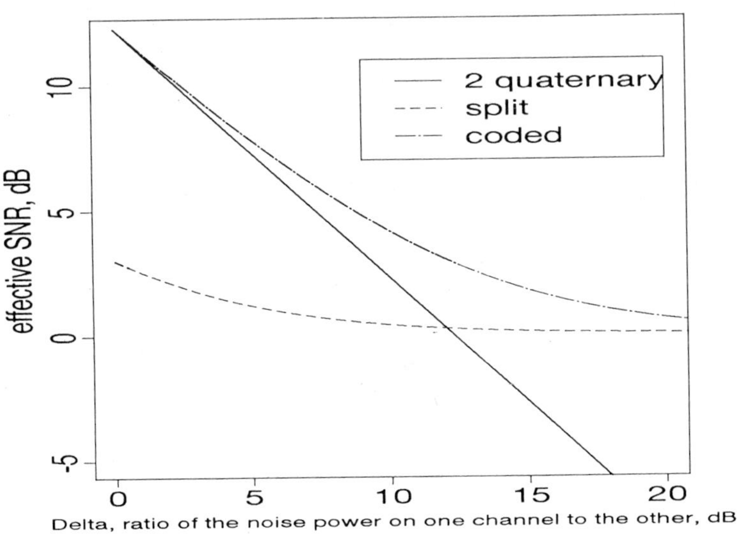

FIGURE 4. Effective SNR of systems transmitting 4 bits on 2 channels. $M = 4$, $L = 2$.

7. Discussion

Coordinated coding is a viable technique for providing diversity while maintaining high performance. The coordinated code may be used to advantage for simultaneous communication over any number of channels with unequal noise powers. No matter what the noise statistics are, the coordinated code essentially performs at least as well as a system with no diversity. As long as any one channel remains reliable, all the transmitted information may be recovered no matter how noisy the other channels are. The coordinated code is also an excellent method of bit allocation for multi-tone or multi-channel systems. The coordinated code may be applied to digital radio to provide diversity and mitigate the effects of fading [**4**]. Coordinated coding provides up to 9 dB SNR gains over symbol splitting diversity.

References

1. R. E. Blahut, *Digital Transmission of Information*, Reading, MA: Addison-Wesley, 1990.
2. J. W. Lechleider, "Coordinated Transmission for Two-Pair Digital Subscriber Lines," *IEEE Journal on Selected Areas in Communications, Special Issue on High-Speed Digital Subscriber Lines*. Vol. 9, pp. 920–930, August 1991.
3. D. D. Falconer, "Simple Reception Techniques for Coordinated Two-Pair Digital Transmission," *IEEE Global Telecommunications Conference 1991, Globecom '92*, Session 2.3, December 2–5, 1991.
4. K. J. Kerpez, "PSK Constellations for Good Diversity on Fading Channels," *IEEE Global Telecommunications Conference 1992, Globecom '92*, Session 20A.2, December 6–9, 1992.
5. W. Feller, *An Introduction to Probability Theory and Its Applications, Volume II*, New York: Wiley, 1971.
6. J. H. Conway and N. J. A. Sloane, *Sphere Packings, Lattices and Groups*, New York: Springer-Verlag, 1988.
7. I. N. Herstein, *Topics in Algebra, Second Edition*, New York: Wiley, 1975.
8. K. J. Kerpez, "Constellations for Good Diversity Performance," to appear in the *IEEE Transactions on Communications*, September, 1993.

BELLCORE, 445 SOUTH STREET, MORRISTOWN, NEW JERSEY 07960-1910
E-mail address: kerpez@aries.bellcore.com

DIMACS Series in Discrete Mathematics
and Theoretical Computer Science
Volume **14**, 1993

Bounded Expansion Codes for Error Control

ALI S. KHAYRALLAH

March 17, 1993

ABSTRACT. We introduce the concept of bounded expansion codes. Bounded expansion codes are linear block error control codes with the property that $w(\mathbf{y}) \geq \min(w(\mathbf{x}) + d - 1, 2d - \rho)$, where d is the minimum distance of the code, ρ is the decoding radius (for a bounded distance decoder), and $(\mathbf{x}, \mathbf{y})$ is a nonzero input-codeword pair. We show that channel errors cause user errors (from source to sink) in a well controlled manner. We also discuss limitations on weight distribution and rate. We give several examples of bounded expansion codes.

1. Introduction

Consider the problem of transmitting information over a discrete memoryless noisy channel. For simplicity we assume a q-ary symmetric channel with crossover probability $\epsilon/(q-1)$, $0 \leq \epsilon \leq (q-1)/q$. The relevant distance is the Hamming distance $d(\mathbf{u}, \mathbf{v})$, where $\mathbf{u}$ and $\mathbf{v}$ are blocks of the same length. Also let the Hamming weight be $w(\mathbf{u}) = d(\mathbf{u}, \mathbf{0})$. In this paper we focus on linear block error-control codes. An $(n, k; d)$ code has input length k, output length n, rate k/n, and minimum distance d. The encoder map f_e is a one-to-one and onto linear map defined by a $k \times n$ generator matrix $\mathbf{G}$

$$
\begin{gathered}
A^k \to C \subset A^n \\
\mathbf{y} = f_e(\mathbf{x}) = \mathbf{x}\,\mathbf{G}
\end{gathered}
$$

where A is the alphabet of size q and C is the codebook. In a typical treatment of error-control coding, the encoder map itself is given little attention. However for the class of bounded expansion codes to be introduced next, $\mathbf{G}$ is of crucial importance.

1991 *Mathematics Subject Classification*. Primary 94A14.

The usual error-control code will be referred to as a minimum distance code. It is easy to see that a code is an $(n,k;d)$ minimum distance code if it satisfies

$$\forall\, \mathbf{x} \neq \mathbf{0},\ w(\mathbf{x}\,\mathbf{G}) \geq d \tag{1.1}$$

$$\exists\, \mathbf{x} \text{ such that } w(\mathbf{x}\,\mathbf{G}) = d\ . \tag{1.2}$$

A code is an $(n,k;d)$ expansion code [**4**] if it satisfies

$$\forall\, \mathbf{x} \neq \mathbf{0},\ w(\mathbf{x}\,\mathbf{G}) \geq w(\mathbf{x}) + d - 1 \tag{1.3}$$

$$\exists\, \mathbf{x} \text{ such that } w(\mathbf{x}\,\mathbf{G}) = d\ . \tag{1.4}$$

For $0 \leq \rho \leq \lfloor (d-1)/2 \rfloor$, a code is an $(n,k;d;\rho)$ bounded expansion code if it satisfies

$$\forall\, \mathbf{x} \neq \mathbf{0},\ w(\mathbf{x}\,\mathbf{G}) \geq \min(w(\mathbf{x}) + d - 1, 2d - \rho) \tag{1.5}$$

$$\exists\, \mathbf{x} \text{ such that } w(\mathbf{x}\,\mathbf{G}) = d\ . \tag{1.6}$$

One can see from the above definitions that an expansion code preserves and expands the distances between inputs, whereas a minimum distance code ignores input distance. Hence an expansion code is most useful when input distance is meaningful. This is the case for instance when the code is a stage in a cascade of codes, or in the context of joint source-channel coding. The price paid for the expansion property is a decrease in coding rate in comparison to minimum distance codes. Performance bounds for expansion codes similar to the Gilbert and Plotkin bounds ([**1**], [**6**]) are derived in [**4**], and the error probability is studied in [**5**].

The subject of this paper is bounded expansion codes, which can be viewed as a compromise between expansion and minimum distance codes: they satisfy a relaxed expansion property in exchange for a higher rate. Later, the cutoff at $2d - \rho$ in (1.5) will be discussed in some detail. The relation between input and output distance for all three codes is illustrated in Fig. 1. From it and from the above definitions, it is clear that

$$\{\text{expansion codes}\} \subset \{\text{bounded expansion codes}\} \subset \{\text{minimum distance codes}\}\ . \tag{1.7}$$

Let $n^{md}_{(k;d)}$ and $n^{e}_{(k;d)}$ denote the smallest n for a minimum distance [**8**] and an expansion code [**4**] with parameters k and d, respectively. Similarly, let $n^{be}_{(k;d;\rho)}$ denote the smallest n for a bounded expansion code with parameters k, d, and ρ. It follows from (1.7) that

$$n^{md}_{(k;d)} \leq n^{be}_{(k;d;\rho)} \leq n^{e}_{(k;d)}\ . \tag{1.8}$$

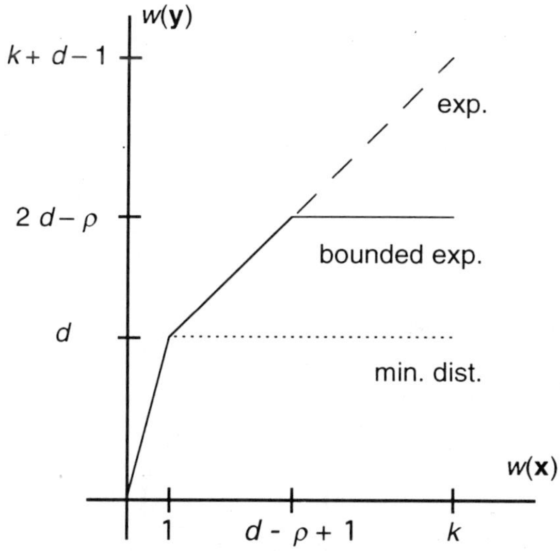

FIGURE 1. Lower bound to $w(\mathbf{y})$ vs $w(\mathbf{x})$.

EXAMPLE 1.1. We give an example of a $(7,4;2;0)$ bounded expansion code. Its generator matrix is

$$\mathbf{G}_{(7,4;2;0)} = \begin{bmatrix} 0 & 0 & 0 & 0 & 0 & 1 & 1 \\ 0 & 0 & 0 & 1 & 1 & 0 & 0 \\ 0 & 1 & 1 & 0 & 0 & 0 & 0 \\ 1 & 0 & 1 & 0 & 1 & 0 & 1 \end{bmatrix}.$$

It is interesting to compare this code to the best minimum distance and expansion code. For the same parameters $k = 4$ and $d = 2$, $n^{md}_{(4;2)} = 5 < n^{be}_{(4;2;0)} = 7 < n^{e}_{(4;2)} = 8$. It is easy to check that every nonzero input-codeword pair $(\mathbf{x}, \mathbf{y})$ satisfies the expansion property except for $\mathbf{x} = (1111)$ and $\mathbf{y} = \mathbf{x}\,\mathbf{G} = (1101010)$ $(w(\mathbf{x}) = 4,\ w(\mathbf{y}) = 4 = 2d - \rho < w(\mathbf{x}) + d - 1 = 5)$.

We give more examples of bounded expansion codes later.

2. Channel Errors and User Errors

We restrict our attention to bounded distance decoders [**2**]. The decoding radius is ρ, $0 \le \rho \le \lfloor (d-1)/2 \rfloor$, and the decoding sets are the spheres $S_{\mathbf{y}} = \{\mathbf{z}, d(\mathbf{z},\mathbf{y}) \le \rho\}$. The total decoding region is $S = \cup_{\mathbf{y}\in C} S_{\mathbf{y}}$.

The decoder can be described in two stages. The first stage is a decision rule

$$f_{d1} : A^n \to C \cup \{?\}$$

$$f_{d1}(\mathbf{z}) = \begin{cases} \hat{\mathbf{y}} & \mathbf{z} \in S_{\hat{\mathbf{y}}} \\ ? & \mathbf{z} \notin S \end{cases}$$

where ? denotes a detected (and uncorrected) error. We assume that in the event of a detected error, the receiver will ask for a retransmission, according to

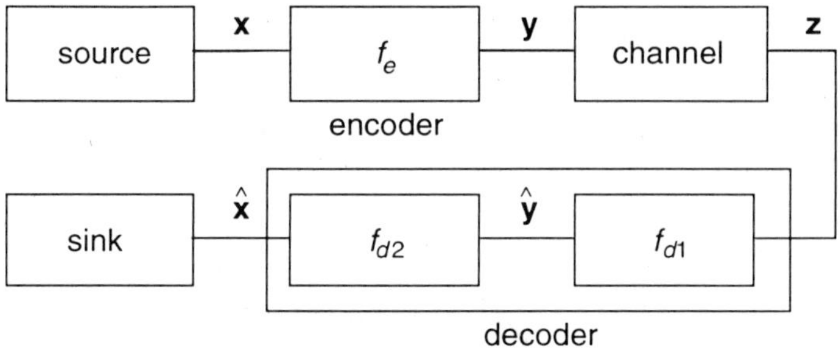

FIGURE 2. Error-control code components.

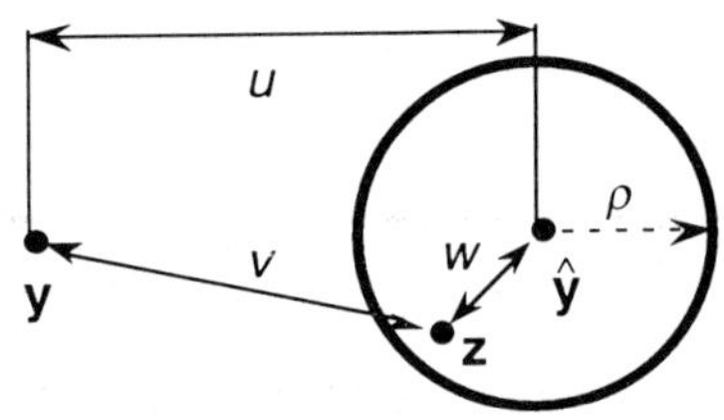

FIGURE 3. Error event in a bounded distance decoder.

some ARQ scheme [**6**], so that $\mathbf{z}$ will eventually fall in S. Then the second stage f_{d2} of the decoder is simply the inverse of the encoder map.

Using Fig. 2 below, we refer to errors between the transmitted codeword $\mathbf{y}$ and the received word $\mathbf{z}$ as channel errors, as usual. We refer to errors between the encoder input $\mathbf{x}$ and the decoder output $\hat{\mathbf{x}}$ as user errors. Our premise is that the users (source and sink) are concerned with user errors, and not channel errors. In particular, they would like $p(\hat{\mathbf{x}}|\mathbf{x})$ to decrease with $d(\hat{\mathbf{x}}, \mathbf{x})$. In a general minimum distance code, the effect of channel errors on user errors is obscure, and quantities such as $p(\hat{\mathbf{x}}|\mathbf{x})$ are very difficult to compute. However for expansion codes, we are able to show precisely how channel errors cause user errors [**5**]. For bounded expansion codes, we will see that the effect of channel errors on user errors is well controlled for low weight error events, and can be ignored for high weight error events, whose probability is very low.

We now discuss the effect of channel error on decoded input errors. Suppose codeword $\mathbf{y}$ is sent over the channel, and some word $\mathbf{z} \in S_{\hat{\mathbf{y}}}$ is received, where $d(\mathbf{z}, \mathbf{y}) = v$, $d(\mathbf{y}, \hat{\mathbf{y}}) = u$, and $d(\mathbf{z}, \hat{\mathbf{y}}) = w$. (See Fig. 3 above.) Then

$$p(\mathbf{z}|\mathbf{y}) = \left(\frac{\epsilon}{q-1}\right)^{v} (1-\epsilon)^{n-v} \triangleq p_v \tag{2.1}$$

which decreases with v for $\epsilon \leq (q-1)/q$. The probability of decoding $\hat{\mathbf{y}}$ given that $\mathbf{y}$ is transmitted depends only on their distance u. That is

$$p(\hat{\mathbf{y}}|\mathbf{y}) = P(\mathbf{z} \in S_{\hat{\mathbf{y}}}|\mathbf{y}) \triangleq \Pi_u \; .$$

The computation of Π_u is discussed in detail in [**5**]. It is shown that Π_u is

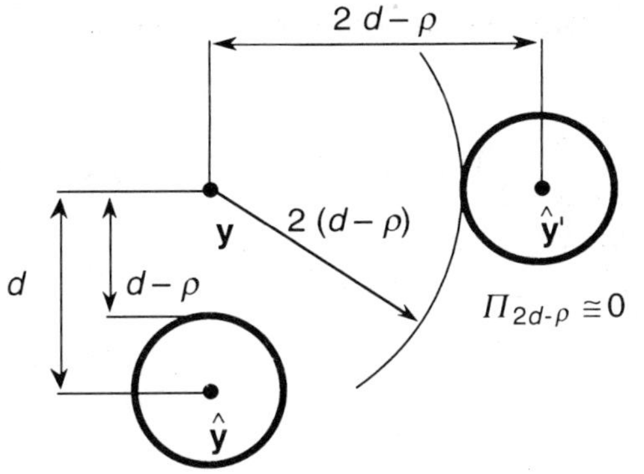

FIGURE 4. Error events with significant ($\hat{\mathbf{y}}$) and negligible ($\hat{\mathbf{y}}'$) probabilities.

bounded by

$$\binom{u}{\rho} p_{u-\rho} \leq \Pi_u \leq s_\rho p_{u-\rho} \tag{2.2}$$

where $s_\rho = \sum_{0 \leq j \leq \rho} \binom{n}{j}(q-1)^j$ is the volume of a decoding sphere.

Now suppose d is chosen so that Π_d is considered "small enough" by the user. Then from (2.2) we know that $p_{d-\rho}$ is also small, and from (2.1) we have that $(\epsilon/(q-1))^{d-\rho}$ is also small. We now argue that the square of a quantity deemed small is negligible, hence $(\epsilon/(q-1))^{2(d-\rho)} \cong 0$, and $p_{2(d-\rho)} \cong 0$. Again using (2.2) we have $\Pi_{2d-\rho} \cong 0$, and we conclude that $\Pi_u \cong 0$ for all $u \geq 2d - \rho$. This is illustrated in Fig. 4 below. This argument is the basis of the cutoff at $2d - \rho$ in (1.5).

We now go back to $p(\hat{\mathbf{x}}|\mathbf{x})$. If $d(\hat{\mathbf{y}}, \mathbf{y}) = d(\hat{\mathbf{x}}, \mathbf{x}) + d - 1$, and $d(\hat{\mathbf{y}}, \mathbf{y}) \leq 2d - \rho$, then $p(\hat{\mathbf{x}}|\mathbf{x}) = \Pi_{d(\hat{\mathbf{x}},\mathbf{x})+d-1}$, which from (2.1) and (2.2) does "approximately decrease" with $d(\hat{\mathbf{x}}, \mathbf{x})$ (in the sense that it is upper and lower bounded by constants times $p_{d(\hat{\mathbf{x}},\mathbf{x})+d-1-\rho}$, which decreases with $d(\hat{\mathbf{x}}, \mathbf{x})$). For the case $d(\hat{\mathbf{y}}, \mathbf{y}) > d(\hat{\mathbf{x}}, \mathbf{x}) + d - 1$, and $d(\hat{\mathbf{y}}, \mathbf{y}) \leq 2d - \rho$, $p(\hat{\mathbf{x}}|\mathbf{x})$ should be even lower than $\Pi_{d(\hat{\mathbf{x}},\mathbf{x})+d-1}$, again from (2.1) and (2.2). If $d(\hat{\mathbf{y}}, \mathbf{y}) > 2d - \rho$, then $p(\hat{\mathbf{x}}|\mathbf{x})$ will be negligible.

3. Weight Density and Distribution

Let a_i denote the number of codewords of weight i, and let b_i denote the number of codewords of weight no greater than i. Then $b_i = \sum_{j=0}^{i} a_j$. We call

a_i and b_i the weight density and distribution, respectively. Let

$$a_i^{be} \triangleq \begin{cases} 1 & i = 0 \\ \binom{k}{i-d+1}(q-1)^{i-d+1} & d \leq i < 2d-\rho \\ \sum_{j=2d-\rho}^{k+d-1} \binom{k}{j-d+1}(q-1)^{j-d+1} & i = 2d-\rho \\ 0 & \text{otherwise} \end{cases}$$

and

$$b_i^{be} \triangleq \sum_{j=0}^{i} a_j^{be} = \begin{cases} 1 & 0 \leq i < d \\ \sum_{j=0}^{i-d+1} \binom{k}{j}(q-1)^j & d \leq i < 2d-\rho \\ q^k & 2d-\rho \leq i \leq n\,. \end{cases}$$

PROPOSITION 3.1. The weight distribution b_i of an $(n, k; d; \rho)$ bounded expansion code satisfies

$$b_i \leq b_i^{be}$$

for all i.

The proof is similar to the one in [**4**] and is omitted. We now define the total weight of a code as $W \triangleq \sum_{i=0}^{n} a_i i$. Also let $W^{be} \triangleq \sum_{i=0}^{n} a_i^{be}$. The next result follows from Proposition 1.1.

PROPOSITION 3.2. The total weight W of an $(n, k; d; \rho)$ bounded expansion code satisfies

$$W \geq W^{be}\,.$$

The next result combines Proposition 3.2 and the fact that the total weight W of an $(n, k; d)$ linear code is $W = n(q-1)q^{k-1}$ (the basis of the Plotkin bound [**7**]).

PROPOSITION 3.3. The output length n of an $(n, k; d; \rho)$ bounded expansion code satisfies

$$n \geq N_{(k;d;\rho)}^{be} \triangleq \frac{W^{be}}{(q-1)q^{k-1}}\,.$$

4. Examples

We give another detailed example of a bounded expansion code. We also include tables of bounded expansion codes for $d = 2, 3, 4$ and 5. All codes were found by computer search.

EXAMPLE 4.1. Our second example is an $(8,5;2;0)$ code. Note that $n^{md}_{(5;2)} = 6 < n^{be}_{(5;2;0)} = 8 < n^{e}_{(5;2)} = 10$. The generator matrix is

$$\mathbf{G}_{(8,5;2;0)} = \begin{bmatrix} 0 & 0 & 0 & 0 & 0 & 0 & 1 & 1 \\ 0 & 0 & 0 & 0 & 1 & 1 & 0 & 0 \\ 0 & 0 & 1 & 1 & 0 & 0 & 0 & 0 \\ 0 & 1 & 0 & 1 & 0 & 1 & 0 & 1 \\ 1 & 1 & 0 & 0 & 0 & 0 & 0 & 0 \end{bmatrix}.$$

The codewords that violate the expansion property are listed below.

$(\mathbf{x},\mathbf{y}) : 2d-\rho \le w(\mathbf{y}) < w(\mathbf{x})+d-1$				
$\mathbf{x}$	$w(\mathbf{x})$	$\mathbf{y}$	$w(\mathbf{y})$	$w(\mathbf{x})+d-1$
01111	4	10101001	4	5
10111	4	10100110	4	5
11011	4	10011010	4	5
11110	4	01101010	4	5
11111	5	10101010	4	6

The weight density a_i and the weight distribution b_i are listed below, along with a_i^{be} and b_i^{be}.

i	a_i	b_i	a_i^{be}	b_i^{be}
0	1	1	1	1
1	0	1	0	1
2	4	5	5	6
3	0	5	10	16
4	22	27	16	32
5	0	27	0	32
6	4	31	0	32
7	0	31	0	32
8	1	32	0	32

We end the paper with code tables for $d = 2, 3, 4$ and 5. From (1.5) it is clear that $k > d - \rho + 1$ is a necessary condition for the existence of strictly bounded expansion codes (that are not expansion codes).

$d=2,\ \rho=0,\ k>3$				
k	$n^{be}_{(k;d;\rho)}$	$n^{e}_{(k;d)}$	$n^{md}_{(k;d)}$	$N^{be}_{(k;d;\rho)}$
1	−−	2	2	2
2	−−	4	3	4
3	−−	6	4	6
4	7	8	5	7
5	8	10	6	8
6	10	12	7	8
7	11	14	8	8
8	12	16	9	8

$d=3,\ \rho=1,\ k>3$				
k	$n^{be}_{(k;d;\rho)}$	$n^{e}_{(k;d)}$	$n^{md}_{(k;d)}$	$N^{be}_{(k;d;\rho)}$
1	−−	3	3	3
2	−−	5	5	5
3	−−	7	6	7
4	9	9	7	8
5	10	11	9	9
6	11	13	10	9
7	13	15	11	10
8	15	17	12	10
9	16	19	13	10

$d=4,\ \rho=1,\ k>4$				
k	$n^{be}_{(k;d;\rho)}$	$n^{e}_{(k;d)}$	$n^{md}_{(k;d)}$	$N^{be}_{(k;d;\rho)}$
1	−−	4	4	4
2	−−	7	6	7
3	−−	9	7	9
4	−−	11	8	10
5	13	13	10	11
6	15	15	11	12
7	16	17	12	13
8	18	19	13	13

$d = 5,\ \rho = 2,\ k > 4$				
k	$n^{be}_{(k;d;\rho)}$	$n^{e}_{(k;d)}$	$n^{md}_{(k;d)}$	$N^{be}_{(k;d;\rho)}$
1	−−	5	5	5
2	−−	8	8	8
3	−−	10	10	10
4	−−	12	11	12
5	14	14	13	13
6	16	16	14	14
7	17	18	15	15

REFERENCES

1. Berlekamp, E. R., *Algebraic coding theory*, McGraw-Hill (1968).
2. Blahut, R. E., *Theory and practice of error control codes*, Addison-Wesley (1984).
3. Clark, G. C. and Cain, J. B., *Error-correction coding for digital communications*, Plenum Press (1981).
4. Khayrallah, A. S., "Expansion channel codes: Performance bounds and examples," *Proceedings of the Conference On Information Sciences and Systems* (1992).
5. Khayrallah, A. S., "The error probability of expansion codes," *Proceedings of The Thirtieth Allerton Conference on Communication, Control, and Computing* (1992).
6. Lin, S. and Costello, D. J., *Error control coding: Fundamentals and applications*, Prentice Hall (1983).
7. Peterson, W. W. and Weldon, E. R., *Error-correcting codes*, second edition, MIT Press (1972).
8. Verhoeff, T., "An updated table of minimum-distance bounds for binary linear codes," *IEEE Trans. Inform. Theory*, vol. IT-33, pp. 665–680 (1987).

ELECTRICAL ENGINEERING DEPARTMENT, UNIVERSITY OF DELAWARE, NEWARK, DE 19716
E-mail address: ali@ee.udel.edu

DIMACS Series in Discrete Mathematics
and Theoretical Computer Science
Volume **14**, 1993

A Bound on the Zero-Error List Coding Capacity

ERDAL ARIKAN

May 1, 1992

ABSTRACT. We present an upper bound on the zero-error list coding capacity. Using this bound, we show that the list-of-3 capacity of the 4/3 channel is at most 0.3512 bits, improving the previously known bound of 3/8. The relation of the bound to the graph-entropy bound of Körner and Marton is also discussed.

1. Introduction

Consider a discrete memoryless channel (DMC) $K = (\mathcal{I}, \mathcal{J}, P)$ where $\mathcal{I}$ denotes the input alphabet, $\mathcal{J}$ the output alphabet, and $P(j|i)$ the probability that $j \in \mathcal{J}$ is received given that $i \in \mathcal{I}$ is transmitted. Let $P_N(y|x)$ denote the probability that $y \in \mathcal{J}^N$ is received given that $x \in \mathcal{I}^N$ is transmitted, which by the memoryless channel assumption is given by $P_N(y|x) = \prod_{n=1}^N P(y_n|x_n)$.

A set $S \subset \mathcal{I}^N$ is said to be *independent* in K if for every $y \in \mathcal{J}^N$

$$\prod_{x \in S} P_N(y|x) = 0,$$

i.e., if there is no output word which can be reached with nonzero probability from each word in S. Note that if $S \subset \mathcal{I}^N$ is independent, there must be a coordinate n, $1 \le n \le N$, such that $\{x_n : x \in S\} \subset \mathcal{I}$—the set consisting of the nth coordinates of the words in S—is independent in K. This follows from the memoryless channel assumption.

A set $\mathcal{C} \subset \mathcal{I}^N$ is called a zero-error list-of-L code for K if each output word of K can be reached from at most L codewords in $\mathcal{C}$, or more precisely, if every $S \subset \mathcal{C}$ with $|S| = L + 1$ is independent in K. So, given the channel output, a

1991 *Mathematics Subject Classification.* Primary 94A15.

This research has been sponsored by TÜBİTAK under project TBAG 1053.

decoder can always produce a list of at most L codewords which contains the transmitted codeword.

Zero-error list-of-L coding was first considered by Shannon [**1**] for $L = 1$, and by Elias [**2**] for $L \geq 2$. Problems equivalent to zero-error list coding also arise in combinatorics and in the design of hash functions (see, e.g., the references in [**5**]).

The major problem of information-theoretic interest about zero-error list-of-L coding is to find a computable formula that gives the zero-error list-of-L capacity, which is defined by

$$C_L = \limsup_{N \to \infty} \frac{1}{N} \log M(N, L),$$

where $M(N, L)$ is the maximum possible size for a list-of-L code of length N. (All logarithms in this paper are to base 2, and all rates in bits.) Unfortunately, no such formula has been found. It is therefore of interest to obtain upper and lower bounds on C_L. The aim of this paper is to present such an upper bound. Earlier upper bounds on C_L have been given by Shannon [**1**], Elias [**2**], Lovász [**3**], Haemers [**4**], and Körner and Marton [**5**].

In the next section we present a new upper bound on C_L and indicate its relation to earlier bounds. In Section 3, the new bound is applied to the 4/3 channel and an improved upper bound is obtained on its list-of-3 capacity.

2. An Upper Bound on C_L

Shannon's capacity bound [**1**], [**2**] is obtained by looking at the zero-error code through a one-user channel; here, we obtain a new bound by looking at the code through a more general type of channel. In this sense, our bound is a generalization of the Shannon bound. The bound here may also be seen as an information-theoretic interpretation of the Körner-Marton graph-entropy bound [**5**]. However, the present bound incorporates an improvement and always yields results at least as good as the graph-entropy bound.

There is a restriction in the applicability of our bound, which we now point out. Given any channel K, its zero-error list-of-L capacities form a non-decreasing sequence: $C_1 \leq C_2 \leq C_3 \leq \cdots$. Also, $C_L = \log I$ for all $L \geq I$ where I is the number of letters in the input alphabet of K. So, for any channel with at least two input letters there is some finite L such that $C_L > 0$; we call the smallest such L the *index* of the channel. The bound here can be used to upperbound C_L only if L is the index of the channel K. This is the only restriction on the applicability of the bound.

To develop the bound, let $K = (\mathcal{I}, \mathcal{J}, P)$ be a fixed but arbitrary DMC throughout the following discussion. Let L be the index of K. For each $m = 1, \ldots, L$, let $\mathcal{P}_m(K)$ denote the set of DMCs $K' = (\mathcal{I}^L, \mathcal{J}', P')$ such that

$$P'(j|i_1, \ldots, i_m, h_1, \ldots, h_{L-m})P'(j|i'_1, \ldots, i'_m, h_1, \ldots, h_{L-m}) = 0$$

for all $j \in \mathcal{J}'$ whenever $\{i_1, \ldots, i_m, i'_1, \ldots, i'_m, h_1, \ldots, h_{L-m}\} \subset \mathcal{I}$ is independent in K.

Fix m and a channel $K' = (\mathcal{I}^L, \mathcal{J}', P') \in \mathcal{P}_m(K)$. Let P'_N denote the (product-form) transition probability for K' over blocks of length N. Note that

$$P'_N(y|x_1, \ldots, x_m, z_1, \ldots, z_{L-m})P'_N(y|x'_1, \ldots, x'_m, z_1, \ldots, z_{L-m}) = 0$$

for all $y \in \mathcal{J}'^N$ whenever $\{x_1, \ldots, x_m, x'_1, \ldots, x'_m, z_1, \ldots, z_{L-m}\} \subset \mathcal{I}^N$ is independent in K.

Fix a list-of-L code $\mathcal{C}$ for K. Let N be the block-length, M the number of codewords, and $R = (1/N) \log M$ the rate of $\mathcal{C}$. Also fix $L-m$ distinct codewords $z_1, \ldots, z_{L-m} \in \mathcal{C}$.

LEMMA 2.1. Let $x_1, \ldots, x_m, x'_1, \ldots, x'_m \in \mathcal{C}$ be any collection of codewords such that
(i) $x_1, \ldots, x_m, z_1, \ldots, z_{L-m}$ are all distinct,
(ii) $x'_1, \ldots, x'_m, z_1, \ldots, z_{L-m}$ are all distinct, and
(iii) $P'_N(y|x_1, \ldots, x_m, z_1, \ldots, z_{L-m})P'_N(y|x'_1, \ldots, x'_m, z_1, \ldots, z_{L-m}) > 0$ for some $y \in \mathcal{J}'^N$.
Then, $\{x_1, \ldots, x_m\} = \{x'_1, \ldots, x'_m\}$.

Proof. Let $x_1, \ldots, x_m, x'_1, \ldots, x'_m \in \mathcal{C}$ satisfy (i) and (ii), and suppose $\{x_1, \ldots, x_m\} \neq \{x'_1, \ldots, x'_m\}$. Then the set $\{x_1, \ldots, x_m, x'_1, \ldots, x'_m, z_1, \ldots, z_m\}$ contains at least $L+1$ codewords, so it is independent in K. This contradicts (iii) and completes the proof.

Let the random variables $X_1, \ldots, X_m, Y$ be defined by the joint probability assignment

$$\Pr\{X_1 = x_1, \ldots, X_m = x_m, Y = y\} = \frac{1}{M^m} P'_N(y|x_1, \ldots, x_m, z_1, \ldots, z_{L-m})$$

for all $x_1, \ldots, x_m \in \mathcal{C}$, $y \in \mathcal{J}'^N$. For brevity, let us write $X = (X_1, \ldots, X_m)$ and $z = (z_1, \ldots, z_{L-m})$.

LEMMA 2.2. The conditional entropy of X given Y, z is upperbounded by

$$H(X|Yz) \leq pmNR + (1-p) \log m!$$

where p is the probability that $X_1, \ldots, X_m, z_1, \ldots, z_{L-m}$ are not all distinct.

Proof. Let $U = 1$ if $X_1, \ldots, X_m, z_1, \ldots, z_{L-m}$ are not all distinct; $U = 0$ otherwise. Then,

$$\begin{aligned} H(X|Yz) &\overset{(a)}{=} H(X|YzU) + I(X;U|Yz) \\ &\overset{(b)}{=} H(X|YzU) \\ &= pH(X|Yz1) + (1-p)H(X|Yz0) \\ &\overset{(c)}{\leq} pmNR + (1-p)\log m! \end{aligned}$$

where (a) follows by the definition of mutual information, (b) since U is determined by X, z, and (c) by the facts that (i) $H(X|Yz1) \leq mNR$ since X takes one of at most $M^m = 2^{mNR}$ values, and (ii) $H(X|Yz0) \leq \log m!$ since Y determines $\{X_1, \dots, X_m\}$ uniquely when $U = 0$ (Lemma 2.1), leaving at most $m!$ choices for X.

We can estimate p by the union bound:

$$\begin{aligned} p &\leq \sum_{i<j} \Pr\{X_i = X_j\} + \sum_{i,j} \Pr\{X_i = z_j\} \\ &= m(m-1)/2M + m(L-m)/M \leq L^2/M \ . \end{aligned}$$

Let X_{in}, Y_n, z_{jn} denote the nth coordinates of X_i, Y, z_j, respectively. Let us write $X^{(n)} = (X_{1n}, \dots, X_{mn})$, $z^{(n)} = (z_{1n} \dots, z_{L-m,n})$.

LEMMA 2.3. The rate of $\mathcal{C}$ is upperbounded by

$$R \leq \epsilon + \frac{1}{mN} \sum_{n=1}^{N} I(X^{(n)}; Y_n | z^{(n)})$$

where $\epsilon = p + ((1-p)/mN) \log m!$.

Proof. $mNR = H(X) \overset{(a)}{=} H(X|z) \overset{(b)}{=} H(X|Yz) + I(X;Y|z) \overset{(c)}{\leq} mN\epsilon + I(X;Y|z)$ $\overset{(d)}{\leq} mN\epsilon + \sum_{n=1}^{N} I(X^{(n)}; Y_n | z^{(n)})$ where (a) is by the statistical independence of X and z (a constant), (b) by the definition of mutual information, (c) by Lemma 2.2, and (d) by the product-form property of P'_N.

The above results can be summarized as follows.

THEOREM 2.1. The rate of any zero-error list-of-L code $\mathcal{C}$ for a channel K with index L is upperbounded by

$$R \leq \epsilon + \min_{1 \leq m \leq L} \min_{K' \in \mathcal{P}_m(K)} \min_{z} \frac{1}{mN} \sum_{n=1}^{N} I(X^{(n)}; Y_n | z^{(n)})$$

The minimum over z ranges through all $(L-m)$-tuples $z = (z_1, \dots, z_{L-m})$ of distinct codewords in $\mathcal{C}$. The mutual information $I(X^{(n)}; Y_n | z^{(n)})$ is computed using the probability assignment

$$\Pr\{X^{(n)} = (i_1, \dots, i_m), Y_n = j\} = Q_n(i_1) \cdots Q_n(i_m) \times$$
$$P'(j | i_1, \dots, i_m, z_{1n}, \dots, z_{L-m,n})$$

where Q_n is the empirical distribution of the nth coordinate of the codewords, i.e., $Q_n(i)$ equals the fraction of codewords $x \in \mathcal{C}$ with $x_n = i$, P' is the transition probability for $K' \in \mathcal{P}_m(K)$, N is the code block length and ϵ satisfies $0 < \epsilon \leq L^2/2^{NR} + (1/N)\log(L!)$.

For comparison, the Körner-Marton graph-entropy bound states that

$$R \leq \epsilon + \min_{1 \leq m \leq L} \min_{P' \in \mathcal{P}_m(K)} \sum_z \frac{1}{mN2^{(L-m)NR}} \sum_{n=1}^{N} I(X^{(n)}; Y_n | z^{(n)})$$

where the summation over z is over all $(L-m)$-tuples of distinct codewords in $\mathcal{C}$. This upperbounds R by the average of the quantity

$$(1/mN) \sum_{n=1}^{N} I(X^{(n)}; Y_n | z^{(n)})$$

over a set of z, while Theorem 2.1 upperbounds R by the minimum of the same quantity over the same set of z.

3. The 4/3 Channel

By the 4/3 channel we mean a DMC $K = (A, A, P)$ with $A = \{0, 1, 2, 3\}$ and $P(j|i) = (1/3)(1 - \delta_{ij})$ for all $i, j \in A$. (δij is the Kronecker delta function, which equals 1 or 0 depending on whether $i = j$ or not, respectively.) Below we apply Theorem 2.1 to show that $C_3 < 0.35116$ for this channel, improving the best earlier bound $C_3 \leq 3/8$ [**5**].

Let $K' = (A^3, A, P')$ be such that for each $j, i, h_1, h_2 \in A$,

$$P'(j|i, h_1, h_2) = \begin{cases} \delta_{jh_1} & \text{if } h_1 = h_2 \\ 0 & \text{if } h_1 \neq h_2 \text{ and } j \in \{i, h_1, h_2\} \\ \frac{1}{4 - |\{i, h_1, h_2\}|} & \text{otherwise.} \end{cases}$$

It can be verified readily that $K' \in \mathcal{P}_1(K)$, and that

$$I(X_{1n}; Y_n | z_{1n}, z_{2n}) = \begin{cases} 0 & \text{if } z_{1n} = z_{2n}; \\ h(\alpha) - Q_n(z_{1n}) - Q_n(z_{2n}) & \text{if } z_{1n} \neq z_{2n}, \end{cases}$$

where $h(\alpha) = -\alpha \log \alpha - (1 - \alpha) \log(1 - \alpha)$, $\alpha = [Q_n(z_{1n}) + Q_n(z_{2n})]/2 + Q_n(i)$ where i is an element of $A \setminus \{z_{1n}, z_{2n}\}$. (For example, for $z_{1n} = 0$, $z_{2n} = 1$, we may take $\alpha = [Q_n(0) + Q_n(1)]/2 + Q_n(2)$ or $\alpha = [Q_n(0) + Q_n(1)]/2 + Q_n(3)$. $h(\alpha)$ has the same value for either choice.)

It is convenient to define

$$d_n(z_{1n}, z_{2n}) = I(X_{1n}; Y_n | z_{1n}, z_{2n}) \ , d(z_1, z_2) = \sum_{n=1}^{N} d_n(z_{1n}, z_{2n}) \ ,$$

and $d^*(\mathcal{C})$ as the minimum of $d(z_1, z_2)$ over all pairs (z_1, z_2) of distinct codewords in $\mathcal{C}$. In this notation, Theorem 2.1 states that for any list-of-3 code

$$R - \epsilon \leq d^*(\mathcal{C})/N. \tag{3.1}$$

We proceed to upperbound $d^*(\mathcal{C})$, which is an unusual type of code minimum distance in that the distance function depends on the code composition.

LEMMA 3.1. Given any $\epsilon_1 > 0$, there exist list-of-3 codes (for the 4/3 channel) of arbitrarily large block-length, with rates $\geq C_3 - \epsilon_1$, and for which $1 - Q_n(i) \leq 2^{-(C_3 - 2\epsilon_1)}$ for all n and all $i \in A$.

Proof. For any $\epsilon_1 > 0$, there exists a finite integer $N_0(\epsilon_1)$ such that all list-of-3 codes with block-length $N \geq N_0(\epsilon_1)$ have rate $\leq C_3 + \epsilon_1$. This follows from the definition of C_3. Fix $\epsilon_1 > 0$, and consider a list-of-3 code $\mathcal{C}$ with rate $R \geq C_3 - \epsilon_1$ and block-length $N > 3N_0(\epsilon_1)$. The existence of such a code for arbitrarily large N is also guaranteed by the definition of C_3.

If there exists n, i such that $1 - Q_n(i) > 2^{-(C_3 - 2\epsilon_1)}$, consider the subcode $\mathcal{C}' = \{x \in \mathcal{C} : x_n \neq i\}$. $\mathcal{C}'$ is a list-of-3 code (any subcode of $\mathcal{C}$ is a list-of-3 code) with $M_1 = M(1 - Q_n(i)) > 2^{N(C_3 - \epsilon_1) - (C_3 - 2\epsilon_1)}$ codewords, where $M = 2^{NR}$ is the number of codewords in $\mathcal{C}$. Let $\mathcal{C}_1$ be the code obtained by deleting the nth coordinate of each codeword in $\mathcal{C}'$. $\mathcal{C}_1$ has block-length $N - 1$, and it is easy to see that it is also a list-of-3 code for the 4/3 channel. Thus, $\mathcal{C}_1$ has M_1 codewords and rate $R_1 = [1/(N-1)] \log M_1 > C_3 - \epsilon_1 + \epsilon_1/(N-1)$. Since $R_1 > C_3 - \epsilon_1$, we may iterate the above process with $\mathcal{C}_1$ in place of $\mathcal{C}$. At the end of the kth round, we shall have a code $\mathcal{C}_k$ with block-length $N - k$, number of codewords $M_k > M2^{-k(C_3 - 2\epsilon_1)}$, and rate $R_k > C_3 - \epsilon_1 + k\epsilon_1/(N-k)$. In particular, if this process could continue for more than $2N/3$ rounds, at round $k = 2N/3$ we would have a code with block-length $N/3$ and rate $> C_3 + \epsilon_1$. But this contradicts the assumption that $N > 3N_0(\epsilon_1)$. So, the process must terminate at some step $k < 2N/3$, yielding a list-of-3 code with block-length $N - k > N/3$, rate $R_k > C_3 - \epsilon_1$, and for which $1 - Q_n(i) \leq 2^{-(C_3 - 2\epsilon_1)}$ for all n and all $i \in A$. Since $N/3$ can be arbitrarily large, this completes the proof.

Let $\mathcal{C}$ be a list-of-3 code with length N and rate $R \geq C_3 - \epsilon_1$ for which $1 - Q_n(i) \leq 2^{-(C_3 - 2\epsilon_1)}$ for all n, i. Then, $1 - Q_n(i_1) - Q_n(i_2) \leq 2^{1-(C_3 - 2\epsilon_1)} - 1$ for all n, i_1, i_2. Since $h(\alpha) \leq 1$ for all $0 \leq \alpha \leq 1$, we have $d_n(i_1, i_2) \leq d_H(i_1, i_2)[1 - Q_n(i_1) - Q_n(i_2)] \leq d_H(i_1, i_2)[2^{1-(C_3 - 2\epsilon_1)} - 1]$ for all $i_1, i_2 \in A$, where d_H is the Hamming distance. Summing over all coordinates n, we obtain $d(z_1, z_2) \leq d_H(z_1, z_2)[2^{1-(C_3 - \epsilon_1)} - 1]$. This, combined with 3.1 and $C_3 - \epsilon_1 \leq R$, gives

$$C_3 - \epsilon_1 - \epsilon \leq [d_H^*(\mathcal{C})/N][2^{1-(C_3 - 2\epsilon_1)} - 1] ,$$

where $d_H^*(\mathcal{C})$ is the minimum of $d_H(z_1, z_2)$ over all pairs of distinct $z_1, z_2 \in \mathcal{C}$. We may choose ϵ_1 arbitrarily small and N arbitrarily large, so in the limit as $\epsilon_1 \to 0$ and $N \to \infty$ we obtain

$$C_3 \leq \delta_H(C_3)(2^{1-C_3} - 1) , \tag{3.2}$$

where $\delta_H(R) = \limsup_{N \to \infty}\{d_H(\mathcal{C})/N : \mathcal{C}$ is a code of length N and rate $\geq R$ over a quaternary alphabet $\}$.

By the Plotkin bound [**6**, p. 545] (as modified for a quaternary alphabet),

$$\delta_H(R) \leq (1 - R/2)(3/4) . \tag{3.3}$$

Substituting 3.3 into 3.2 we obtain

$$C_3 \leq (1 - C_3/2)(3/4)(2^{1-C_3} - 1) .$$

This gives the bound

$$C_3 \leq \sup_x \{x : x \leq (1 - x/2)(3/4)(2^{1-x} - 1)\} < 0.35116 .$$

Clearly, even better bounds can be obtained by using sharper estimates of $\delta_H(C_3)$, e.g., the Elias bound in its general form as discussed in [**7**, p. 410].

References

1. C.E. Shannon, 'The zero error capacity of a noisy channel,' *IEEE Trans. Inform. Theory,* vol. IT-2, pp. 8-19, 1956.
2. P. Elias, 'Zero error capacity under list decoding,' *IEEE Trans. Inform. Theory,* vol. IT-34, pp. 1070-1074, Sept. 1988.
3. L. Lovász, 'On the Shannon capacity of a graph,' *IEEE Trans. Inform. Theory,* vol. IT-25, pp. 1-7, 1979.
4. W. Haemers, 'On some problems of Lovász concerning the Shannon capacity of a graph,' *IEEE Trans. Inform Theory,* vol. IT-25, pp. 231-232, 1979.
5. J. Körner and K. Marton, 'On the capacity of uniform hypergraphs,' *IEEE Trans. Inform. Theory,* vol. IT-36, No.1, pp. 153-156, Jan. 1990.
6. R. G. Gallager, *Information Theory and Reliable Communication.* Wiley: New York, 1968.
7. R. E. Blahut, *Principles and Practice of Information Theory.* Addison-Wesley: Reading, 1987.

Electrical Engineering Department, Bilkent University, Ankara, 06533, Turkey
E-mail address: arikan@trbilun.bitnet

DIMACS Series in Discrete Mathematics
and Theoretical Computer Science
Volume **14**, 1993

Geometric Vector Quantization for Subband-based Video Coding

CHRISTINE PODILCHUK AND ARNAUD JACQUIN

May 20, 1993

ABSTRACT. A new video coding technique based on three-dimensional subband coding is described. The coder is based on decomposing the video data into spatio-temporal frequency bands and then encoded. Encoding the data in this domain allows us to take advantage of reducing the data based on perceptual criteria. The coder also implements a new type of vector quantizer – geometric vector quantizer (GVQ) – that takes advantage of the very sparse and highly structured data that is typically found in the high frequency subbands for image data. GVQ can also be used to quantize any other type of data that is characteristically sparse and edge-like. The coder described here was applied to several image sequences of varying complexity at a bit rate of 384 kbps.

1. Introduction

Video coding based on three-dimensional subband decomposition and a new form of vector quantization — geometric vector quantization (GVQ) — is described. The tree-structured subband decomposition used here was originally introduced in [**1**]. The three-dimensional decomposition consists of two temporal subbands followed by a cascade of spatial decompositions as shown in Figure 1. The 2-tap Haar filterbank is used for the temporal decomposition. The spatial filtering is based on 10-tap quadrature mirror filterbanks (QMFs) of Johnston [**2**]. We will refer to subband 1 as the lowpass band while subbands 2–11 will be referred to as highpass bands. A more extensive study of the effects of different filter types on the coding results in a subband framework has been discussed in [**3**].

The bits are adaptively allocated to the subbands based on a local energy criterion and frequency ranking. More bits are allocated to subband 8 when the

1991 *Mathematics Subject Classification.* Primary 94A29.

motion activity is high. Bits are dynamically reallocated to subbands 2–6 when the motion activity drops. Conditional replenishment is also implemented in the low-temporal frequency bands in order to code static objects and background at a very low bit rate. This results in a locally adaptive frame rate coder. The lowest frequency band, labeled subband 1 in Figure 1, is allocated a large portion of the bits and is encoded using PCM. The significant highpass subbands are encoded using a new form of vector quantization called Geometric Vector Quantization (GVQ) which takes advantage of the sparse and highly structured characteristics of the upper frequency data. GVQ was first introduced in [**4, 5, 6**]. GVQ consists of purely deterministic codebooks. We will examine a codebook consisting of 2-levels with no constraints and also a codebook of 3-levels with some constraints on the levels in order to reduce the search complexity.

Section 2 discusses the bit allocation, conditional replenishment and encoding of the lowest frequency band. Section 3 describes the generalized GVQ method and results based on 2 and 3-level quantization. Section 4 consists of the conclusion.

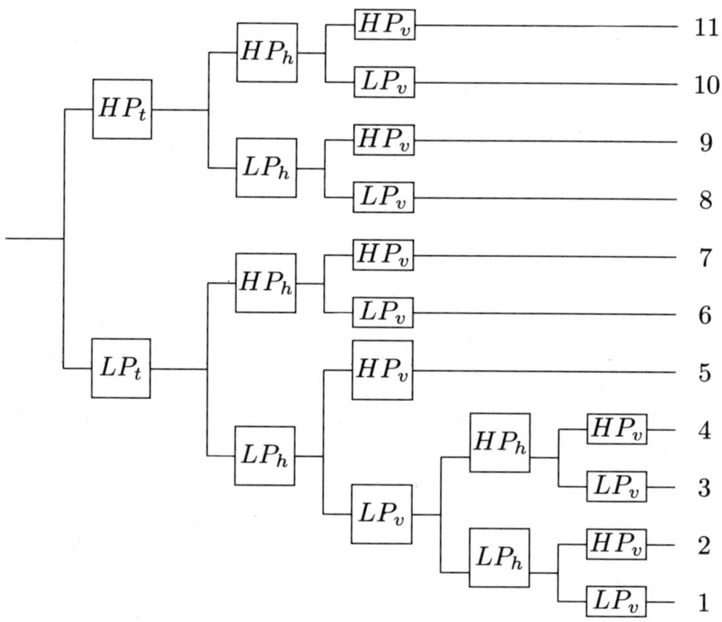

FIGURE 1. 11-subband tree-structured decomposition

2. Dynamic Bit Allocation and Coding Scheme

The coder described here is based on the 11-subband decomposition illustrated in Figure 1. For the results presented here, subbands 7, 9, 10, and 11 are discarded due to the low signal energy found in these subbands. The bits are adaptively allocated to the remaining subbands. In subband 1, conditional replenishment is implemented on a pixel basis using the following condition:

$$\hat{x}(i,j,t) = \begin{cases} \hat{x}(i,j,t-1) & \text{if } |x(i,j,t) - x(i,j,t-1)| \leq T_{cr} \\ Q\{x(i,j,t)\} & \text{otherwise} \end{cases} \tag{2.1}$$

where $x(i,j,t)$ is the original pixel in the ith row, jth column and tth frame and $\hat{x}(i,j,t)$ is the quantized pixel. $Q\{\cdot\}$ is the quantization operator and T_{cr} is a scalar threshold that is empirically derived. Conditional replenishment allows the coder to operate at locally adaptive variable frame rates. The static background does not need to be updated each time and by using conditional replenishment, we are effectively decreasing the frame rate to 1 frame per scene change. The most dynamic areas of the picture (such as the lips and hands in a teleconferencing scene) are updated regularly and may be kept at the original frame rate. For the higher frequency subbands, CR is implemented on a block basis.

Due to the perceptual significance and high signal energy concentration in subband 1, we encode this subband accurately using 6 bit PCM. Conditional replenishment is first applied to the data in subband 1 as given by Equation (2.1) followed by 6 bit uniform quantization. Subband 8 is encoded using GVQ in every block where the local average energy value exceeds a predetermined threshold T_8. When none of the local block energies exceed the threshold T_8, subband 8 is not encoded. This results in discarding subbands 8–11 which is equivalent to reducing the frame rate by a factor of two. This coding schemes automatically lowers the frame rate when motion activity as given by subband 8 is detected as being low. The remaining bits are allocated to the blocks in subbands 2–6 with the highest energy content. In this scheme, when there is a lot of activity in the form of apparent motion, subband 8 contains more signal energy and gets allocated more of the available bits. When the activity drops, the bits are shifted from subband 8 to subbands 2–6 to yield better high spatial frequency encoding. The next section will describe the vector quantizer used to encode the high frequency subbands.

3. Geometric Vector Quantization

By working with a range of head-and-shoulder video sequences, we notice the following characteristics. In the lowpass temporal, highpass spatial subbands (2–6), the non-zero pixels cluster into *edges* or *Moiré patterns* corresponding to object boundaries or edges and fine textures. Geometric vector quantization (GVQ) attempts to take advantage of the characteristically sparse and highly structured data found in these high frequency bands. Two schemes were examined here. A 2-level GVQ applied to 3×3 blocks and a constrained 3-level GVQ applied to 4×4 blocks. The results show that 3-level GVQ yields better encoding results than 2-level especially pronounced in scenes with more high frequency data. Selected areas in subbands 2 through 6, and 8 are encoded with

GVQ. Each of the original blocks in these subbands is either repeated from the same location in the previous encoded frame, coded with GVQ if it is a high energy block, or set to zero if it is a low energy block or if all the bits have been allocated. The coding status associated with each block is transmitted as part of the overhead.

In this section, an original data block extracted from one of the highpass image subbands (subbands 2–11) will be denoted by B. It consists of a square block of $P = N \times N$ pixels. An *ordered block* is the arranged P pixel values of the block B, ordered from "most negative" to "most positive", along with their location within the block. A *quantized* block will be denoted B_q. The quantized block B_q will consist of three regions: R^0, R^1 and R^2 with associated levels I^0, I^1 and I^2. The constrained 3-level GVQ always constrains level $I^0 = 0$.

The problem of optimal L-level quantization of a source with unknown distribution has been addressed in [**7**], in the context of the quantization of LSP parameters for LPC speech coding. Here, the data source is a list of P pixel values of a data block B. The optimal L-level quantizer is found for each block B. The data is sent as a codeword from the GVQ codebook which gives the pixel to quantizer level configuration for each block and the optimized (in the mean square error sense) L-levels for each block. GVQ was first introduced in [**6**] for the 2-level case. The optimum L-levels and best codeword are found using a fast search technique. The P pixel values of the original data block B are ordered in a list:

$$p_1 \leq p_2 \leq \cdots \leq p_P. \tag{3.1}$$

Let,

$$b_0 = 1, b_L = P$$

denote the indices of the first and last pixels in the list. The problem is to find the overall "best" set of $L - 1$ indices

$$b_1, \cdots, b_{L-1}, \tag{3.2}$$

along with the "best" L intensity values or *levels*

$$I_1, \cdots, I_L. \tag{3.3}$$

This can be formulated mathematically as finding the optimal partitioning in the minimum mean squared error (mmse) sense, of the ordered list into L regions of constant level, which minimizes the mean-squared distortion:

$$E(B, \underline{b}, \underline{I}) = \sum_{k=1}^{L} \sum_{i=b_k}^{b_{k+1}} (p_i - I_k)^2, \tag{3.4}$$

where $\underline{b}$, $\underline{I}$ indicate the vectors defined in (3.2) and (3.3) respectively. The *quantized list* is the set of P values:

$$\underbrace{I_1, \cdots, I_1}_{b_1 - b_0 + 1}, \cdots \underbrace{I_L, \cdots, I_L}_{b_L - b_{L-1} + 1}. \tag{3.5}$$

The indices $b_0, \cdots, b_L$ which specify L connected regions in the ordered list also specify L *geometric regions*

$$R_1, \cdots, R_L, \tag{3.6}$$

in the original data block. It turns out that the optimum indices form well defined regions of horizontal, vertical and diagonal strips of varying thicknesses due to the inherent structure associated with each frequency band. The number of pixels of the quantized block at each level will be referred to as the *population* of the level:

$$\begin{aligned} pop(I_1) &= b_1 - b_0 + 1 \\ &\vdots \\ pop(I_L) &= b_L - b_{L-1} + 1. \end{aligned} \tag{3.7}$$

It is straightforward to show that given the L regions $R_1, \cdots R_L$, the best levels in the mmse sense, are the respective averages of the pixel values over these regions, i.e.

$$I_k = \frac{1}{pop(I_k)} \sum_{i=b_{k-1}}^{b_k} p_i, \tag{3.8}$$

for $k = 1, \cdots, L$.

The fact that the mean–square error minimization in Eq. (3.4) only has to be performed over *connected* regions in the ordered list in order to achieve a globally optimal minimization results in a *fast search GVQ* which makes the scheme practical for image coding. Note that if *all* L-ary patterns had to be considered as candidates for "block matching", the search would be among L^{P-1} codewords. Instead, it is easy to see that GVQ with a fast search requires mean-square distortion computations on the order of P^{L-1} for the 3-level case.

We noticed that for a great majority of 4×4 blocks, the optimum mmse 3-level GVQ yields a partitioning into three regions with 1 level ≈ 0 surrounded by 2 "strongly non-zero" regions. This allows us to constrain 1 level to zero *a priori* resulting in an only slightly suboptimum solution while reducing the search complexity tremendously. Below, we describe the algorithm for the quantization of a block B into three regions R^0, R^1, R^2, with the zero region R^0 constrained to have the associated level $I^0 = 0$. The algorithm is best described in three stages. The algorithm is illustrated for a sample highpass 4×4 data block in Fig. 2

Stage 1: Block ordering (see Figure 2.a)
The pixel values of the data block B are ordered according to increasing pixel values. The initial "border point" which separates the initial negative region R^-_{init} from the initial positive region R^+_{init} is found. If zero value pixels exist, the initial zero region is split in half.

Stage 2: Constrained 2-level GVQ (see Figure 2.b)
Perform a fast-search 2-level GVQ on the region R^-_{init}, with one level constrained to be zero. The result of this procedure is a segmentation of R^-_{init} into a "best" region R^1 with associated level $I^1 \leq 0$, and a zero region R^{0-}. Repeat this procedure with R^+_{init}, and obtain R^2 with associated level $I^2 \geq 0$, and R^{0+}. Merge the two zero regions R^{0-}, R^{0+} into a single zero region R^0. The quantized block B_q consists of the triplet:

$$B_q = \{(R^1, I^1), R^0, (R^2, I^2)\}.$$

The algorithm is modified slightly to handle the case when all the data is negative or positive.

The number of bits required for the addressing of a block described here is computed based on the assumption that 3-level GVQ is done on 4×4 blocks and that the 2 levels to be transmitted are each quantized to five bits. The levels therefore require:

$$b_l = \frac{2.5}{16} \approx .63 \; bpp. \tag{3.9}$$

The geometry of the 3-level block can be addressed with:

$$b_g = \frac{log_2 S}{16} \; bpp, \tag{3.10}$$

where S indicates the size of the purely deterministic *geometric codebook*, which in this case consists of all possible ternary 4×4 patterns. The total number of bits per pixel needed to address a quantized block in a GVQ codebook is the sum:

$$b = b_l + b_g. \tag{3.11}$$

Clearly, there is a total number of

$$S_1 = 3^{16} \tag{3.12}$$

different ternary pattern for a 4×4 block. Note that this number is very large ($\approx$ 43 million !). It is the combination of the very specific nature of the data to encode (highpass data), along with the existence of a fast search which make 3-level GVQ practical. Also note that this set of all ternary pattern for 4×4 blocks constitutes a simple 16-dimensional *lattice* commonly referred to as Z^{16} [**8**].

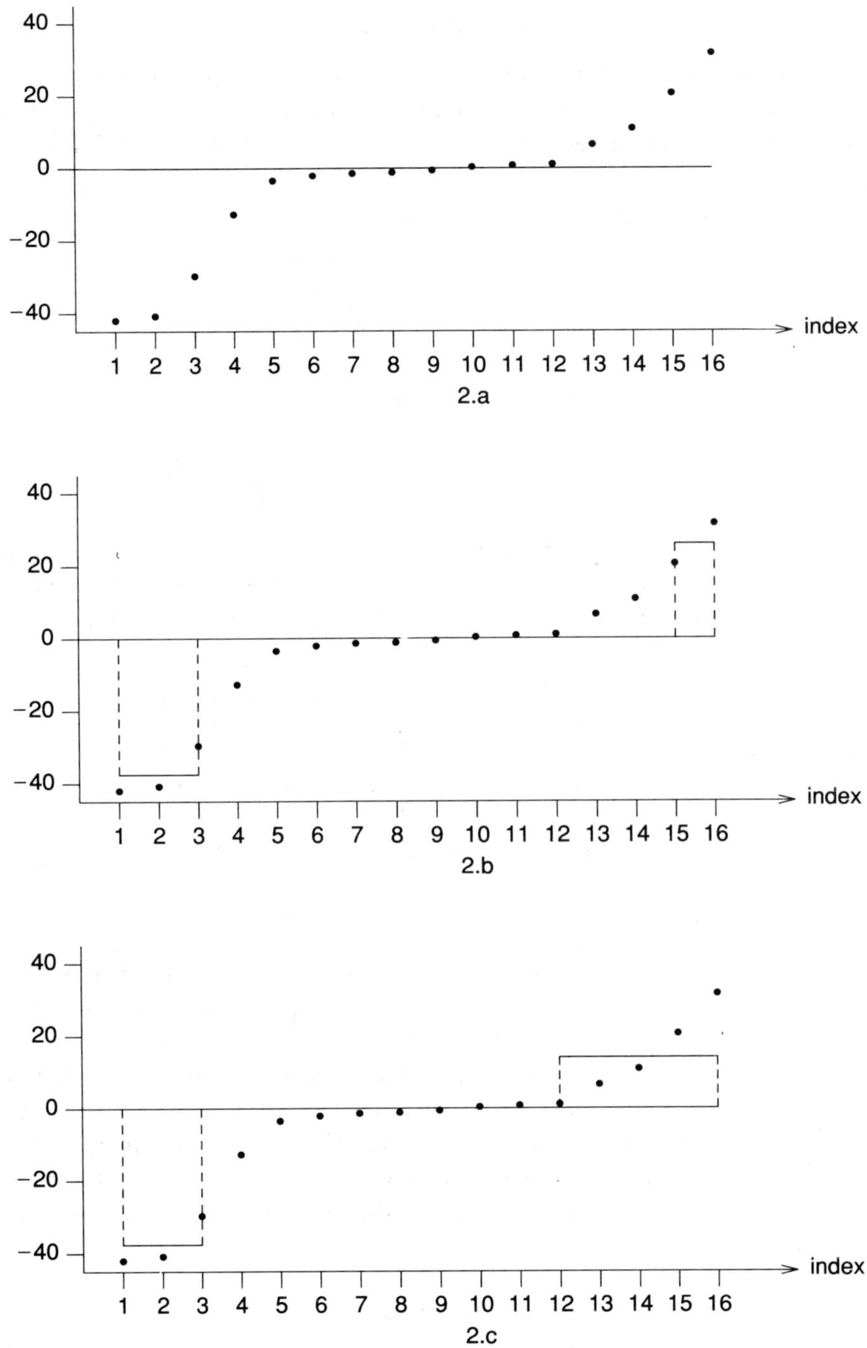

FIGURE 2. 3-level GVQ of a data block: (a) stage 1: ordering, (b) stage 2: quantization on three levels I^-, 0, and I^+, (c) stage 3: enforcement of population constraint $\Delta P = 8$.

4. Conclusion

We used the CIF 360×240 video sequence "Melanie" for our simulations at 15 frames per second. The overall bit rate is assumed to be 384 kbps so that the high frequency subbands are given a bit allocation as shown in Table 1. It

	bit rate
Speech	16 kbps
Color	40 kbps
LP Subband (1)	50 kbps
Overhead	20 kbps
HP Subbands	256 kbps
Total	384 kbps

TABLE 1. Overall bit allocation for 384 kbps coding.

seems that encoding the highly visible high frequency details more accurately using 3-level GVQ outweighs the advantage of encoding more high frequency components using 2-level GVQ. The average SNRs for 2-level vs 3-level GVQ are given in Table 2.

	SNR	PSNR
HP data coded with 2-level GVQ	16.1	27.8
HP data coded with 3-level GVQ	17.5	29.2

TABLE 2. Average SNRs over reconstructed "Melanie" sequences for different GVQs.

The results at 384 kbps look promising. One area of investigation in order to increase the quality or decrease the bit rate is the examination of different spatial filter types and different subband structures; ideally, matched to both the human visual system and the video signal characteristics. Another extension of the present work is to use an adaptive generalized GVQ, adapting the number of levels and block size according to local signal characteristics. Finally, an idea that looks promising in the 3-D subband framework is taking advantage of the redundancy between subbands and several different schemes are presently being investigated.

REFERENCES

1. G. Karlsson and M. Vetterli, Three dimensional subband coding of video. In *Proceedings ICASSP*, 1988.
2. J. D. Johnston, A filter family designed for use in quadrature mirror filter banks. In *Proceedings ICASSP*, 1980.
3. Arnaud Jacquin and Christine Podilchuk, Comparative study of different filter banks for low bit rate subband-based video coding. NJIT Wavelet Symposium, 1992.

4. Christine Podilchuk and Arnaud Jacquin, Subband video coding with a dynamic bit allocation and geometric vector quantization. In *Proceedings SPIE — Human Vision, Visual Processing and Digital Display III*, 1992.
5. C. I. Podilchuk and N. Farvardin, Perceptually based low bit rate video coding. In *Proceedings ICASSP*, 1991.
6. N. S. Jayant C. I. Podilchuk and P. Noll, Sparse codebooks for the quantization of non-dominant subbands in image coding. In *Proceedings ICASSP*, 1990.
7. F. Soong and B. H. Juang. A globally optimal quantizer design. In *Proceedings of Inter. Sym. Inf. Theory*, 1988.
8. J Gibson. Lattice quantization. *Advances in Electronics and Electron Physics*, 1988.

Signal Processing Research Department, AT&T Bell Laboratories, Murray Hill, NJ 07974

E-mail address: chrisp@@research.att.com, arnaud@@research.att.com

DIMACS Series in Discrete Mathematics
and Theoretical Computer Science
Volume **14**, 1993

Recursively Indexed Differential Pulse Code Modulation

KHALID SAYOOD AND SANGSIN NA

January 10, 1993

ABSTRACT. We study the performance of a DPCM system with a recursively indexed quantizer (RIQ) under various conditions, with first order Gauss-Markov and Laplace-Markov sources as inputs. We show that when the predictor is matched to the input, the proposed system performs at or close to the optimum entropy constrained DPCM system. We also show that if we are willing to accept a 5% increase in the rate, the system is very forgiving of predictor mismatch.

1. Introduction

Differential pulse code modulation (DPCM) is often used to efficiently convert an analog source such as speech, music or images into a digital form for communication or storage. Its efficiency is due to the exploitation of the memory in a source by the use of a predictor, which estimates the present source sample to be encoded, based on the previously quantized source samples. The performance of DPCM depends on two factors

1. How well the predictor exploits the source memory, i.e. , how closely it can estimate the actual source samples.
2. How well the quantizer is matched to the prediction error (the quantizer input).

In order to maximize the goodness of prediction, the predictor is usually chosen based on the statistical properties of a given source. However, many physical sources, such as those listed above, exhibit statistically varying local properties which are usually quite distinct from their global ones. If this is the case and DPCM happens to operate on a segment whose statistics differ from

1991 *Mathematics Subject Classification.* Primary 94A29.
This work was supported by NASA Lewis Research Center under grant NAG 3-806, and NASA Goddard Space Flight Center under grant NAG 5-1615.

the global ones, it operates in a mismatched state, which results in additional degradation in the reproduction [**1**].

Various schemes have been devised to handle this mismatch between the source and the predictor. These involve some form of adaptation of the quantizer and/or the predictor, by which DPCM quickly follows up the changing statistics of the source and prevents overloading of the system. However, this quick response of DPCM is not without its cost: the adaptation requires more implementation and operational complexity.

Matching the quantizer to the statistics of the prediction error is even more difficult, as the quantizer structure itself effects the statistical properties of the prediction error. One way to obtain the statistics of the prediction error process is through the use of an orthonormal expansion [**2, 3, 4, 5**]. This has been used to optimize the quantizer through an iterative procedure [**4, 6, 7, 8**]. However, under operational circumstances this might not be a viable option.

In this paper we study the performance of a DPCM system operating on a Gauss-Markov source and a Laplace-Markov source. The DPCM system considered here, called a recursively indexed DPCM, consists of a uniform quantizer with infinitely many output levels, a recursively indexed binary encoder, and a first-order linear predictor. The quantizer is designed simply by specifying its step-size, and the predictor is non-adaptive. The Gauss-Markov and Laplace-Markov sources are chosen because of their use in the modeling of physical sources. The goal is to observe the rate distortion performance of this system, as well as the performance degradation when the predictor and the source are mismatched. We compare the rate distortion performance of the proposed system to the optimum results in the literature [**6**], where the quantizer was optimized using the iterative procedure mentioned above.

The simulation results show that the rate distortion performance of the proposed system achieves or comes very close to the optimum performance at all rates studied. In the case of mismatch the simulation results show that only a 5 percent increase in the rate allows a rather wide range of the predictor mismatch to first-order Gauss-Markov and Laplace-Markov sources. They agree with a result in [**9**] reported for a 2-level optimized DPCM that the predictor coefficient does not significantly effect the optimality of DPCM. But unlike [**9**] it is observed that a lower predictor coefficient than the source correlation coefficient is better for the low rate case.

In Section 2 a recursively indexed binary encoder is discussed. In Section 3 DPCM is briefly reviewed and the DPCM mismatch problem is posed. In Section 4 the performance of a recursively indexed DPCM is considered and numerical results are presented. Conclusions follow in section 5.

2. A Recursively Indexed Binary Encoder

The DPCM system discussed here uses a quantizer with infinitely many output levels. This requires binary encoding of a countably infinite alphabet, which poses obvious problems in design and operation. An obvious and reasonable approach is first to represent the input alphabet using only finitely many symbols and then to encode these symbols either using a fixed-to-fixed or fixed-to-variable length encoding. A recursively indexed binary encoder is used for just this purpose.

The recursively indexed binary encoder considered in this paper is a two stage binary encoder: recursive indexing followed by an optimum (the minimum average codeword length) symbol-to-variable length binary encoder for the output of recursive indexing.

Recursive indexing is a mapping of a countable set to a collection of sequences of symbols from another set of finite size [**10, 11**]. Given a countable set $A = \{a_0, a_1, \ldots\}$ and a finite set $B = \{b_0, b_1, \ldots, b_{M-1}\}$ of size M, the recursive indexing of A by B is a mapping I of A to the collection of all sequences of symbols from B such that

$$I(a_i) = \underbrace{b_{M-1} b_{M-1} \ldots b_{M-1}}_{q \text{ times}} b_r \text{ if } i = q(M-1) + r \tag{2.1}$$

where q and r are the quotient and remainder of i when divided by $M-1$. Set B is called the representation set. Defined as such, recursive indexing is a one-to-one mapping, a symbol-to-variable length, M-ary, prefix-free code and therefore uniquely and instantaneously decodable.

Since the second stage of the recursively indexed binary encoder is an optimum symbol-to-variable length encoder (the Huffman algorithm is used to design such), the statistic of the representation symbols must be computed. For this purpose we first compute the number of representation symbols needed to describe a typical source sequence $X_1, X_2, \ldots X_n$ of the length n from set A. Define $p_k = Pr(X = a_k)$, then the number n_0 of the occurrences of symbol b_0 is computed as follows. Observe that b_0 occurs once whenever a_0, a_{M-1}, $a_{2M-2}, \ldots$, $a_{k(M-1)}, \ldots$ occur. The number of times these symbols occur is given by np_0, np_{M-1}, $np_{2M-2}, \ldots$, $np_{k(M-1)}, \ldots$ and so on. Therefore,

$$n_0 = n \sum_{k=0}^{\infty} p_{k(M-1)}. \tag{2.2}$$

In a similar manner the number n_j of the occurrences of symbol b_j are found to be:

$$(2.3)\qquad \begin{aligned} n_j &= n\sum_{k=0}^{\infty} p_{k(M-1)+j} \quad \text{for } j = 0, 1, \ldots, M-2, \\ n_{M-1} &= n\sum_{k=0}^{\infty}\sum_{j=0}^{M-2} k p_{k(M-1)+j}. \end{aligned}$$

From (2.3) it is seen that on the average the number of representation symbols needed for n source symbols is

$$(2.4)\qquad \sum_{j=0}^{M-1} n_j .$$

Therefore, the average number of representation symbols to represent one source symbol is

$$(2.5)\qquad \frac{1}{n}\sum_{j=0}^{M-1} n_j = 1 + \frac{n_{M-1}}{n} = 1 + \sum_{k=0}^{\infty}\sum_{j=0}^{M-2} k p_{k(M-1)+j} .$$

It is convenient to define the above expression as the expansion factor, denoted e, of the recursive indexing I. It is the factor by which one source symbol is expanded by the recursive indexing. The relative frequency q_j of representation symbol b_j, is computed as follows:

$$(2.6)\qquad q_j = \frac{n_j}{n} .$$

An optimum symbol-to-variable length binary encoder after the recursive indexing takes one representation symbol at a time and produces the corresponding binary sequence from a set of variable length code words. It is designed for example using the Huffman algorithm. Then its rate R_{RI} , the number of binary digits per representation symbol, is bounded by

$$(2.7)\qquad H(B) \le R_{RI} < H(B) + 1 .$$

For the symbol-to-variable length code generated by the Huffman algorithm it is observed that rate R is almost equal to $H(B)$, the lower bound, when M is large.

The overall rate of the recursively indexed binary encoder then is bounded as follows:

$$(2.8)\qquad eH(B) \le R < eH(B) + e .$$

3. DPCM with Recursively Indexed Binary Encoding

3.1. Source and DPCM. Let us consider the encoding by a DPCM system of a first-order Gauss-Markov process,

$$X_k = \rho X_{k-1} + W_k \tag{3.1}$$

where W_k is an independent identically distributed Gaussian with mean zero and variance σ_w^2 . The source correlation coefficient ρ is between -1 and 1.

The DPCM system consists of a quantizer, a predictor and a binary encoder In a typical operational cycle the difference Z_k between the source output X_k and its prediction $\hat{X}_k$ is quantized by quantizer Q yielding $Q(Z_k)$, which in turn is binary encoded. The predictor considered in this paper is a first-order linear predictor and therefore it is given by bY_{k-1} for some constant b, where Y_k is the reproduction for X_k.

We will say that DPCM is matched to the source if the source correlation ρ equals the predictor coefficient b and that it is mismatched otherwise.

The binary encoder in ordinary DPCM is either a fixed-to-fixed length or a fixed-to-variable length binary encoder. In the former the binary encoder takes the index of the quantizer output level, produces its binary representation and sends the binary sequence through the channel. In the latter blocks of quantizer outputs are buffered and (usually) entropy-encoded.

The performance of a DPCM system will be measured by distortion and rate. The distortion incurred is defined to be

$$D = \limsup_{N\to\infty} \frac{1}{N} \sum_{k=1}^{N} E\Big\{(X_k - Y_k)^2\Big\}. \tag{3.2}$$

It is well-known that the error of the DPCM system is that incurred by the quantizer alone and nowhere else, i.e., $X_k - Y_k = Z_k - Q(Z_k)$. Hence the distortion can be rewritten as

$$D = \limsup_{N\to\infty} \frac{1}{N} \sum_{k=1}^{N} E\Big\{(Z_k - Q(Z_k))^2\Big\}. \tag{3.3}$$

The rate is defined to be the average number of binary digits used to transmit one source symbol. In case of a fixed-to-fixed length binary encoder it is given by $\lceil \log_2 N \rceil$, where N is the number of quantizer output levels. In case of a fixed-to-variable length entropy encoder it is approximately H(Q), the entropy of the quantizer output process.

3.2. Recursively Indexed DPCM. The DPCM system considered in this paper is a recursively indexed DPCM system. It is different from an ordinary system in the following two ways:

1. The quantizer Q is an infinite level uniform quantizer with the thresholds being the mid-points of output levels.

2. The binary encoder is a recursively indexed fixed-to-variable length encoder.

The quantizer with infinitely-many output levels uniformly spaced yields granular distortion only. The magnitude of the distortion is bounded by $\Delta/2$. Therefore, no matter how large the input to the quantizer is, due to bad prediction, its output is at most $\Delta/2$ different from its input. Since an unoverloaded quantized value is available to the predictor at the next prediction, the system can track the source output, thereby yielding lower prediction errors. Due to this quick response the system does not have catastrophic error propagation, which DPCM with a finite number of quantizer output levels has when a pathological source sequence is encountered.

As discussed in Section 2, a recursively indexed binary encoder is necessary because the quantizer used has infinitely many output levels. We note that the encoder is not necessarily an entropy-encoder for the quantized process.

The distortion for this system is given by (3.3), while the rate is simply the entropy of the representation symbols multiplied by the expansion factor.

4. Simulation Results

To test this system first order Gauss-Markov and Laplace-Markov random number generators with correlation coefficient ρ were used. The Laplace-Markov process was defined as in [**6**]. The variance of the innovation sequence was chosen so as to get a source variance of unity. For each realization of the process 100,000 samples were used.

4.1. Rate-Distortion Performance. To obtain the rate-distortion performance, the predictor was matched to the source correlation coefficient and the step-size was varied. Each step-size Δ generated a distortion-rate pair which was then plotted. The results were overlaid on the optimum results from [**6**]. The results for $\rho = 0.8$ are plotted in Figures 1 and 2.

For the Gauss-Markov source the rate distortion performance of the proposed system achieves (or almost achieves) the optimum performance for the entire range of rates. This is true for both the experimentally obtained rates from [**6**] as well as the asymptotic results. Recall that for the optimum results the quantizer was designed using a relatively complex iterative procedure, while for the proposed system the quantizer was designed by simply specifying the step-size.

For the Laplace-Markov source, the proposed scheme again performs as well as the optimum scheme for almost all rates as far as the experimentally obtained results are concerned. However, the proposed scheme provides *better* results than the asymptotic results in [**6**]. We presume this is due to an error in the asymptotic results (or our interpretation of them!).

Similar results were obtained for ρ= 0.5, and 0.2 for both sources. The results seem to indicate that the problem of matching the quantizer with the input

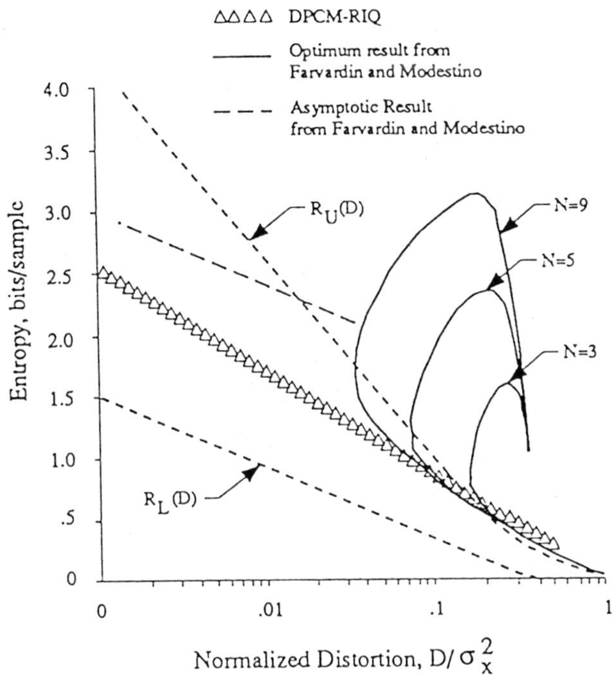

FIGURE 1. Performance comparison of optimum DPCM and the DPCM-RIQ coding scheme for first-order Laplace-Markov source with $\rho = 0.8$.

statistics can be easily resolved by the use of a recursively indexed quantizer. The quantizer can be easily designed by simply specifying the step-size Δ, which in turn can be specified based on the distortion requirements.

4.2. Performance Under Mismatch Conditions. To investigate the effect of mismatch between the predictor and model coefficients we used three values for the spacing Δ of the uniform quantizer: $2.5\sigma_x, 1.5\sigma_x, 0.2\sigma_x$. These correspond to low, medium, and high resolution (rate) quantizations, respectively. For each spacing for uniform- quantization, the source sequence is applied to the recursively indexed DPCM system with various values for the predictor coefficient. The quantizer output sequence is fed to the recursively indexed binary encoder with M representation symbols. The value of M ranges from 5 to 31. The results are shown in Figure 3, where the horizontal and vertical axis are respectively the predictor coefficient and the product of the rate and distortion.

For the Gauss-Markov source, for low rate ($\Delta = 2.5\sigma_x$) the distortion is about 0.44. The best performance is obtained when the predictor coefficient is around 0.6, where the rate is 0.58 bits/sample. This value is far below the source correlation 0.8. Note that in [**4**], the best performance was reported around 0.815, slightly higher than the source correlation. If 5% increase in rate

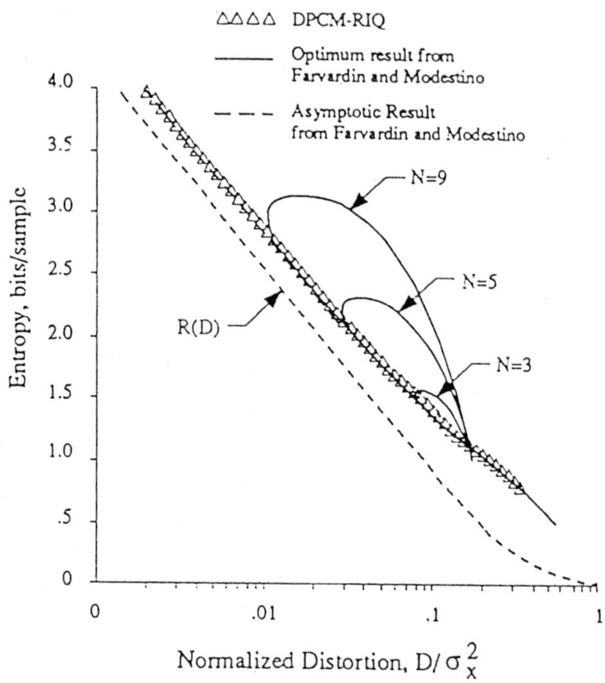

FIGURE 2. Performance comparison of optimum DPCM and the DPCM-RIQ coding scheme for first-order Gauss-Markov source with $\rho = 0.8$.

is allowed, then Figure 3 shows that the predictor coefficient can be anywhere between 0.4 and 0.8.

For medium rate ($\Delta = 1.5\sigma_x$) the distortion is about 0.186, while $\Delta^2/12$ is 0.1875. The best predictor coefficient is around 0.7. The rate for this value of Δ and b is 1.12 bits/sample. The value of b is again lower than the source correlation. Again a 5% increase in rate allows the predictor coefficient anywhere between 0.48 and 0.88. For high rate ($\Delta = 0.2\sigma_x$) the distortion is about 0.00333, while $\Delta^2/12$ is 0.00333. The best predictor coefficient is around 0.8, where the rate is 4.2 bits/sample, and can range from 0.0 to 0.99 if 5% increase in rate is allowed.

We observe that the best predictor coefficient moves closer to the source correlation from below as resolution increases. This may be because for larger values of Δ the quantization noise tends to accumulate when the predictor coefficient is larger, and the memory of the predictor is longer.[1] Also we note that the distortion expression ($\Delta^2/12$) is quite accurate even for large Δ. Similar results are observed for the Laplace-Markov source.

[1]Thanks to Dr. J. Johnston for his suggestion.

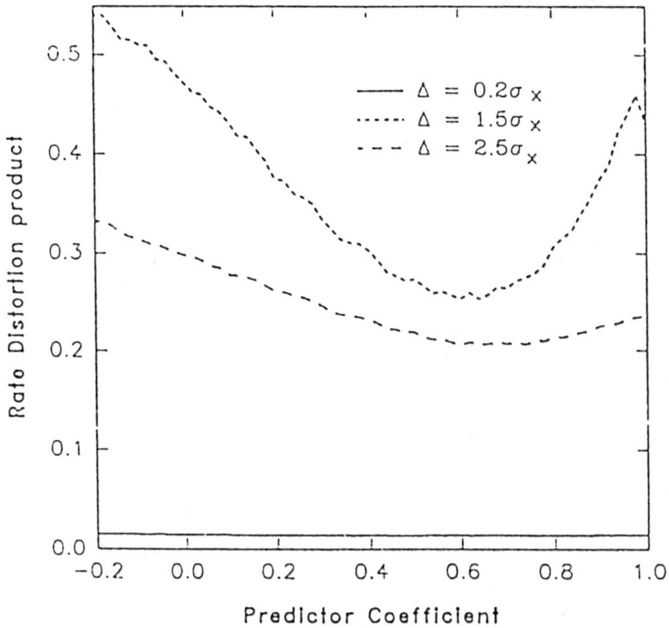

FIGURE 3. Effect of Predictor Mismatch for first order Gauss-Markov source with $\rho = 0.8$.

4.3. Effect of the Alphabet Size M. Finally we look at the effect of the size of the representation alphabet on the rate. Note that the larger the representation alphabet is for a certain value of Δ the less likely it is that the encoder will enter the recursive mode. This implies that given a value of Δ larger values of M will tend to lower the value of the expansion factor e closer to 1, thus lowering the rate. If this is a very strong effect, recursive indexing looses some of its charm, as the smaller alphabet size of the reproduction alphabet makes it more amenable to entropy coding. The recursively indexed DPCM system was simulated with representation alphabet sizes 7,9,11,13, and 15. The results for a Laplace-Markov source are shown in Figure 4. Note that at low rates (large values of Δ)there is no difference between these sizes. At higher rates, there is noticeable difference as we increase the alphabet size from 7 to 11. After that point there is very little improvement obtained in the rate when the alphabet size is increased.

5. Conclusions

Recursively indexed DPCM, which features an infinite level quantizer coded with a finite alphabet entropy coder has been shown to be an efficient encoder for first order Gauss-Markov and Laplace-Markov sources. The use of a recursively indexed quantizer in a standard DPCM system seems to provide a solution both to the problem of matching the quantizer to the prediction error statistics, and

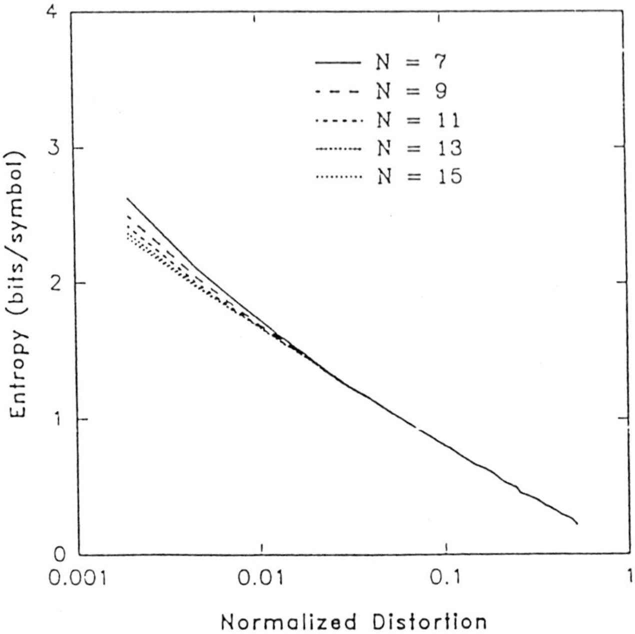

FIGURE 4. Performance of the DPCM-RIQ system as a function of alphabet size for a first order Laplace-Markov source with $\rho = 0.8$.

the problem of exactly matching the predictor to the source, at least for these simple sources.

REFERENCES

1. N.S. Jayant and P. Noll. *Digital Coding of Waveforms.* Prentice-Hall, 1984.
2. L. D. Davisson. Information Rates for Data Compression. In *IEEE WESCON.* IEEE, 1968.
3. D. Slepian. On Delta Modulation. *Bell Syst. Tech. J.*, 45:2101–2137, December 1972.
4. D. S. Arnstein. Quantization Error in Predictive Coders. *IEEE Transactions on Communications*, COM-23(4):423–429, April 1975.
5. M. Naraghi-Pour and D. L. Neuhoff. Convergence of the Projection Method for an Autoregressive Process and a Matched DPCM Code. *IEEE Transaction on Information Theory,* 36:1255–1264, Nov 1990.
6. N. Farvardin and J. W. Modestino. Rate-Distortion Performance of DPCM Schemes for Autoregressive Sources. *IEEE Transactions on Information Theory,* IT-31:402–418, May 1985.
7. N. L. Gerr and S. Cambanis. Analysis of Adaptive Differential PCM of a Stationary Gauss-Markov Input. *IEEE Transactions on Information Theory,* IT-33:350–359, May 1987.
8. E. Janardhanan. Differential PCM Systems. *IEEE Transactions on Communications,* COM-27:82–93, January 1989.
9. M. Naraghi-Pour and D. L. Neuhoff. Mismatched DPCM Encoding of Autoregressive Processes. *IEEE Transactions on Information Theory,* pages 296–304, March 1990.
10. K. Sayood and S. Na. Recursively Indexed Quantization of Memoryless Sources. *IEEE Transactions on Information Theory,* IT-38, November 1992.
11. K. Sayood and S. Na. Recursive Quantization. In *24th Annual Asilomar Conference on Circuits, Systems, and Computers,* November 1990.

Department of Electrical Engineering, University of Nebraska, Lincoln, NE 68588-0511

Department of Electronic Engineering, Ajou University, Suwon, Korea